EXPERIENCING MUSIC VIDEO

CAROL VERNALLIS

(Film Studies, Arizona Uni)

EXPERIENCING

 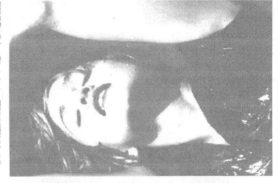

 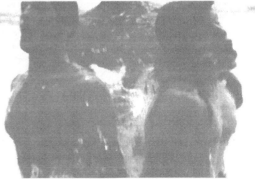

MUSIC VIDEO

AESTHETICS AND CULTURAL CONTEXT

COLUMBIA UNIVERSITY PRESS / NEW YORK

Columbia University Press
Publishers Since 1893
New York   Chichester, West Sussex

Columbia University Press gratefully acknowledges permission to reprint
selected poems (pp. 253–269 passim., this volume) from Anne Sexton,
The Complete Poems (Boston: Houghton Mifflin Company, 1981). Reprinted
by permission of Sterling Lord Literistic, Inc. Copyright by Anne Sexton.

The music and lyrics for Peter Gabriel's "Mercy St." are published by
Real World Music Limited (PRS) for the World, Pentagon Lipservices Real
World (BMI) for N. America. Used with permission of Lipservices Music
Publishing, Brooklyn N.Y.

Library of Congress Cataloging-in-Publication Data
Vernallis, Carol
Experiencing music video : aesthetics and cultural context / Carol Vernallis.
p. cm.
Includes bibliographical references (p.) and index.
ISBN 978-0-231-11798-2 (cloth : alk. paper) —
ISBN 978-0-231-11799-9 (pbk. : alk. paper)
1. Music videos—History and criticism.
2. Music videos—Social aspects.   I. Title.
PN1992.8.M87V47   2004
780.26′7—dc22
2003064605

Printed in the United States of America

Designed by Lisa Hamm

CONTENTS

ACKNOWLEDGMENTS

I WOULD LIKE to thank the many friends and colleagues who shared their ideas with me on the subject of music video and read all or parts of the manuscript: David Bordwell, Nicholas Cook, Ken Dancyger, Simon Frith, Todd Gitlin, DeeDee Halleck, Dan Hallin, Ken Hillis, Tim Hughes, Anahid Kassabian, Stevan Key, Helene Keyssar, Eric Lyon, George Lipsitz, Jeff Melnick, Richard Middleton, Ann Miller, Mitchell Morris, Will Ogdon, Cate Palczewski, Jann Pasler, Leenke Ripmeester, Joseph Rubenstein, Ron Sadoff, Jonathan Schwabe, Jesse Swan, and Margaret Vernallis, as well as my students at the Richard Stockton College of New Jersey and the University of Northern Iowa. I dedicate this book to Charles Kronengold in recognition of all that his interest, criticism, and support have meant.

Chapter 2, "Editing," was previously published as "The Kindest Cut: Functions and Meanings of Music Video Editing" in *Screen*; chapter 7, "Lyrics," was previously published as "The Functions of Lyrics in Music Video" in *Journal of Popular Music Studies*; and chapter 11, "The Aesthetics of Music Video: An Analysis of Madonna's 'Cherish,'" was previously published as "The Aesthetics of Music Video: An Analysis of Madonna's 'Cherish'" in *Popular Music*.

INTRODUCTION

I **LOVED MUSIC VIDEO** before it existed. As a young teen, I would stay up to watch *Don Kirshner's Rock Concert* or *The Midnight Special* on television. Not much was happening in those programs, it now seems clear, but at the time I was transfixed by the image of the musician performing on camera. One day, as a graduate student without cable, I was at a friend's house, and the television was on. He mentioned MTV, and I turned toward the set. What I saw, Steve Winwood's "Higher Love," was beautiful somehow. As a doctoral student in communication, I was well aware of the role of mass media as a shaper of ideology, with its aims to turn Americans into consumers and to inculcate a way of thinking that made the wide gap between the wealthy and the poor appear appropriate and natural. But I felt excited about this video, which seemed to me to possess humanistic and celebratory features. I became an avid watcher.

Music video fit my needs. I have a B.A. and M.A. in music and had been working across departments, putting music to films and writing music for my own images. I wanted to discover what kinds of relations music, image, and lyrics might create. I knew the ways music functioned in the service of narrative film, but I wondered whether music could play a predominant role, or at least an equal one. Such a body of work existed—experimental film and video that explored music-image relations—but it was small. Music video seemed the thing to study in the 1980s because it resembled a laboratory where relations among music, image, and text could be tested. All kinds of videos seemed possible, those in which the tonality of the video changed so that viewers found themselves somewhere new, or somewhere in which the stars never showed up.

I stayed with music video while earning my doctorate in communication and have continued with it as a college professor. My research has demanded that I become an omnivore: music video belongs somewhere among music, film, television studies, cultural studies, ethnic studies, and communication studies, as well as philosophy, theater, and dance. Many scholars have worked on the topic of music video, including Ann Kaplan, Andrew Goodwin, Simon

Frith, and Robert Walser.[1] Andrew Goodwin's *Dancing in the Distraction Factory* contains a good review of the literature up until 1992, and my dissertation provides one as well.[2]

My work draws on this literature, but it departs from it in significant ways. I treat music video as a distinct genre, one different from its predecessors—film, television, photography—a medium with its own ways of organizing materials, exploring themes, and dealing with time, all of which can be studied through close analysis. This book provides both a description of the ways that musical and visual codes operate in music video, and in-depth analyses that show these operations at work in a temporal flow.[3] These two modes work together to inform us about music video as an artistic practice and as an ideological apparatus. If we attend to features held in common by many videos, and features particular to a single video, we can begin to understand how music video works. It is through this attention to these features that we can learn about music video's distinct modes of representing race, class, gender, and sexuality.

Experiencing Music Video differs from previous work on music video because it takes the music of music video most seriously. I argue that music videos derive from the songs they set. The music comes first—the song is produced before the video is conceived—and the director normally designs images with the song as a guide. Moreover, the video must sell the song; it is therefore responsible to the song in the eyes of the artist and record company. Music videos have many ways to follow a song. They often reflect a song's structure and pick up on specific musical features in the domains of melody, rhythm, and timbre. The image can even seem to imitate sound's ebb and flow and its indeterminate boundaries. Videomakers have developed a set of practices for putting image to music in which the image gives up its autonomy and abandons some of its representational modes. In exchange, the image gains in flexibility and play, as well as in polyvalence of meaning. Many of the meanings of music video lie in this give-and-take between sound and image and in the relations among their various modes of continuity.

A remarkable thing about music video is the fact that any visual element can come to the fore at any time. A viewer cannot predict the kind of function a particular element will perform or the degree of preeminence it will obtain in a video; nor can a viewer assume that its function or status will remain consistent over the course of a video. A video may provide a detailed depiction of some character at the beginning only to abandon him later in favor of a rhapsody on green, which may in turn give way to a precise visual articulation of a percussion part—or we may find that the final section reveals a big chair as the video's true subject. It might be helpful to imagine the various elements of music video's mise-en-scène as separate tracks on a recording engineer's mixing board: any element or combination of elements can be brought forward or become submerged in the mix. These elements form a dynamic system in which a change in one part of the mix may be compensated for by a change in another. Inasmuch as any element can come to the fore, the world that a video depicts can become very strange. Some of music video's excitement stems from the sense that anything can happen—even an insightful or progressive image of social relations.

Critics have noticed the disorienting style of music video, but they have not often looked carefully at whence this discontinuity derives. Are all videos equally confusing? At every moment? Are the shots that depict performance coherent and all other shots incoherent? Chapters 1 through 10 move from an acknowledgment of music video's changing surface to an investigation of how it is created. Chapters 11 through 13 continue this investigation by looking closely at individual videos. I pay attention to the dramatic effects an element can create, but I attempt to describe the full range of its functions: although an element such as editing or the song's lyrics may come to the fore only once in a video, it is present, working in the background, throughout. This approach reflects the fact that no single element is allowed to predominate. An element that might be thought to dominate the video, such as narrative, advertising, or dance, may govern only isolated moments or aspects.

Chapter 1 considers the function of narrative, an element that has been taken at times as the prime determinant of music video. Some writers on music video have claimed that videos work primarily as narratives, that they function like parts of movies or television shows; others have wanted to say that music video is fundamentally antinarrative, that it is a kind of postmodern pastiche that gains energy from defying narrative conventions. I examine a number of videos along a continuum from strongly narrative to nonnarrative or anti-narrative. I pay close attention to techniques derived from Hollywood film in order to see how their functions and meanings change when employed in music video.

Chapter 2 concerns the editing in music video. My discussion will make clear that music-video editing does not simply assemble images and place them in sequence: it constitutes a distinct visual domain, even a realm of expression, that can operate on an equal footing with those visual parameters to which we habitually pay more attention. I begin with the observation that edits in music video come much more frequently than in film, that some stand out as disjunctive, and that many provide a rhythmic accent against the song's beat. These last two features—that music-video editing is sometimes meant to be noticed and that it brings out aspects of the song—suggest at once that it does something different from, and a good deal more than, the editing in film. Music-video editing bears responsibility for many elements. Not only does the editing in a music video direct the flow of the narrative, it can underscore nonnarrative visual structures and form such structures on its own. Like film editing, it can color our understanding of characters, but it has also assimilated and extended the iconography of the pop star. Music-video editing is also strongly responsive to the music. It can elucidate aspects of the song, such as rhythmic and timbral features, particular phrases in the lyrics, and especially the song's sectional divisions. More subtly, the editing in a music video works hard to insure that no single element—the narrative, the setting, the performance, the star, the lyrics, the song—gains the upper hand. Music-video directors rely on the editing to maintain a sense of openness, a sense that any element can come to the fore at any time. Although the editing in music video often becomes noticeable, it also uses precisely those invisible techniques most common in film. The interest of music-video editing derives not only from the sheer number of functions it serves, I argue, but also from the way that it moves unpredictably among these functions.

Chapter 3 considers the use of human figures in music video. The presence of star performers points to the strictest and most pervasive of music video's conventions: a video must provide a flattering depiction of the singer lip-syncing the song. I look carefully at instances of this convention for the way they are shot and edited. The investigation shows that the use—one might say overuse—of this convention has allowed for a range of meanings to emerge. The varied mise-en-scène of these images can raise questions about a performer's status in the video: is she a character in a narrative, or does she stand only for herself as star? Are we to imagine that the song influences her behavior or that it reflects her thoughts and feelings? I also show the ways that these stylized depictions of the star can suggest when a performer possesses the authority of an omniscient narrator, when she functions as part of the story, and when she exists in isolation from the world the video depicts.

The conventions of music video do not generally allow the figures really to speak. The lead singer must lip-sync, and the other figures—the band members and extras—do not speak at all. These conventions complicate a video's attempt to tell a story or to depict ordinary human activities. Videomakers have made this limitation into a strength by developing techniques that tease a variety of meanings out of the scheme of lip-syncing singer plus silent figures in the background. Sometimes the extras simply play roles that naturalize the absence of speech: mermen, people overcome with emotion, even librarians. At other times their silence becomes not merely conventional, but dark and uncanny. These silent figures can appear mute or possessed. Their isolation from the musicians and each other can make them seem like allegorical figures, representative of some emotion or principle. The extras exist in a changing relationship with the musicians and the video's setting, sometimes sharing space with the lead performers, sometimes receding into the background of the space. This changing relation can draw attention to the play of foreground and background elements in a song's texture. My discussion of extras attempts to piece out this complex system of visual and musical relations.

Chapter 4, on the settings of music video, focuses on genre and ethnicity. A look at current videos reveals that different modes of address are available to different constituencies. Alternative bands often inhabit huge, fanciful spaces and display generalized emotional and physical suffering, while R&B videos operate within a nexus of action/adventure films, melodrama, and Hollywood musicals. Rap videos usually take place on the street and use realistic modes of depiction. These images, apart from the music, might suggest that the alternative groups are asserting a form of white privilege, that the R&B artists are practicing wish fulfillment, and that the rappers are depicting "reality." Taken with the music, however, these images acquire a more complex dimensionality. The locations that appear most in music video tend to be generic depictions, representing a *kind* of place or suggesting a *concept* of place rather than providing a detailed view of a specific setting—a beach, concert hall, apartment, bar, or street corner. Settings may be generic in order for the videos to make musical claims; many videos use generic settings to draw upon cultural associations between a type of place and the musical elements of a song. A small group of examples, in the genres I have mentioned, shows the way that the interaction among music, lyrics, and image creates complex social meanings.

Chapters 5 and 6 discuss several elements crucial to mise-en-scène, including props and costumes, along with more abstract considerations: space, color, texture, and time. Props can carry an excess of meaning in music video, almost as compensation for the absence of dialogue. The heightened importance of props creates an odd inversion of roles, whereby a figure shown in close relation to a prop can be reduced to statuary while the prop seems almost to serve as a character. Space, color, texture, and time each possess their own logic and cultural codes. Because these elements are so malleable, they can be made to respond to musical features. Videos often begin by soliciting a viewer's identification (through interesting characters, animals, stick figures, and the like) and creating a concern for the future (by providing glimpses of a narrative). Once these tasks have been fulfilled, however, the video can focus on matching the music's flow, and it does so by modifying parameters such as color and texture. Each parameter can respond to the music at a particular moment, and to the song's larger processes.

Like narrative and advertising, lyrics have been called the prime determinant of music video.[4] Chapter 7 looks at how music videos respond to a song's lyrics. I argue that the lyrics constitute no more and no less than one of many strands a video must weave together. Of course, listeners attend to lyrics in different ways, and the same is true in the case of music video. Not only that, the relative importance of lyrics varies from song to song, as well as within songs. In a music video both the song and the image play shifting roles in articulating the lyrics. The image can render certain words more obscure and others more apparent. If we look closely, we notice that, like other elements, lyrics can come to the fore for a moment and then fade away. The lyrics fragment, and thus they become mysterious and unreachable. Nevertheless, lyrics serve a number of structural functions, existing in varied relations with the music and the image and casting a narrow or wide range of influence. In this way, they can exert a special power over music videos. Because of this fragmentation, the lyrics can take on what Antoine Hennion, a popular-music scholar, describes as a "shimmer."[5]

Any musical parameter, from a song's arrangement to its sectional divisions, can be represented in the image. Chapter 8 considers the way that videos can reflect musical parameters. Music-video imagery often responds to musical parameters in a serial fashion—drawing our attention to the rhythm first, say, and then to a musical "hook"; by the end, many aspects of the song will have been articulated in some way by the image. The relations of music, image, and lyrics raise questions of cause and effect, and the lack of clear causes may partly explain why music video's world seems strange. Striking music/image relations can catch a viewer's attention, and their return in some form can draw attention to the development of song materials, as well as to the progress of the song as a whole. Chapter 9 examines modes of connection among music, image, and lyrics. Early on, scholars described these relations in music video as mostly one-to-one or as based on similarity and contrast. Drawing upon more recent scholarship by Nicholas Cook and Michel Chion, I show that these three come together in more varied ways. This chapter describes some of these ways and explores both local and large-scale connections. This chapter suggests how multiple strands of connection among music, image, and lyrics create form.

The previous chapters suggest that a good way to begin an analysis is to consider one aspect of a medium in light of another. One might ask whether musical space is reflected in the song's rhythm, or some aspect of the color or space of the image, or a few words in the lyrics. Chapter 10 provides other means of beginning an analysis, some drawn from popular music studies, phenomenology, and advertising. A short discussion of advertising is included as well as some more speculative models for music video. Musical and visual processes unfold in time and work in relation to other processes. Therefore, in chapters 11 through 13, I provide close readings of three videos: Madonna's "Cherish," Prince's "Gett Off," and Peter Gabriel's "Mercy St." "Cherish" and "Gett Off" both held the top spot in MTV's Top Twenty countdown and frequently appear in MTV's Top One Hundred of all time. "Mercy St." has seldom been screened on cable but is available on compilations of Gabriel's videos. All three videos are readily accessible on Madonna's *Immaculate Collection,* Prince's *Diamonds and Pearls,* and Gabriel's *CV.* These are very different videos, partly because of the generic differences among the songs—one is a retro-sixties pop song, one constitutes a complex fusion of African American styles, and one represents a kind of subdued "world beat."

The commonalities among these three videos, too, serve a methodological function. Each fits squarely within current practices and elucidates features that can be recognized in many videos. What makes these videos noteworthy may be the play of conflicting forces that characterizes their respective textures. Herb Ritts, who directed "Cherish," might be described as a videomaker with a classical impulse: the image track of "Cherish" reflects many musical parameters with a sense of clarity and balance. "Cherish" can therefore serve as a model to describe the music/image relations within many videos. In contrast to the classical simplicity of the "Cherish" video, both the music and the image of

"Gett Off" are dense, ornate, and full of references to musical and visual styles. The song has no one "center" but rather embodies an ensemble of forces. The video, too, is constructed to reflect multiple perspectives. The density of materials in "Gett Off" can dazzle the viewer in its own right, but it allows for reactionary as well as progressive messages. Like "Gett Off," Peter Gabriel's "Mercy St." creates a relation among several musical styles, but in a different way and to different ends. Gabriel here takes isolated elements—a flute melody, a drum pattern, performed in styles outside of Anglo-American popular music—and blends them into the mix to create less a song than a kind of incidental music. The video's imagery is grounded in sentiment as well as in sentimentality and reflects upon privacy, incest, death, and epiphany. Yet the video seems resistant to a reading that would piece out this constellation of themes, because the creation of mood as such overwhelms the particularities of historical and cultural origins.

I hope to slow down the viewing process so that we have something to talk about. It may be said that I discuss too many older videos and not enough recent ones. A good new video excites me today as much as ever. Yet music video's waning availability frustrates me, as I am sure it does other viewers. The difficulties of obtaining videos flow into this book.[6] Nevertheless, I believe that the strategies I propose succeed as well for today's videos as for those of the 1980s and 1990s.

I am not arguing that music videos should be treated ahistorically. Videos are not purely formal: they are subject to the influences of institutional structures, technology, and cultural context. It may be simply that the period I am looking at is rather short—about twenty years—and certain techniques have held up very well. Perhaps music video developed its aims and practices quickly; but to acknowledge this is not to give up hope that music videos may yet evolve.

PART I | THEORY

1

Telling and Not Telling

SOME WRITERS about music video have claimed that videos work primarily as narratives, that they function like parts of movies or television shows. Others have wanted to say that music video is fundamentally antinarrative, a kind of postmodern pastiche that actually gains energy from defying narrative conventions.[1] Both of these descriptions reflect technical and aesthetic features of music video that remain worthy of discussion, but they need to be placed in context with techniques drawn from other, particularly musical and visual, realms; we should consider music video's narrative dimension in relation to its other modes, such as underscoring the music, highlighting the lyrics, and showcasing the star.

Music video presents a range all the way from extremely abstract videos emphasizing color and movement to those that convey a story. But most videos tend to be nonnarrative. An Aristotelian definition—characters with defined personality traits, goals, and a sense of agency encounter obstacles and are changed by them—describes only a small fraction of videos, perhaps one in fifty.[2] Still fewer meet the criteria that David Bordwell and Kristin Thompson require in their *Film Art: An Introduction*: that all of the events we see and hear, plus those we infer or assume to have occurred, can be arranged according to their presumed causal relations, chronological order, duration, frequency, and spatial locations. Even if we have a sense of a music video's story, we may not feel that we can reconstruct the tale in the manner that Bordwell and Thompson's criteria demand.[3]

Music videos do not embody complete narratives or convey finely wrought stories for numerous reasons, some obvious and some less so. Most important, videos follow the song's form, which tends to be cyclical and episodic rather than sequentially directed. More generally, videos mimic the concerns of pop music, which tend to be a consideration of a topic rather than an enactment of it. If the intent of a music-video image lies in drawing attention to the music—whether to provide commentary upon it or simply to sell it—it makes sense that the image ought not to carry a story or plot in the way that a film might. Otherwise, videomakers would run the risk of our becoming so engaged with the actions of the characters or concerned with impending events that we are pulled outside the realm of the video and become involved with other narrative possibilities. The song would recede into the background, like film music. Music-video image gains from holding back information, confronting the viewer with ambiguous or unclear depictions—if there is a story, it exists only in the dynamic relation between the song and the image as they unfold in time.[4]

This chapter divides into four sections. It begins with a sketch of the continuum from narrative to nonnarrative videos, tracing some of the familiar forms and providing descriptions of particular examples. Second, it considers why music videos most often do not embody narratives. The penultimate section offers models for understanding nonnarrative modes such as the "process" video, the catalog, and the use of techniques such as contagion. Finally, advice is given for parsing meaning in examples where the message is particularly elusive.

FROM NARRATIVE TO NONNARRATIVE

As a short form with few words, a music video must fulfill competing demands of showcasing the star, reflecting the lyrics, and underscoring the music. If a director wishes to insert a narrative within such confines, she must employ certain techniques and devices. This section examines several narratively oriented videos in order to extract these techniques and devices.

Aerosmith's "Crazy" is a video that flaunts its narrativity, even if it only creates the appearance of a narrative rather than really delivering one.[5] Endowed with some of the proper elements—a beginning and a middle (though not an end)—it has characters who possess volition and encounter obstacles. The video tracks the exploits of two teenage girls as they play hooky, shoplift, enter an amateur strip contest, spend the night in a seedy motel, and then drive off to pick up a hitchhiker and skinny-dip in a lake[6] (fig. 1.1).

"Crazy" departs from convention by conveying its tale in the present tense; videos that tell stories most often situate them in the past, stringing together noncontiguous moments by interpolating images of the artist poised in the act of remembering. As in many music videos, the narrative elements are established in the opening images, well before the song begins: a "bad" Catholic girl kicks out a door, revealing her underwear as she escapes from school through a bathroom window. Thus, most of what happens during the video proper— the shoplifting and strip contest—does not represent narrative drive so much as a spinning out of material. Once the characters have committed their greatest transgression—the striptease—there is nowhere else to go. Although a trace of the premise lingers, the rest of the video veers toward a more episodic structure; here, not knowing what might happen, we are taken along for the ride. (At this point, the video begins to operate in a more familiar mode.) Although the supporting characters we encounter in the opening sequences (the gas station owner and his clerk) have some degree of agency and autonomy, characters that appear later (a k.d. lang look-alike and a handsome country bumpkin) are only mannequins—stock figures that elicit less of the viewer's curiosity.

"Crazy" creates the semblance of a narrative through a clever technique: exploiting the fact that characters lack dialogue. The video alternates between the girls' lip-sync performances and situations in which they cannot or do not speak. In the former case, the young women sing along as the song blasts over the car radio and mouth the lyrics while stripping in a karaoke talent show; in the latter case, when the girls shoplift, they pantomime to one another to prevent the old man who sits idly in front of the gas station from overhearing. Later in the production, when the two girls prepare for a show, they gaze at one another in mutual affection; here, in the throes of a homoerotic moment, they say nothing because words would be superfluous.

Most often in music video, performance footage of the band has the effect of blunting narrative drive. Here, however, the director, Marty Callner, is able to incorporate incidents involving the women and the band to further the story. The images of Aerosmith, shot so dark that the group is set off from everything else, carry almost no weight, and they almost escape our vision. At one level, when the band appears—as pauses between narrative moments—it becomes irrelevant, like an afterthought; yet at another level the band's appearance carries deep psychological resonance. The band's gestures match those of the girls. The lead singer, Steven Tyler, spits, and then so does one of the girls; he throws forward a microphone with attached ribbons, and the other girl tosses her handkerchief into the air. Tyler's own daughter, Liv, plays the role of one of the rambunctious young women, and in some subtle way, a twinning effect is manifest, with the band imagery suggesting an anxiety lodged in the subconscious of both young woman and singer. For the father, there are thoughts

FIGURE 1.1 (A–H) Aerosmith's "Crazy." Furthering the narrative through devices appropriate to music video: karaoke, radio singalongs, pantomime, match cuts, signage, quality of light, and the like.

about a child's actions, as well as a desire to be young again himself, while the daughter dreams of the father who worries about her or of the band member for whom she wishes to become a groupie.[7] That characters' personalities and internal desires feel so palpable makes "Crazy" exceptional; the viewers are able to follow the trajectory of their aims. In most music videos, where music rather than personality is primary, the characters appear too sporadically for the viewer to get a sense of a throughline, or the figures in the frame seem pushed along by the musical flow.

"Crazy" is remarkable for conveying a plot by drawing not from techniques of television programs and film but rather from those of television commercials and movie trailers, both of which are carefully storyboarded. Such techniques work with temporal compression, including precisely choreographed movements of the figures in the frame, and the condensation of what might take three shots in a movie—establishing shot, middle, and close—into a single shot. The mise-en-scène of "Crazy" also borrows from the intertitles of silent film. Throughout the video, signs—the nightclub's marquee and the gas station's sundry store—help to show us where we are; to conclude, a tractor plows the word "crazy" onto a field. Other temporal cues reflect specific kinds of daylight: escaping from the schoolyard is linked to the afternoon; stripping in a seedy club to evening; sleeping in the motel to late evening; gazing out of the hotel doorway into the bright sunlight and the seedy hotel's pool to late morning; picking up a hitchhiker and skinny-dipping to late afternoon. To advance the story, there is a reliance on shots of objects—cars, gas pumps, a photo booth, lipstick, a microphone—and a kind of overgesticulation, or ham acting, that would be out of place in most film genres.

The song does create an ambience that allows the image to diverge from the music and lyrics. Connections might be established between the title and the activities of the characters (the girls are rambunctious, therefore "crazy," or the father is mad with grief) or between the song's genre—the road ballad—and the video's picaresque structure and emphasis on driving, but the narrative world of the video leaves the lyrics far behind. Without an incursion into psychoanalysis, it would be difficult to imagine the song being performed by or addressed to the characters. The effect of this treatment is to make the music seem superfluous: at certain moments of extreme narrative interest, the song as such becomes almost impossible to follow; any effort to concentrate on it in these moments founders, as it might if we were to force our attention onto the soundtrack of a movie during a crucial moment of revelation. Because music videos are not in business to turn our attention away from the song, "Crazy" remains an exception to current practice.[8]

Of other existing narrative videos to consider, only a handful are fully developed; they usually tell the story in the past tense, and most adopt tragic themes such as murder, adultery, or incest, as in Aerosmith's "Janie's Got a Gun," R. Kelly's "Down Low," and Snoop Doggy Dogg's "Murder Was the Case." Questions of how the hero will vanquish the villain elicit the viewer's curiosity, and therefore empathy and involvement—perhaps more than is useful for a music video. When, how far, and in what way the hero will fall can be more thinly sketched and therefore more appropriate to the genre. These videos work well because they are tragedies; they possess a hint of inevitability, as if the outcome were already embedded within the opening of the tape. Often, the hook line helps to focus our attention on the narrative trajectory, telling us what we already know will occur, and leading us inexorably to the main character's unhappy fate. Accompanied by ominous visual imagery, the lyrics keep us moving forward. Another such example, "Bad Girl," borrowed from the plot of the 1977 film *Looking for Mr. Goodbar,* is a video in which Madonna goes out with a number of stray men and is eventually murdered by one. The lyrics "bad girl" as well as iconic imagery let us predict the outcome as the singer passes through a series of tableaux: Madonna's black dress, encased in dry cleaner's plastic, looks like the body bag that she will eventually be wrapped in; her cat, who fails to recognize her, hisses like a wild animal, suggesting that she is already a ghost or a figure who bears a curse; and the singer walks through a doorway that looks like the entrance to Hades.

The particularity of epithets like "bad girl" or, even better, of proper names can be emphasized so that the video's figures take on greater dimensionality, as with the Dixie Chicks' "Goodbye Earl," in which the band members hunt down an abusive husband.[9] Lyrics can serve the narrative, but in a partial, incomplete manner. The fit between words and other constituent parts of a video—a musical hook, close-ups, a particular object or person in the frame—range from close one-to-one connections to those that are elliptical or disjunctive, and these shift constantly. Although it is possible to separate the lyrics from the image and the music in a limited way, words are largely transformed by image and sound. Because their role varies—lyrics sometimes come to the fore and are sometimes buried deep in the texture—they have a kind of occult quality. Most productions direct our attention to so many different parameters that lyrics do not stand out as a single mode of continuity. For example, in Janet Jackson's "Love Will Never Do (Without You)," a heterosexual romance is created out of almost nothing—Jackson, several men, a bed sheet, a gargantuan crescent, and a similarly gigantic wheel, all on a desert—and the flimsy plot is quickly derailed. The video opens with Jackson's maypole dance around a lover, then men and Jackson give chase, suggesting a romance. Jackson's lyrics and the characters' shifting facial expressions, as well as a camera that presents different perspectives of the body, can encourage us to piece out a story about the lovers. When Jackson sings, "We're always falling in and out of love" and "Others said it wouldn't last," with a perturbed, slightly weary expression crossing her face, she may be prompting the viewer to consider those off screen— family or friends—who might be too critical. The suggestion of a sexually satisfying relationship is conveyed by the words "like you do-do-do-do," by the gestures of bending forward with hands on knees and shaking her hips. When she sings, "We've always worked it out somehow" and "Love will never do without you," points a finger, and then the lovers embrace, we assume they have gone through their trials and solidified a union. But can we stake a claim on such an assumption? We have enough time to make a conjecture but not to settle on an interpretation before we move on to the next frame— the narrative structure has already turned in another direction. It becomes fragmentary and volatile: at the bridge and the final chorus, we start seeing more men in swimsuits diving from the sky in a celebratory spectacle.[10] All of a sudden, we are really in the Weather Girls' music video "It's Raining Men." To encourage repeated viewing, a video may need tantalizing imagery, or perhaps just additional imagery of another sort. Those who are sensitive to gay iconography will recognize that the imagery is more the director's fantasy than the star's.

Strangely, instances when the musician performs while illustrating the lyrics through gestures can encourage the viewer to participate in the narrative in ways that an enactment of the lyrics' content through a staged scene cannot. (Such scenes—which take on the quality of tableaux—work poorly, in part, because they cannot match the temporal and spatial conditions under which the music was originally composed and recorded.) In his "Little Red Corvette," Prince's hands and face show off lyrics like "pocket full of condoms." The viewer may begin to create a picture for the scene and want to see more of it. But Prince's bass player is cute: soon one's attention is diverted elsewhere.

Prodigy's "Smack My Bitch Up" contains several narrative devices to add to our toolkit on how to construct a music-video narrative. The video creates the sense of a narrative, in part, by presenting the point of view of someone who remains behind the camera. As the camera continually tracks forward, a hand stretches before its lens. Without seeing the body that would ground our sense of this figure, we do not consider the figure's past and future, aims and desires. The Prodigy song works like techno, bringing elements in and out of a relatively stable mix without establishing sharp sectional divisions. (As such, the videomaker does not need to wrestle with strongly contrasting song sections that might suggest changes of consciousness, activity, or mode of being.) The video's director combines diagetic sound effects with the prerecorded audio track; these sound effects play against and echo material in the song proper, creating a dense soundscape that rests in neither the song's world nor the real one. Depicting a single night out, the video unfolds from early evening to sometime at night. The advancing hour is shown through darkening skies and rooms, people who look more and more disheveled, images of clocks, an increasingly shaky camera, and copious ingestion of drugs and alcohol. The drug and alcohol consumption suggests unpredictable shifts in consciousness for which no account need be provided. Most videos that emphasize a story contain an enigmatic ending, and "Smack My Bitch Up" is no different. At the video's close, a glimpse in a mirror reveals a woman who should be our sexually rapacious, physically abusive protagonist. Attentive viewing shows, however, that the hands before the camera alternate between male and female. How do we reconcile our sense of a unitary male point of view with these differently gendered hands (see fig. 1.2)?

Videos like "Crazy" that present full-blooded stories remain exceptions; it is only through the director's canny and careful deployment of narrative techniques that such videos can succeed in keeping our attention on the song rather than having it preempted by the image. More commonly, music video directors choose imagery reflective of the particular form and scale of a pop song. Janet Jackson's "Anytime, Anyplace" creates the effect of narrative drive from the ways that the image shapes itself to the pop song's form. Most obviously, the video depicts a love story described in the lyrics, and Jackson both sings the song and plays the protagonist. Although she does not lip-sync the entire song or take up all of the narrative space, the video tells the story from her perspective—using such traditional narrative techniques as the point-of-view shot through the keyhole—which is patently not the case with Steven Tyler in "Crazy." A more telling aspect of the Jackson video is evident if we acknowledge the form of the song as it relates to moments of narrative revelation or closure. Specifically, Jackson always initiates a meeting with her lover at the beginning of a verse, sits isolated on the bed in her bedroom during the bridge, and then unites with her lover during the chorus. The minimal nature of the narrative—girl apart, girl together—fits well with the song's three-part structure. Accordingly, Jackson moves repeatedly among three psychological states, finally achieving happiness with her lover just in time for the final chorus, which (quite typically for a pop song) conveys feelings of fulfillment and jubilation.

A particularly satisfying and successful handling of musical material in the service of a narrative trajectory occurs in Marvin Gaye's "Sexual Healing." The work makes use of a device common to many music videos: it possesses mul-

FIGURE 1.2 (A–E) Prodigy's "Smack My Bitch Up." Unusual point-of-view shots assist the narration.

tiple types of setting—performance space, story space, and televisual space—and its cleverness derives from the way that the "story" occurs within the last of the three types, the space most fictional and marginal. On the way to a Gaye concert, a woman watches a silly television show from the back seat of a fancy limousine. Because the show is presented not as the video's main concern (the concert and arriving on time are) but as only a small diversion, we feel less obliged to stake a claim to it. In the show, a spoof on low-budget porn and children's games, the woman and Gaye play "doctor," she being the nurse, he the patient. The nurse checks Gaye's blood pressure, the meter rises, and the lyrics say "Get Up, Get Up." She brings him a giant bottle marked "love potion" with an oversized spoon, and the viewer can guess how this might keep going. The childish visual narrative, which appears only intermittently, is not crucial to the video's flow. Whatever pleasure or anxiety it may elicit from us, the nurse/patient scene is posited as a daydream, disposable and fleeting.[11] Because the music is by Gaye, we already have the arousal and satisfaction that the inset narrative promises the actors. No narrative contests the song's power.

As we move toward nonnarrative videos, it is important to consider those that present some sort of problem or inconsistency and fail to yield a satisfying resolution. Even if we watch these videos repeatedly, we may never feel that we can put the characters and events in clear relation to one another. For me (and for many of my students), these problem narrative videos create a sense of pleasure but also anxiety and trauma. At the end of the video, I will feel as if I have grasped the video at some fundamental level but cannot articulate who, what, where, when, how or why. Such videos exploit two important aspects of the genre: (1) that each shot possesses its own truth value—a truth that cannot be undermined by another shot's; and (2) that each shot has only a vague temporality. Because of these ambiguities of truth value and temporality—and because a pop song's form and lyrics can undermine one another's authority—the viewer is hard pressed to decide a video's ultimate meaning.

Michael Jackson's "Thriller" is an example where each shot possesses its own truth value. Jackson performs in a number of roles: 1970s-style leader of a dance troupe; 1980s-style self-absorbed moviegoer, sidewalk escort, and stay-at-home boyfriend who has yellow eyes; werewolf; and zombie. Although Jackson's first personas might be explained away as a role in the movie within the video, the music lends this imagery integrity: Elmer Bernstein's movie music soundtrack harkens back to 1940s and 1950s classic films and possesses a significant amount of cultural cachet. Rod Temperton's music, on the other hand, though it occurs in the song proper and seems better suited to Jackson's roles as escort and as zombie (in the latter, the plucked acoustic guitar seems to warm up his character), does not have as much authority as Bernstein's music, which has served so many films so well. Here, viewers may have difficulty hierarchizing fantastical images with auctorial music, and pop music against real-life depictions. Not until the video has been watched many times do the different images of Jackson as predatory, flirtatious, and shy gain coherence and weight (see fig. 1.3).

"Like a Prayer," a video that combines a murder filmed in docudrama style alongside footage that looks more like a stagy passion play, is a similar example. At the opening, Madonna runs over a hill past fires, as we hear a guitar solo that sounds desperate and raw. Next, in the midst of a storybook environment, she sings a recitative that recalls operetta. (Although the scene was shot inside a real church, the colors are lurid, and light from a painted sky-blue backdrop peeks through a window above the door.) Throughout the video, Madonna wanders in and out of the church, looking on rather than participating in the action. (Wearing a nightgown, she seems to be sleepwalking.) The curtains that close in on the set at the end of the video suggest that what has just unfolded, including the murder, has been only a play. Yet the viewer may feel less than satisfied. Perhaps the obvious attempt at closure comes too late, and the framing device of the curtains seems too casual. By contrast with this theatrical device (a second order of narrative), the music and image of the opening seems so heartfelt that we cannot reconcile the ending with the beginning. This irreconcilability is not atypical for music video. After watching a narrative film, when we reflect on its opening, the ending most often colors our understanding of the characters and their motivations. In a pop song, however, the ending may cast but little light on the beginning: a jubilant final chorus will not seem to have been influenced by a subdued tone at the outset. This illustrates that the music video shares an important property of music—namely, that no musical moment can annihilate another (as characters can affect one another in film).

LESS THAN NARRATIVE

Thus far we have remained on the side of the continuum where a video's story takes on such precedence that it threatens to overtake the song. Most videos,

FIGURE 1.3 (A–E) Michael Jackson's "Thriller." How should disparate images linked to different musical features be placed in relation?

however, are not so ambitious, choosing rather to suggest the hint of a story and letting the song remain ascendant. A filmmaker may create continuity through moments of narrative closure or revelation that are satisfying but do not take over the action. Madonna's "Cherish," for example, has narrative devices calculated to create peaks of interest rather than to develop the plot. In this video, images that carry a strong emotional charge—one of impregnation and one of birth—encourage us to seek the rest of the story. The sensationalized imagery implies developments that never happen; like certain musical hooks that attempt to shock us, it serves to provoke our interest in development or continuity—to get us into the video. The moments of narrative are so distanced from one another that the video can foreground flow and pattern.

The narrative devices used in Lenny Kravitz's "Are You Gonna Go My Way" are likewise subliminal. The video is ostensibly a performance tape; the site is an indoor coliseum, and only on many viewings is the viewer likely to see the Christological imagery—a crown of thorns, Mary, Judas, and Magdalene figures, the little children, and (last) Kravitz, who is killed symbolically in the end. Because this imagery is so hard to see, it serves more to build flow than to create a narrative. The hook of the song suggests the Christ theme, but even the most committed fans will need to watch it repeatedly to uncover the connection.

In many videos that hint at a story, the functions and meanings of a particular image may seem unclear and even unstable, and viewers may watch the whole of the tape only to discover that they have watched with the wrong kind of attention. The literary and filmic references in the Rolling Stones' "Love Is Strong" are so richly drawn that we assume a narrative is forthcoming. As part of the video's conceit—that the members of the band and other characters are as tall as the buildings in New York City—we see the idle young and beautiful playing in a labyrinth sized to a giant's proportions, along with visual allusions to *Godzilla, Attack of the Fifty-Foot Woman, The Creature from the Black Lagoon, Lolita,* and *Gulliver's Travels.* The cinematic references and the figures' size suggest a payoff—sort of like Mothra versus Mecca Godzilla; however, by the video's close, the Rolling Stones simply show up together in Central Park. By the end of the video it is clear that these are only quotations that fail to add up. By contrast, in U2's "With or Without You," the band members perform in an empty studio while patterns of light are projected before and behind them. The murky patterns suggest fleeting and ornamental images of thorns, waves, a woman, a hand, a box, and possibly a casket. As the video concludes, the lead singer wields his guitar as if he were pushing the light away, and suddenly we realize that these ornamental light patterns might actually represent our protagonist's memory, the encounters from which he wishes to free himself. By pursuing this possibility, we can reconsider the things we have seen and piece out a recounting of a story.

Even more enigmatic is Smashing Pumpkins' "Disarm," in which some elements become more narrative and others more like thematic processes, depending on what the viewer chooses to accept as a ground. The band floats above the steeples and roofs of a city. We see the image of an old man walking slowly down a cobblestone road. There is also footage from grainy home movies of an angry little boy. It is not clear how the two figures relate to each other or to the band. Perhaps they are intended as memories and projections about the lead singer's life. But it could be just an old man and an angry little boy who have little or no relation to the band. Quite possibly the performance footage is only stock music-video imagery where the band extends its presence throughout the space—merely aural and visual filler. We do not know whether the band is moving toward something or whether it is in stasis.

In the Beastie Boys' "Sabotage," there is a deliberate use of narrative techniques, but for the sake of a particular narrative style—that of '70s cop shows—rather than to tell a story: the video brings out the extent to which the borrowed mode was itself as much interested in style and feel as in plot (for example, the television shows *The Streets of San Francisco* and *Kojak,* especially the opening sequences).

EXPLAINING THE ABSENCE OF NARRATIVES

Music videos avoid Aristotelian narratives and fully drawn stories for several reasons: (1) the genre's multimedia nature, (2) the lack of appropriateness and applicability of narrative film devices, and (3) the necessity of foregrounding the song's form (in order to sell the song).

THE GENRE'S MULTIMEDIA NATURE

Videos that foreground changes in fortune, conflicts that matter, and ellipses in the narrative may always introduce an element of trauma: the viewer takes part in the video's unfolding and notes the shifts of activity, affect, and time, but cannot fill in the context. Here, music video's multimedia nature may be the major determinant. Each of music video's media—music, image, and lyrics—are to some extent blank. (Are the lyrics for me or a lover, or are they the singer's personal reflection? To whom do the empty sets and characters belong? What are the music's uses, and what spaces should it fill?) Music, image, and lyrics each possess their own language with regard to time, space, narrativity, activity, and affect.

The rest of the book will explore this topic, but I would like to give one example of how each medium possesses its own language with regard to time, space, narrativity, and affect. Music video's narratives are constructed by not only the tangled accumulation of music/image conjunctions, each of which may possess its own point of view and truth value; music, lyrics, and image even possess a distinct sense of time, whether suggestive of the future or the past, of time spent languidly or nervously. The sense of time created by music, lyrics, and image is always indefinite rather than exact, never definitive of the day or the moment. Each medium can suggest different types of time, and each can undercut or put into question the temporality of another medium. Not surprisingly, therefore, in "Take a Bow," a video in which Madonna falls in love with a bullfighter, the music for the verse opens with a broad, open feel and closes with a touch of hesitation. The accompanying images show Madonna, the matador and the people of the town meticulously preparing for a bullfight over the course of what appears to be a single day. (The music and imagery match closely but not exactly. The music has a sense of grace, yet the image carries the scent of dull, repetitive labor.) A secondary staging presents Madonna standing or sitting alone in a room, hunched below a single light source, or passing her hands in front of a television set; here time seems painful, a suggestion that Madonna has engaged in this activity for a very long time. The music for the chorus, relaxed and lyrical in a ruminative way, could extend over a day or months. Even more oblique is the imagery featuring hands flowing over the matador's cape and Madonna's face and arms falling through the frame. This imagery is almost devoid of temporal markers: they might suggest a particular instant, a reoccurring moment, or a passing thought. Later, when Madonna and the bullfighter have what looks like demoralizing sex, there is no way to draw on what we have learned to tell if this is a one-time fling, a repeated event, or a figment of the star's imagination (see fig. 1.4).

Even when the three media of lyrics, music and image seem to combine seamlessly into a new whole, some aspects of music, image, and lyrics may move to the background (as time, space, narrativity, activity, and affect), where they linger in an almost palpable way. Each medium may also change in relation to the others, making the multimedia object ambiguous. Finally, each element—music, image, and lyrics—is, moment by moment, riddled with its own ellipses. What happened between the cut from the image of the face to the shot

FIGURE 1.4 (A–E) Madonna's "Take a Bow." An image imbued with the rhythms of dull, repetitive labor, and languorous music evoke two different senses of time.

of the fingertips? From the line "she knew me well" to "I've always been there for you"? Or in the shift from the verse to the chorus?

The video often begins with the establishment of a ground, with a sense of stability and coherence. Although I cannot immediately understand the movement from one shot to another, the music begins to give me some feel for it, and the lyrics help me to piece it out. Once the music video starts developing a sense of history, however, and musical, visual, or lyrical elements begin to draw upon what the video has presented thus far, I note that I cannot find these sources from earlier in the video. One such source may be locked in the visual track in the fourth beat of the third measure of the first chorus. Another may be found in the lyrics of the second verse, third line. A third may reside in the music's texture, somewhere in the introduction. These moments are quite disparate, and between them stretches an archipelago of different events. These three moments from the video's past, and the moment in the video's present that has sent me back to them, are linked to other such complexes, each contributing to the present moment's sense of culmination. The best way for me to grasp the video is to learn the patterns inherent in the music, lyrics, and image, as well as the relations among these patterns, and to make conjectures about what happens in the gaps—time lapses, activity not shown, unexplained motivations. The template thus created (out of both depicted and inferred material) cannot be experienced in real time, because music videos are designed to be almost constantly engaging: the image draws us on as it rushes forward. Cognitive research on film has suggested that we cannot simultaneously track every medium of a multimedia object. We may only hear and see moments of congruence among media, for example. Perhaps we may thereby edit out the most crucial aspects of a video.[12]

TECHNIQUES FROM FILM

Because music videos often lack essential ingredients—place names, meeting times, a link to both past and present, and fully realized protagonists and villains—they cannot be described as possessing a classical Hollywood film narrative. As a rule, music videos do not help us to predict what will happen— in the next shot, or the following section, or at the close of the tape. To engage the audience in a feature film, many directors adopt a technique known as the narrative plank. An appointment is set, after which the character engages in some routine activity in preparation for the important meeting: she packs a suitcase and then walks or drives to the next scene. This gives the viewer ample time to predict how the upcoming encounter will unfold. If the director is able to intuit the viewer's guesses, and even incorporate an unusual twist on these expectations, he or she will seem competent and worthy of the viewer's respect. But because the objective of music video is to be continually engrossing, there is little time for a narrative plank. The music demands attention at every instant; a pressing future takes away from an interesting present. Music video typically elicits some protensive activity, most often on a local level—within spatial terms or within broadly sketched outlines of interpersonal relations (which also feel spatial). The viewer might chart how long it will take for the melodic line to reach its apex, or for the musical section to close, or for the figure to move across the room, or for one stock character to "get with" another.

Often the imagery that occurs at one of the high points of the video will have been disclosed somewhere in the opening third. As we move past the opening imagery, however, we can seldom identify an object, person, or setting as the "marked" material that will round out or clinch the piece. The satisfying rhythm of concealment and discovery so crucial to film narrative is less present in music video. Likewise, videos almost never give us enough information to predict one outcome over another (even if, in retrospect, the narrative appears to have unfolded in a coherent fashion). All outcomes seem possible—including an abandonment of the narrative in favor of a dance sequence.[13]

As it is, the superficiality and brevity of a pop song mean that truly evil antagonists are almost always absent, and background figures can be only mildly threatening; their power and reasons for implementing it remains unclear. Some examples include the stone-faced judges in Nine Inch Nails' "Closer" and the factory owner in Madonna's "Express Yourself." Given the absence of villains and, correspondingly, so few elements with which to define them, music-video figures become shadowy.

Music video's protagonists are strange. Video directors I have interviewed note how rare it is for viewers to become truly curious about the lead character. By common consent, a handful of Mark Romanek's videos form a rare exception. (Michael Jackson's "Scream," Fiona Apple's "Criminal," Madonna's "Bedtime Stories" and "Rain," and No Doubt's "Hellagood" are good examples.)[14] Romanek's videos contain a series of tantalizing glimpses into some offscreen world, whole within itself but opaque to viewers. His characters possess special powers and often partake in illicit behavior. Yet, although viewers may be curious about the characters, they do not know enough about them to form more than the beginnings of a story.

To understand the elusive qualities of a character in a music video is to accept a music video as a short, almost mute form whose purpose is to showcase the star, highlight the lyrics, and underscore the music. This requires that the viewer's attention be directed to various parameters; constant shift of focus precludes the construction of a unified subject. In addition, music video possesses multiple senses of time and space. A music video's star is a phantasmagoric multiple: the songwriter, the performer, and the figure on the screen embody different subjectivities. When the video is finally an edited whole, the image follows the music, and there is the eerie sense that the music, rather than the subject's intent, animates the figure. Generally, the image, in order to match the speed and energy of the music, reflects a more heightened experiential state than ordinary consciousness, and the characters seem like mythical automatons.

FOREGROUNDING THE SONG'S FORM

Thus far, I have discussed how music video's multimedia nature and the applicability of Hollywood narrative film devices shape music video narratives. Now I would like to consider this question in relation to popular songs. Pop videos are rarely teleological, and the same is true of pop music. Reflecting different aspects of a single topic, the verse might lay out the situation, while the bridge presents a solution to the problem, and the chorus, a crystallization of it. When a section repeats, we seem to know it more clearly. Similarly, as a musical and visual section repeats in a music video, we return to a related set of interests. More generally, videos mimic the concerns of pop music, which are usually a consideration of a topic rather than an enactment of it. If the intent of music-video imagery lies in drawing attention to the music—whether to provide commentary on it, or simply to sell it—it makes sense that the image ought not to carry a story or plot in the way that a feature film might. Otherwise, videomakers would run the risk of our being so engaged with the actions of the characters or so concerned with impending events that we are pulled outside the realm of the video and become involved with other narrative possibilities. The song would recede into the background, like film music. Music-video imagery gains from holding back information, confronting the viewer with ambiguous or unclear depictions. If there is a story, it exists only in the dynamic relation between the song and the image as they unfold in time.

The problems of superimposing a fully wrought narrative on the episodic, cyclical structure of a pop song can be seen in videos that derive from feature films—for example, Paula Abdul's "Hush Hush" (borrowed from *Rebel Without a Cause*), Meatloaf's "I'd Do Anything for Love, but I Won't Do That" (*Beauty and the Beast*), and Blues Traveler's "Runaround" (*The Wizard of Oz*). In all of these, the opening two-thirds of the video follows the original source, and we can recognize the themes that will eventually collide to create a new status quo. But the videos fail to take up the encounters that truly count. They devolve instead into randomness and confusion. Perhaps such an encounter and its aftermath would suggest a sense of time and a type of structure different from that of the song.[15] In an interview with me in spring 1998, director David Fincher noted that when he first started to make videos, he tried to tell straight stories but soon abandoned the throughline approach. Rather, he began to create six or seven separate segments, each evoking a unique mood configured as an autonomous unit. This stylistic feature establishes the context for what most clearly distinguishes the character in a music video from a character in narrative film. Whereas an action of the latter spawns a series of effects that reflect back on him, thereby encouraging him to act again, the impetus in music video resides episodically in the song or in the way that the figures move in concert with the music. Moreover, a clear sense of time and movement must belong to the music in order for us to bestow our attention on it. Assuming that the figures in video are not characters in a story—they are the band or extras—and that we will not be told what led up to the situation of the video and what will follow from it, our best course is to examine how music videos foreground a play of relations among figures, rather than the unfolding of a story; thus, we will likely have a place, a group of figures, and perhaps a few objects to which our attention is drawn. As the video unfolds, the relations among the elements will shift, and these elements will become clearer or vaguer, closer to or more distant from one another. No matter the degree of shift in these relations, the process will seem to have evolved out of elements that were present in the opening. By the end of the video, we may feel as if we know the place, the figures, and the objects more definitively, even without anecdotal underpinnings.

The unfolding of relations among figures in music video resembles the manipulation of materials in popular music. In a pop song, each musical element can both exist within its own sphere and become transformed over the course of the piece. For example, after a flute line is introduced, it will then be varied, extended, or simply repeated so that, by the end of the song, it stands in a new relation to other musical elements, like the bass line and the voice. Or, if the flute line disappears, it becomes submerged in the unfolding of the piece. Even when there is a dramatic break—when the music cuts out, the image shifts realms, sound effects and dialogue are added—the music will quickly resume, and the work remains intact. There is no annihilation of materials in music, as there is in narrative film.

Does music and video image here mimic some of the properties of music? In "Thriller," "Like a Prayer," and "Take a Bow," the contradictory evidence and lack of temporal cues may make viewers doubt the existence of a "true story." When a video's attention to narrative seems to fade, does the viewer's engagement shift elsewhere, perhaps toward a focus on a certain type of personal relationship? Music video's indifference to causality can best be seen in "Like a Prayer," which devotes little attention to questions of whether the murderer will be caught, whether Madonna will testify, or whether the saint will go free. Just as Aerosmith's "Crazy" eventually becomes not a story but a study of the closeness between two girls and "Take a Bow" explores the connection between two sadomasochistic lovers, "Like a Prayer" reflects mainly on Madonna's involvement with the saint, singer, and gospel choir. Details about Madonna and the black lead singer are drawn with particular care: the relationship is highlighted by seamless, graceful editing and by similarity in lighting, hair, clothing, and facial and bodily expression. (As with the Aerosmith video, "Like a Prayer" has its homoerotic moments.) In contrast to that bond, Madonna and the black saint are separated by tears, edgy editing, handcuffs, and prison bars. While "Like a Prayer" has these satisfying moments based in a detailed here-and-now relationship—the past and future becoming uncertain and dissolving away—the obvious narrative devices work less successfully.

Some musicologists have claimed that music can suggest a narrative in its own language. Here narrative contains a succession of integrated events, repetition, and calls to the listener's recollections to integrate the work into a significant whole. Childs points out that music can have a narrative curve similar to those found in conversation. He notes that there is often an introduction, development, climax, and concluding gesture.[16]

Yet most pop songs are so blocklike and hook-driven that they may not suggest a narrative curve.[17] Pasler grants music a narrative through a more generous description. Any time we can make out a figure against a ground— a person standing in front of a building or a melodic line against its accompaniment—we might grant this figure a sense of agency.[18] Popular music can possess a subtly constructed soundworld that suggests a physical environment with which a voice or melodic line must contend. Yet finding a narrative for a pop song can be trickier than finding one for a classical piece. Often the music is so carefully shaped that it imitates and echoes features of the voice, thereby suggesting that the sonic bed in which the voice lies is more like a part of the psyche than like an external environment. Melody and accompaniment may not divide easily into a person and a physical environment. Philip Tagg has suggested that the drive and propulsiveness of a song alone can suggest a narrative, and I do agree that songs leave us with a sense that something is being told.[19] With this model, the notion of a number of micronarratives interspersed across the video might be more helpful. The rock star moving against the music with varying degrees of energy and self-possession can suggest a relation of figure to background. In addition, the rock star's image and recorded voice can suggest two different personas, one divided against the other. Both may be struggling against musical lines recorded on separate tracks. These momentary struggles may collide with the video's large-scale narrative, which might be concerned simply with making it to the concert on time. Not only that: these micronarratives are episodic, and we must follow them in tandem with many other lines of development.

But Jean-Jacques Nattiez argues that if there is a narrative in music, it is only because the listener put it there. Music has no method for communicating a past tense (we are always in the present), a technique commonly used in literary narratives.[20] He points out that music may unleash in the listener a string of narratizing behaviors much in the same way as when we see initials carved in a tree and we think, "John loves Mary, or Mary loves John, or John and Mary are in love, or here on the spot, John met Mary, or John remembers Mary, or Mary remembers John."[21] Interpretive freedom remains immense because, as in music, the narrative here is only a virtual object. All the capabilities to join subject and predicate, to recollect, expect, to resolve, are made by the listener. "Music," said Theodor Adorno about Gustav Mahler's music, "is a narrative that narrates nothing."[22] In music, we do not know who, what, where, or why. Music is not a narrative, says Nattiez, "but rather an incitement to make a narrative, to comment, to analyze."[23] As Suzanne Langer remarks, "Music is an unconsummated symbol."[24]

In music video, what is concealed and what is revealed serve to encourage multiple viewings by engaging the viewer in a process of reconstructing, interpolating, or extrapolating a story behind the scenes that are actually visible. When the narrative mode is present even fleetingly, it creates an aura of mystery, a sense that things need to be puzzled out; it also raises questions of continuity, of how the video unfolds, especially by encouraging an engagement with figures. Both the distance from cinematic narrative depiction and the proximity to it play a role in this creation of a sense of engagement.

TYPES OF NONNARRATIVE

If narrative models fail to capture a large portion of music video, what models can we put in their stead? Many videos are devoted to completing a single process: getting everyone to the party on time, ensuring that the plane gets off the ground or that the baby is born, and so on. (Here, we might define process as the act of carrying on or going on, a series of actions, changes, or functions bringing about a result, or a series of operations performed in the making or treatment of a product.) Such music-video projects do not feel like narratives, in part because they are arbitrary; one activity might have been picked as well as another. In addition, the focus on a single task often becomes apparent only in retrospect. The presentation of this process is fragmented, attenuated abruptly by images of the band performing or lip-syncing against an amorphous background. The sustained treatment of the activity comes suddenly, at a time when we do not expect it, and its duration may be unusually prolonged or drastically abbreviated. The video's main project is dispersed across a number of the song's sections. When footage of this material appears over the course of the video, carrying the process forward, these appearances gain an uncanny sense of return. In such videos, the emblematic characters, appearing intermittently with ferocious attention to a simple task, create qualities of volition and determination befitting musical materials that function similarly.

A related type of music video involves categories, series, or lists. The performers might walk through a series of tableaux or separate rooms, or down the street as they encounter different people. The musician might be seen recounting a number of previous relationships. Like the laundry list, the catalog is not a narrative; events or settings simply fall one after another. The catalog works well in a music video because the addition of a new yet familiar item (one that has a similar shape) can be compared with musical material that returns regularly but also incorporates variation.

The travelogue has elements of both the "process" video and the category or list—the performer driving, sailing, walking, and seeing or fantasizing things along the way. Sting's "Desert Rose," Matchbox 20's "Ben," and Bon Jovi's "It's My Life" are examples. Of special note is a species that blends process and list with a vaguely mysterious sense of cause and effect. One example is the mechanical chain of causality in which the camera tracks the flow à la Rube

Goldberg's machines. In Nice Day's "The Story of a Girl," after a woman in a bathtub tosses and turns, the overflowing water seeps through the ceiling and shorts out the television set of the apartment below. The couch bursts into flames, triggering the fire extinguisher. The ceiling pipes start to shower, and the party in the apartment one floor below breaks into a celebratory dance. Like the protagonist of the Bon Jovi video, the woman in "It's My Life" shows up at the party in her own way. Such a chain demands that we consider every event, and even compare one against another. Like most pop songs, the episodes emphasize continuity and flow but also contain transformations. This chain of events may be purely a function of gravity, but we cannot be sure; the movement of the camera from one surface to another almost resembles the passage of sound through water or walls.

In music video as a whole, any visual reference to an unusual mechanical cause seems to suggest that the music possesses the greatest authority. R.E.M.'s "Shiny Happy People" takes place in a high school auditorium, and a man pedaling a stationary bicycle rotates a pulley that draws back the curtains on the stage and shifts the rolling painted backdrop behind the actors and musicians. To ascertain whether this could really happen, we examine the music for possibilities. In fact, almost any technical, mechanical, or physical link between two spaces in relation to the music—two-way mirrors, rear-screen projections, pipes, satellites, computer terminals, television sets, and antennas—creates a question about effects.

Music-video directors add richness and complexity to the simple structures of processes and lists in several ways. One is to include a number of threads (for example, organized around lists, processes, or series) in a music video and make sure that at some point at least one becomes linked with another. Many music videos work on the principle of contagion: an element in one of the strands seeps into another—it might be a color, a particular prop, a way of feeling or moving. For example, in Ben Folds Five's "Brick," the splashes of red that appear in the performance space (which function purely as an arbitrary, decorative touch) gradually invade the story space (we see a red Christmas bulb). Rage Against the Machine's "Bulls on Parade" presents a much more complex example. The video weaves eight threads into the texture in an unpredictable way: (1) generic, black-garbed freedom fighters wielding flags make their way up a mountain (a la "king of the hill"); (2) the band performs, becoming more agitated as time progresses; (3) the crowds surge; (4) iconic political propaganda flashes on the screen; (5) text hand-scratched on film jitters on the screen; (6) a printing press churns; (7) an anonymous person writes graffiti on institutional walls proclaiming "long live the Los Angeles revolution"; (8) close-ups of earnest, highly photogenic young people of various ethnicities appear. Many of these threads contain material or processes that seep into the others. The torn red flags that become more worn as the video progresses connect to the last close-up of the lead performer, who stands firm, though looking completely exhausted. The red from the flag starts coloring the black and white footage of the crowd and the performers. The guitar necks begin to angle upward in the frame, as does the scribbled text, matching the movement of the freedom fighters as they make their way up the hill. (Over the course of the song, the tessitura shifts from low to high.) Even though they are clearly in a different space, the youthful ethnic types begin to bestow greater definition on the generic black-garbed freedom fighters. A crude line drawing of the graffiti artist strips them bare (fig. 1.5).

The technique of using several threads of material that intersect later works well for constructing music videos. As the music shifts or a shot's novelty liquidates, the director can choose imagery from one of several strands and slot that imagery into the video based on what most fits the needs of the song at that particular moment. In this way, she is able to build a visual track that closely follows musical changes. "Bulls on Parade" as a riff-based song on its own may catch our attention more than does "Crazy," but it is also remarkable how many more of the song's nuances we hear while watching "Bulls on Parade" than from viewing "Crazy."

A consideration of a video's use of processes, threads, and contamination is helpful for analyzing videos that we judge as narrative. "Thriller" contains several long vamps. We can compare what happens in each vamp—what Jackson does when he has a date and when he is a zombie—and why one section might end with a sexy kiss and the other with the touch of death. With "Take a Bow," we might look at the ways characters fulfill their daily activities. In the case of Madonna and the matador, it culminates in sex or slaying a bull. Why would one thread be slotted in at this musical moment versus another?

Another way to add complexity is to flesh out (and/or strip down) the

FIGURE 1.5 (A–I) Rage Against the Machine's "Bulls on Parade." Several threads help to construct a form.

various threads, as in DMX's and Sisqo's "What You Really Want," where DMX recites a litany of past girlfriends and we see them one by one. A third of the way into the video, we see rows of women's legs; toward the end of the video, in the middle of the street, in a pyramid structure are Sisqo and numerous women in various complicated physical contortions; and finally, a close-up of DMX appears against the barren, cold background of sound baffles. DMX seems to be thinking about Sisqo and the women but is not able to participate. He has taken up the mantle of the hardworking musician, yet his thoughts dwell uneasily elsewhere; hence some sort of contamination has occurred, even if it is only within a psychic realm. Although visual strands may quickly come together and then depart and head their own way, an elaboration and playing out of material will seem to have taken place.

There are a few more nonnarrative modes still left for consideration—some more purely processual and some more based on tableaux. Many music videos simply extend performance settings: the performer might appear in a dolled-up high-school theater, and then some activity will play out backstage or in the wings. Performance videos are discussed in chapter 4; however, it is worth mentioning here that although the depiction may be static, the relation between the performer and the setting can seem unusually charged, as if the activity within the frame is somewhat taboo, and the police or a parent might rush in on the scene at any moment. In "Virtual Insanity," Jamiroquia occupies a silvery, boxlike setting. He does little except move back and forth along a floor resembling a conveyer belt, yet around him hover a number of ominous elements: a crow, a pool of blood, a group of techno/science-fictional men appearing and then disappearing. While the objects have little meaning, they present a bit of threat or danger for the performer.

Similar to the performance video is the "slice of life." The slice of life functions in music video more as an extended tableau than as documentary, however: a single image will be highlighted in time rather than revealed at once, with only one or two elements shifting slightly. In Dishwalla's "Charlie Brown's Parents" a stock situation is set up—a candidate for public office appears with his unhappy spouse at a fundraiser while the band performs. In a vague way, the dynamic between the couple changes when the wife heads down the corridor, possibly to pick up a young campaign worker. Given numerous uncertainties—the viewer sees footage of the band only intermittently, does not know the time in which all of this is happening, and might guess that one thing might occur as well as something else—we may feel that we are simply seeing one tableau after another. We may connect the dots between instances, but what happens in the interim might be arbitrary.

Music videos often suggest a story, but in a somewhat static way: we obtain no more visual information than we might derive from a single narrative painting. One such example is Faith Hill's "Breathe," in which the singer, swaddled in white cotton sheets, lies voluptuously on a bed in the desert. She also stands on the sand in a sheer satin dress. The video takes on a gold tone, and two-thirds into the piece, the singer takes two or three steps toward the camera. In the last shot, she stands wearing what resembles a white wedding dress with strips of lace, satin, and cotton—a composite of her earlier clothes and bed linens. "You Oughta Know" shows Alanis Morissette performing in the foundations of a burned-down house, walking around in the desert with a suitcase, sitting on a bench, and lying in a poppy field. Neither of these two videos tells a story, but the faintest allusions to domesticity—to brides, lovers, and housekeepers—are enough to suggest the possibility that a story is being generated.

Music videos encourage us early on to seek out a narrative, and by the video's close, they suggest that something crucial has transpired. But where, when, and how did this transformative event occur? Perhaps the evidence is buried in too many different places, and the clues are too elliptical. How much do we really know about what happens? A viewer may believe that some moment of density and richness is locked somewhere within this tape. But where is it? And what was it?

DISCOVERING NARRATIVES THROUGH CLOSE READING

When confronted with a Hollywood film, we can assume the existence of a narrative; anxieties about the kind of movie we will see are usually put to rest by the end of the opening credits. Given the likelihood that a music video will lack certain narrative drive, it is not clear, at first, with what kind of attention we should watch. During the accretion of details that shape the production into a narrative, documentary, or performance video, the initiate will look intently for cues to determine the genre of the video—action adventure, sitcom, musical, fashion magazine, advertisement, soap opera, B movie, or whatever. Yet the sources of music video are quite disparate, and even if the genre appears to be narrative, a story may not materialize. Generic cues may provide no more guidance for the viewer than do other unfolding narrative elements.

A look at how easel painters handle depiction will be helpful to our understanding. Educated audiences know that if a portrait includes a particular cluster of icons like a lily, a cross, and a swan, there will be no story conveyed about the person depicted in the painting; rather, by drawing on biblical and mythological references, the painting will point to a generalized truth—an ideal such as faith, beauty, or chastity. If detailed attention is paid to the depiction of the figure, however—one focused more on specifics than on an idealized image—we might instead ask questions involved with narrativity: who is the person, how does he live, and so on.

To comprehend the ways that characters function in music video, we can learn from the film theorist Jean-Louis Comolli's discussion of the difference between cubist painting and traditional film.[25] He claims that no one looking at a still life by Georges Braque seeks further information about the objects that make up the composition—what the fish may be telling each other, why they are there and not in the sea, to whom the lemon belongs, and whether the plate is exploiting them. In cinema, he says, the opposite is true: an actor cannot put one foot in front of the other without a spectator wanting to know where he is going, why, whether the woman he loves has broken with him, and whether that is his last pair of shoes.

Music-video characters resemble the lemon, fish, and sea in Comolli's description of Braque's painting. Each figure is integral and whole, yet also opaque and mysterious. Nothing can be added to a music-video character, and nothing can be taken away. Perhaps the sketchy, obscure nature of music videos helps to create the sense that most often they are kept at a threshold below which a narrative commences. Without enough material to get us started, we spend time simply deciding what to make of the characters and whether to take them as allegorical figures, as musicians who find themselves in a strange situation, or as actors within a complete fiction. To see the characters as self-possessed and well-formed agents, we must feel that we can become acquainted with them. The ability to know what the characters will do next, or how they will meet the next obstacle before them, depends on this choice.

Music videos often challenge us at the first moment we must try to read them. It takes a certain skill to determine where to place a work because depictive modes collide within the same video. For example, in Monica's "Before You Walk Out of My Life," the scenes of her walking in the city are too emblematic to suggest anything but a fashion shoot. Monica walks a large Dalmatian, and she wears matching raincoat and boots. The umbrella she carries over her shoulder is tilted just so, and the New York City locations are chosen for their graphic values rather than for their sense of place. She and her dog constitute an emblem rather than characters in a narrative. By contrast, Monica and her boyfriend appear in cutaways against a simply lit, plain black background, and they appear to be placed there in order to document their relationship for a family portrait. The exchange of gestures between the pair seems nuanced and intimate, and the look is reminiscent of the photo spreads that accompanied serious biographies for *Life* magazine from the 1950s to the 1970s. To make sense of the two depictive modes, the viewer will have to decide what the languages we associate with style and intimacy have to do with each other, and part of the answer may lie in how the music plays against both.

Another telling comparison can be made between Boyz 2 Men's "On Bended Knee" and Jodeci's "Gotta Get on Up." The Boyz 2 Men video deals with the separations and reconciliations of band members and their lovers. We watch for a story, yet the pastel colors, the soft focus, the forced perspective, the lack of differentiation between individual women and men, and the very generic things the couples do—baking cakes, writing on a mirror with lipstick, drawing portraits with the lover as model, hiding sheet music, and breaking a record in half—signal that these are tales about all lovers rather than any particular ones. By contrast, the Jodeci production presents a much more fleshed-out

narrative, although its subject matter is restricted to people listening and dancing to live music, and its conceit makes it look like a common type of performance video. By showing the band coming into town on a bus and holding a
block party, the video suggests that these particular people have a significant
relation to the place where they live. The cinematographic style is documentary,
and many of the shots echo the WPA photographs of Dorothea Lange. In
actuality, this neighborhood had recently suffered from a great deal of racial
strife, and the anxiety on the faces is real. Although the depictions are relatively
static—a woman looking through a window onto her front porch, a young
child with a ball—the viewer would like to know more about the underlying
context for these people and this place. The previous two examples show that
realistic codes drawn from sources such as painting, fashion, and news photography may ground our understanding of video.

2

Editing

WHEN CRITICS of film and television say that something is "cut like music video" or refer to "MTV style editing," what do they mean? They might mention quick cutting or editing on the beat. And indeed, one can see that the edits in music video come much more frequently than in film, that many stand out as disjunctive, and that the editing seems to have a rhythmic basis closely connected to the song. These last two features of music-video editing—that it is sometimes meant to be noticed and that it brings out aspects of the song—suggest at once that it does something different, and perhaps something more, than does the editing in film. Music-video editing bears a far greater responsibility for many elements than does classic Hollywood film editing. Not only does the editing in a music video direct the flow of the narrative, but it can also underscore nonnarrative visual structures and form such structures on its own. Like film editing, it can color our understanding of characters, but it has also assimilated and extended the iconography of the pop star.

Much of the particularity of music-video editing lies in its responsiveness to the music. It can elucidate aspects of the song, such as rhythmic and timbral features, particular phrases in the lyrics, and especially the song's sectional divisions. Because it can establish its own rhythmic profile, the editing can provide a counterpoint to the song's rhythmic structures. More subtly, and most importantly, the editing in a music video works hard to ensure that no single element (the narrative, the setting, the performance, the star, the lyrics, the song) gains the upper hand. Music-video directors rely on the editing to maintain a sense of openness, a sense that any element can come to the fore at any time. The editing does so in part simply through being noticed. By demanding attention, it prevents powerful images from acquiring too much weight and stopping the flow of information. The editing thus preserves the video's momentum and keeps us in the present. A striking edit can allow one to move past a number of strange or disturbing images while neither worrying about them nor forgetting them completely.[1]

Music video's complexity stems not only from the sheer number of functions it serves, but also from the way that it moves unpredictably among these functions. It may be helpful to picture the succession of images in a video, and the edits that join them, more as a necklace of variously colored and sized beads than as a chain. This picture not only emphasizes the heterogeneity of shots in music video, but it also suggests the materiality of the edit itself. Indeed, sometimes the edit seems to function as a part of the image and sometimes as a gap.

This chapter is divided into five sections: (1) an introduction to the grammar of shots and edits, and a discussion of how their functions differ between film and music video; (2) an analysis of the role of editing in making meaning, creating narrative, and establishing other forms of continuity; (3) an explanation of how music-video image adapts to the processual nature of sound; (4) an examination of the ways that music videos treat close-ups of the star; and (5) a presentation of the means by which editing can reflect musical features. Because it deciphers types of shots and edits, this chapter functions as a grammar for music-video editing; however, it also contains a theoretical component. I argue that the edits in music video mean something different—and create meaning differently—from their filmic counterparts. Even when a shot and edit in a music video remind one of classic narrative film, their function may have undergone a change of valence. Music-video editing, like camera movement and camera placement, enables relations between the song and the image.

SHOTS AND EDITS

When constructing a taxonomy of shots and edits in music video, one can begin with traditional narrative film practices. The continuity system forms the basis of film editing but is much less common in music video. Common continuity edits in film include the 180-degree rule, which preserves screen direction, as well as the thirty-degree rule, which prevents a jump cut between two shots, and shot/reverse-shots, over-the-shoulder shots, and matches on actions.[2] Such edits attempt to naturalize the movement from shot to shot and render the break as seamless as possible. Continuity editing seeks to preserve the flow of time and the coherence of spaces. The ultimate goal of continuity editing is to create a single, clear path through a film's world. Because music videos seem to benefit from providing a multiplicity of incomplete, sometimes obscure paths, continuity editing will serve different functions and govern only isolated sections of a video.[3] Perhaps music videos avoid continuity editing because such techniques would give the visual track too strong a forward trajectory: the image might seem to overtake the song. A music video's aim is to spark a listener's interest in the song, to teach her enough about it that she is moved first to remember the song and second to purchase it. Music video's disjunctive editing keeps us within the ever-changing surface of the song. Though such edits may create a momentary sense of disequilibrium, they force the viewer to focus on musical and visual cues, allowing the viewer to regain a sense of orientation. In addition, the dense, oblique quality of a string of images can serve to showcase the star. The viewer may experience a jolt of accomplishment and pleasure as she passes through a thicket of imagery to come upon a clearing where she finds herself alone with a close-up of the performer. One of the most narrative music videos, Aerosmith's "Janie's Got a Gun," comes the closest to following the rules of traditional Hollywood continuity, yet it also extends and breaks these rules. The video concerns incest. At one point, the father stands at the threshold of his daughter's room while the mother watches. In this sequence, sightlines do not match. Consequently, it will take a while for the viewer to notice that, based upon the position of the characters, the mother is watching the father, yet he does not see her. In addition, the thirty-degree rule is violated between the medium and close-up shots of the father. (The camera angle between shots is narrower than thirty degrees, and the object in the frame appears to jump.) Music videos avoid matches on action, often extending or abbreviating a shot to give the sense of a cut in the "wrong place." This effect blunts narrative progress and creates a rhythmic emphasis on the moment when the edit occurs[4] (fig. 2.1).

It will be helpful to widen our consideration of editing techniques to include not only those of classic Hollywood films, but also those in the Russian formalist film tradition. Karel Reisz's description of Eisenstein's *October* works as a characterization of music-video editing.

Indeed, as a piece of narrative, [*October*] is extremely unsatisfactory. The incidents are loosely constructed and do not follow each other with the dramatic inevitability which a well-told story demands: we are not, for instance, shown Kerensky's character through a series of dramatically motivated episodes but through a number of random incidents, each suggesting a further aspect of Kerensky's vanity or incompetence. The time relationship

FIGURE 2.1 (A–E) Aerosmith's "Janie's Got a Gun." Departures from the continuity system—breaking the thirty-degree rule and sightline matches.

between consecutive shots and scenes is left undefined and no sense of continuous development emerges: the cut from [shots] 108 to 109, for example, takes us—without reason or explanation—from the Czar's study to a staircase somewhere in the palace. No attempt is made to explain or to conceal the time lapse between the shots, as could easily have been done with a dissolve.[5]

It seems intuitive that the Russian film formalists (precursors to the experimental filmmaking tradition) should share a lot with music-video directors, but some of the reasons why this is so may not be immediately clear. We should remember that the early Russian film directors Lev Kuleshov, Vsevolod Pudovkin, and Sergei Eisenstein worked with minimal resources (film was so valuable that it was recycled for its silver), and they used almost no intertitles because they were making films for a largely illiterate public. Even though music-video directors can command great resources in the era of late capitalist production, they too struggle with limitations. These limitations may seem trivial by comparison: music video is a short form; the music and lyrics may be banal; the singer must lip-sync while the rest of the figures remain silent; much time must be spent showcasing the star. Like the early Russian filmmakers, they have to make the most of the brute materials of film, and to make frames and cuts as expressive as possible.

One kind of edit, graphic match, appears frequently in music video and Russian formalist films, but much less often in traditional narrative film. Such an edit joins two shots through shared compositional elements such as color or shape, irrespective of content. In film, graphic matches are normally used to join scenes. Strikingly formal, they appear unnatural in most other contexts. Whereas we might see one or two graphic matches in the whole of a Hollywood narrative film, we often find two or three in a five-minute music video. Music video can use graphic matches so freely because the genre has reason to draw attention to its materials and production methods: the viewer can revel in an interesting edit, in a nice shape shared by two images, and in the cleverness of the director's and the editor's work, any of which might draw us away from the narrative of a Hollywood movie.[6] The graphic match can highlight elements of a popular song. As just mentioned, in the graphic match most visual parameters remain the same while one changes. In a pop song, a melody might be sung by the voice and be picked up by a flute. In this case, the one feature that has changed is timbre. Both sound and image share qualities of transformation and continuity (fig. 2.2). The concentration of imagery in music video has led

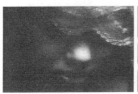

FIGURE 2.2 (A–B)
Peter Gabriel's "Mercy Street."
A graphic match.

to an expanded role for the visual principles of graphic match. In particular, videos will contain groups of nonadjacent shots that share bold compositional elements. (I will discuss the nature and structural role of these groups of shots later in this chapter.) Film editing generally seeks to avoid placing a series of shots that contain motion against one another; films will interpose a static shot when possible. When films cut between shots with motion, the editing tries to keep the viewer's eye in the same location to minimize the disjunctive effect.[7] Only in action sequences or heightened dramatic scenes does the editing compel the viewer to shift focus rapidly from one edge of the frame to another. Music videos place movement against movement much more promiscuously, juxtaposing motion within the frame to camera movement and mixing speeds, directions, and durations (fig. 2.3).

Unlike films, music videos frequently employ intentionally disjunctive edits. A jump cut, which is generally unacceptable in film, can be avoided by shifting the camera at least thirty degrees between two adjacent shots that contain a change in scale. The jump cut makes us feel that we are lurching forward or back. This kind of edit has been much discussed since its occasional deliberate use in films of the French New Wave (fig. 2.4). Music videos use jump cuts liberally, along with a variety of other disjunctive edits. There are brusque edits that demand attention through a drastic shift in scale, color, or content. Some-

FIGURE 2.3 (A–D) Janet Jackson's "Love Will Never Do (Without You)." Music videos place movement against movement promiscuously, juxtaposing motion within the frame to camera movement and mixing speeds, directions, and durations.

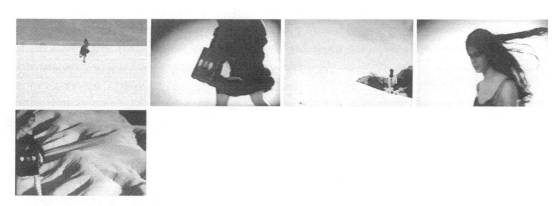

FIGURE 2.4 (A–E) Alanis Morissette's "You Oughta Know." Jump cuts.

times we see an even stronger edit, one so clearly aestheticized that it separates itself from the flow of the video. This edit might contain a roughened edge (say, a bit of film leader and a white flash sandwiched between the shots) that makes it work like a jump cut.

It is important as well that videos can create confusion about what is an edit and what is not. There are many ways to produce a meaningful articulation, both in camera and through postproduction: the lens can continually change focal planes, or an element of the frame can pop forward, almost as though there had been an edit that affected only part of the frame. When other effects help to do the work of the editing in a video (defocusing, fading to black, strobing) the editing can perform other roles, such as creating an aesthetically pleasing visual line or drawing the viewer's attention to the music (fig. 2.5).

FIGURE 2.5 (A–B)
R.E.M.'s "Losing My Religion."
An aestheticized flash-frame raises
questions about the role of editing.

Just as editing changes in the shift from film to music video, so does the function of shots. Music videos and Hollywood films share a basic premise: that visual information can best be communicated by cutting among three kinds of shot—long, medium, and close-up. One can describe these shots according to the relation each establishes between the figure and the space around him. In long shots, the space obtains a greater prominence than the figure; in medium shots, the relation is roughly equivalent; and in close-ups, the figure dominates the space. Hollywood film has virtually standardized the cropping of the figures in these shots. Most textbooks recommend that the proportion of the figure to the space in the frame fall within set guidelines to achieve a sense of balance: if too much or too little space surrounds the figure, a shot is said to look awkward. Further, the camera should not frame the body in such a way that the frame's edge passes through a join of the body, such as the neck, elbows, knees, or ankles.[8] Music videos do not follow these rules. Not only is the relation between figure and space frequently off kilter, but the camera bisects the figure in places that would be unacceptable for classic Hollywood film. In film, the framing helps to draw attention to the content of a shot, rather than its composition, and to render the editing process invisible. The framing in music video makes us as aware of the edge of the frame (and of what we cannot see) as of the figure itself. This kind of framing can give a shot a precarious quality that the succeeding shot cannot always put right. In this way, the image moves forward, matching the momentum of the music (fig. 2.6).

Viewers still learn the grammar of traditional shots from watching films and television. Music videos make use of these shots but give them different functions and meanings. Our knowledge of film and television practices still provides a reference point and can lend excitement to a shot in a music video that violates the rules of these practices. In Hollywood films, the extreme long shot frequently serves to set the context for a new scene or to adopt a character's point of view. Such a shot might appear at any point in a music video as a way of exposing a space otherwise revealed only in fragments or of creating visual contrast. It may even help us to listen past the song's foreground elements to acknowledge the totality of its sound space. The absence or oblique presentation of master shots in music video means that the viewer does not own or know fully the space, but is taken through it. The close-up, in classic Hollywood film, will disclose something intimate about a character. In music video, the close-up can work similarly to showcase the star, but just as often it serves to underscore a lyric, a musical hook, or the peak of a phrase. It may even be chosen simply to fit a pattern of shots already established within the edited sequence. In general, Hollywood cinematography's language of confrontation plays a greatly diminished role in music video. Over-the-shoulder shots, separation shots and the 180-degree rule tend to make the relations between figures clear and specific in a way that would be inappropriate for most videos.

The use of camera angles can tell us much about the visual language of music video. Low-angle shots are used more extensively in music videos, partly because they reproduce the relations among audience, performer, and stage. Such shots confer authority upon performers and assert their sexual charisma, often crudely, by highlighting the erogenous zones of performers. High-angle shots in music video, as in film, give the viewer a sense of power and mobility (fig. 2.7). These shots perform other functions in videos. Sometimes an overhead or extremely high-angle shot is edited in to create a rhythmic unison with a key moment in the music, like the crest of a melody. Classic Hollywood film employs high-angle and low-angle shots sparingly; the camera quickly returns

FIGURE 2.6 (A–F) Janet Jackson's "Love Will Never Do," Alanis Morrisette's "You Oughta Know," Nirvana's "Smells Like Teen Spirit," and Mariah Carey's "Honey." Music video inappropriately frames the body.

to a level perspective. A music video, by contrast, may contain a long series of high-angle or low-angle shots. When high- and low-angle shots are mixed together to form a series, the video will lack a sense of ground. The viewer turns to the music for additional spatial-temporal cues.

Traditionally, in forms like the Hollywood film, opera, the stage and oratory, the singer is placed in the center and on a level field as a means to establish centrality, stability, importance, and clarity. When the singer is placed off center (through framing and so on), we might assume a different experience of the song. It is important to note that many music videos have parodied or deconstructed proscenium framing, for example in Nirvana's "In Bloom," the band performs before an Arabian Nights backdrop on an episode of the *Ed Sullivan Show*. The scene is particularly humorous because the set, which the men, wearing skirts, quickly destroy, was shot with low-resolution black and white video. Music videos often contain a long series of low- or high-angle shots that create a different relation between listener, music, and image. For example, when there is a long series of medium, low-angle shots (so that the performer appears from the waist up) as well as with an image that lacks stability—for example, with both camera movement and movement within the frame—one may have the sense that the song buoys the performer. In music video, there is no clear causality concerning which came first, music, lyrics, or image, and at any moment, any media can be seen to influence the other. In this case, the performer is no longer the unambiguous source of the song. It can seem almost as if the image floats above, and is carried by the music, literally as if sonic waves passed along the bottom of the screen, and the image bobbed up and down accordingly.

Camera movement in music video also differs from that of film. Most music videos make such extensive use of the dolly that a static shot seems anomalous. The dolly shot keeps the video moving; it starts almost invariably as soon as a video begins and ceases only toward the end. It provides a simple way for a

FIGURE 2.7 (A–E) Guns N' Roses' "November Rain." When high- and low-angle shots are mixed together to form a series, the viewer turns to the music for additional spatial-temporal cues. The figure seems to be buoyed by the music.

video to match and sustain a song's momentum. Director Marcus Nispel says that his work derives its musicality from a clever deployment of the dolly. He employs the dolly to create what he calls "moves within moves"—the simultaneous use of tracking and panning.[9] Nispel sometimes uses this scheme while a figure turns in the frame (fig. 2.8). He thereby interposes three types of motion into one shot. A more common scheme places the artist at the center of a circular track. The camera, often positioned at a low angle, moves back and forth along the track at various speeds. This scheme can create the sense of a performance space in almost any setting, while the low-angle and varied speeds give the camera a responsive, even performer-like character. Videos can present a number of dolly shots edited together in order to build toward key moments in the video.

One type of music-video camera movement that contrasts strongly with the continuity editing system is the tracking shot. Often used for special emphasis, it frequently dominates a segment toward the middle of the song and is punctuated by a few dissolves. Tracking shots play a crucial role in music video because they provide relief from a typically shallow sense of space. (In videos, we almost never pierce the background or stray far from the star.) The movement of the camera provides a change in point of view: instead of experiencing the music from a stationary position, as it rushes past, the viewer can get the sense of running alongside the soundstream. The tracking shot embodies perfectly the music video's attempt to match the energy of the song, to approach the song's rhythmic drive, even if the music remains just out of reach. The tracking shot can also constitute a distinct rhythmic stratum that will go in and out of synchronization with the song's other rhythmic strata (fig. 2.9). Other

FIGURE 2.8 (A–I) Amy Grant's "House of Love." Creating a sense of flow: camera moves within moves.

kinds of camera movement function similarly. Cranes, pans, tilts, and dramatic reframings are usually done by hand and can achieve the intimate effects associated with handheld camera work. These shots provide possibilities for textural detail and subtle expressive nuance. They can also mimic the ways that sound approaches and fades away.

Different types of shots and edits can be mixed to create variety, and although one gets the sense that any shot can follow any edit, some shots and edits are particularly complementary. An edit or camera move can anticipate a gesture in the shot that follows. A tracking shot can complement a subsequent shot of a strutting figure. A crane shot that starts low and rises through the space seems to match a figure reaching outward. A brusque edit works well preceding a shot that contains a series of sharp rhythmic gestures performed by the dancer or musician. Videos can create this kind of play simply between shots and edits, almost irrespective of what a shot contains. A dissolve can pair nicely with a tracking shot, and the effect of a jump cut can be extended by an unbalanced shot. This isomorphism or exchange of gestures and shapes teaches the viewer to move fluently from parameter to parameter while watching a video. Such movement can occur across many parameters, leading the viewer directly into the structure of the song. In pop music, materials are commonly shared among different domains, for example, a melodic line in the voice will be taken up by the guitar, though the rhythmic values may be expanded. The drums will be performed "out of the pocket" (off the beat) to showcase breaks in a singer's voice.

The syntax of shots in music video, taken as a whole, is less conventionalized than that of shots in film. In the traditional Hollywood film scene, the camera begins at a distance and gradually moves in—from long or master shots to two-shots and medium shots, to close-ups like separation and over-the-shoulder shots. We seem to learn more about the film's world and the characters' inner lives as we narrow our focus in this way. The music-video camera shifts more freely among types of shots. Because a shot decision is made partly according to the form of the music and the pattern established by preceding shots, the search for knowledge about people and places takes second place. One cannot construct a typical shot order for music video. One might thrill at a twirling overhead shot that appears two-thirds into the video. In retrospect, the viewer

FIGURE 2.9 (A–C) Missy Elliott and Janet Jackson's "Son of a Gun." A tracking shot.

will realize that this is a good choice within the structure of the video; however, while viewing the tape, he would not have been able to predict the appearance of the shot. Unlike films, music videos do not divide neatly into scenes. The song's sectional divisions provide a stronger basis for parsing a video. If one had to generalize about the syntax of music-video image, one might take the musical phrase as the most significant unit. Music videos typically present segments of six to nine shots that last roughly the length of a musical phrase. Although the beginnings and ends of these segments do not always align with those of musical phrases, they can be recognizable to a viewer because they contain internal repetition and often possess a kind of symmetry (fig. 2.10).

MEANING, NARRATIVITY, AND CONTINUITY

How does music-video image create meaning, and in what ways does editing contribute to that creation? The meanings of music videos have been thought to present a puzzle. Most often, music-video image is relatively discontinuous. Time unfolds unpredictably and without clear reference points. Space is revealed slowly and incompletely. A video will hint at a character's personality, mood, goals, or desires but will never fully disclose them. We seldom see an action completed—a figure's movement is often cut off by the edit. Stories are suggested but not given in full. Nor can the lyrics tell us what we need to know—they may be banal or purely conventional. A famous performer can also pull at the video's meaning—we cannot tell beforehand how or to what extent our knowledge of a star is intended to come into play in a given video.

Music-video editing plays an interesting role in producing this effect of discontinuity. The editing in Hollywood film seeks to fill the gaps in our knowledge, to stabilize the meaning of an image. In music video, the editing seems rather to help create the discontinuity and sense of lack. If, as I have suggested,

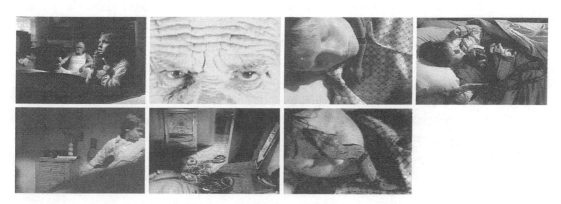

FIGURE 2.10 (A–G) Metallica's "Enter Sandman." Lengths of visual sections often follow that of musical phrases.

editing constitutes a distinct visual parameter of music video, we should expect that it can contribute to the creation of discontinuity. Because it, too, reveals things incompletely, makes promises it does not keep, it should be understood as but one of the elements fighting for attention in a video. And the case becomes more complicated. Edits happen between images; they are not part of the image. Edits can literalize the discontinuity by making us aware of the space between images.

Scott McCloud, in *Understanding Comics,* writes about the pleasure of reading into incomplete images.[10] He celebrates the interpretive work needed to transform black and white lines or spots of color into meaningful characters. Music-video images can provide the same pleasure. We know very little about the figures we see, but we still attempt to make sense of them based on how they look and what they are doing, as well as the setting, the lyrics, and the music. We must decide whether a figure functions as a character or merely as part of a *tableau vivant.* Extending the notion of the reader's share in the interpretation of the image, McCloud discusses the gap between panels of the comic. In this gap, the reader calculates the amount of time elapsed, the distance traversed, and any change in the figures. The edits in music videos work similarly. Partly by attending to the song, the viewer decides what has happened in the cut from one shot to another. The disjunctive force of the edit compels this decision: how do these two shots relate? On what basis does the edit link them together? And what is the net effect of these disjunctions on the video as a whole?

A video like Marilyn Manson's "Beautiful People" highlights how difficult it can be to make sense of music-video editing. Manson first became known for a version of The Eurythmics' spare synth-pop hit "Sweet Dreams." His version recast the song as a gothic metal dirge with a video that placed the androgynous singer in a decayed warehouse, wearing a variety of abject and incongruous costumes. "Beautiful People," the band's next video, extended the gothic punk aesthetic of the first to encompass a much broader range of imagery and more serious themes. Where "Sweet Dreams" played with and against the singer's rock iconography, "Beautiful People" remakes him as a Faustian figure who, we find out, experiments on human and animal subjects in order to gain control of the masses. The video's theme emerges quickly, and its plot can ultimately be pieced together. "Beautiful People" tells its story at an unpredictable rate, however, complicating the narrative with imagery whose origin and function are difficult to determine. The opening shots of the video demonstrate the *modus operandi* of music video's particular narrativity—the suggestion of a narrative along with a clear indication that this narrative will proceed elliptically and be rendered only in fragments.

The video opens with fifteen rapid static shots, many of which show parts of a human figure, prostheses, or medical appliances (fig. 2.11). Beakers and electronic devices suggest a laboratory. A worm, in close-up, dangles off the edge of a shelf. The video's theme of Faustian mad science is clear enough, but the elements are rendered with such detail that they begin to suggest a narrative. But which elements will be elaborated narratively, and which simply provide color? The video does not let on. Videos generally seem unable to mark images as important or unimportant in the ways that film can.[11] The laboratory shots, which one might expect to return, are not really taken up. The worm never reappears, but it is echoed by images of bootlaces and metal cables twisted around a microphone stand.[12] The remainder of the video never seems to take stock of this opening, but rather moves forward to present three types of material: shots of the singer; images of dancers on stilts; and shots of the other band members, a crowd, or people with prostheses, all of whom are shown to serve as experimental subjects. These strands proceed unpredictably—we do not know which will appear when, or whether a given appearance will provide any new information. The viewer will realize at the video's close that the "Beautiful People" concerns process: Manson grows creatures out of stolen body parts. Yet, the clues are scattered across different domains and embedded in a variety of locations.[13]

Claims that videos lack coherence center on wildly disparate juxtapositions and abrupt changes of style or production values. As "Beautiful People" suggests, however, the connection between shots is sometimes clear, sometimes obscure, and many of the most interesting juxtapositions lie in between: we can have a vague understanding of a connection but be unable to specify its nature. Metallica's "Unforgiven" provides another example of a video that bor-

FIGURE 2.11 (A–J) Marilyn Manson's "Beautiful People." Music video's elliptical narration: narrative clues are scattered across different domains and embedded in a variety of locations.

ders on incoherence precisely because, at some moments, the shooting and editing work as they do in film. It takes place in an abstract space with richly textured surfaces of sooty black and gray. A little boy and an old man perform repetitive tasks that seem impossible to complete. The band is set off from these characters, although the tonality of their surroundings remains consistent with the rest of the video's settings. Separation shots of a traditional sort imply a relationship between figures, but the video provides no way to determine which is the best of several possibilities—are they grandfather and grandson, allegorical figures of youth and old age, or do they represent one subject as child and adult? The matter is complicated further by separation shots of the singer and the old man (fig. 2.12). In a film, these shots would presuppose a relationship between the two figures. We would not expect such a connection between musician and nonmusician in a video that isolates these figures spatially, but the style of the shooting and editing almost demands that we imagine one. What is remarkable about these two shots and the edit between them is that each exists within a separate discourse. The shot of the lead guitarist belongs to the language of documentary, the shot of the old man to allegorical painting, while the edit between them derives from the realm of narrative filmmaking. When one recognizes these three elements, one becomes aware of an unbreachable rift among different modes of expression.

FIGURE 2.12 (A–B)
Metallica's "Unforgiven."
The editing features three modes of
address: documentary, allegorical
painting, and narrative filmmaking.

That "Unforgiven" compels a viewer to pose these questions explicitly already marks it as different from Hollywood Film. Very few videos allow these conventions to perform their traditional functions unnoticed, and seldom present two adjacent shots that resemble paired shots in Hollywood cinema: we are unlikely to see two characters gaze at each other so that the sightlines match, each character takes up the same amount of space in the frame, and we can identify both and understand what their gestures mean. When this happens, the viewer may feel a shock of recognition. She may think, "This feels like a film!" The same is true for paired shots that carry clear narrative implications in film. Imagine a suspenseful sequence in which one shot shows a protagonist approaching a door and the following shot shows the door from the protagonist's perspective. If we were to see this sequence in a music video, we would know to feel suspense, but we would be so relieved to see something familiar, that we might well experience a sense of increasing rather than decreasing certainty. These moments often work as a pastiche of cinema.

In both "Beautiful People" and Unforgiven," the editing verges on inscrutability. A typical video contains a broad range of connection, with the clear and egregiously unclear connections appearing unpredictably. The particular quality of videos may derive from those juxtapositions in which there is obviously a connection, but from which something is left out. Such juxtapositions represent the middle of the continuum. We see successive shots of people, whom we can identify by type, in a single space, but the people do not acknowledge one another and we cannot determine their relation. Or we might see people in different places and be unable to tell whether they are meant to relate at all. We must often extrapolate from what the shots provide if we are to give meaning to a juxtaposition. The early Russian filmmakers understood that this kind of extrapolation was crucial to cinema and argued forcefully that the editing could actually create a meaning in situations where the shots could not themselves provide one. Kuleshov performed an experiment in which he paired shots of an actor and coffin, an actor and bowl, and an actor and children. The results showed that the meaning created by placing one shot next to another could be that of a proper emotion directed toward an object: these pairs seemed to signify, respectively, mourning the loss of a beloved, yearning for food, and enjoying children at play. In music video, adjacent shots often relate but loosely; when separated by dramatic edits, each image will seem enclosed within its own semantic realm. Even paired shots of figures often withhold something. Such pairs of shots can resemble the images in the Kuleshov experiment. In these cases, the affect of the song provides the context for the image. The music cannot define the meaning of objects, but it can surely suggest the animating desire that characters bear towards objects or others. We read emotions into the image before us, and, with the help of the song, make connections between this image and others in the video (fig. 2.13).

FIGURE 2.13 (A–B)
Brian McKnight's "Miss You."
Music helps to fill the gap between
ambiguous images.

Eisenstein gave the word *montage* a special sense, to signify the way in which two shots edited together could create a new meaning that could not inhere in either shot alone. Eisensteinian montage, like the Kuleshov experiment, is predicated on an absence or incompleteness of meaning, but it establishes connections based on conceptual relationships. In a famous sequence from Eisenstein's *Battleship Potemkin* (1925), a ship's cannon fires, accompanied by shots of a stone lion reclining, crouching, and standing upright, signifying the uprising of the proletariat against the tsar. Andre Bazin notes that montage disappeared from cinema when sound arrived, to be replaced by the seamless editing we now take for granted.[14] One can see how the silent image track of music video might lend itself to montage. Montage occurs with some frequency in videos, but the collision rarely creates more than a mildly humorous or clever effect. (If montaged images possessed the force that Eisenstein expected of them, they might detract from the song.) In Don Henley's "The End of the Innocence," two girls, about sixteen and seven, sit alone in a movie theater. We can see the projectionist's light behind them, and on the screen we see a shot of a train with people sitting as passengers. The cropping of the shot makes the image look like a strip of film. In Nine Inch Nails' "Closer," the eel stands in for a phallus (fig. 2.14).

⌈The precarious relation of shot to shot, and the varied bases for this relation, affects a video's larger structures of meaning.⌋The polysemic image track creates expectations it frequently leaves unfulfilled; we do not always know where—or how—a video is going. Films teach us to assume that we gain information as the narrative progresses, that we move steadily closer to revelation. Music videos work within this assumption but play against it by progressing haltingly and unpredictably, and by contradicting what has already been shown. Videos also draw us away from the narrative by foregrounding other structures (especially formal and musical ones) and fulfilling other responsibilities (as to the star). We will therefore be unable to guess, as the video unfolds, whether a given shot will bear heavily, somewhat, or not at all on a video's narrative. If narrative fulfillment does come, it will be at a time and in a form that cannot be predicted. This kind of expectation and interrogation of individual shots can suggest the way that videos build larger structures.⌋The relationships between shots have more various bases in music video than in film: they can relate not only because they present the same character, object, or location, but also because they share projection values, a lighting and color scheme, a sense of scale or the use of a camera position. A single shot gives only an incomplete representation of that feature which makes it stand out, whether a character or a color scheme. Successive appearances of this feature—even if not contiguous—therefore form a structure of partial revelation in which some questions are answered while new ones are asked. Indeed, the relation between noncontiguous shots linked by a single feature is unexpectedly potent in music video,

FIGURE 2.14 (A–D) Don Henley's "The End of the Innocence" and Nine Inch Nails "Closer." Eisensteinian montage: shots evocative of a film strip and a phallus.

sometimes closer than the connection between adjacent shots. Larger structures made of half a dozen or so shots, irregularly spaced and connected by the way they treat some visual parameter, play an important role in creating continuity.

A music video can interlace several of these structures, which, like adjacent shots, may be unified by disposition of the figure, shape, color, setting, theme, and so on. It is important that they are not flat and featureless. They manifest changes of intensity as they unfold. A value may increase and decrease, in the case of color, light, size, speed, height, or depth; if we are considering plot, location, or character development, it is the amount and nature of revelation that will vary. Some of these structures contain a shot that can function as a high or low point. The high points sometimes form tears in the musical-visual texture (by jutting out above an established level of intensity). This effect is momentary, and afterward a viewer may quickly invest attention in some aspect of the song's texture in an attempt to prolong the moment of intensity. This prolongation takes place in the instant after the high point has been reached but before the cut to the next shot. The song can provide something to latch onto—a melodic high point, a sectional division, or the entrance of a new timbre. This musical feature takes on new meaning, in this heightened moment, which it carries into its subsequent occurrences. One may consider the feature's history, and in retrospect, invest it with a special meaning. The structures formed according to principles of graphic match are particularly interesting. One might be tempted to call these irregularly spaced graphic matches "visual rhymes," inasmuch as a match interrupted by a group of shots that do not share the feature held in common by the two matched shots carries a chime of recognition and creates a momentary sense of completion. Nirvana's "Come as You Are" connects shots according to graphic similarities. Each of these shots contains an oblong shape with appendages, and in tandem with the music, suggests a stunting of potential (fig. 2.15).

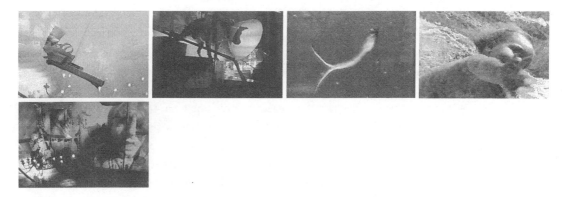

FIGURE 2.15 (A–E) Nirvana's "Come as You Are." Shots connected according to graphic similarities create a momentary sense of completion or recognition.

EDITING AND THE EXPERIENCE OF IMAGE AND SOUND

I suggested earlier that music-video editing exceeds the functions of film editing largely through its responsiveness to musical features—rhythmic, timbral, melodic, and formal. I want now to expand on this suggestion. When early discussions of music video mentioned music/image connections, they tended to notice simple rhythmic correspondences: "cutting on the beat." In order to show that the connections between the editing and the music of music videos can be more subtle and more various than this, it will be helpful to take a step back and consider those elements of music-video image—crucial, in my view—that reflect the experiential properties of sound. This deep connection between image and song in music video allows for the responsiveness of editing and other visual parameters to musical features.

Theorists such as Edward Branigan, Michel Chion, and Walter Ong have reminded us that sound and image possess different properties.[15] Sounds ebb, flow, and surround us. The cinematographic features and mise-en-scène of music video—extreme high, low, and canted angles, long-tracking shots, unusual camera pans and tilts, and the lively features within the frame, glittering surfaces, rippling light—can mimic sonic processes. The types of shots used in videos do not just reflect sonic processes, but they also suggest a listening subject as much as a viewing one. We actually see figures turning, as if to listen, toward people and objects in the space. The camera's perspective often suffices to imply a listening subject. In order best to see something, we might want to be placed squarely before it. If we want to listen attentively to a sound, however, a frontal position is unnecessary. Many positions may be satisfactory—above, below, off to the side. In fact, turning an ear toward the object will take our eyes away from it. One of the most common camera positions in music video—below the subject and to one side—may privilege listening over viewing and grant greater authority to the soundtrack than to the image. The camera in music video also seems to mimic the ways that we direct our attention in a sonic space. We can throw our attention to focus on a sound that interests us. When we shift our focus among various sound sources in our environment, we experience a greater sense of mobility than viewing offers. The kinds of shots and editing that we see in music video—jumping from one location to another even before an image catches our eye—resembles what we do when we listen.

The camera normally takes time to explore the extent of video's setting, so that a setting is only partly revealed in any single shot. How does this practice influence our hearing of a song? A pop song creates a sense of a space through arrangement, production, mixing, and mastering. The acoustical properties of this constructed musical space seldom seem to match that of the video's setting. This lack of fit creates some confusion and some interest. How could the song's soundworld inhabit the space of the video? The camera, as it explores the space, suggests possible ways that parts of the arrangement might be distributed within this environment. Many music videos exploit our curiosity about how a song might sound in the actual space of the music video: walls, floors, and ceilings are placed at odd angles and covered with materials that imply specific acoustical properties; objects that resemble speakers and baffles may be distributed throughout the space. Despite the fact that the camera never quite reaches the sides or the back of the setting, these videos encourage us to imagine the sound waves rolling into the walls and bouncing off them, much like dye moving through water (fig. 2.16).

If the very walls and furniture can seem to respond to the music, what of the figures we see interacting with it through dance and other, more subtle kinds of movement? Sounds can seem to come through, or from them. But how? All gestures in music video—the flick of a wrist, the flickering of light, or the fluttering of fabric—become like dance. We use sound to register the interiority of objects, whether hollow or dense. The way that the camera in music video hovers over the figures, slowly taking in their bodies, may look pornographic, but it might also be a way to register the sounds emanating from these bodily sources. If we think of a singer's voice as reflecting the rhythms of her body, and the instruments as extending the voice, then the camera can be thought of as creating a fantasy of what lies inside the body—the spring of the muscles, the heartbeat, the flow of blood.

To sell the band and the song, a video most often places the singer front and center. Some of the time, however, figures begin to turn away from us and show us only crowns of heads, crooks of necks, and elbows. These parts of the body seem to carry as much authority as does the face, and any part that is turned toward us can seem to lead us into the music. Indeed, the figures do not look at each other so much as they turn receptively toward one another as if to listen. The singer remains perpetually in motion, turning sometimes to address us, sometimes toward the figures in the background. The supporting figures may continue to turn toward and away from us, helping thereby to continue the image's rotation. This continuity of motion works to maintain the flow of the image against that of the music.

The description that I have laid out thus far suggests that music video creates an experience more like listening than viewing. As such, it encourages some of the receptiveness and sense of connection that sound creates. Music videos draw us into a playful space where attractive objects are distributed across the

FIGURE 2.16 (A–D) Usher's "Make Me Wanna." Music video's strange spaces are shaped to a song's soundworld.

visual field. In the absence of a strong narrative, videos have other means to maintain a viewer's engagement. The figures, the camera, and the edits each find ways to participate, but they do not always work together harmoniously to achieve this goal: the three often fight among themselves for attention, with the song's formal and rhythmic structures as the stable ground. It does not matter, in a sense, whether an elbow comes forward, an edit occurs, a camera tracks, or a figure walks—all are felt as articulations against the music. The bodies of the figures are often the first element to engage us. Music video reveals the body as an enormous but incomplete surface. We may feel tempted to extrapolate beyond the edge of the frame in order to fill in the missing arms and legs. At the same time, the intense focus on a fragment of the body invests it with a special expressive weight. We can imagine feelings and desires—a thinking subject—by watching the rate of release in the shoulders or the spring of the hips. As the video unfolds, we piece together what we have seen to make the body whole. We might remember a longer shot of the body, perhaps torso to feet, a close-up of the head and neck, and a high-angle shot that captures the figure from above. The image also creates associations with the song, matching sections or other musical features with particular visual materials. We see the body bob up and down during the third verse of the song, say, and we might recall the way it moved during the previous verse. As the video progresses, features of the song become associated with elements of the image: a rhythmic motive with the swivel of the performer's hips, a lilting instrumental melody with a character in the background. By recalling what we have seen and heard, we imagine a phantasmagorical body (fig. 2.17). If a video gives us

FIGURE 2.17 (A–J) Mariah Carey's "Honey." Phantasmagorical bodies: music helps to depict the heft and feel of parts of bodies that remain offscreen.

enough material to create a picture of one body, we can attribute moods to other characters in the space who have been rendered more partially, and who often have been chosen because their carriage and gestures are so different from those of the lead performers. As a video progresses, we participate kinesthetically in the video. We compensate imaginatively for what we do not immediately see in the frame.

The camera functions similarly to create the sense of a consciousness. It is silent and invisible, yet it moves so concertedly—searching, jogging back and forth—that we imagine these movements adding up to something like a narrative voice. As the song unfolds, we can try to guess what the camera is hearing and what it will follow next. The edits balance the camera's movement, keeping things on track. Almost like a downbeat, the edit creates a new beginning. The edits form patterns that the viewer can project into the future. Such patterns are formed by the camera and the body as well. The body, the camera, and the editing thus build a kind of momentum that can carry the viewer through a video.

Along with those features that attract and hold our attention, music videos have several ways to keep us at bay. The moving camera and the patterns formed by edits are among the techniques that engage us. We are also engaged by the ever-changing surface of music video, in which a lyric might come to the fore at one point, then a close-up, followed by a striking edit, and then some hook in the music. The song's unfolding and the performers' movements may draw us in. Though music videos rarely contain fully wrought stories, they can interest us in a narrative by inciting curiosity about who the characters are and what they might do. Videos distance us in a variety of ways. The borders of the television screen block our entry into the visual space. The figures move obliquely against the music and do not speak; their gestures are abruptly cut off, so one never knows what the next shot will be or how the rest of the video will evolve. We may get the sense that the figures are not quite human but not fully emblematic. What animates them seems strange. It is almost like looking at an aquarium. The mechanisms that draw us forward and keep us at a distance exist in constant tension in music video. One may have an urge to follow the unfolding of the image and the music, to enter the space of the music video. One can also feel as though one is locked forever outside, looking in. The body seems restrained somehow, glued to the chair.

SHOWCASING THE STAR

A focus on editing can help us to understand the relation between music video's star-making dimension and its modes of continuity and signification. Close-ups of the star, and the ways they are edited into the flow of a video, provide useful cases to study. The music-video close-up possesses its own rhetoric. It has developed a unique look, revealing each wrinkle of the brow and blink of the eyelid as if to capture every emotion crossing the face. Music videos break down visual, lyrical, and musical elements to their smallest constituent parts: a prop, a color, a gesture, a few words, an intriguing riff. In this light, the close-up can be understood to serve specific structural functions. Close-ups can leave a viewer with just a face and a moment of the song; unlike actors in narrative film, who bear a past and future that press in on them as we view them in close-up, the music-video performer stands in a kind of temporal isolation. As the face fills the frame, it is subjected to so much visual analysis that it seems to move very slowly, almost to suggest the song's slowest rhythmic stratum. This rhythmic effect can serve a grounding function. The close-up of the singer's face is often shot and edited in such a way as to leave us with a single gesture. In its abbreviated simplicity, this gesture suggests a way of grasping hold of some musical element, which might be the main hook or a small detail.

Music videos often present a flow of images that are too rich and materials that seem to dissolve too quickly. The close-up gives us something to commit to memory. The music seems to set certain faces in amber, preserved and just out of reach. The face becomes a mask, drawn into contortions we associate with the most hyperbolic silent screen acting—more an archetype than an expression of the performer himself. This intense isolation keeps the viewer in the present, blocking access to the past or the future as the music rushes by. The compositional features of the close-up, particularly the relation of the figure to the edges of the screen, contribute to this sense of the figure's being held in isolation. Rudolf Arnheim has taught us to recognize the force of the frame on the composition of a painting. He defines the balancing center as the point "around which the composition organizes itself. It is created by the con-figuration of vectors issuing from an enclosure such as the frame of a picture."[16] One can liken this force or pressure from the frame upon the picture proper to that of the song upon the close-up of the star. Here the song drives toward the downbeat, the beginnings of phrases and sections, or the tonic chord. When a performer is shown in close-up moving a bit with the music, the music seems to buffet the figure, like rip tides pushing and pulling in different directions. One wonders whether the figure will hold position or be sucked into the center.

This effect of a push and pull within an unyielding frame makes the close-up precarious. The moments of stability that close-ups provide become high points of the video. The video brings us towards these peaks, holds us against them, and then releases us. Only a few moments of the video will provide this much pleasure, and as I, the viewer, reach for them they will be gone. As I watch a video and follow the song, I casually study the performer's body, just as I do when I look at models in magazines. I admire the lines of the jaw, the look in the eye, the light. Suddenly the performer's head turns toward me, the eyes gaze into mine, the singing voice demands my attention, and I am struck. Music can transgress both physical space and the borders of the body, changing our sense of time and of these boundaries themselves. At this moment, the performer crosses the limits of the screen and addresses me as a person, and I can no longer view this face and body as an object. Just as quickly, the head turns, the rhythm changes, the soul has gone, and again I am simply watching a blank human form.[17]

In the absence of a strong narrative, music video creates tension by varying basic visual materials, such as shots and edits. Much of music-video editing consists in finding new relationships within space and among persons. When a video presents an alternation between shots that display a body and shots that emphasize the space around it, the body becomes the video's ground. One of the most sustained discussions in film theory concerns how a viewer is sutured into the diegesis of film through editing. A series of sightlines and shot/reverse shots, most commonly, place the viewer in the position of the protagonist or the privileged onlooker. Music video, it seems to me, is much freer in terms of viewer identification and perspective. In the Backstreet Boys' "Show Me the Meaning of Being Lonely," the viewer's empathy switches from figure to figure simply because someone is within the frame and/or lip-syncing. Identification occurs quickly—within one or two shots. In the most extreme examples in music video, the viewer's empathy and identification moves between multiple elements in the frame. A series of shots can all contain movement on the beat—a bob of a head, a slap of a wrist, a raising of a glass, a throwing of a ball—and the viewer's attention will seem to skip across the surface like a skimmed stone, following the movements and feelings of everything that moves within the frame.[18]

EDITING AND THE MUSIC OF MUSIC VIDEO

Through its varied roles, editing loosens the representational functions filmed images traditionally perform, opening them up to a sense of polyvalent play. The editing thereby places the video's images and the song's formal features in close relation.[19] I doubt the numerous ways that music and image can be put into one-to-one relations would surprise musicians or pop music scholars. Obviously, editing can reflect the basic beat pattern of the song, but it can also be responsive to all of the song's other parameters. For example, long dissolves can compliment arrangements that include smooth timbres and long-held tones. A video can use different visual material to offset an important hook or a different cutting rhythm at the beginnings and ends of phrases. And, of course, these effects can switch from one-to-one relationships to something that is more contrapuntal.[20]

Tempo is one feature readily taken up by music-video editing. Music videos tend to underscore the most arresting features of a song, and if the song is striking for its sprightly rhythmic feel or its languorous, plodding tempo, the image will often unfold especially quickly or slowly—the image will seem actually to exceed the song's extreme speed. Green Day's "Jaded/Brain Stew" is really two short, connected songs. During the slower first part, the video shows a tractor dragging a couch across a landfill in slow motion, along with shots of a dead horse and a sullen old man. The performers' lack of engagement enhances the sense of lassitude. When the music changes to a faster tempo for the second part of the song, the camera starts whipping around and the pace of the editing increases. The concentration of energy also derives from squeezing the performers into a small room and from using lurid, overheated colors (fig. 2.18).

The editing can draw our attention to the general contours of the song's phrase structure. Long takes underscore broad melodic phrases, while quick cutting is used to keep us focused on the beat of songs that emphasize smaller rhythmic elements. Maxwell's high, pure falsetto floats over the arrangement in his "Ascension." His singing suggests that he can extend the melodic line for measures on end. The video unfolds in a performance setting typical for music video—a stark space with an enormous winged backdrop. The phrasing is reflected in two principal ways. Editing occurs very infrequently, especially while Maxwell sings. The breadth of the melodic line is also matched by the long strides of models in close-fitting metallic suits who walk resolutely toward the camera (fig. 2.19). The vocal hook for Tag Team's "Whoomp, There It Is," on the other hand, is constructed of short, rhythmic vocal interjections. The camera correspondingly adopts a high-angle point of view over a crowd of dancers who vigorously bob up and down. The camera darts in and out over the dancers, while the editing serves to break up the camera movement.

When the editing diverges from the rhythm of the song, the departure can serve a number of functions. In most pop songs, the beat pattern is omnipresent and easy to follow. When the editing moves from coincidence with the beat pattern to divergence or vice versa, the effect can be keenly felt. Occasionally, editing off the beat can create a rhythmic counterpoint to the song's beat pattern. Prince's "Gett Off" presents a high level of rhythmic complexity. The video contains cutting before and behind the beat, which establishes an-

FIGURE 2.18 (A–H) Green Day's "Jaded/Brain Stew." A song can be striking for its sprightly rhythmic feel or its languorous, plodding tempo. Correspondingly, music video image will often unfold especially quickly or slowly.

other rhythmic voice and brings out the cross-rhythms created by the figures' movements.

⌈Editing can, of course, carry on two roles simultaneously, like reflecting musical features and shaping the meaning of the video.⌋ In Madonna's "Oh, Father," the verse is sedate, and the editing occurs regularly, separated by long intervals. On the other hand, the chorus, which narrates the story of a child being tormented by her father, is much more tumultuous. The rapid editing occurs sporadically and off the beat, while Madonna's voice cracks, and the drums are "out of the pocket" (not squarely in time). Because the image alone in music video cannot narrate a story (figures cannot speak, the form is short, and time and place are rendered incompletely), the other parameters must do the work of telling the tale. In this instance, the editing bears much of the brunt of describing Madonna's distress, and it also functions musically, underscoring both the jagged quality of her voice and the rhythm arrangement.

⌈In the last example, the editing reflects musical structure and at the same time conveys meaning. But editing can perform even more sophisticated functions. By emphasizing certain sounds and images, a filmmaker can provide a path through the image.⌋ In one scene from Jacques Tati's *Monsieur Hulot's Holiday,* vacationers relax at a resort hotel. In the foreground of the shot, some guests quietly play cards, while in the background, M. Hulot plays ping-pong. Early in the scene, the guests in the foreground are murmuring softly and Hulot's ping-pong game is louder. The sound encourages us to watch Hulot. As the guests become louder and we hear less of Hulot's ping-pong ball, our attention shifts to the front of the set.

⌈Let me now give a similar example from music video. In a video, our attention to the song shapes the way we perceive the image, but, to an equal extent, what we attend to in the image helps to determine how we hear the music. When a star jams his face in front of the camera, or when a hand or foot threatens to break through the viewing plane, we suddenly hear the music

FIGURE 2.19 (A–H) Maxwell's "Ascension" and Tag Team's "Whoomp, There It Is." The editing can draw our attention to the breadth of a melodic line or the brevity of a vocal hook.

in a different way. We become aware that we should pay attention right now. If the same moment in the song were accompanied by a less assertive image— say, a long shot, we would more likely attend to the overall arrangement of the song than focus on any particular element. This experiment can work in reverse, with the music influencing our attention to the image. Imagine a scenario with two types of music. The first contains a city scene, shot in slow motion, with people walking down a busy street; a medium shot in slow motion is cropped so that we see the people from their knees to just above their eyebrows. Let us say that the song contains a pounding jungle beat and short synthesizer flurries. We might notice the intensity of the pedestrians' faces or the muscular armature of one or two people. On the other hand, if we hear a flowing synthesizer pad with a minimal rhythm arrangement, perhaps some innocuous "CD jazz," we might attend instead to the spring and sweep of the bodies in motion, and to the flow of the crowd as a whole. Music videos frequently crop images such as the example above, breaking bodies at the joint or rendering them partially, so that more of the context must be supplied by the music than by the image.

In music video, the musical or visual element with the sharpest profile tends to claim the viewer's attention. As a video unfolds, our attention shifts continually among music, image, and lyrics, as each provides novelty at some point and then recedes into the background. A deployment of mixed shot sizes, some with very clear content, and some cropped so that they are vague or unspecific, can thus establish a path through the formal and timbral space of the song. The editing can even complicate the matter further by controlling the deployment of shots so that as we move toward a moment of culmination in the song, the editing can tease us with the possibility of spoiling the peak moment's arrival, or feign disinterest by drawing attention to other features of the song. By anticipating what the song will do next, the image can create a sense of expectation. A change of shot sizes can also allow us to circulate within a musical parameter such as rhythm or the arrangement. A viewer might first notice the music's smallest rhythmic value and then jump down one level to the basic quarter note pulse. If one sees a long shot of performers in the background against an ornate curtain or a waterfall, one might attend to the microrhythms of the music. Imagine that the video cuts next to a medium shot in which the singer's face and chest are foregrounded and her head moves side to side, while she crosses and uncrosses her arms as if clocking to the music. The two shots together might encourage such a leap. The image can then serve as a guide to teach us about salient features of the song.

■■■

I hope that I have provided a glimpse into the world of music-video editing. As the video unfolds, the editing can shift rapidly in function, foregrounding musical structure, showcasing the star, reflecting experiential features of the sound, conveying meaning, and even constructing aesthetically pleasing visual strands in its own right. It is helpful, as one watches video, to be attentive to the way that the editing sometimes plays an equal role with other elements, like color, narrative, and the treatment of the star, that sometimes vie for attention and sometimes recede into the background, and also to how editing will play a uniquely superordinate role, functioning as a switcher. Editing controls as it has traditionally served to control the order and duration of shots, and therefore helps to determine when and for how long another parameter will come to the fore.

The investigation of music-video editing should be understood as one example of a kind of study that might be performed on any element. Such a study would acknowledge the field on which all elements interact without forgetting that each has its own cultural history within and beyond music video, its own set of functions (traditional and nontraditional), and its own technical means. A group of these studies would allow us to appreciate music video as a discursive form without imposing a false unity or unjustly privileging one element over the others. When we follow the changing surface of a video, we can try to remember that a momentary effect that claims our attention is part of a structure that traverses the whole of the video, and that this effect is created within the context of that structure: it may mark the high point of some value or constitute a departure from a traditional role. If a video seems discontinuous, it is not because the image track consists of autonomous shots that do not relate to one another, but because the video interlaces a number of such structures in an unpredictable way. The sheer density of this interlace provides one of music video's greatest pleasures.

3

Actors

RECORD COMPANIES and videomakers will try anything once, if only because novelty can break through the onslaught of commercial messages and grab the viewer's attention. Why, then, has there not been a video that makes it difficult to find the lead singer? Such a video might place the singer in a crowd in order to obscure her, or in a large group of performers, with each character acting slightly out of phase until the real performance is almost unrecognizable. There are videos that do without the performers, most of these being either clay or line-drawn animation, and a few that seem nearly to abandon the need for a band, such as Chemical Brothers' "Setting Sun." Several contain only cameo appearances of the star or leave out the band entirely, drawing on experimental films instead (like the found footage with gigantic superimposed printed lyrics in R.E.M.'s "Fall on Me"), but no video offers the goods and then fails to deliver.[1]

Whereas both the sets and the supporting characters in music video typically have an indeterminate nature, the star is most often foregrounded in bold relief. The camera showcases every curl of the fingertips and bend of the elbow, every wrinkle of the brow and blink of the eyelid. When the shot is a close-up, it seems that the lens captures every emotion for our own private scrutiny. At first glance, the glitzy depiction of the star serves only as an advertising technique, and the critics' complaint that a performer's mugging before the camera is overwhelmingly tiresome carries real weight.

Yet close-ups have an important role to play in the overall experience of the video. Because music videos break visual, lyrical, and musical elements down to their smallest constituent parts—an object, a color, a few words, a turn of the wrist, a funny or intriguing riff or sound—the close-up can be as important a structural element as anything. Close-ups give us just a portion of a sound-track and a face; unlike the protagonists of narrative film, who have a history and a future, desires and intentions, the music-video performer stands in temporal isolation. Often, as the head fills the frame, it is subjected to so much visual analysis that it seems to move very slowly, so slowly that the face alone can suggest the slowest rhythm of the music. In this musical fashion, the close-up has a grounding effect. The close-up of the singer's face is shot and edited to emphasize one simple gesture—a gesture that in its abbreviated simplicity will indicate a way of paying attention to or grasping some element of the music. It may be the main hook, a lyric, or a small rhythmic or melodic feature. [1] And as it unfolds, we have something to commit readily to memory. Some faces have the torching poignancy of photographs, and the music seems to set them in a pool of liquid amber, preserved and luminous but slightly out of reach. By contrast to viewers of narrative films, a fan will wish to watch and wait unendingly for this moment in the music video. [2] We can teach ourselves where the sublime instance is—one-third into the verse on the fourth beat—but we can experience it only in passing and can never own it.

In real time, while watching, we can recreate the pleasures of the performer singing and performing endlessly: Nate Dogg's operatically mournful expressions in "Regulate" and Bono's "With or Without You"; Janet Jackson's expressions of bliss in "Love Will Never Do (Without You)" and "That's the Way Love Goes"; Busta Rhymes's unbridled fury in "Woo Hah" and Kurt Cobain's in "Heart-Shaped Box," respectively; and the cavernous, empty corridors of the mind that Madonna evokes in "Rain" and "Cherish." The viewer reads the image and pours the music into the nooks and crannies of archetypically expressive faces. The mask, pulled into the contortions that we associate with the most hyperbolic of silent film acting becomes more a sign of the song at this moment than an expression of the artist per se. In these heightened moments, the face is animated by the song. [3] The earlier music and images in a video set the viewer on a path that will bring her toward, lock her into, and then release her across and over these peak moments.

An isolated gesture can be nearly as memorable, lending a fetishistic appeal: Shirley Manson's kick in the back of the frame in Garbage's "Stupid Girl"; Des'ree's birdlike hands in "You've Gotta Be"; the turn of Chili's hip in TLC's "Waterfalls"; Kurt Cobain's lunge in Nirvana's "Heart-Shaped Box" and dangling, passive arm in "Smells like Teen Spirit"; Toni Braxton's arms thrown out to the sides in "You Mean the World to Me" and held close to the chest in "Breathe Again." But isn't it the particular moment within the well-placed close-up that possesses special power and allure? [4]

Many people disparage lip-sync as the cheesiest aspect of music video, but the practice also constitutes an element in counterpoint. As a purveyor of similarity and contrast, lip-syncing creates a space for the other subtle shifts and transformations that occur in the medium. With lip-sync, the prerecorded music is played back over speakers, and the singer tries to match her original performance. She will sometimes be right on the mark of the original performance, but sometimes ahead or behind. These slight shifts can create a rhythmic feel and become distinctive in their own right. Lip-sync also renders something like a visual and auditory blur. A music video contains a history of articulations: first the recording session, where the singer(s) and instrumentalist(s) lay down separate tracks, with the producer and engineer adding additional nuance; then the mixing and mastering to prepare the song for release, both of which can greatly affect the sound; then the video shoot, where the music is played back, and the director and crew bear witness to the musicians' performance and impose their own touches, particularly through the work of often very mobile lighting and camera; then the editing, which makes a signal contribution by putting shots into relation; and finally the screening in a nightclub or on cable TV, which allows the viewer to project his or her own rhythms and musical understanding on the performance. The viewer enters this blur, trying to find the moments of origin by bouncing against the many iterations—against the walls, so to speak—of the song and video as they were made. In a fraction of a second, we have the entire sweep of the changes that occur in all of the parameters of music video. These slight shifts in every parameter form the core of experiencing music video as on and off, coming into and going out of focus, the sense of resolution and of dissolution, of being found and then lost again.

HOLLYWOOD FILM'S CONVENTIONS VERSUS MUSIC VIDEO'S CONVENTIONS

The conventions of rock and roll imply that the singers in music videos are trying not to act but to speak truthfully. We assume that they draw on their own emotions and experiences. Whether they excel or not, we should keep faith in their honesty even though we know that record companies and videomakers put artists in roles they feel confused or embarrassed by and have little control over. The very fact that artists in music-video settings are vulnerable to embarrassment may even elicit our sympathy. Knowing that the performer has put herself at the mercy of directors, cinematographers, set builders, and so on, and seeing that the work has, in some ways, spun out of her hands, we can identify with her predicament. Thus, music video's persuasive force functions like this: if a person I admire for her music is willing to endure such a strange context, I might as well leave aside my critical disbelief and go along for the ride. There are a few clear exceptions, as when cinematic codes tell the viewer that the video is a spoof or parody; here, the performers appear within TVs, dress like politicians or shysters, or leer and wink at the camera. Another is with performers who have enjoyed long, well-established careers and have become cultural icons: Madonna, Aerosmith, Prince, Rolling Stones, and ZZ Top all carry a trace of the self-referential with them. In whatever they do, we assume that they wear some sort of mask.

Music-video performance differs markedly from acting styles in film and television. For a number of reasons, the genre brings to the foreground candor, self-disclosure, and direct address. Perhaps the situations in music video are streamlined because the performer lacks a clear goal that would encourage us to place her in a competitive context with others and distance her from ourselves. In addition, the setting often seems organic, as if it were a projection of the performer's own psyche. (Directors talk about showing off the performer's best side while also including some aspect of the character of which he is unaware.)

Yet another aspect that heightens the intimacy of music video is the variety of ways that the performer can break the viewing plane or, as is said in the theater, the fourth wall. In Hollywood film, to reveal the scaffolding of the production or to acknowledge the viewer is not allowed. Yet in music video, we often see the cameras, and band members address us routinely. Some of music video's most provocative examples of breaking the frame include the wet kisses the star and the little girl give the camera lens in the Stone Temple Pilots' "Vaseline" and Nirvana's "Come as You Are," respectively. Dr. Dre likes to cover the lens with his palm in "Gin 'n' Juice" and "No Diggity." Similarly, Busta Rhymes smashes his face into us in "Woo Hah," and Cypress Hill's B-Real gleefully threatens to poke out our eyes with his finger in "Insane in the Membrane."

A number of other codes breed familiarity and comfort; these resemble film in that the lead character remains autonomous, integral, and predictable. The principal roles music video performers play can be sketched roughly as overseers, dreamers (or somnambulists), neutral observers, and participants embedded within the action of the piece. Whatever role a performer adopts, it becomes set in place as the video gets underway and remains stable until nearly the end, when boundaries occasionally threaten to dissolve. (In the latter case, the shift functions primarily as a framing device.) The musicians do not pull a Hitchcock on us; they do not pop in on their actors' tableaux, and the actors do not intrude on the performers' private space unless they are arriving as part of a band rehearsal. The band's performance space and that of the story rarely interpenetrate. Recent videos flirt more with these boundaries than have videos of the past; however, the sense of a boundary is teased but remains firm.[5] Almost all videos maintain a sense of coherence. For example, it would be surprising if TLC's "Waterfalls," Pearl Jam's "Jeremy," or Green Day's "When I Come Around" integrated the star into the narrative. In a Madonna video, it would be strange for the background figures to move into the star's contemplative space. As in many videos, Chaka Khan plays the role of both narrator and participant in the action of "When the Water Runs Dry," but this is established from the outset. If she withdrew from either role, it would be just as surprising.

It is instructive to watch videos and imagine what it might be like for the performer to move into and then quickly out of the collective, action-oriented space, or for supporting characters to flow in the other direction. This inflexibility of role and address may have to do with the homogeneity of tone in a pop song (of a uniform emotional pitch), as well as the need to preserve structural boundaries, to showcase the song's sectional divisions. It might also be a way of preserving suspense. Once performer and characters have bridged settings, there is nowhere else to go. Or the formulaic functions might constitute a form of advertising: the message must be decipherable. The most important rules for music video—the clear and limited role a performer plays—differ little from those of classical Hollywood film in this particular way. Not only can we predict that the performers will stay in their own realm, but we can also expect them back at the same section, often at the same point, on or near a hook line.

Another rigid convention is the way that the performer acknowledges the musical environment in which she or he exists. This convention can be illustrated by contrast with opera. Whereas characters in an opera would not be surprised to discover that they were part of a given scenario, they would be shocked to find out that they were singing, not simply speaking within their present context.[6] In music videos that extend past the documentation of performance, that are more narrative, the singers would not be surprised to find out that they were singing. They are forbidden, however, to acknowledge the sonic environment in which they exist. Within the communicative resources of a video, this might be signaled quite subtly; the singer might play "air guitar," pretend to listen to the music, and then smile appreciatively or frown, or initiate one of those typical interruptions when the music stops and voice and sound effects kick in.[7] Two examples: in John Cougar Mellencamp's "It's Just Another Day" and Sheryl Crow's "Every Day is a Winding Road," the performers engage in musical gestures reminiscent of performance, but they do not seem to hear the music around them. Strangely, they seem to be listening to some private song inside their heads, rather than what we are listening to. In almost all videos that neither foreground live performance nor depict the speakers carrying the song, the song is something like room temperature and humidity, something that is so much a part of the setting that no one attends to it. But the song functions as more than ambience; by the video's close, the singer will most likely have been put through paces—asked to look happy or sad, wistful, thoughtful, or reckless. Some of music video's charm derives from the myriad moods the performer displays. Because the star cannot acknowledge the role of the music in affecting her emotions, we are left to conclude that the image and music have acted on her. This is remarkable especially when the performer is the songwriter or producer. Toward the end of Janet Jackson's "If," the singer suddenly looks more joyous. The transformation in mood is completely unmotivated by the setting; Jackson's dance has not taken a new turn, nor has her relation with those around her shifted or the background changed. The shift, which remains mysterious, can be attributed only to the song's culminating in a larger chorus at the end. (The shift was in fact made by compositing many different outtakes; however, within the logic of cinema, and to some extent, that of music video, editing cannot be the cause of changes, and the viewer must look elsewhere to find her sense of orientation.[8])

A number of threads that are easy to follow run across the whole of the music video's fabric. One is the character who maintains a single activity that carries out a process, such as going to or getting everybody ready for a concert. Another is a shift in time or weather, such as from day to night or from clear skies to cloudy ones. A third is the star's face as it shows a number of moods from happy to sad. In all of these cases, we must make guesses about what has happened and about how much time has elapsed. By the close of "If," Janet Jackson becomes ebullient; in Nine Inch Nails' "Closer," Trent Reznor becomes relaxed and somber; Kurt Cobain becomes exhausted in Nirvana's "Heart-Shaped Box"; in "You Were Meant for Me," Jewel becomes less aggrieved. The image does not reveal why such shifts have occurred, so we must turn to the music for additional narrative, temporal, and affective cues.

THE STAR IN RELATION TO OTHER CHARACTERS

It may well be unclear whether music video has a narrative and what the figures mean to each other. Much of the charm and challenge comes not from the often futile task of determining what the figures might be searching for and where they have been—providing answers to these questions may be beyond the capabilities of the form—but rather from observing the relations among the figures: who is listening to whom and who refuses to hear, who remains approachable and who impenetrable, who has insight into or influence over unfolding events, who is aware that he is singing to the viewer and whether he seems to think the viewer can contribute solace or approval. Without enough words, such relations are established through textural, musical, and visual codes that are finely nuanced, but finally, equivocal. In "Cherish," Madonna sings from the shoreline while the mermen swim far out to sea. We assume that the mermen know Madonna is singing, but they remain relatively unimpressed, concerning themselves with their own affairs. This is an inversion of the episode in Homer's *Odyssey* that describes the warriors' stopping up their ears as their ship passes by so as not to be seduced by the enchanting but deadly sirens who sing to them.[9] Also contributing to our understanding of the mermen's indifference are the filmic codes of sightline matches (rare) and the great distances between Madonna and the mermen. Musical codes, however, are equally essential to our understanding of the video; if Madonna were to sing Aretha Franklin's "Giving Him Something He Can Feel," a song with more sexual lyrics and music, the relations would be different. Perhaps the men would be seen as available, just playing coy. It is the music that fills the gap between ambiguous figures.

The example of "Cherish" suggests that music-video images are blank, and that it is the song that defines or places the image. Here the style of music video dictates that such shots be related loosely to one another and set apart by quite dramatic edits, isolating each image in its own realm, to some extent. What provides the context for the image are not adjacent images but something more immediately at hand: the song, which carries the emotional import that belongs to the images. The song may not be able to describe objects, but it can represent the animating desire toward objects—feelings of lust, grief, hunger, or fury. We read these emotions into the image and interpolate links of affect between one image and others. The music video image places us in a context; facial expressions, posture, and clothing clearly identify characters as types. The image helps us find the general vicinity, but it is the music that fills in the more nuanced meaning. An amusing use of stereotypes is Ginuwine's "Pony." Because the characters performing on stage are young African American studs dressed up as cowboys, and those who watch disapprovingly from the audience are old, beer-drinking Okies, we can guess the video's general concerns. But the video's unarticulated themes of youth and sexual prowess can be fully understood only with recourse to musical codes; the swagger and the disdain that these young men display toward older white males is expressed in the sly bass line.

Music videos raise questions about how the sounds in the song's mix are to be distributed throughout the spatial environment. Some of the decisions about what sounds go with what are based on visual cues. The viewer must decide how much the music reflects the performer's own feelings and how much it simply describes the outward manifestations of other characters' actions or of the whole setting. Such choices reflect visual as much as musical and textual cues. Human League's "Don't You Want Me," U2's "With or Without You," and R. Kelly's "Down Low" present music that seems to reflect private thoughts of the characters. In these videos, environments revolve mechanically around a relatively immobile performer. Because the song is so personal and expressive, however, we assume that it comes from the deep recesses of the performer's psyche. The unresponsive environment and static performer encourage us to believe that the music depicts thoughts and feelings. In other instances, the burden of creating meaning remains with the star but falls more heavily on the settings and the other characters. In Pearl Jam's "Jeremy," we can assume that we are seeing the thoughts of the protagonist. The lead singer tilts his head back, bends his body forward, and furrows his brow, signaling that he is engaged in the act of reviewing images in his head. In cases like "Jeremy," background figures depicted specifically as characters are apt to move more stiffly or dreamily than we might expect, drifting through the unfolding events rather than acting as agents. If figures in tableaux gesture out of sync with the music—and it is significant that often the activity has been shot MOS (without sound)—they may reflect the way we sometimes daydream, reviewing silent pictures rather than experiencing images with sound.

There are rare cases when the music does not seem to latch on to any character or any element in the set. A very different message is transmitted by TLC's "Waterfalls," in which the song serves to underscore the moralizing tone of the video and describes in a totalizing way the impoverishment of the community. In other cases, like Bryan Adam's "Have You Ever Loved a Woman" and Green Day's "When I Come Around," the music seems dissociated from the situation altogether, a disavowal of the context.

When the lyrics, music, and environment of the video refuse to disclose a story, we are often able to determine the lead character's relation to the supporting cast by the disposition of the figures. In Tom Petty's "Free Fallin'" and LL Cool J's "Hey Lover," the background figures cannot hear the star. The stars in Green Day's "Come Around" and Nirvana's "Heart-Shaped Box," know what is going on around them but do not much care. In Lisa Stansfield's "I Can't Find My Baby" and Jill Sobule's "I Kissed a Girl," the singers try to tell the viewer something others should not know. TLC's "Waterfalls" suggests that the stars can influence events; in Aerosmith's "Janie's Got a Gun," the stars choose not to. In ZZ Top's "Legs" and R.E.M.'s "Everybody Hurts," the performers will most likely intercede only as a last resort. Music provides additional information about the feelings of the characters and will extend their reach or deepen their receptiveness.

By examining the ways in which characters are designed two-dimensionally in order to be fleshed out by music, we see more clearly the subtle inflections that define the lead and supporting roles, even without the help of dialogue. A surprisingly large number of videos cast the singer in an overseeing role—most often benevolent, sometimes neutral, paternalistic, or hostile. That it is impossible for the singer to know what is going on in the context of the video as a whole never becomes an issue, nor does the fact that the background figures seem attentive or sensitized to the singer's voice (challenging credibility because in most cases the distance between the performer and supporting cast puts everyone out of aural range). Visual codes help us to understand the complexities of the singer's role. Stars often possess greater mobility than do the supporting characters—they patrol the streets or ride dollies, sit in cars or stand on airplane wings, and they are usually placed on a frontal plane. They may also gesture with authority, pointing a finger in the air or raising a palm upward. Foregrounded in the frame, they may gain added presence by being dressed with imagery from folktale, myth, or religion, and through clothing, props, or demeanor. In these cases, the link between the singer and the supporting figures is typically created through the visual codes of light and editing. For example, Smashing Pumpkins' "1979" shows the group's lead singer driving in a car with shots of rowdy suburban kids in a car of their own. No clear connection is established between these two sets of shots, save that dusk falls on the singer as well as on the kids. The only other similarity between the two groups of shots is that we see the kids turning their heads and the lead singer turning his head as well. These two groups of shots remain distinct, in separate spaces, but are matched through the editing, which creates continuity between head turnings in adjacent shots. In Melissa Etheridge's "Come to My Window," the camera cuts between Etheridge, strumming her guitar, and a woman in a locked room; Etheridge looks up, and in the subsequent shot the other woman in the subsequent shot continues the direction of her gaze.

A more liminal case is that of Madonna. In many of her videos—"Express Yourself," "Vogue," "Open Your Heart," and "Bedtime Stories"—her knowledge of what is going on extends quite far, but there are nooks and crannies where figures can cavort beyond her gaze. Our ability to judge Madonna's capacity to oversee events has to do with her status as a star, our notions of gender, the disposition of the figures, as well as musical codes. It is instructive to imagine how the figures might move slightly differently, how the setting might be laid out in another manner, or how Madonna's music might take on a greater sense of power so that her presence would cast a wider net.[10]

Yet another type can be identified in which the star becomes a fully integrated member within the video. Through a subtle choreography between star and background figures and the kinds of claims that the music and lyrics make on them, all appear to be concerned more with each other than with us. Here the stars do not acknowledge the viewer, their space is not set off from supporting roles, and they act unaware that they are singing. The codes for this can be very nuanced, as in Madonna's "Take a Bow," a video where the star is more fully a part of the scenario than an informant speaking to us. Although she is clearly part of the story world, she is also placed in a stripped-down, possibly artificial setting—an empty room with a television set, the latter a reflexive object, the status of which is unclear. If she were to perform Extreme's "More Than Words," however, or Lisa Loeb's "Stay" (keeping true to the original arrangement and vocal production, as well as to the same type of sight lines and framing), we might be more likely to place her in the second of the two performance categories, speaking directly to the audience.

As for the aforementioned one-dimensionality of music-video figures, music videos seldom contain characters as richly articulated as the femme fatale in film noir, or as the tired private dick who chases after her. Perhaps the conventions of pop songs require a uniformity of tone, along with a short duration, that precludes the variety of material and depth of character that can be achieved in opera, which offers a great deal of exposition through the recitatives. Or it might be because pop songs tend to be upbeat and the singers too self-congratulatory. Theorists such as Edward Cone have said that in the traditional presentation of a song, both the accompaniment and the singing voice are part of the composer's psyche.[11] We cannot as easily make this claim for a music video because so many people play a role in its creation. The director is inclined to insert his or her own presence, and in certain instances, such as the videos of Matt Mahurin and Mark Romanek, the vision is so all-encompassing that the song's voice sometimes seems to slip away. Compare, for example, the loving treatment that director Mark Romanek gives his videos for Janet Jackson and Macy Gray, against the troubled portrait of Michael Jackson and his sister in the video "Scream." The song title, sound effects, vocal performance, and music make Jackson appear to be throwing a tantrum. Romanek places him in a sealed-off space far from the earth and treats the subject with extreme distance, as if Jackson's anger is without merit. Because the background and cameras are seamlessly aligned with the singer and the song, we seem to see numerous elements simultaneously: the most flattering parts of Jackson's personality, the part of himself that he wishes to submerge, as well as those elements that viewers feel more supportive of and frightened by. This complex portrait frequently happens at points when an image pokes fun at or criticizes the singer, perhaps for misogyny or pompousness. Madonna's "Cherish" and LL Cool J's "Six Minutes of Pleasure" are two such examples. Often the image expresses more than what the singer dares say, though sometimes it conveys it less. In the Red Hot Chili Peppers' "Under the Bridge," we can sense, as the lead singer walks along the desolate streets and alleyways of Los Angeles, how deep his grief goes, deeper than his own awareness, and this grief somehow finds its realizations in the way that the music spreads across the background of the setting.

■ ■ ■

If there is one parameter that juts out too far in the music video's texture, it is the star's close-up. Its prominence is more a function of the record companies' imperative to advertise than properties inherent to music video's form.[12] I have described the aesthetic merits of including the star in a music video. However, I wish the star's appearance were not so rigorously enforced. We can imagine videos that would do quite different things. The star might not focus on self-disclosure, but rather attend to the arrangement of the song as she hears it in playback or acknowledge people who exist offscreen; boundaries between settings might be more fluid, as could the relations among the star and the background figures, especially in terms of modes of attention and listening. We could imagine videos in which the star constituted only one small element, or in which the song became supplemental, sometimes disappearing, sometimes letting text and/or image take on greater weight. In the last twenty years, the role of the star has become more limited and codified rather than more varied. Our culture would benefit if there were support for independent music video-making, but considering how little support there is for independent filmmaking, a second stream of music-video practice seems unlikely.

Dido's "Thank You" exemplifies many of the issues discussed in this chapter. In this video, Dido thanks someone for giving her the best day of her life while a wrecking crew moves in and destroys her tiny, white-picketed house, which sits between two taller buildings. Dido sings earnestly to the viewer rather than attend to the audio mix or the background figures. She has her own private "star" space (which no one else visits) where her intimate self-disclosure is finely nuanced. The wrecking crew, even though they exist in the same story space, are either slightly sympathetic or oblivious to Dido. It would take only a subtle shift in the image track to change the relations among figures: a slightly longer held pair of shots where sightlines between characters matched, the removal of a shot of an African American construction worker who stares blankly at nothing at all, or the addition of a shot where the workers waved goodbye (perhaps lifting a high-five to Dido). Perhaps the background figures might lip-sync a bit, but then they might seem as if they were dreaming their own words. A different song would also produce a different effect: perhaps one of Moby's, whose mixes feature reverberation and multitracked voices (thereby, perhaps drawing our attention to the back of the set and the supporting characters), and whose arrangements are evocative of proletarian angst. The fact that we are not quite sure about the relations among the wrecking crew and Dido encourages us to watch the tape repeatedly.

ONE SINGS, THE OTHER DOESN'T: MUSICALITY AND THE HUMAN FIGURE IN MUSIC VIDEO

Anyone who has even casually watched music video would notice that the star performer is most often foregrounded in bold relief. The camera showcases every curl of the fingers and bend of the elbow, every wrinkle of the brow and blink of the eye. A close-up captures every emotion that crosses the face for our own private scrutiny. On the other hand, supporting characters in music video typically have an indeterminate nature about them. I want to spend time with the background figures, discussing how they work politically and socially as well as formally and musically, taking some time also to discuss the role of dance in music video and issues of representation, particularly that of African American women.

So, as I have just mentioned, whereas the lead performers in the video are likely to be granted emotional range and shading, the nonperforming accompanying figures are sketchier. Much about them remains unsaid, by contrast with the stars, who tell us more about themselves than we ever wanted to know. Background performers often seem strange and uncanny: as a whole, they are music video's underclass, as if from a caste different from that of the lead.[13] Some of the reasons for the laconic supporting characters are obvious, and others are surprisingly subtle: in the former case, supporting roles have no lyrics and therefore no dialogue. The resources with which these people can assert themselves are much more meager than those of the star, mirroring the fact that we, as a society, are predisposed toward speakers (and all able-bodied individuals) and away from the mute, passive, or silent. Understandably, record companies want to tie the band to the song, and since the lead singer most often sings the hook line, we can see why the star is placed under our immediate gaze. Yet it is also true at times that a character's move to the background will have to do with the formal properties of music and lyrics. To explain the reasons for that, let me lay out some types of background figures—for example, those who, at least for a moment, resemble the bit players in a movie and those who are silent or in a position where they cannot speak, including mannequins and statuary.

When a video's scenario has a strong narrative charge, the supporting characters can look real, fleshly, and unaffected by the music. If those in R. Kelly's "Down Low" resemble real people, it may be because the video is a rare example of a full-blown narrative. (It relies on breaks in the sound track to make way for movie music, a long, dialogue-rich introduction with the plot clearly laid out, and occasional moments where the characters silently mouth dialogue). The two subsidiary roles, Mr. Big's white girlfriend and the number-one hit man, both extremely small, are derivative of roles that we know from movies; they are placed strategically within key moments in the musical and visual flow, and their parts are full of emotional charge—one with imagery of miscegenation, the other of violence. In this case, the viewer may be supplying much that has been gathered from films in order to construct a character (fig. 3.1).

Another person we see in "Down Low"—Lila, the girlfriend of R. Kelly—is a type more common to music videos. Perhaps overcome by infatuation from having just received a stroke on the cheek or a bouquet of flowers, she is unable to speak. Here, her silence is naturalized; she is mute, but she can be nuzzled or receive gifts. At other moments, her silence seems like a wound conveying a helplessness about her—she is put in a position where she cannot speak, and the lead performer must articulate the feelings for both of them. Alongside such passive lovers, there are the general nondescript background figures portrayed as enigmatic and shadowy. Except in dance-party videos, the characters seem mute, as if they have had their tongues cut out or are milling around in the scene with not enough to do, limbs dangling a bit limply at their sides. My observation of shoots reveals that directors take great care in shooting background characters, disposing their bodies in a deliberate manner, having them turn their heads from one side to another with the music, and asking them to move slightly out of sync with the music during playback, so they will

FIGURE 3.1 (A–G) Ron Isley and R. Kelly's "Down Low." Music-video characters drawn from those found in narrative film can seem somewhat fully fledged.

possess their own sense of time. For all these efforts, however, a moment arises in most videos when the character of the background figure seems thin or wanting.

Sometimes one solitary figure will be especially emblematic—for example, an old man wearing overalls and sitting in a rocking chair in the middle of a bar. Placing such a figure in the background compels the viewer to search him out, as in Dr. Dre's "Keep Their Heads Ringing," in which a copilot, shrouded in darkness, with curlers in his hair and birdlike gestures, speaks in a high squeaky voice. A comparably unapproachable type, this time set in the foreground, is the custodian in Nirvana's "Smells like Teen Spirit," a figure who, in his own setting, churns a mop obsessively in a pail (fig. 3.2).

For all the emphasis on beauty in music videos, there are a surprising number of characters who are plump or grossly overweight; who might be called ugly or too old; who stand in as stereotypes for class, ethnicity, sexuality, gender, avocation, or occupation; or who seem freakish, comical, or absurd. Such figures are essential to the genre in part because their tempo differs from that of the principal performers; they possess a different force against the music. Nothing can enable the viewer to experience the range of materials in a pop song as successfully as a variety of people mingling together. For example, in the beach-party scenes in Coolio's "Fantastic Voyage," the camera, tilted up from below the sand's surface, reveals a series of figures emerging from the trunk of a car. Alternately, we see the bikini-clad crotches of beautiful young women, and then the front torsos of a much more varied group of men—dumpy, slovenly, exotically dressed (as mariachi musicians), or shrimpy. Such a contrast encourages the viewer to feel a graceful flowing movement as well as something awkward and leaden against the music. At the beginnings of phrases, an obese African American man appears against the noisy, even flatulent, bass line; a woman or a figure holding a small child appears at the ends of phrases—highlighting the upper register. Our attention is drawn to particular elements on the musical surface, as well as to stereotypical notions about the ways these bodies move and feel (fig. 3.3). One might hope that this broad range of humanity would increase the viewer's sensitivity to the others, but they seem not to. Unlike the star, whom the camera lingers over and who appears from a variety of angles, the background figures are experienced most often in passing; the viewer literally glances over them. The figures help to define what the star

FIGURE 3.2 (A–C) Nirvana's "Smells Like Teen Spirit." Music video's emblematic figures.

is not and set the outer limits to a system of representation. Looking through the video for characters that color our relation to the star is an important part of understanding how music video works as a whole.

This brings us to one of the commonest and most striking types of supporting figure in music video: static emblems like mannequins, statues, or robotic workers. By placing such figures in libraries, prisons, mental asylums, schools, offices, and factories, directors make calculated use of these figures' inability to speak. Directors also exploit this muteness by introducing what can be called "paraspeak": gestures that resemble speaking—opening and closing mouths, chattering teeth, or broad gesticulations. Fine gestures are generally reserved for the star. The movement of the star's hands before her face provides the most useful example of refined expressivity because it closely reflects speech and can also possess the rhythmic qualities of dance.

How does the relegation of supporting characters to the background help show off a pop song? Most obvious is the tendency, through choices made at all stages of production—composing, arranging, and producing—to bring the voice forward over other sonic elements. If the star performer begins to stand for the primary voice, other figures may become associated with the accompaniment and slip beyond our attention. Rudolf Arnheim, in *The Power of the Center,* describes how the frame exerts a centrifugal force upon any object depicted within it.[14] The moving image extends the force-field metaphor much further. In film, there are not only moments of stress and relaxation created by the ways visual material falls within the frame, but also spatial and temporal nodes of stress.[15] In addition, the music exerts its own qualities of pressure: harmonic pulls, metrical accents, changes in dynamics, rises and falls in melodies. All of these create pockets of tension and release in the image. If a subsidiary figure lacks authority (is not dancing or performing) and is devoid of charisma, he will, like a doll, seem to be danced by the music or, worse, left aside by the momentum of the music and the lyrics, as if he did not have

FIGURE 3.3 (A–H) Coolio's "Fantastic Voyage." Imagery placed in relation to music assists in marginalizing the background figures.

sufficient energy to rail against an unceasing flow. (By contrast, the lead performer seizes the music; he is slightly in front of—pushed onward by—the
music, as if he were catching hold of and riding a tiger.)

Possessing a stillness that complements some of the more extroverted qualities of the star, mannequin figures can also mediate between silence and becoming. Videos establish a continuum from stillness and silence to constant
flux: the inanimate decor and the quiet out of which the song begins; still
figures and the slowest tempos; moderate physical movements such as shallow
knee bends, heads turning to one side, or steps forward; frenetic visual elements
such as the showy, fluttery gestures of the star, the rapid movement of small
turning objects, and shifting patterns of light. If a music video reflects a world
where no object or person acts quite as we expect, the still figures help to bridge
the gap between inanimate and animate—the gap between setting and star.
Another reason that directors make such use of the mute figure is that these
figures help to create a more richly nuanced psychological portrait of the star.
They play the Hyde to the performer's Jekyll. When the lead character is lip-
syncing and carrying out all kinds of demonstrative business, it is helpful for
others to hold down the scene and act as a receptive audience (even when they
are not listening, their bodies are turned receptively toward the star). The use
of background figures as a type of Greek chorus is exemplified in Nenah
Cherry's "Under My Skin" and En Vogue's "Whatta Man."

Richard Middleton has argued that one of the defining features of popular
music is its high degree of repetition—rhythms, timbres, iconic materials, and
sectional divisions repeat endlessly and build to a state of *jouissance*.[16] At some
level, the whole and parts of a music video's character also becomes material
to be used for musical purposes. With such a small palette to work with—a
short, circular, and episodic form and little narrative or dialogue—the distinc-
tion of the video becomes secondary to the characters' controllable parameters—props, hairstyle, costume, color, and makeup. Hundreds of photographs
and hours of tape will be scanned to find extras with the right look. After
choosing physiques and facial features that play off, echo, or complement those
of the star, directors will have created one more type of visual/thematic variation to support the varied representations of the lead performer: the varied
iterations formed through posters, TV appearances, Claymations, statuary,
photographs, and extreme close-ups; the musician performing and the musician in dramatic situations, the musician wearing one type of clothes or hairstyle versus another. If the star constantly shifts between something that we
might recognize as a narrative character or a real person to something that
hardens into a close-up shot, so, too, does the background character become
alive and then dead, hard and then soft, functioning as a second layer of articulation. The relation between star and subsidiary character creates a bleed-
through; as in many elements in music video, the local connections across
parameters first link and then supersede larger formal devices, weaving a vast
subtle network, a fine skein. In the Robbie Williams video, representations and

transformations between character and supporting figures run thick through the texture. Williams, sporting black-slashed tattoos, dances with a woman dressed in a zebra-striped costume; he showcases his tiger-headed underwear, and then the video cuts to an African American woman dressed in gold lamé; Williams's groin becomes fuzzed out, and then we see a woman with soft, blurry underwear. The star pulls back his pink flesh to reveal red, bloody musculature underneath, and the video then cuts from a woman dressed in pink-tinged glasses and a baby-pink halter and shorts to a woman with gaudily painted matte red muscles with striated yellow veins. (She looks as if she belonged in a medical diorama) (fig. 3.4).

The supporting characters—women roller skaters—in the Robbie Williams video "Rock DJ" exemplify a key principle of music video: that almost every musical and visual parameter, such as props, camera movement, lighting, melodic hooks, and lyrics, can serve a dual purpose. How much do they serve to accentuate a musical function? And to what extent do they work as cultural objects—things that try to tell us how we should get on in the world? We never know. And, in fact, the most magical moments in music video occur when a parameter simultaneously fulfills both functions in a virtuosic manner—the activity of the figure furthers the story (often through a transgressive gesture intended to undermine a socially contested norm) and illuminates musical structure. The visual element becomes magical because it can negotiate between two worlds—a real world and a musical world. At the end of the section in "Rock DJ," when the women nod their heads as they stand in the doorway, we are unsure if they do this because the video wants to make a social point—that

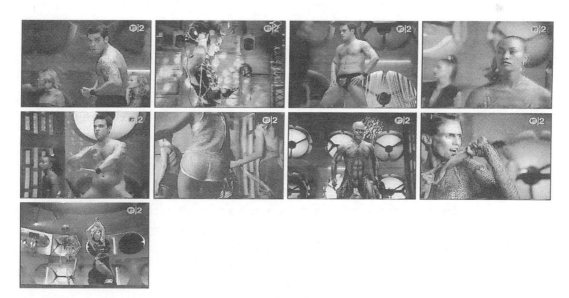

FIGURE 3.4 (A–I) Robbie Williams's "Rock DJ." Visual rhymes help transform figures into malleable musical material.

women, as much as men, objectify and judge the other for their sexual attributes as commodities—or because it wants to draw our attention to interesting musical material—the break when the rhythm arrangement comes to the fore.[17] (Music-video image frequently draws our attention to different features of music almost like a tour guide.) Much of the pleasure of this video comes from its critique of capitalist culture—its ability to articulate the flip side of consumerism, which is to say the death drive—and the video makes this critique in a very formalistic manner through the way material unfolds and becomes manipulated. Do these formalistic permutations in some way remind us that our social order is also a highly constructed system?[18]

The background figure who is out of rhythm with the rest of the video contributes important qualities to the video. In music video, the music track is a stern master. Once into the song, the listener will measure every moment of sync and divergence from it and will gauge the scale of the song—how long it will be until the phrase ends and the verse closes, how soon the next chorus will arrive and the song as a whole will drive to a close. The image can tarry, match, or run ahead of the music, but at some level it must subject itself to the track's steadfastness. The image most assists in the process of closing sections, of finding an end, almost certainly on the first beat four or five measures from now. If the image and music in the first verse had ended with a striking build-up or fade, we hope for the same or even more in the next. No wonder that, with the unyielding current of the music, the image is forced into frenzy. There is a need to move, to try to obliterate and transcend what one is yoked to. The background figure suggests the possibility of an exit.

What about the question of dance? Dancers rarely perform fully choreographed work; their movements might be described as "clocking," that is, small, repeated, or varied gestures with about the same desire of effect as many other parameters in music video, such as a few words in the lyrics, a melodic hook, or a prop. With music-video directors' financial and time constraints, it is not surprising that dance is so often thinly articulated; there might be two planes of action, with one group of figures in the foreground moving one way and another just at the edge of the periphery moving another, but the choreography is rarely more nuanced than that.[19]

Perhaps the schematic approach to dancers in music video is a function of television, which is a thinner medium than film: containing fewer pixels within a very compressed gray scale, the small, square television frame forces directors to depend upon close-ups. Or perhaps music-video choreography both attempts to match the sparseness of today's R&B and pop songs and draws attention to the song's formal properties. Featuring rapid editing and schematic imagery (a different scenic background and varying numbers and types of figures in the frame), a video encourages a type of perception based on scanning: this focuses the viewer's attention on repetition, sequence, movement, and speed. The few planes of dancers may raise questions of sync: performers' bodies cannot articulate musical gesture at a value much finer than the eighth note (as John Cage notes, limbs possess a different rhythmic hierarchy from that of the music) and a sense of rhythmic nuance may derive instead from the slight fluctuations created by gestures that pass from one performer to another. When the star and background figures perform in lock step, the moments of synchronization and slight departures from that can resemble the very fine differences between performers' movements and playback—between the body and the music, and between the lips and sung text. The foregrounding of the horizontal plane also contributes to some of the greatest pleasures in music video: in the cut from a long to a closer shot, the viewer gains a sense of prowess, of being able to hold onto that sweeping visual and musical line against the small bumps or dislocations offered by a perceptual shift at the edit. If all the figures are moving the same way, the editor may similarly have more control over the eyes' visual path through the image and may then be able to move the viewer more successfully into the material in the next shot, which is often the close-up. Last, the figures dancing as one unit grants more autonomy to the music: it raises the question of whether the music or the characters have volition, and when the figures begin to look like automatons, the music can seem to take over. (Remember, music videos want to grant more power to the music. If the music can seem to have agency, the viewer will listen as much as they watch.) Though professional dance instructors disdain music-video dance for both its rudimentary nature and its damaging effects on bodies (the hard marble or concrete surface is unforgiving), dance is essential to music video because it teaches how the music is to be experienced in the body. Journalists have noted that it was only when people saw Missy Elliot move could the viewers really get behind her music. The characters' dance in music video also instructs us how we should feel about our bodies within a certain cultural epoch. Certainly the small, fluid gestures—the "jerk, jerk, jerk"—and arms spread wide of today is different from the sinuous S-curves of the early 1990s and the broader, wooden, robotic movements of the early 1980s.

And what about the frequent occurrence of highly sexualized imagery of dancers and background figures, almost invariably of African American women? How does this imagery affect the perceptions, beliefs, and imagination of many different groups of Americans, young and old, whites and nonwhites, straight or gay, male or female (for I assume that the responses are not the same)? In defense of a more moderate stance toward, at one level, such unquestionably sexist imagery, one could say that the body, music, and pleasure have always been closely linked, and pop music historically has always dealt with transgression: one of the most powerful ways to do this is through race and sex. African American women's bodies in videos are often eye-poppingly beautiful, Amazonian sculptural forms that achieve a semiotic pitch that the image needs in order to match the speed and density of the music. (Another way is through a concatenation of disparate visual references, a costuming touch from one era against a setting from another, a prop against an unusual color.) And we should note, of course, that this type of imagery is used so often because not only men but also women like to look at women. Perhaps the particular depictions of African American women's bodies and contemporary pop sound are linked somehow, rap music sits in the lower registers with heavy drum and bass beats and the women are strong and voluptuous, which stands in stark contrast to the soaring guitar and vocal work of the 1980s metal videos with thin, gazelle-like women with long, thin white legs. (If music in the context of a video can possess agency, the sounds can threaten to topple these appendages over. This imagery can also reveal a latent fragility in the sound itself.)

None of the previous explanations will serve as any consolation for those who are oppressed by this imagery, who are left feeling inadequate with the types of bodies that they have, and certainly that is almost all of us. It must be especially hard for African American women because the imagery so stridently argues that their bodies are for ogling and sex. When we consider the imagery of African American women, we need to be sensitive to the ways their bodies are used in each video, where they fall within the music, and what other kinds of imagery surrounds them. Sut Jhally, in his *Dreamworlds 2* video, offers an incisive and far-reaching analysis of the objectification of women in music video, but, as he admits, he leaves out the sexualization of men and fails to consider an image within the context of a whole video.[20] Directors often make at least the weak nod toward other viewing subjectivities when they include African American women who are on site and who simply watch or listen and offer a nonsexualized presence. In music video, the trope of the woman's body has been played with, spoken for and argued against. Nelly's video "Country Grammar" stands out as a surprise, because a woman of average build dances around a rapper with T-shirt and jeans: she is fully clothed—she even sports a kerchief. Madonna bends both gender and sexual roles in "Music." Looking tanned and wearing full-length furs and several pounds of gold chain jewelry, she looks like Goldy in the 1970s black action film *The Mac.* She plays an empowered masculine role and ogles, fondles, and has fun with the dancing women, whose bodies do not exactly mimic but instead resemble the stereo-typical African American figures who most commonly appear in music videos. The image is carefully worked to suggest transgression, but to avoid the real taboos as well.[21]

Though such highly sexualized imagery is objectionable, I am not in favor of shutting it off with its attendant pleasures. Rather, I would be in favor of a greater range of visual imagery in videos, those that stress other types of beauty and sexuality, and would include the disabled, the overweight, or the aged. I would like to see more videos focus on politics rather than sex and on relationships besides romantic ones. Most of all, I would like to see videos that dare to be slow and reflective, that approach a quality of wisdom, perhaps even the state of silence. These states may be achievable with the liberation of the background figure.

4

Settings

MUSIC VIDEO'S HISTORY shows that different modes of address are available to different constituencies. An avid viewer will recognize the studio set of a living room with worn wallpaper; the industrial site with naked pipes and debris on the floor; the high-ceilinged hotel with marble staircases, and "the street." Why do alternative bands inhabit huge, fanciful spaces or squeeze into cramped ones? Why do they get to display generalized emotional and physical suffering, while R&B artists must operate within a nexus of action/adventure films, melodrama, and Hollywood musicals? Rap videos, meanwhile, have traditionally taken place on the street and used realistic modes of depiction.[1] Settings are segregated, and the ways of inhabiting them seem strictly codified (fig. 4.1). R&B singers Toni Braxton and Brian McKnight would never back themselves into the corner of a lower-middle-class house; alternative groups such as The Goo Goo Dolls, Green Day, or The Offspring would never perform a choreographed sequence in a high-ceilinged hotel.[2] These images alone—apart from the music—might suggest that the alternative groups are asserting a form of white privilege, that the R&B artists are practicing wish fulfillment, and that the rappers are depicting "reality."

In a generous mood, we might take such settings as providing a way for viewers quickly to identify what genre a song belongs to, much as an album cover can. Such representations start to pile up and become insidious stereo-

FIGURE 4.1 (A–D) Blur's "Song 2 (Woo Hoo)," Marilyn Manson's "Sweet Dreams," Keith Sweat's "Twisted," and Redman's "Funkorama." Alternative, heavy metal or gothic, R&B and rap settings, respectively.

types, however. Not only the settings themselves, but also the use of space, props, and especially the disposition of figures, become problematic. And it has as much to do with the absence of certain kinds of representation as with what we do see. Only in the rarest instances would an African American look slovenly and depressed, like the protagonist of Metallica's "Hero of the Day." No European American would be at such risk of being blown up or sucked down to the depths as Dr. Dre and Puffy Combs, nor would they always be restricted to homemade technology (fig. 4.2). Few European American female artists are as strongly compelled to be people-pleasers as Janet Jackson or to be as highly sexualized as Christina Aguilera, Eve, or Foxy Brown. Britney Spears might be considered an exception, but her sexiness is counterbalanced by her virginity and Barbie-doll surface. African American women who play supporting roles are much more frequently objectified as sexual objects than are their European American counterparts. For the most part, African American artists must work with a much smaller set of materials. The whole history of film, literature, and television does not seem available to them in the way that it does for European Americans.

Although I cannot deny the hegemony of these stereotypes in music video, I would like to complicate our understanding of this imagery by acknowledging the specificity of music video as a medium and by looking at strategies employed in specific videos. Although music videos arise out of complex institutional structures and elude the complete control of videomakers and musicians, it remains useful to begin where music videos ask us to begin, with the possibility that a video will present a departure from the norm. A first look at a video may yield a quick gloss on its intended effects, but its meaning can become unstable with closer viewing: we may not be able to determine to whom a video is directed or for what it is arguing. An image that might be objectionable alone can cut across a stereotype when taken with the music and the lyrics.

The functions of music-video settings differ from those of classic Hollywood

FIGURE 4.2 (A–H) Dr. Dre's "Been There, Done That" and Metallica's "Hero of the Day." Settings tied to genre and ethnicity. Imagine a European American figure in the first tape or an African American in the second.

film. The locations that appear most often in music video tend to be generic depictions, suggesting a concept of place, or representing a kind of place, rather than providing a detailed description of a specific setting—a beach, train station, concert hall, bridge, toilet, apartment, bar, or street corner. These generic settings are often stripped down, reduced to their barest essentials: in videos such as Lil' Kim's "I've Got a Crush on You," the schematic character of the setting allows other elements—color, texture, props, costumes, and extras—to come to the fore. Features such as the video's intense use of color help blunt the viewer's desire for narrative. Nevertheless, the modes of depiction for individual settings can vary greatly, and the moment when a setting appears in the course of a video can help to determine its meaning. At certain moments in Snoop Doggy Dogg's "What's My Name," the locations seem highly particularized, like the opening high-angle shot of a South Central bungalow with Dobermans picking through trash on the front lawn. Later, however, an image of Snoop standing before a graffiti-emblazoned wall looks like an emblem of all inner-city spaces. The tires and trashcans behind Snoop seem to have been arranged just so, as if the art department has had a field day. Our understanding of the artist, the setting, the song and video changes in response to this more generic and perhaps didactic depiction (fig. 4.3).

Many elements affect the choice of a setting, its presentation, and its meaning. Music videos present objectionable images of class, gender, ethnicity, disability, and sexuality. When we come across a particular video, however, it seems harder to make an assertion about what kind of cultural work it does. This difficulty derives from music video's unique features: the formal compression, the elliptical or banal lyrics, the music's determinative effect on the video, the incompletely rendered visuals. The video seems to take on too many tasks, showcasing the singer, enticing the viewer with the promise of a story, revealing the music, and highlighting the lyrics. More than other genres, music video seems porous to what impinges upon it.

This chapter aims to raise viewers' awareness to the features involved in settings, genre, and ethnicity in music video, and to help them make a critical judgment concerning how the video creates meaning. In order to understand how setting and ethnicity work in a video, we should first consider a number of features: what kinds of musical practices are suggested? In what ways does the video underscore or play against generic norms? How does the video appeal

FIGURE 4.3 (A–D) Snoop Doggy Dogg's "What's My Name." A video's varied settings, both realistic and stylized.

to particular viewing communities? Does the video simply adopt hardened stereotypes, or does it reflect upon them? We should also attend to the formal properties of music video: how does the music video work within the common types of settings? How does ethnicity and genre reflect this choice? Where does the setting appear within the song's structure? How does visual space play against musical space? We should consider the role of institutional pressures and production practices: how does the personal voice of the director affect the uses of figures and can the director convey a sense of visual and musical space? Last, we want to address, in a more theoretical way, whether music video is a form different from narrative film. Do music-video settings serve less as a documentary real space and more as a one-dimensional backdrop? Do the characters function differently from that of classic Hollywood narrative?

The body of this chapter divides into three large sections in order to address several of these questions. The first section considers the ways that settings are shaped by references to musical features and music making practices, and follows with questions of audience, the role of the star, and cultural stereotypes. The second section takes on the formal features of music video. It treats more carefully the ways that settings are explored over the course of a video, focusing on the use of space, the placement of settings within the song's flow, and the movement of the camera. The third section looks briefly at some of the factors that impinge upon the creation of settings: production practices, institutional pressures, budgetary considerations, and the personal style of the director. The chapter closes with a more speculative discussion on the interaction of music, lyrics, and settings, which I hope can provide a way to consider some larger issues: the role of the figures in videos, and the question of how and to what extent the settings of music video can create a sense of place.

MUSICAL CONNECTIONS, MUSICAL PRACTICES, REPRESENTATION, AND THE ROLE OF COMMUNITY

Settings can serve different functions, such as making social points, showing the artist's status in some community, foregrounding musical features, or highlighting production practices. Attention to the last two functions can help us to understand individual videos, differences among musical genres, and the medium as a whole. Many videos use generic settings to draw upon cultural associations between a type of place and the musical elements of a song. Several of D'Angelo's videos, for example, may take place in after-hours clubs because of his musical connections with jazz organ trios of the 1960s. R.E.M.'s "Losing My Religion" is set in a log cabin partly because the song's use of folk instruments like mandolin and fiddle constitutes a musical departure for the group. References to musical features can be extremely direct, as with the extreme close-up of a guitarist's fingers on the fretboard in metal. They can mislead the viewer by showing a performer on an instrument the song does not contain. A video may contain a DJ, keyboardist, or drummer, even though the song was produced using Pro Tools software. Music videos can even swap acoustic instruments, such as an alto sax for a flute, as in Prince's "Gett Off." (The alto sax looks more exotic.) Music videos can be elliptical but revealing: a song's borrowings from flamenco may be reflected visually by nothing more than a Seville orange under a sunset backdrop at a staged photo shoot. Certain videos derive energy from a visual scheme that actually conflicts with the song's genre. (I discuss three examples later in this chapter.) Settings reflect not only musical practices but also a song's sonic features. Mark Romanek's videos show respect for a song's soundworld: the pedal-point vamps and wet synthesizer timbres of Madonna's "Bedtime Stories" and the dry, percussive rhythm tracks of Michael Jackson's "Scream" are matched with a resonant and nonresonant space, respectively (fig. 4.4). The range of these approaches suggests something more fundamental about settings in music video: that there is no predetermined degree of proximity between song and setting, despite the repetition of a small number of stock locations from video to video. Many videos will reward a viewer's efforts to piece out the relation between music and image.

Rap videos reflect musical features and production practices in interesting ways while maintaining a commitment to place. Images of the street are especially useful to study. Not only do these images provide a realistic ground for audiences, they serve a thematic function as well: by recalling the block parties and sidewalk performances with which hip-hop began, they symbolize rap's origins, keeping it close to its roots. These videos can also complement musical features by depicting the street in certain specific ways. One often sees a long tracking shot in slow motion, with the camera placed at a low angle and mounted with a wide-angle lens. The breadth of the image is frequently underscored by black mattes at the top and bottom of the frame. The wide-angle lens and camera position suggest a peripheral vision, allowing us to notice

FIGURE 4.4 (A–G) D'Angelo's "Brown Sugar," R.E.M.'s "Losing My Religion," No Doubt's "Don't Speak," Madonna's "Bedtime Stories," and Michael Jackson's "Scream." A video's setting can correspond to the song's materials.

elements beyond the rap and the basic beat. The tracking shot's momentum, along with the use of slow motion, creates a sense of flow that reflects both what rappers call the "lyrical flow" and the groove underneath. One might also take the slow-motion footage as reflecting the relatively relaxed quality of the speaking voice as against the singing voice.

Rap videos have many ways of responding to the song, whether or not they take place on the street. This emphasis on visual detail and on the political and cultural functions of place resonates with the practices of hip-hop. Although rap videos may seem at first glance to depict "the city" or "the ghetto," broadly defined, they work hard to represent specific places and people. Rap is the single genre consistently committed to creating a sense of place: the videos often feature identifiable housing projects, small businesses, and street signs.[3] Even if one is unfamiliar with a location, one senses that its particularity matters. More generally, one can pick out the difference between East Coast and West Coast videos through architecture and quality of light.[4] Nor do these videos make the performers seem like tourists, or reduce the extras to mere "local color": the performers appear to belong to the place. The level of detail in the lyrics seems also to call forth the particularity of the settings. Samples in hip-hop sometimes contain surface noise or otherwise show their age, lending the song a nostalgic quality that the image can match with an amber tint.

It is not naive to claim that rap's commitment to place derives in part from the fact that words are spoken rather than sung. In this regard, videos bear some kinship with documentary voiceovers that are accompanied by a soundtrack. If raps were sung rather than spoken, we might imagine that the videos would look different.

A sizable number of rap videos have turned away from street footage, partly because the record companies have granted larger production budgets. One thematic departure is action/adventure movies, with some videos alluding to particular films such as George Miller's *The Road Warrior* and James Cameron's *The Terminator*, as well as crime films such as Brian De Palma's *Scarface*. This focus on a few primary texts resembles certain musical practices in hip-hop. Rap songs frequently sample, quote, or embellish upon a handful of songs by James Brown, P-Funk, and earlier rappers such as Eric B and Rakim. This point of origin acquires its status as much for its multiplicity and richness of possibility as for its authority.

Videos in other genres emphasize different musical practices and musical features. In alternative videos, one might see a small, boxy set, built in a studio or warehouse, covered with murky green wallpaper, and decorated with shabby furniture. The run-down look of these settings underscores an interest in rawness and spontaneity and an ambivalence about such practices as writing attractive, accessible hooks. Alternative groups are typically imagined to play in low-rent spaces, like garages and small clubs, and these sites become associated with specific musical practices. Contemporary R&B is built up in the studio, and many videos pay homage to this institution. Even when the videos do not literally depict the studio, the smooth surfaces and high ceilings of many R&B videos seem to fit the carefully crafted textures of R&B songs.

Heavy-metal videos are often situated in abandoned industrial sites, with exposed pipes and debris on the floor, and are often shot in long shot with a blue tint. This setting may reflect metal's posture of the outsider as well as sonic features. The music is meant to be played so loudly that it cannot reside where people live and work.

Some of the most interesting songs and settings are those that straddle two genres, such as rap and smooth R&B or rap and alternative. Such a video can reflect two different dispositions—toughness, suavity, or knowingness—and raise the question of which genre the song reflects more strongly. One type of rap and R&B mixed setting features a contemporary casino floor in Las Vegas with the men decked out in fedoras and the women in flapper outfits of beaded obsidian. Videos can play against expectations by departing from a genre's iconography, while those poised at the edge of a viewer's consciousness succeed because they tease the viewer into watching the tape many times. In Mariah Carey's "Sweetheart," the singer performs atop the Guggenheim Museum in Bilbao, almost challenging the viewer to connect the imagery with that of typical R&B videos; here, it is only the sheen of the shaped metal that recalls R&B's smooth surfaces. In Oasis's "Do You Know What I Mean?" in which the band perform before enormous bombed-out buildings, the setting still connotes alternative rock's worn, boxy settings. Despite the setting's gigantic scale, it still recalls the confined spaces of typical alternative videos. Some videos depart even further from their genre, retaining only a color, costume or prop, while some flaunt conventions altogether.

In a music video, neither lyrics, music, nor image can claim a first origin. It can be unclear whether the music influences the image or the lyrics influence the music. For a form in which narrative and dramatic conflicts are hard to come by, some of the excitement stems from the way each medium influences the others. Smooth R&B pop song writing might be considered well crafted, but too cold and calculated. The videos often present overmanicured surfaces that reflect both the elegance and the coldness of the musical surface. The expensive interiors and statuesque figures can be a bit austere and off-putting, but they, in turn, are changed by the music: as the camera moves with a sense of agency and the music fills up the space, the setting seems to warm up. The result is one of cooperation: the setting gives the song and the camera something to do, somewhere to go. Similarly, the music affects the images of ennui in alternative music, waking them up as if they had been jammed into an electric socket.

I have shown so far that the image concretizes sonic and performative features. In so doing, the image brings to light power relations already encoded in the music. Yet we should also note that these images also add their own ideological content, often restricting the song's range of meaning. This aspect of music video brings us to the next issue in our discussion—the cultural import of the video's representations. Rap and R&B often draw our attention to the presence or absence of money, while alternative and metal seem locked in an eternal middle class: a few alternative bands hint at working-class culture (Evergreen and Green Day); metal bands, even within their neglected sites, seldom address urban decay (Pantera) and almost never depict the unemployed. Why is it that African American genres raise the question of how capitalism shapes American consciousness? One could argue that the lyrics within African American song tradition have dealt frankly with sex and getting paid, dating back to the early forms of the blues. But I bet the settings more reflect the record industry's cynical exploitation of how youth uses music.[5] The largest share of the buying public is made up of young European Americans who turn to alternative music for lessons in how to conduct oneself and how to brood about philosophical issues; hence the lyrics can be ponderous and the imagery encompasses a vast range. In this musical universe, rap and smooth R&B are for pleasure—for partying and sex—and for voyeurism—for imagining oneself as or flirting with the Other. Thus, the imagery must occupy a much narrower compass.[6]

The settings are often influenced by an appeal to the star's particular status. Images of class affect the settings of music video—rap is posed against R&B and metal is posed against alternative. A carefully constructed class hierarchy exists within any genre (metal's Soundgarden is of a higher class than Rob Zombie), though a performer's status may change as he or she becomes more famous. Mary J. Blige started as a slightly tough working-class woman and became a high-class diva as her record sales improved. Once a pop star has become a multimillionaire, he cannot truly return to the streets. Both Dre and Jay-Z have made videos that incorporate street footage, but the directors have been careful also to place them in situations that show off wealth.

The images not only signal the star's status but also appeal to specific audiences. Videos attempt to create a sense of community particularly by picking up the communal implications of genre. Record companies and videomakers use settings to connect their performers to musical communities. For example, the black British singer Seal sells records primarily to white audiences; placing him in an empty environment, apart from black culture, distances him from other black artists. The late singer Aaliyah has been shown in settings reminiscent of the villains' lairs in James Bond films despite her tender age and sound. This depiction works to distance her from R&B singers of the same age who have opted for a more wholesome persona (Brandy, Monica) (fig. 4.5). Sometimes the appeal to a neighboring genre will entail the use of specific images and themes derived from that genre's videos. This appeal can be made ironically, as in Coolio's "1, 2, 3, 4," a video that depicts the rapper's attempt to get to a house party across a vast, unspecified distance. This video contains simulated found footage of a '50s TV newscaster, spaces that recall videos for alternative bands, large patches of primary colors, and a number of sight gags. Thematically, the video shows that Coolio does not belong to the world through which he must pass. The video's mise-en-scène helps to depict this homelessness by placing Coolio in the spaces of a genre not his own. At the same time, the video is clearly designed to attract viewers who do feel at home with the imagery for alternative videos. More generally a director may use cliché imagery as a mode of critique, for commercial purposes, or simply because she cannot, or may not, do anything else (fig. 4.6).

Music videos often reflect cultural stereotypes. In fact, they sometimes exaggerate them. A good example is the way the industry gives distorted representations of homosexuality. It is almost as if music videos still operate within the American Hayes code system for film—homosexuality does not exist. Gay imagery is more heavily censored in music video than in film or broadcast television. In part, advertisers and stations believe music videos are intended for a younger audience that needs to be protected. Because videos are just commercials, this line of thinking goes, there is no reason not to edit them. Advertisers are already anxious about what might be considered as threatening content in popular music, and they therefore try to wield greater control over the image. There is a substantial body of tapes with gay imagery, but these tapes have been heavily censored or rejected from playlists, circulating underground instead. From my interviews with music-video directors, I have discovered that not only gay imagery, but also imagery that makes an issue of race, class, and gender, is subject to censorship.[7]

FIGURE 4.5 (A–D) Seal's "Crazy" and Aaliyah's "One in a Million." Appeals to communities of viewers.

FIGURE 4.6 (A–H) Coolio's "1, 2, 3, 4." A setting drawn from a neighboring genre.

Music videos also reflect gender stereotypes. The most common setting of a music video for women is within the domestic sphere—most female artists make at least one video in which they appear alone, beside a bed. As is also true for the music-video genre as a whole, this setting can have a range of meanings, from sexual provocation to revelation of a woman's private space and parody of domesticity. The visual depiction of the set can be schematic or ornate. But this variety should not be allowed to obscure the pervasiveness of this association between women and bedrooms, which therefore comes to seem natural, and a natural subject for videos. When women perform in videos, their bodies frequently remain passive, existing in a state of being rather than action; they reside in a no-man's land or stand detached while activity swirls around them.[8] Such imagery of still or vulnerable women has historical precedents: John Berger famously announces, in his discussion of European oil painting, that "men act and women appear."[9] We might link this imagery to production practices. Women rarely play an equal role in both songwriting and instrumental performance, hence an image of cooperative labor may be hard to find. It is also possible that the static representations of women serve to foreground the uniquely prized female voice.

Questions of gender are of course inflected by ethnicity. Contemporary female soul singers—Whitney Houston, Janet Jackson, Anita Baker, Toni Braxton, and many others less well known—are placed in isolation more frequently than are performers of any other sort. Several sites seem to recur with particular frequency. These singers often appear in a desert setting that carries no narrative weight—it is not the desert of *Mad Max* or ancient Egypt one finds in many other videos—and sometimes no implications of heat or dryness. This static depiction lends the image a painterly quality. Other videos place the singers against plain backdrops. Perhaps the most common form of isolation for African American female singers is the grand, old, usually empty theater. These varied settings share the capacity to foreground these women's power as singers. The stratification of singer and backdrop—a visual device with a long heritage—gives the sense that their voices can fill these spaces, whether vast, empty, or simply undifferentiated. At the same time, by separating the singer from the civil sphere, and specifically from other African American women, these videos may also make her less threatening to white or male audiences.[10]

Imagery of European American woman artists has coalesced into depictions of pure and quiescent saints. In late '90s videos, Alanis Morissette, Jewel, and Sarah McLachlan pass effortlessly through cityscapes and wastelands. These videos embody the particular cultural formation Richard Dyer has termed "whiteness"—intellectualism, restraint, and asexuality. One wonders whether this impassiveness constitutes an attempt to claim the stature granted to African American female singers.

Lisa Lewis praises the way that women in early '80s videos moved boldly through the street, thereby claiming it as their own.[11] (Lewis mentions Cyndi Lauper's "Girls Just Want to Have Fun," Tina Turner's "What's Love Got to

Do with It?" and Pat Benatar's "Love Is a Battlefield.") In the 1990s, women artists such as Morissette, Björk, Queen Latifah, and Brandy still took to the streets as a way of claiming the civil sphere, but they did so with a quirky touch, such as riding a horse, performing somersaults, or sprinting across a series of cars. The first three of these women also made innovative use of fantastic spaces. Such videos suggest that representation in music video is not mono-lithic, that progressive videos, ones that run against the grain, also exist.

THE MECHANICS OF SETTINGS: USE OF SPACE, SETTINGS AGAINST MUSIC, AND CAMERA MOVEMENT

Music videos include many different types of places, but they consistently reuse a small number of them. These types appear more frequently in some genres than in others and thereby take on particular cultural meanings. It will be helpful to consider five basic types of place: (1) an extension of a performance space; (2) a space that suggests specific acoustical properties; (3) a schematic representation of a familiar type of site; (4) a composite space that combines more than one type of site within a single setting; (5) a fundamental contrast between two types of shot: one an elaborately constructed setting, and the other an empty shot with a simple backdrop; (6) a series of sites that culminate in a final destination like a party or the beach.

The vast majority of music videos simply extend performance contexts. These performance spaces might resemble arenas or smaller venues, but a video will most often depict them as more handsome than they would normally be, making use of a historic movie theater, for example, or an auditorium dolled up with ornaments. Videos that place the star against a white background or in a desert also seem to return us to a performance setting. Barren spaces—empty hallways and rooms, alleyways—can serve as a stage or simple backdrop. Sometimes musicians are shown performing where they might normally re-hearse—a studio, a hotel room, backstage. They often appear in contexts that involve a kind of performance—fashion shows, classrooms, brothels, revival meetings. Screenwriters speak of "opening out" a play when they adapt it for cinema by adding additional scenes and locations. Similarly, music video's de-pictions of rehearsal sessions, the green room, and other backstage sites work to open out the documentation of performance. All performance settings, how-ever, respond as much to changes in fashion and styles of depiction as do other types of setting: distorted performance spaces—walls with off angles, tunnels with doors at the far end—were as common in the 1990s as canted stages were in the 1980s. It is important as well that performance settings have different meanings in each genre: power and authenticity in metal; a desire for history in the case of alternative music; musicality and charisma in R&B.

A good example of the way that genre and ethnicity impinges on a setting's meaning, and the value of a more careful reading, can be found in Janet Jackson's "If." If we try to read the video without much contextualization, we would notice that, in the crass terms of the video, technologically advanced Asians ogle African Americans performing a sexual dance in a bordello. (If we change the terms so that African Americans ogle Asians or African Americans ogle European Americans, the video would not work.) However, a closer look at the video reveals a much more complex reading. The setting is of type 1, an extension of a performance space, one most common to metal and, in particular, alternative videos. (The renovated, slightly prissy performance space is the most common to alternative.) By working against the grain, Janet Jackson, as an African American woman coming out of smooth R&B, has the ability to transcend this type of place and become somewhat of a heroine. The set is extremely detailed, and a number of nuances seem to complicate the imagery, such as the strange rhyming of the dancers' hands and the fans of the onlookers, which makes everyone more of a participant, rather than one ethnicity functioning as the viewers or as the performers.[12] The music is dense in cultural references. This song is based in R&B and contains elements of both Eastern music and heavy metal, providing the image with multiple possibilities for emphasis. But most important, much as in opera, the power of the female voice seems to raise Jackson's character above her compromising position. The camera and editing against the song's form support this power. Shots of the setting and of the singer's and dancers' bodies predominate in the verse and pre-chorus, while the chorus features close-ups of Jackson's face and hair. In the more jubilant chorus, she seems to have achieved a sublime state beyond the pleasures and limitations of the body (fig. 4.7).

Type 2 can be understood as an extension of the recording studio, just as type 1 is an extension of performance spaces. Instead of the studio's acoustical tile, baffles, and speaker cones, one will see slanted walls or unusual surfaces that can reflect the timbral or spatial qualities of the song. This kind of setting is most closely associated with African American musical genres, perhaps due to budgetary limitations, a confusion concerning where to place African American stars within a real world environment, or the sound world of the song itself.

Type 3, the schematic representation of a familiar place, might put a couch in a warehouse to suggest a living room. Such is the case in Monica's "First Night," in which the song provides the ambiance for a first date. This approach

FIGURE 4.7 (A–C) Janet Jackson's "If." Do relations among media ameliorate a racist construct?

may encourage the listener to use the music and lyrics to make the site complete. This type of setting most frequently appears in alternative and R&B videos and depicts domestic spaces such as bedrooms and living rooms—settings over which the viewer may feel some sense of control—rather than the corporate spaces of offices and boardrooms of big-business America.

Type 4 yokes together incongruous sites within a single setting—imagine a cathedral, bisected to reveal its interior, set within an African plain. Such a scheme can draw our attention to contrasts within the other media, particularly with respect to the multiple influences impinging on the song. The most striking uses of composite settings have been in rap and R&B songs, like Prince's "Gett Off," Salt-N-Pepa's "Shoop," and Janet Jackson's "Together Again." These videos contain a form of political critique—they hint that the world can be imagined differently while maintaining a connection to real places.

Type 5 juxtaposes two types of shot: a complicated set with many figures in the frame, and a plain background or a corner of a makeshift set with the singer alone. This scheme can lend the music video a degree of psychological complexity. Music videos cannot convey a character's depth—they cannot suggest conflicting emotions, as can classic Hollywood film. A good example of how film conveys a rich psyche, according to James Naremore, is dissembling—here, a character plays a social role that conflicts with her thoughts and feelings, for example, the spurned lover who wears a brave face, or the calculating and deceitful businesswoman who possesses a smooth facade.[13] Music-video performers act differently than film actors, they sing plainly to us. Mixed spaces can establish a movement between public and private space, leading the viewer to infer a richer subjectivity. Similarly, they can pose questions of whether the performer really sees, or only thinks he sees, what is around him, and can suggest a temporal disjunction. In addition, such settings create contrasts between sparseness and density that might correlate to nascent and more fully developed musical material. This type of setting seldom appears in heavy metal videos where a sense of interiority is left aside in favor of action.

Type 6 is a series of sites—room after room or location after location—often reaching a destination alluded to in the video's opening. Such a visual approach matches the music's speed and continuity, but also its variety of material. It often reflects sonic features—sounds penetrate surfaces that objects cannot. (For music video, a wall is no obstacle.) Serial places also bequeath an aspect of virtuosity upon the song and the performer. Both song and performer possess volition and mobility and can flourish in many places. Such an approach also raises questions of where we will land and what we can call home. The device of serial locations is a common one to all genres, yet rarest to metal, and most common to alternative and pop. Freed from commitment to place, it can suggest a type of white privilege.

I have described a number of types of settings, though the list is by no means complete. What about questions of size, proportion, and fit? How do these apply to music video's settings and songs? A place's meaning derives from an ensemble of elements: where shots of a place occur within the song's structure; the scale of the setting and its level of detail as it plays against a song's form; the ways that the video's places are revealed by the camera and inhabited by the characters; and the nature and scale of the video's landscape against the scale of the song. Each of these elements influences a setting in its own particular fashion, and I will look at them in turn. Most commonly in music video, the chorus is matched with a more public space than is the verse. Duran Duran's "Rio," for example, shows a lone musician stalking a shadowy woman during the verse, while the chorus shows the whole band and a bevy of attractive women perching on the helm of a yacht. Madonna's "Bad Girl" inverts this rule, with the result that the video suggests the protagonist's lack of control and impending doom. Throughout most of the video, Madonna is shown going to work during the verses and partying while the chorus takes place. Toward the end of the video, she subverts these patterns of behavior: she brings stray men to her apartment during the last verse and bridge, and finds herself alone during the final chorus. Her murder at the video's end does not surprise us because the settings and the song's form have been strangely out of joint.

Music videos often figure the bridge as a space outside of the video: in the Red Hot Chili Peppers' "Under the Bridge," there is a section in which the camera departs from the scene to speed down city streets. Many videos for women artists cut in their most provocative images during the bridge—Madonna dancing before burning crosses in "Like a Prayer," Fiona Apple crouching inside a limo in "Criminal."[14]

A video's landscape helps to determine the meaning of an individual setting. The gradual disclosure of this landscape, against the song's form, complicates this creation of meaning. The relationship between the video's landscape and the song's form can give a location a specific ideological slant. For example, TLC's "Waterfalls" and Coolio's "Gangster's Paradise" both preach on social problems using a visual that places the artist in one location while presenting action in another. Although both videos deliver a social message—"Waterfalls" deals with AIDS and "Gangster's Paradise" with inner-city schools—"Gangster's Paradise" seems more effective because of how the director places the terrain against the scale of the song. In the chorus of "Waterfalls," the members of the group stand in the midst of an enormous stretch of water and adopt a position of wise distance. The verses, depicting gang violence and AIDS, occur in completely different spaces, in terms of both location and color, and are separated from one another by the chorus's broad, blue expanse. No intermingling of visual materials occurs across song sections—each section exists in isolation. The artists thus seem far away from the people in distress, and we are encouraged to think that we also are at some distance from the problem. The video's attitude might even be called smug. On the other hand, in his "Gangster's Paradise," Coolio sits next to the woman he lectures at. Because this white woman (Michelle Pfeiffer) appears unfamiliar with her surroundings and shows both concern and a little anxiety, we might assume that she stands for white, middle-class, suburban viewers. The recurring images of classrooms are edited around shots of the dark, empty room in which Coolio and Pfeiffer sit. These two spaces bleed into each other through similarities of layout, music, and decor, and most primarily through a swish pan of the camera that seems to link both worlds. Unlike "Waterfalls," the sets of "Gangster's Paradise" seem cozier than the song, so that the problems of inner-city youth seem near rather than far, our problem rather than someone else's.

In general, each musical genre develops a repertoire of settings; some advance musical ideas, while others make territorial claims. A visual claim for the numinous or the simply big can also assert that the music possesses great weight. R&B videos often occupy large interiors to underscore the professionalism of the artists and producers as well as the breadth of the song. When an R&B video emphasizes exteriors, the artists are often placed in isolation, not only to speak about social limitations but also to make the artists less threatening. The opposite is true of much alternative rock video. The cramped interiors reflect the artists' ambivalent feelings about their status as musicians and their unwillingness to let the song be dominated by its musical hooks. When alternative videos employ more fanciful or expansive settings, the groups appear to assert white male privilege despite themselves.

The history of exteriors in music video, especially, can be read as a series of territorial claims. We might even say that the genres are dialogic, or even that they compete with one another. In a series of videos released in 1993, Guns N' Roses roamed freely among a group of settings one might see in the course of a feature film. The mise-en-scène worked to suggest that these men had every right to be where they are, that they have power over these places. It was not until a year or so later that African American artists ranged over the same extent of territory, and their power was figured differently. These artists often hovered far above the ground and projected their influence from this height. Instead of claiming territory, they seemed to cloak the world below. But the suggestion always remained that they cannot land for fear of capture or reprisal. It was as if the videomakers wished to acknowledge the gap that exists between the typical depictions of these African American stars and those of everyday African American women and men.[15] A newer kind of territorial claim was then made on cinematic and televisual history, as groups like Hanson were shown moving with aplomb through disparate settings from different periods. The Hanson video "Mmm Bop" reflected the singers' European American ethnicity. It remains hard to imagine a video with African American teenaged boys tearing up the space in similar fashion (fig. 4.8).

The question arises whether movement across schematic settings can create a sense of place, and if settings matter—whether music videos simply zip across a number of cartoon stills. I argue more fully later that music videos do indeed create a sense of place, if only momentarily. Music video emphasizes constant motion, and if we become too firmly rooted to a single site, we may not be able to follow the musical and visual flow. Yet music video does tease us with a more secure sense of place. Without a narrative, and with so few devices to create drama, many videos hinge on questions of place—what it means to get from here to there, from the bedroom to the back yard, the bus to the building, the street to the studio. These depictions respond to the music—we tend to reach the party in time for the rousing outchorus. They are also culturally constrained. Though we may move from the bedroom to the party, we rarely move from the home to the political arena: music videos make some trajectories more imaginable than others. Music video may chart a path haltingly, interrupting forward motion to draw our attention to different visual and musical features, but, almost like Dorothy's journey in *The Wizard of Oz*, we almost always return near to the point at which we left off. As such, videos emphasize quality of movement, the way that we get from one place to another. But also important is a constant motion—how a sense of instability can be momentarily arrested by a return to a more secure place. Some of a video's pleasure may lie in discovering these more favored places and moving among them.

Movement within a place also colors our understanding of it. R&B contains the most sinuous and intimate camera movement. Despite the cold surfaces, R&B's receptive, tracking camera seems much more generous than the darting camera that documents an alternative band exclusively from the front. In her

FIGURE 4.8 (A–P) Guns N' Roses' "November Rain," Wu Tang Clan's "Triumph," and Hanson's "Mmm Bop." Territorial claims along the lines of genre and ethnicity.

"Nobody's Supposed to Be Here," Deborah Cox moves only from the bedroom to the backyard, yet the camera work (a dramatic crane shot sweeps from low to high) responds so sensitively to the key change near the end of the song that when she plants herself outside, she seems to own the space.[16] A closer look at Beck's "Where It's At" shows how an alternative video can incorporate a distanced, sardonic stance that shifts to an engaged point of view. In this video, all media—music, lyrics, and image—contribute to a camp aesthetic. The song features '60s instruments such as a Wurlitzer electric piano, a Hammond organ, and a guitar played through a fuzzbox, along with a drum sample associated with hip-hop. Some of the lyrics sound like Stevie Wonder's 1973 hit "Living for the City." The organ—with the left hand performed rather squarely and the tremolo turned on too fast—sounds the most humorous and archaic. The irreverent imagery is organized in blocklike sections (mostly composed in long shot) and contains '70s sex films, prison road crews, and a bargain-day celebration from the mall parking lot. In spite of the heavy sarcasm, however, our relation to the video changes near the end, primarily through a new orientation to place via camera and music. As the video closes, line dancers do the two-step on what looks like the Nashville Network. The camera, for the first time, enters the space and tracks alongside the upturned feet of the performers. The camera angle and movement relate closely to a musical feature—they mimic the contour and placement of one of the song's primary hooks, now transposed into the bass. (The audio visuals also spark desire: we can spy on Beck and his band at the back of the room.) At this point, the viewer participates in the music and the image. Thus far, we have maintained ironic distance, but following the music and camera, we are asked to dance, to participate deeply in white working-class culture.

INSTITUTIONAL PRESSURES, PRODUCTION PRACTICES, AND THE ROLE OF THE DIRECTOR

Knowing the ways that videos come into being through a unique set of institutional constraints will also sharpen our understanding of their settings. The speed and volubility we experience as we move across sections of a video extend to production practices; the instability and sense of incompleteness that characterize music video stem from the way that they are made. The production process exerts a centripetal force upon music video. Record companies solicit one- to two-page "treatments" from video directors that contain a prose description of a mood and a concept, along with supporting illustrations often cut from magazines or art books. These treatments are produced on spec, and the process as a whole seems to encourage a guessing game on the part of the director, who must design images that match the record company's expectations. Treatments accepted by the record company then become subject to contentious negotiations among the director, the musician, and record company personnel, with the satellite services' screening process looming in the background. This complex production system often necessitates strange, seemingly minor additions and subtractions that can have a profound effect on a video. A record company may demand, for instance, that an intimate video for R&B girls-next-door like Changing Faces place the women in full-length fur coats.[17] Here, the fur coats threaten to undermine the mood and the point of the video. In an alternative video like Filter's "(Can't You) Trip like I Do," an image of hanging mannequins dressed like policemen was censored. Without this shot, the video loses its gothic quality, political edge, and sense of culmination. A Polynesian-themed video set in Hawaii must be revamped suddenly for the south, in part, because Janet Jackson's schedule suddenly precludes extended travel time. This process describes the way that music videos often seem to contain a message, but also something missing or superfluous.

Often the director will attempt to negotiate with the record company to preserve what he or she considers essential, or will fulfill the record company's request in such a way as to transform its meaning. One such instance can be found in the choice of setting for Lil' Kim's "No Time." The record company had demanded that the video look "street." Marcus Nispel, the director, got the record company to agree to the subway as a location without describing what precisely he would do. He then lit and shot a subway station's escalator in such a way as to transform it into a glamorous hotel lobby. In an interview in spring 1997, Nispel told me that he intended to confuse white viewers about the identities of the performers—are they buppies or drug dealers? He felt also that he had played a kind of trick on the record company by using the stereotypes they were comfortable with to achieve subversive ends. The malleability of space in music video allows for this transformation: without having to serve a function in the plot or even having to be revealed as a physical space, the subway escalator could become more enigmatic. For record companies, the raw image of the street had become too familiar—when the record companies' A&R representatives ask for something raw or new, they often seem already to have an image of what that rawness or newness should be.

The more elaborate music videos are produced in a hothouse atmosphere, for at any one time the same dozen or so directors will get the most prestigious gigs. This practice might seem to have a constraining effect on music video, but it in fact exerts a centrifugal force on the medium as the top directors riff on and try to outdo each other's work. The meaning of a setting can change drastically within a year. Marcus Nispel's politically progressive use of explosions as a backdrop for the rap group Fu Schnickens was censored by MTV. Within eight months, numerous videos had used explosions, culminating in Puff Daddy's "Can't Nobody Hold Me Down," directed by Paul Hunter. This video created no problems for the censors, probably because it exists comfortably within the mode of action/adventure films. In the fall of 1997, Hype Williams turned the backdrop of explosions into a more hopeful image. In "Mo Money, Mo Problems," by Puff Daddy and Mase, Williams mixes the bombs with shards of mirrors and a deep blue tonality to create the sense of an emergence from danger (fig. 4.9). Certain motifs dominate videos for a few seasons only to be replaced by others. One of the most obvious tropes is the mid-1990s rapper in the kingly chair. These images function more as references to other videos than anything else.

Although I am fully aware that music video is still written off as an advertisement by many theorists, I wish to claim that a directorial voice can play a major role in the videomaking process. Though I do not have the space to make a full counterargument concerning how music videos are designed to sell commodities, I would like to point to the fact that contemporary culture has made it hard to determine what is designed to promote what: movies sell dolls and songs as much as these dolls and songs sell movie tickets, for example. Similarly, the consumption of recorded and live music, videos, and other multimedia prevents one from saying that one of these forms—the album, typically—constitutes the central text and the others the periphery. Industry insiders tend to say that a good video cannot sell any song—they will not go further than to say that a well-crafted song and a compelling video make a potent combination. We should remember that the men and women who direct music videos also direct movies and commercials, and that many of them characterize music video as a place for experimentation, play, and relative aesthetic fulfillment. This characterization derives partly from the fact that the director of a music video can oversee and participate in every phase of its planning, production, and postproduction: unlike a director of film or commercials, a videomaker can develop a concept, design a budget, create a storyboard, scout for locations, choose actors and props, act as cinematographer, and edit the footage.

Settings may appear opaque to an audience, but they can take on a heightened meaning for directors and record industry personnel. I was surprised to hear from a record company's head music-video commissioner I was inter-

FIGURE 4.9 (A–F) Fu Schnickens' "Breakdown," Puff Daddy's "Can't Nobody Hold Me Down," and "Mo Money, Mo Problems." Cases of music video's heightened intertextuality.

viewing, in the midst of a lengthy description of how important it was to keep budgets in check, "But you know, if the director proposes a site which a review committee member does not know—say, Joshua Tree Monument—we'll send one of our people out to take pictures there."[18] Record industry personnel want information about a site because they can then envisage and start to gain control over the project. Directors, whether they have chosen a site at the treatment stage or soon after, when the video involves location shooting, send out for a large series of site-specific photographs. Detail concerning set, props, color, movement, and the like, can then be sketched in. For Floria Sigismondi, the discovery of an abandoned distillery helped bring together her video for Marilyn Manson's "The Beautiful People"—the domed main space and catacomb-like basements suggested what could happen in the verse, chorus, and bridge. Francis Lawrence has spoken proudly about finding a particular abandoned shack on the rolling hills at the outskirts of Los Angeles, or building a set for an R&B video based on a ceiling from the public library, walls from a corporate building, flooring from a loft, and so on.[19]

But we should still keep in mind, as the example of the Marcus Nispel Lil' Kim video shows, to what degree settings are malleable. They are subject to props and décor, lenses and lighting, camera framing, position and movement, editing, and postproduction effects. Settings, by the time they reach the television screen on the satellite television service, recede, carrying only a bit of nuance or color. They are rendered partially, quickly, and unpredictably. The music makes the environment strange—gridding it (almost providing time and space coordinates for it). Joshua Tree National Monument in a music video, for most viewers, becomes the generic desert. Perhaps some viewers will notice an interesting cactus. Settings become iconic—representative of many "somewheres." Form, shape, and light come to the fore.[20]

I want now to discuss how a director can use music, lyrics, and settings to create a personal voice against the institutional backdrop that I have just sketched. In Solo's "Where Do You Want Me To Put It," director Hype Williams uses an enhanced performance space as the setting for a song with deep cultural and musical resonances, and demonstrates its videomaker's individual approach. The song and video partake of the anthemic mode, which allows us to begin with a consideration of the video's racial dimension. European American artists often invoke an anthemic quality by occupying space. The anthemic videos for African American artists tend to use strongly coded settings, like a crowd gathered in the street, a church, or a basketball court. Videos by Guns N' Roses, Stone Temple Pilots, and Alice in Chains sweep across a vast terrain, suggesting the mobility of white male subjectivity. Similarly, the music in these tapes might be seen as aggressively anthemic. At first glance, Hype Williams's "Where Do You Want Me to Put It" seems far from the anthemic mode. The video's small, low-ceilinged nightclub and playful lyrics, at first glance, would seem to suit a song about sex. The music, however, recalls Curtis Mayfield's politically conscious work like "People Get Ready." Famous black actors, performers, and record producers make stunning entrances, and the crowd and musicians, who come from a variety of backgrounds, form a happy, cohesive group. The set's low ceilings and the closely interlocking gestures of the all-male vocal group draw our attention to Mayfield's well-constructed harmony and voice leading. At some level, the Mayfield echo still lingers, perhaps more strongly than the lyrics or the nightclub. Even if the setting and lyrics are playful in tone, the music and image seem to convey a more urgent sense of social purpose. Though Mayfield's lyrics have been left behind, one still recalls his message (fig. 4.10).

Even with the most banal settings, Hype Williams has a way to give them force. When Williams places his performers in real environments, the backgrounds often seem unusually close or too far away, and the image is cropped in such a way that the space is only partially disclosed, and when he uses constructed sets, the walls tend to slope inward precariously, lending his spaces an unstable quality. Williams makes frequent use of the wide-angle lens, lending his figures a comic book quality, yet this should not take out attention away from how deeply connected his figures are to the ground. His performers—almost all African American—possess a degree of warmth, self-possession, and pride, regardless of circumstance. His use of the figure against the setting suggests a worldview that differs quite markedly from those of other well-known directors. David Fincher's figures are dwarfed by gigantic sets, which suggests a concern with patriarchy. Matt Mahurin, whose figures and backgrounds disappear into what looks like a murky, one-dimensional, chalk drawing, focuses on the alienation of the individual from the community.

■■■

Thus far I have argued for a number of factors that we should take into consideration when we try to read the cultural resonance of a video's setting: the

FIGURE 4.10 (A–H) Solo's "Where Do You Want Me To Put It." A music video evokes a sense of community and history.

musical practices and sonic features of the music; appeals to audiences and community; the video's cultural import; the formal relations between song and image; the role of the record industry, the star and the director. I have argued that music video is both generic and specific and that it straddles the imaginary and the real. Though videos are coded by genre, an individual video often exceeds a genre's boundaries. Music videos contain a degree of complexity that demands we consider more than the images themselves: we must attend to the ways that each medium inflects and diverges from the others, and respect the fragmentary quality of music, lyrics, and image. It will be useful to think a bit further about the interaction of music, lyrics, and settings, in a more abstract theoretical way, in order to consider the ways that the settings of music video can create a sense of place.

Each medium in music video—image, lyrics, and music—is deficient in itself. The camera sways back and forth, often out of focus, and the edits come suddenly and rapidly; watching a video silently, one can guess at its genre, but one misses the sense of the video: the image seems barren. The lyrics by themselves are similarly banal. "I love you now and forever" is not so much different from "I will love you always" or "You were meant for me." The music of today's pop songs, considered alone, tends to have a patchwork quality, suggesting multiple meanings inconclusively. As Nicholas Cook might say, each medium is gapped for the other, has an emptiness that the other media can attempt to fill.[21]

Even when music, image, and lyrics are put into relation, a sense of vagueness remains. One cannot always tell whether a setting is documentary space, a narrative element, an allegorical space, a historical reference, a backdrop, or simply a placeholder. Though the music and image keep us engaged, the disclosure of space can seem almost willful; the camera reveals space only partially and unpredictably. We are never sure if we will see the whole setting or be placed firmly within it. Taken with the other media, the lyrics lose some of their grip. At particular moments in the video, a line like "I feel for you" might belong to the singer, the band as a whole, or the singer as a character; the line might be addressed to a lover, a friend, the crowd, or the television audience. Chunks of lyric separate from the whole, exerting a local influence on the music and image. Stylistic allusions in music are always debatable, and videos reflect these unpredictably.

On another level, each medium subtly influences and even can be said to define the others. By naming specific characters and objects, the lyrics can draw our attention to the back or the front of the frame, or toward offscreen space. The lyrics pull our focus toward the past, present, or future. The music can suggest how characters feel, and how time is experienced. It can seem to color the distance between objects. Though a setting is often heightened by surrealistic or expressionistic touches, and only partially disclosed, the music can help us to determine how safe or dangerous the space might be. In Trent Reznor's "The Perfect Drug," a chromatic chord sequence creates a sense of malevolence; we may hear the reiterating triangle in Puff Daddy's "All About the Benjamins" as dangerous; the three-note vocal hook in Smashing Pumpkins' "1979" seems gently nostalgic. Somehow, these musical touches help to color a place in subtle ways, much like humidity, air pressure or scent.

At any one moment in a music video, there can be a range of connections among media, some formed by literal relations, and some more tangential or elliptical. The sonic space of a song can bear an interesting relation to the real space of the setting; the lyrics and physical gestures can make the same point. (The singer sings "I love you" and places her hand over her heart.) All three media can convey the same affect using different strategies. The connections among music, lyrics, and image can be quirky as well. A song's lyrics may say "I can't live with or without you" in a romantic spirit, but the imagery may focus on how the lead singer will get by without the band. A funny hook from a song might be associated with the mechanical sounds of a Slurpee machine at a 7–11, though a Slurpee machine only remotely sounds like this. Media can also be quite at odds with one another. The color can seem wrong for the timbre, or the editing can carefully follow local syncopations but leave other rhythmic structures unexamined.

On a larger scale, music video's settings can depart quite significantly from a song's cultural associations. Fiona Apple's "Across the Universe" and Radiohead's "Karma Police" are good examples of videos in which the music, lyrics, and setting are distinctly at odds. Apple's version of the Beatles song preserves aspects of the arrangement and certain touches in John Lennon's vocal performance, but also includes a hip-hop beat. The video serves as a promotion for the film *Pleasantville,* and the slo-mo black-and-white images of thugs smashing up a '50s diner bears little relation to Lennon's oeuvre. Perhaps Stanley Kubrick's film *A Clockwork Orange* is an intermediary point of reference here, as are Fiona Apple's waiflike looks, and the dreamy way that the camera rotates 360 degrees in the air. This, however, is a song stuck to an image to sell a film and soundtrack. The video functions perfectly well on the satellite services, yet it stages a tug-of-war between the content of the song and the images we see. The chorus of Radiohead's "Karma Police" recalls The Beatles' songwriting more subtly. The video was filmed from the back seat of a '60s Chevy traveling a dirt road at night, somewhere in the Southwest. The car sits on a flatbed, and as it rolls forward against the darkness it matches the relaxed tempo of the song. However, there is a conflict among the song's pop songwriting values, the desert setting, and the lyrics' distinctly urban tone. These slight disjunctions create a pleasantly strange effect. Perhaps the video's solitary human figure in the empty desert suggests a hunger for a referent beyond the frame—in this case, John Lennon.

The Dave Matthews Band's "Crash into Me" is more gently disjunctive. The music brings out the band's affinities with the acoustic, bluesy side of groups like The Grateful Dead and Buffalo Springfield. The lyrics reflect sexuality and aggression: "tie me up," "crash into me," "hike up your skirt a little more." As in many videos, the setting refuses to align itself with either music or lyrics. The scene might resemble something out of *A Midsummer Night's Dream* or Ingmar Bergman's *The Seventh Seal*: figures cavort in a clearing, while a skeleton with a horse's head peers from behind a tree. The group's African American violinist wears only a skirt of violins and raises his hands, affecting the posture of a crucifix. Women in long silk dresses dance among the trees, but they look a little spoiled—their mascara has smudged, and the color runs from the hems of their dresses. The lead singer sits regally in a giant chair wearing an enormous wide-brimmed hat. Two geisha girls ride hobbyhorses. With such images of violence and colonialism, the place no longer seems so idyllic. The place, the lyrics, and the music share some features (sweetness, courtliness, a sense of loss) and diverge on others (personal relations, aggressiveness, and sexuality). The viewer may watch repeatedly in an attempt to fuse disparate elements into a whole.

Music videos arbitrarily impose a setting upon a song. Many settings are possible for a given song. Music-video directors like to say that there is no right visualization of a song, only a number of readings; with the dense network of connections and disjunctions among music, lyrics, and image, no perfect fit exists. Videos that seem quirky or somehow wrong in terms of setting but are still interesting suggest that we have a pool of associations for the proper use of music, and that this propriety can readily be extended.

Surprisingly, schematic, banal, and even reactionary settings can work well in music videos, partly because of the setting's relation to the musician. On the one hand, the places in music video are tightly constrained. Nothing may seem more overly familiar than the rapper placed in the midst of city streets. However, the clichéd, overly schematic quality of the setting, and the way it doesn't quite fit with other music video elements, including the musician, can allow for some possibilities of representation of character. In music video, the characters often fail to mesh with the settings. Unlike films, music videos show us the mechanisms with which a character fulfills a social role. A performer can try to fill the part, but the fit is never exact. As we watch the performer sing what should be spoken, and as she wanders through a strange, incomplete environment, it is not quite clear to us why she is there. One cannot help but think that the performer might as well be doing other things like visiting a talk show, or recording in the studio; perhaps the setting reflects not hers, but the inspiration of the record company or director. Even if this performer once composed the sounds and rhythms, the body is now carefully monitored so that it fits in with the music, camera framing, and editing. Such moments remind us of our own attempts to play the part of a role society has given us, and the gap between what we present, and the way we experience ourselves inside.

Music video can inspire a kind of Brechtian distance: the space is revealed incompletely, the figures always remain in between things, the edits come before gestures are complete. Too much is elusive for the viewer to become fully involved in the video, and one may have the sense that one is looking in on an aquarium, where the lives of the creatures inside are a bit obscure. The viewer cannot fall into a lull as they do with the classic Hollywood narrative, but must think about the modes of production and the roles of the director, the musicians, the industry, and the audience. On the other hand, music video possesses many features that deeply engage the viewer in the form. The lip-syncing, music, and sensual surface of the partially revealed body that the viewer will put together to make whole, can draw the viewer in, creating a type of deep empathy, a sense that one actually knows and feels the rhythms of the bodies of the performers. Though the kind of empathy that music video elicits is undirected and diffuse, music video viewers may experience a sense of connection to the communities whose music they listen to and watch.

I want now to return to the question of the role of the character within the social spaces in music video—the ways that people inhabit places in music video, and how these behaviors work with and against practices of everyday life.

First, the performer, music, and camera have the power to color or reinflect a schematic place. Music video is ultimately a vaudevillian scheme where the figure is foregrounded against a static background. Compensatory techniques obscure this scheme through partial views, a wandering camera, abrupt editing, postproduction techniques, and so forth. These techniques reaffirm the primacy of the body, however: they encourage the viewer to follow the body and build a complete picture of the performer's form while presenting the background even more schematically, through surprising shifts of context and partial, arbitrary, and slow disclosure. As such, the body seems to mediate our knowledge of the setting and thereby to wield authority over the place.

Music videos also provide an account of the performer's body. Within a scheme that reveals the body bit by bit, the music and camera can work together to show the spring of a shoulder and the release of a hip. As the viewer puts together the whole of the song he or she also constructs an imaginary body whose processes seem to animate the video—to make it hospitable. In this way, music videos suggest how one might feel within a place. The arrangement and the singing voice, along with the movements of the star, provide a road map for how one might move within a setting: would one breathe shallow or deep? How would one walk—forcefully? gracefully? awkwardly? Videos can provide suggestions about how to inhabit our bodies—in the bedroom, at a party, in a car, on a city street, or on a suburban lawn. Constance Penley has argued that film viewers can extend their sense of identity to include other characters beyond their own gender, ethnicity, or sexual orientation.[22] I would argue that subjectivity can be extended even further in music video because a music video asks us to participate with the bodies we see. In this way, I imaginatively construct myself as someone who participates in rap or R&B or alternative or metal. The scenarios that I move through may be less important than the possibility of imagining myself as someone else.

I do not want to argue that a music video is a completely open text. African American bodies are projected as more angry and sexual than European American bodies, and most women's bodies are presented as more passive than men's. Settings are restricted. Though music videos can demonstrate how to walk in suburbia with a sense of ironic distance, they seem unable to suggest attitudes of rage or commitment. Cultural critics may well become frustrated with music videos, because they most often do not make good on the songs' liberatory possibilities. The music may feel utopian, but the image rarely follows suit: more typically, the video will provide cramped imagery, as at the moment in "Ironic" when Alanis Morissette crawls out of a moving car, or in "You Get What You Give" when The New Radicals release dogs from a mall pet store, or it will give us the razzle-dazzle of glittery surfaces and T&A. Music videos, much like musicals, do not really reimagine the world; but videos present images of how to exist deeply in a space, how to move with feeling and self-possession.

Music videos create the illusion that one can inhabit a place authentically, with some sort of grace and authority, even in socially unsanctioned ways. Henri Lefebvre suggests that a society cannot be changed without changing its use of space, but music videos hold out the possibility that if you change your approach or attitude toward the world, space, and place may also undergo transformation.[23]

Videos may make us wonder whether what we see before us is a performance space or something more abstract; what musical genre we are hearing and what communities are being appealed to; or how the setting relates to musical features. Nevertheless, at some moments there may be a perceptual shift. Music video is about motion; it features continual change and uneven surfaces. The music has moments of culmination, the image groups into larger patterns, and the lyrics sometimes possess charm or clarity. There are moments in music video when image, music, and lyrics come into relation in such a way that we feel we have come upon a special place. These moments are elusive, they come suddenly and unexpectedly, yet they are extremely powerful. One gets the sense that one can find a moment of rootedness in almost any environment. This is perhaps a meaningful image in a world where "space/time" is shrinking, and so much about place is contested and in flux.

5

Props and Costumes

OBJECTS IN MUSIC video can carry an excess of meaning and exist outside the flow of the tape. As such, they take on a heightened role. Like the ballet slippers in *The Red Shoes,* they appear to possess a mysterious power, as if their silence contained some truth about the video beyond what the characters embody. Certain props come to the foreground as mysterious but unknowable, graspable but unobtainable. Witness the needle, blouse, bowl of water, and glove in Madonna's "Take a Bow"; the glittering and metallic butterfly in Smashing Pumpkins' "Bullet for Butterfly"; the twirling trumpet in TLC's "Creep"; the crystal ball in Boyz II Men's "Water Runs Dry"; the pig's head and apple, and the chair on which is nailed an impaled heart in Nine Inch Nails' "Closer"; the pears, bowl, and coins in Live's "Lightning Crashes"; the speaker, picture frame, and bowl of milk in Madonna's "Express Yourself"; the record player in Janet Jackson's "Anytime, Anyplace."

Music-video sets are usually stripped down to the essentials; only occasionally are they dolled up, and the few items that are brought to the fore stand in isolation. This strategy is taken to an extreme in some videos from the late 1980s and early 1990s, where the frame is stripped to a nicely painted wall and empty windowsill, or to a corner of a room. Natalie Merchant's "Wonder" simply shows a woman's hands dangling over a washbasin and a praying mantis resting on a woman's forearm. The effect of such a shot's featuring a single gesture—and being separated from the video's stream of events—is that the object and performer are both made strange. Each defines and limits the other's meaning, the object more lifelike and the performer less so. Music assists us in understanding this uneasy relation by revising our assumptions about the object, its uses and purposes, its internal disposition and rhythms in relation to spaces and persons.[1] Without much narrative drive, character development, or dialogue, meaning derives in part from the music and the way that the object is placed in relation to the performer.

With so few clues to a video's meaning, we are often left to puzzle out the role of the things presented in it. Any object possesses a set of culturally determined meanings, values, and uses. Music video's brief, multivalent form may not provide the viewer with enough time to pick a good match from this set, leaving the viewer wondering what the props signify. When Coolio turns off the kettle in "Too Hot," it is not clear whether the kettle helps to create an ambiance of self-sufficiency and domesticity or whether it portends danger. (In the course of the tape, vaporization becomes a metaphor for AIDS.) By analyzing the musical context, we can guess at the ways that different kinds of sexuality are suggested through fruits—apples, grapes, and strawberries—in LL Cool J's "Doin' It," Amy Grant's "House of Love," SWV's "Ladies' Night," Dionne Ferris's "Passion," Biggie Smalls's "Get Money," Janet Jackson's "Anytime, Anyplace," and Nine Inch Nails' "Closer."

That the role of the blemish, disability, mark, or imperfection already suggests the function of strangeness in music video becomes obvious when we consider the treatment. In narrative film, a funny detail—a crooked hat, a facial scar, a limp—helps define the character and, no matter how gruesome or startling, does not usually break the surface of the film. In music video, however, such details are not integrated; rather, they buzz around the performer aggressively, asserting their own bizarre presence. As the image conforms to the soundtrack, musical forces—the thrust of harmony, melody, arrangement, and rhythm—fracture the image into individual components.[2]

That objects recur in videos of a particular genre or period suggests the gradual development of generic repertoires functioning within a sign system unique to the medium. Objects in videos of the mid-1990s included thrones, couches and chairs, canes, heads of animals (pigs and wolves), clowns, and toilets. In the 1980s there had been diaphanous cloth, wind, figures dancing in formation, big hair, sketchily drawn windows and doors, canted stages, and horses. What is interesting is not the answers to the question of what these objects "mean"; it is the role that this question plays, how persistently it is asked, and whether—in different genres and periods and in individual videos—it is answerable.

Like settings, costumes in music video fulfill a number of functions—a quick sketch of a character type or a general statement about the world—before evoking a particular place inhabited by a character who possesses peculiar foibles and assets. More than advancing a story, clothing can serve to mark off the boundaries between performer, supporting characters, and viewer. In TLC's "Creep," the women's silk pajamas suggest sexual availability, but the low-angle camera placement, and the texture and movement of billowing silk fabric suggest a phallic sexuality. Somewhat similarly (allowing for the shift in associations conveyed by gender and power), Bono wears a French-cut T-shirt in U2's "With or Without You," and Vince Neil wears a tie and no shirt in Mötley Crüe's "Primal Scream"; both men flaunt their sexual prowess, but they are also inaccessible. In "Express Yourself" and "Vogue," Madonna makes claims to wealth, power, or authority; she is clearly distinct from the other subjects of the video. An empire-waist body suit and a highly coifed hairpiece enable

Prince to remain aloof from the orgy of philistines in "Gett Off." Janet Jackson flaunts Flintstones-like animal bones as jewelry in "If" to distance herself from the technologically savvy Asian audience in the foreground; the bones also suggest a raw sexuality. In all of these examples, clothing functions as a signpost and a means of separation among figures. Like the use of color in music video, which immediately signals mood, song identity, and timbre, clothing here quickly shows a character's role and its relation with others. Clothing can also signal musical genres. R&B record company personnel and directors often complain that too much of their budget is consumed by Versace clothing. (They speak longingly about alternative videos in which the musician can show up in a T-shirt and jeans.)[3]

There are times when costuming is used simply to complement the formal features of the set. In Bush's "Swallowed," the delicate pattern of red flowers in the singer's shirt rhymes elegantly with the wallpaper. Madonna's see-through blouse in "Vogue" rhymes nicely with the diamond-shaped windowpanes in the background. The director Floria Sigismondi has described using a basic shape that crosses many musical and visual parameters—music, decor, costuming, and props—as a means of unifying the tape. In her video for David Bowie's "Little Wonder," "it is all about spikes."[4] (Mark Romanek's video for Michael Jackson's "Scream" works similarly.) Here, an iconic shape crosses from song to image, rendering the boundaries between both indistinguishable.

One of this book's main arguments is that the materials in music videos fracture into ever-smaller units. And so it is with performers' clothing. We can quickly spot the nurse's uniform, the business suit, or the prom dress, but perhaps because of music video's unique ways of approaching its media—the music's unfolding and the performers' twists and turns, coupled with a mobile camera—we can soon focus on the costume's material. Immediately after the outfit signifies a social function, our attention turns to its material—the severe, guarded quality of thick black leather; the generosity of movement and comfort that a cotton T-shirt provides; the luxurious frictionlessness of satin; the splashy, playful, aggressiveness of plastic, rhinestones, and metal jewelry. So often in a music video, we follow the performer's fabric, and we compare it with whatever texture covers the rest of the set. Why does the moment when we see a medium shot of a woman in a fishnet-stocking shirt in a Naughty by Nature video carry power? Beats me, but it surely does. We hear the music, follow the body, and feel the cloth. As we try to find visual correlates to sound, it makes sense that we would turn to surfaces.

Costuming, dance, and music are intimately bound together. Let me discuss dance and music first. Music theorists have argued that particular musics call for particular body movements—Alan Lomax's work focused on how an African highlands tribe danced with light, seemingly weightless gestures and a corresponding music, while the music and movements of the lowlands were oriented toward the earth. Headbanging seems good for heavy metal, and knee- and hip-bending for rap. Of course, the possibilities for movement are not fixed. We should rather imagine a range of possible movements for a music—one can pogo to heavy metal and perhaps even twist, though the tango or the bourrée might fit poorly. Costuming can function as an intermediary between the dance and the music; in music video, it can complicate our reading of the body and sound. Attractive movements for Salt-N-Pepa's "Push It," a rap song, might include a drop from the knees into the balls of the feet. In the video, however, the group's three women performers wear red leather boots that ride up above the calf; one-piece, body-hugging, shiny black Lycra leotards, cropped like tanks at the top; bulky gold necklaces and bracelets; and large, heavy bomber jackets that drape down below the hips. The women often lean back, and the viewer cannot make out much—skin and tank merge, and the viewer must guess at what happens underneath—most likely a key movement is a graceful bent-back type of S-curve. We miss almost all of the sync of the body and music. Instead of having our attention drawn toward what we want to see—hips, knees, waist, and balls of feet—the clothing against the music draws us toward the shoulders, neck, wrists, and ankles. We are out of luck.

Slightly modifying the costume would help draw the eye toward an easy audiovisual correlate—if the leotard from waist to calf were red rather than black (and the boots black), or if the leotard sported racing stripes that turned out toward the hips, that would help us imagine the rest.[5] In "Push It" a mismatch in costume, gesture, and music tantalizes us. It is not a matter of how much flesh is available. The performers could wear clothes that were less revealing in toto—baggy b-ball shorts (parachute material) that draped below the knee and cinched at the waist, over which hung matching, straight, loose, tank-tops. (A lot of the body would be hidden under the billows, but we could still make out the correlates between body, dance, and music.) The director seemed up on the signifying power of the clothes for "Push It," because the backing male dancers wear clothes that echo the leading ladies'—black cotton turtles and pants that closely follow their bodies from neck to toe. The camera does not hang with the men very long, and their movements are less sensual (more sharp and vertical). We are not much interested in the men, anyway, and keep turning our attention back to the women. We will watch the whole of this tape until we unpiece the relation between music, clothes, and movement. If the women were wearing the male performers' costumes—outfits that are more revealing—the sync between music, image, dance, and costume would be easy, and the video would lack its punch.

So here we are in cloth and bodies, yet this book has emphasized the fluidity of the viewer's attention—its constant flux, following the line of the cloth to the swish pan of the camera, from a lyric to a vocal timbre or a drum solo, from the person as actor to the person as performer, from an inkling of a narrative to a focus on spectacle, from hearing the music alone to hearing music in relation to image, and so on. After remaining a while on the surface, the viewer will return to questions of signification, yet as she tries to procure a meaning for the video, some costuming touches may remain inscrutable: what does it mean that the performer darkens his hair and wears black lipstick and nails in a video? How do we interpret a dangling monocle, cross, bone, or pacifier? What about the strange suit with beaded embroidery, or the thick eyeglasses or gold-rimmed, tinted shades? Like props, clothing and accessories can seem to contain a secret that the video never discloses. The film theorist James Naremore argues that props in classic Hollywood film support stage business—and he therefore calls props expressive objects.[6] The way an actor fusses with a briefcase, dangles a cigarette, or fluffs a pillow helps her to submerge herself inside her character, suggesting both a character type and a nuanced portrait within the confines of a character type. In music video, however, we seldom know how to read the costume accessory. Perhaps the cigarette that the protagonist holds is there for thematic purposes, as an emblem, as an item that looks cool, or as an indication that the performer is a smoker.

Music videos can sustain touches that are personally meaningful to the director but inscrutable to an audience. Hype Williams puts a colored light, so brilliant and dense it looks like crushed paint, under the brim of the star's hat. We can choose to read this image as a sign of exoticism, fetishization, and general unknowability of African Americans for the European American population. Yet, in the context of his other videos, the touch is so striking that it becomes purely his own signature. Similarly, for Marcus Nispel, an aviator's cap was such a redolent image that he tried to get his musicians to wear one, even when the scenario was untenable and his musicians balked.[7] Such examples suggest that music videos are not whole but rather structured around bricolage, odd bits drawn from numerous sources that do not gel into a unified whole.[8]

Occasionally questions of the outfits' social function consume a lot of screen time. (I am thinking of the body bags and doctor's uniform in Korn's "Make Me Bad.") The question is not what costumes signify, but where, when, and how often. What devices undercut the signification of clothing? (Frequent costume changes that draw our attention to texture and color may be one example.) When outfits do signify particular social roles, they read like billboards. Film rarely uses costuming so overtly to broadcast the psychic relationships among a character, other figures, and the viewer, but there are some noteworthy exceptions. In Alfred Hitchcock's film *Notorious* (with costumes designed by the redoubtable Edith Head), Ingrid Bergman wears a variety of outfits, each one tailored to say something different about her persona and situation. At one point, she has a veil over her neck and head, as if she were trapped in a spider's web. Later, she appears in a white dress with black gloves that reach above the elbows. (Although trying hard to become a suitable mate for Cary Grant, she is still marked as a doomed, alcoholic woman.) In a nightclub scene, Bergman wears a dress with a thin slit down the front (telegraphing that she is only slightly available to the evil advances of the suitor, Sebastian). When we see her in an extremely low-cut dress, we know that she has been had. Her hair is rolled up in tight, rigid curls that rhyme with the severe Greek columns and vases adorning Sebastian's opulent mansion. With most films, however, we do not take costumes as readable, like stop signs, and even in the case of *Notorious,* the costumes are woven seamlessly into the texture of the film. What marks the contrast with music video is that in the latter we are left, at the first strange encounter, wondering what on earth is being signified.

HOW PROPS ARE CHANGED BY THE MUSIC AND BEGIN TO FORM A MUSICAL LINE

I have suggested that props possess strange valences. Perhaps they, more than any other visual element in a music video, are transformed by the music and threaten to break away from the surface. In chapter 8, I discuss the relations among music, image, and lyrics. Crucial to our understanding of the role of props in music videos is the relation of metaphor, in which the attributes of one object transfer to another, and the yoking together of concepts from different semantic realms creates a new meaning.[9]

Let me discuss this metaphorical relation in terms of props. Music videos may be so ephemeral, in part, because we never have a grip on their ambiguous materials. We never know for what purpose a pop song was composed (hence, retelling or fabricating of tales about songwriting experiences on the VH1 series "Story Tellers"), to whom the music is addressed or what it concerns, how it is to be used, and what types of spaces it should fill. Jennifer Lopez's "If You Had My Love," with references to salsa, elicits images, feelings, and thoughts linked with happiness, parties, weekends, dancing, and sex. Yet the song might be more militant than this (a feminist anthem)—a calculated bid for the Top Twenty or a personal statement. Where and to whom does this work belong? We are uncertain. And so it is with a music video prop—a chair, a flower, or a knife. Let us take the case of a flower. Depending on whether a chrysanthemum is painted by Piet Mondrian, photographed by Robert Mapplethorpe, projected against a photographic light box, arranged by the FDS florist, sprouted from a planter as part of a Doris Day movie set, illustrated on a Hallmark greeting card, sold at the local fruit market, or held as a single stem by singer Macy Gray in concert, the object signifies differently. Take any item from the previous list—perhaps the Doris Day flower planter—and pick a song—perhaps one by White Zombie. When music video's materials are placed together, they often commingle: the flower assumes some aspects of the music. The results can be quite surprising: the flower can seem kitschy, old-fashioned, exotic, or ordinary. One wonders if meaning here becomes untethered, as if the viewer draws upon everything that she has known about chrysanthemums—their texture, shape, and the kinesthetic response they elicit (which is, in part, culturally determined)—heavy metal and movie musicals, lighting and camera, the 1950s and now, the song's and film's title and the song's lyrics, the names of the actors and of the band. It is similar to the first time a viewer sees Godzilla and hears his cry. What kind of strange beast is this?[10]

Perhaps because music videos must take hold of viewers and the elliptical can prove so haunting, musical multimedia's outcome can be a complicated alchemy, often bringing forth tangential details, attributes that are based on difference, and even those from realms that are unfamiliar. Let us now try the experiment with examples from actual videos. Imagine a black crow in three different videos—Jamiroquai's "Virtual Insanity," Guns N' Roses' "Don't Cry," and the Chili Peppers' "Otherside." Although the crow appears in different settings and in different positions vis-à-vis the camera, the music makes the bird an embodied spirit, a harbinger of death, or a mean cuss. These roles come not from the music's most obvious features, or even those that are submerged in the mix—I would not associate Jamiroquai with spirituality, Guns N' Roses with death, or the Red Hot Chili Peppers with this *particular* brand of ferocity. Nor do I think these qualities are particularly crowlike. We are talking about alchemy. It is also important to remember that the music as well as the imagery is transformed, with the music taking on a strange luster, more powerful, sly, or quiet.[11]

To see how music directs our attention to the image, consider a thought experiment in which the music changes and the image remains constant. Imagine, for example, a knife dangling with a variety of songs (like "The Battle Hymn of the Republic," a tango, or Carl Stalling's work for the *Looney Tunes* cartoons). Although the surrounding context defines somewhat how we understand the image, the degree to which the knife becomes dangerous or magnificent will be shaped by musical materials. Do we notice the knife glistening? Is it hanging, weighted toward the ground? What about the blade's edge? Is it sexy, terrifying, slow, or brutal? Is it about to be brought into action, or is it passive? What surface of the knife do we pay most attention to, and which play of light? Now, against our various selections of music, let us cut in a different image—this time, a slimy, green slug. Suddenly, we experience the music, the image, and our bodies differently. Something may shift or contract within us. And then let us cut in a third image, of a blooming sunset—a horizontal vista, palm tree, and lots of sherbet colors. We expand outward again. The way we expand and contract within our string of images differs based on the musical accompaniment. If the reader remains unconvinced, he can imagine alternating images of a dark, narrow closet and a wide-open blue sky against a music of his own choosing. This sense of inhabiting visuals on the screen may be linked to some sort of kinesthetic muscular response within the body.

That music wields great influence over filmed images may have to do with the fact that the latter are two-dimensional, lacking spatial attributes. The music can fill in qualities that are missing—weight, density, scale, and even deportment and affect. It can direct our attention to particular surfaces—the object's side, edge, or front. In rap and smooth R&B videos that feature a shot of a Jeep's front end, I feel that I am riding either on the vehicle's top or its bottom, toward its back or front, depending on the musical accompaniment. As with the previous examples of slug, knife, and sunset, the front end of the Jeep can draw our focus to certain musical materials—for example, one timbre and register over others. The music has changed in relation to this image.

The ways music narrows down and enriches the meanings of objects create secondary, strange effects. Against the music, objects can seem to be reduced to a mood or flavor or speed, to some sort of existential part of their beings (almost as if we were experiencing objects through a different medium—listening to a sounding body under water or watching an object move within zero gravity). Directors will carefully pick one object versus another to create the right kind of feel against the music. It is not uncommon for a van's worth of props to be hauled out to a music-video shoot (with the prop budget in the tens of thousands) so that the director can pick the best prop based on the immediate context—shoes slightly larger or smaller, darker or lighter.[12] When I have made music videos, I have found at a certain point that I needed a prop of a certain ilk—a dull, large, fattish fish, rather than a sleek, tiny silvery one, the falling blonde hair of a woman, not red or brunette, and it is because of the weight of the image. Music seems transformed also. It seems a bit more dimensional and alive, more tangible, more spatial.

The musicality of images is shaped by its context. If a visual line has been set up against a musical one, and then suddenly one image carries a dramatically different sense of weight than other images, the viewer may have a palpable response, almost as if one could hear a sound emanating from the object against the background that does not fit within the visual/musical line. The imagery of music video suggests types of tonality and weight—bright or dark, light or heavy, joyous or solemn. These "tones" can be discerned running alongside the music, riding above it, momentarily residing in tandem or sinking below. In Madonna's "Take a Bow," two shots—showing drops of blood falling into a bowl (the star has pricked her thumb) and showing her buttoning the back of her dress—possess a dark, slow solemnity that has specific musical equivalents. In addition to the images that exist as a "bottom"—a type of lowest register for the video, in both the musical and visual domains—there are comparable tones for top-register emotional states.

To envision better how objects can form a musical line, we might imagine, as an example, the accompaniment of a harp (similar to the opening of Brandy's and Monica's "He's Mine"), along with a medium close-up of a thimble tumbling along the edge of a log, a quilt falling in slow motion through the air, and a piano crashing onto cement pavement—each of the images with its distinctive weight and phrasing: lilting, floating, and finally resounding with a thud. The viewer makes a guess about the weight and feel of the image, its propensity to turn within flight, and catches hold and follows the progress of pitches, timbres, dynamics, harmony, and rhythms that are most amenable to the object's path. It is a simulacrum of hang-gliding or bungee jumping. The act of gauging the motion and direction of the visual image and finding a corresponding path through the music creates a visceral response that bears a shadowy resemblance to the real thing.

The viewer's projection of her attention into objects and sounds can be guided by one or several musical and visual parameters. Let us first focus on rhythm. Imagine that we hear a rather static swatch of music (house music with a straight four on the floor accompanying a synthesizer pad, for instance) alongside four different shots all framed in close-up and cut to the beat: a giant front of a powder puff, the sharp tip of an ax, a sheet of smoke, and the blunt head of a hammer. Here we will hear two and four articulated more sharply than one and three, and each beat of the drum will have a different sound. Thus, deliberately composed series of images can suggest which beats within a measure should receive emphasis, and they can establish musical and visual lines.

Images that are chosen to create a path through the music can highlight the natural grain of the song. For example, in the beginning of Metallica's "Unforgiven," an enormous desk falls and crumbles to pieces against concrete, while, at the same time, Lars Olsen's sticks pound the drums; here we attend to the heavily mixed beat. Two-thirds into the song, a fine nib of a pen writes illegible prose against a smooth stone surface suspended high in the air, after which thin lines of black ink dribble downward and wispy puffs of smoke fill the frame. Now our attention is directed to the upper partials. The song is about impotence and shame, and the images push us gently away from the masculine frontal drums to the vulnerable high registers of the song and make us more receptive to the video's message: macho posturing limits our ability to connect with others.

Faces and bodies, too, have a weight. Music videos often feature a male singer who moves between two or three different women as a potential lover. On one hand, this reaffirms the sexism of male privilege and desire; on the other, the order of faces does make an aesthetic difference. The movement among people's faces and bodies suggests a movement toward and away from something. In D'Angelo's "Cruisin," the women whom the performer woos, all beautiful, become more exotic and atypically handsome as the video progresses. We feel a movement toward another realm, even if it is expressed simply through images of posed women. A less benign video, Hootie and the Blowfish's "I Will Wait," features frequent appearances of a black boy and a white boy whose faces provide some of the formal structure for the video. Unfortunately, the white child's face, used transitionally to lift the viewer from the relatively placid, static verse into the more upbeat and expansive chorus, reads (partly through exploiting latent cultural associations) as brighter, happier, and lighter than that of the black child.

In Godley and Creme's "Cry," the weight of faces is used against the music for a progressive effect. When the highest pitches of the melody sound, we see, one after another, a number of different types of faces: a young boy (the only black character in the video), a young girl, an effeminate old doctor, and a nerdy little boy. The lowest pitches are reserved for a burly, working-class man;

a masculine, broadly featured woman; and another woman with dark hair and a cat mask. We can sense the temptation to judge whether people match well with the lower or higher registers, and some of this has to do with images of heterosexuality and of masculine authority. A frail old man would be placed up high, but as a doctor, he has some authority and therefore belongs low. A woman belongs high, but the one with dark hair and a cat mask might have some dangerous power, which would put her into a low register, and so on.

The previous discussion suggests that people in music video become more like objects, while props become more animate. Is this liberating or frightening? When props, costumes, or people are placed in relation to music, the mix is unpredictable. My students and I have often performed experiments, taking a song and simultaneously marching different objects across a screen. Objects that were intuitively the most congruent, in the context of a musical multimedia relationship, seemed not to be, and those that bore only tangential relations seemed to work best. Why should mittens and mints feel so alive here? Does the latter work better because a metaphorical link is created—a relation emphasizing similarity and difference? Or is it that something unappreciated in the song comes to the fore? Perhaps music videos raise questions concerning our relation to things in the world and why we feel about them as we do.

6

Interlude: Space, Color, Texture, and Time

ONE OF MUSIC VIDEO'S pleasures lies in tracing a trajectory through space while following along with the music. As the camera cranes, the performer's body twists, and the eyes follow, the viewer can pursue one thread (the music, say) or another (for example, the camera as it tracks through space or the line of the body as it leans backward). This experience raises an important question: can we apprehend more than one medium simultaneously, or are we always more grounded in one? The unfolding spaces of music video—conveying possibility, autonomy, and prowess—stand in marked contrast to contemporary lives, which can be locked into patterns of repetition and stasis, caught within binds of hierarchy, decorum, and surveillance that structure both the social and the familial realms. By enlarging our sense of space, at least in the unfolding moment, music video can leave us dissatisfied with our predicament and lead us back into the video to search for something better; at other times a video's space serves as a mirror of our distress. This chapter suggests how by artful editing—juxtaposition of body to body or setting to setting—music video can free us through its unceasing trajectory; the chapter also explores the medium's spatial limitations. In order to accomplish this, I will first consider the ways music-video space departs from that of classic Hollywood narrative film. The chapter closes with a discussion of the ways space can be used toward musical ends, and put in the service of the star, the director, and the genre.

SPACE UNFOLDING IN TIME

Does time organize space, or does space organize time? Is space four, five, or even more dimensions, curved or Cartesian, quantum or mechanical, out there, in the body, or somewhere in between? In cultural geographer Yi Fu Tuan's characterization, "Space is experienced directly as having room in which to move. Moreover, by shifting from one place to another, a person acquires a sense of direction. Space assumes a rough coordinate frame centered on the mobile and purposive self. . . . Place is a special kind of object. It is a concretion of value, though not a valued thing that can be handled or carried about easily; it is an object in which one can dwell."[1] Tuan's description suggests why music video might be more about space than place. Always in flux as it attempts to match musical processes, the music video image rarely offers us a place to inhabit. The elaborate recording and postproduction techniques of popular music create sonic environments that almost never resemble lived spaces. Correspondingly, music video's settings, camera movement, and editing depart from ordinary lived experience. We must throw ourselves into a music video's environment if we want to make a guess about how these spaces feel.

Music video can return us to simple pleasures, like the exploration of space, as narrative is pushed aside. U2's "With or Without You" suggests a character groping through a misty fog; Prince's "Gett Off" moves through an ornate maze; Peter Gabriel's "Mercy St." traces a slow, winding path out to sea; Madonna's "Cherish" suggests an arrow shooting across the sea. At moments, these videos suggest some character's subjectivity (wounded, virginal, devout), but a viewer may still feel adrift. The camera keeps moving. These experiences do not derive just from setting or the images' unfolding. Music colors the nature of the path.

Viewers follow a music video's progress in a way that differs from their experience of Hollywood cinema. We can begin to understand this difference through a comparison of camera and editing in the two genres. In the traditional Hollywood film scene, the camera begins at a distance and gradually moves in—from wide to over the shoulder to the face. This structure allows the viewer to create an ever-widening base of knowledge about plot and characters.[2] Often, the camera in music video moves much more freely and unpredictably. The close-up most often highlights an intensification in the music and fits within an unfolding sequence of shots. Because shot decisions are made to suit the music and the pattern of close-up, medium, and long shots already chosen, the search for knowledge about space and plot takes second place. Unpredictably, one sees a new setting with a different color scheme, followed by a sudden return to the original setting. These shot sequences produce the effect that the viewer does not own or know the space but rather is taken through it.

One might imagine that the viewer, continually encountering new terrain, turns to the music as a guide, almost as if the soundtrack were a guardrail. Why make such a claim? Tuan notes that, for us, space is out there, and our connection to it is our ability to move into it.[3] But television space is poorly tinted, pixilated, and flat. In the music video, camera and editing are unstable— it is treacherous space. Even when a song is poorly recorded, it wraps around us much as music does in the real world, and it thereby resembles lived experience more than does the image on television. (Many television scholars, including John Ellis, have noted the heightened role of the television soundtrack in relation to the screen.⁴) And music video possesses additional special relations between image and sound. The unfolding landscape appears to reflect the music's teleology: objects such as pixie dust, cloth, and tumbleweeds fall away after musical entrances, suggesting a cause-and-effect relation. A wandering or slithering camera turns in response to the music. The music seems to be a good thing for the viewer to identify and follow. Numerous philosophers of music have noticed that music seems like movement in time—that ironically goes nowhere. Eduard Hanslick describes music as "tonally moving forms,"⁵ and Suzanne Langer makes the claim that music's primary illusion is "an order of virtual time, in which its sonorous forms move in relation to each other."⁶ "Music is the sonorous image of passage."⁷

Music seems to carve out an imaginary space: it seems as if we can almost map the line of the music onto the unfolding space of the music video. Phenomenologists have claimed that one of the unique properties of music and the listener is the way that the listener and music become intertwined. According to Thomas Clifton, music is "something through which we live, something which, in a certain sense, we become. [It] has value because I possess it, and it possesses me."⁸ If the viewer travels through space, so might he travel with music. Whether the viewer places himself within visual space is another question. Viewed silently, music-video imagery at least carries the eye, with its striking, off-kilter shots, objects and figures torqued at odd angles within the frame, and rapid editing. Philosopher Hans Jonas suggests that a viewer is drawn into space when he says that only sight continuously blends its present array into ever more distant "background-planes": there is a "co-represented readiness of the [visual] field to be penetrated, a positive pull which draws the glance on as the given content passes as it were of itself over into further contents."⁹ Philosopher Mark Johnson could be said to make a similar claim through a different argument. Johnson states that the question of inside/outside remains a powerful metaphor that shapes our experience of the world; our sense of inside/outside extends beyond that of concrete physical boundaries.¹⁰ The viewer might experience placing herself, to some extent, within the visual field.

I experience myself tracking through the image with music as a guide, and I notice music shaping my trajectory through space. For me, music's capacity to guide us through an unfolding space is one of music video's great pleasures. Not *every* music video shot can offer such an experience. Music-video space appears in many iterations as the image multitasks—showcasing the star, highlighting the lyrics, underscoring the music, and so forth—and keeps up with the speed and transformational processes of the music. The relationship can work in reverse, for example, with the image guiding the viewer's path through a song—a hall or doorway can serve as a visual metaphor for the onset of new musical material, often a new section of the form. Dimming the lights can suggest the end of a phrase or section.

That the space in a music video can be revealed in a strange way can be shown through several examples. First, the camera and the music control us through the way we experience bodies and settings. With performers turned toward us, we are too often left gaping at their chests and chins, while a wall looms behind them, preventing us from moving deeply into the space. Strangely, we rarely feel that we can reach out and touch one of the set's walls. We are also relatively unconcerned about offscreen space. Transfixed in the moment, we do not worry about the other side of the performers' bodies, the walls, or the adjacent room. In Aerosmith's "Crazy," two girls, after a night in a seedy hotel, stand in the doorway in the glaring sunlight with their shades on, prompting us, perhaps, to wonder how cruddy the outside of the hotel is. But this is an unusual moment in a music video. Unless the music and the image have somehow come up short or used time poorly, we are unlikely to think about the settings we have seen or will see. If we do, the thought will flash unexpectedly, a momentary distraction in which we lose concentration on the video's line. Second, in general, music videos do not exceed their own boundaries, as films do. The characters have no life outside the video's context; it is as if the music barely keeps them alive and moving, as if some unseen mechanism might suddenly hit a catch, causing the musicians and supporting characters to tip over, deflate, or crumble.

When extensive crosscutting is used in a music video, we are likely to see a particular configuration unlike those of classic Hollywood cinema. A character approaches a stationary object or person. In such cases, with sight lines that often match and with slow-motion cutting back and forth between the stationary and the moving figure, we begin to measure how much distance has elapsed as the character approaches its target. The image possesses both clarity and ambiguity; we can quickly judge the shortest line from point to point, yet not what kind of time should be experienced within the slo-mo. For this determination of elapsing time, we turn to the music's temporal and spatial cues.

In order to keep the viewer immersed in a narrative, Hollywood directors often render parameters such as lighting and editing invisible.[11] In music videos, however, shots and edits become tangible. The image's materiality assists in drawing the viewer to the soundtrack. Inasmuch as musical continuity matches the eye's adjustment from one shot to the next, it encourages the viewer to follow the music as well as forge a visual path. A series of shots in Madonna's "Take a Bow" contains separate images of bodies, a matador cape, a sword, a shawl, and broken glass falling toward the floor; on the soundtrack, a pentatonic melody similarly curves downward. These shots are edited prismatically to suggest a shape and feel for the eye's trajectory. The edit, that moment of silence between two images, becomes in itself an aesthetic moment. The edits become hurdles; we must jump them and regain our balance.

Yet, though we can do no more than "go along for the ride," we still have some preconscious idea of where we have been and where we might go. Suddenly, at the end of a verse or phrase, the camera might move into a large, open space—a panoramic view of a theater, or a glorious image of rolling plains and a river. We had been hemmed in, and now, as the music and image have unfolded, we feel a slight frisson, but not too much, for at some semiconscious level we had been measuring the scale of the music and the image all along. When the space opens up, we can look back and find some justification for it, if only because the thematic possibilities of the previous section have been exhausted or because the image has borrowed something from the music, perhaps a sense of momentum from the bass line or a yearning quality in the voice. Similar to an interesting narrative twist in a film, such a change may lead us to admire the music-video director's skill at taking us into a wider sphere—one that reflects more power, agility, physicality, and/or subjectivity. We, too, had been tracking that thread but had been unable to articulate such a development.

Vast, thrilling spaces are often the money shots in music video—as much so as close-ups. With only a limited ability to generate suspense from goals or conflicts, a lot of the dramatic force derives from the ways figures are disposed toward one another in relation to the environment in which they are set. Placing figures precariously high above a ground creates immediate excitement within a primarily nonnarrative form. As images of height, they elicit feelings of glee or vertigo, physical reactions in response to the music, thereby drawing our bodies further into the video. In ordinary life, when we cannot get our bearings, we not only look around us but also listen attentively to the sounds in our environment; placing the viewer in such a predicament helps turn our attention to the soundtrack. When a number of different settings are juxtaposed, the viewer can determine where these spaces belong. She may not think about these places much, or expect them to return, but she will still possess a sense of a landscape or a map of the territory.

COERCIVE AND NONCOERCIVE SPACE

Although these music/image associations have a certain power, they cannot always liberate the viewer from the image's control. The jump from one shot to the next can be dictatorial; the image's vector directs the eye where it does not wish to go, and the use of the human figure can suggest claustrophobia. In the most utopian video, the camera may seem very free, as if it were linked not to a body that walks, but rather to one that can dance, jump, or fly from place to place, as if attention might be thrown in the fluid ways that sound does—over the cranium and under the chin—a 360-degree movement, followed by an extreme low angle, then a point of view taken from behind a hand, cuff, or ankle. But in the typical music video, space may not be as egalitarian. The most potent spot is front and center in the frame, and it is the lead performer who owns it. The performer's movement around the center, synchronized with the frame's corresponding moments of stability and instability, creates the video's sense of drama: can the performer stay ahead of the driving forces in the music and in the frame—the rush to the downbeat of the measure, the pull and push of objects in relation? When a supporting character fills the space, the moment often seems transitory and unstable; often the centered interloper becomes an object for study, as if a title—"silent boy" or "old man"—could be placed at the bottom of the frame.

Similarly, the larger organization of space in a video often turns toward the workmanlike and banal. One of the commonest and simplest means of choreographing figures within the frame could be called a "proscenium arch." The singer moves along a z-axis, while supporting figures fill in the front left and right edges of the frame, creating a portal. An arc or semicircle fans outward from these foreground edges toward the back. This fanning configuration (ornamenting the lead performer) can occur within a single frame or it can also be constructed through a series of edits with different figures and/or types of spaces that gradually fill in to compose a virtual space.[12] By lending the star an audience as well as a sense of plentitude, the arc shape flatters the performer; it also mimics sound sources like speakers, the throat, and the bell of a brass instrument. Although this arrangement provides fluidity and momentum, it reduces the other choices for organizing space. The star's face and body are the primary hooks, and the constant return to the star's face as the video's ground may restrict the video's peripheral vision. A video that does not use this bell-like structure is Celine Dion's "All Coming Back to Me Now," which places greater emphasis on a single site (a generic castle) and long tracking shots; the video also favors medium shots of the star over close-ups, however—a tactic many video producers cannot afford to adopt.[13]

David Bordwell and Kristin Thompson note that "editing usually serves not only to control graphics and rhythm but to construct film as well." They go on to describe the way that the possibility of such spatial manipulation was explored by the Soviet filmmaker Lev Kuleshov, who during the 1920s shot and cut "experiments" in constructing spatial relations by eliminating establishing shots. Kuleshov cut together shots of actors, "looking at each other" but on Moscow streets miles apart, then meeting and strolling together—and looking at the White House in Washington. "Although filmmakers had used such cutting before Kuleshov's work, film scholars call 'the Kuleshov effect' any series of shots that *in the absence of an establishing shot* prompts the spectator to infer a spatial whole on the basis of seeing only portions of the space."[14] Because music can suture images, according to the Kuleshov principle, we assume that music video images are related more closely to one another than to images we might see in another context. For example, in R.E.M.'s "Everybody Hurts," separate shots reveal car passengers who contemplate futile lives, their thoughts written in subtitles at the bottom of the screen. As part of the context of music, these thoughts are linked more tightly than if the images were silent. The Kuleshov effect can sometimes help further positive political ends: Madonna adopts a series of conflicting poses—some daring, some submissive—and makes them appear to be all part of the same identity. But music video's relation to the Kuleshov principle carries negative implications as well. Character facets can seem trivial, easily obliterated, or substituted for by something else, each one just the fanciful spinning out of some nonessential part of self. It is helpful to compare the radical Maya Deren film *Meshes of the Afternoon* with Mela's music video "The Gentleman Who Fell," which uses the same imagery. Everything strange and frightening becomes fanciful or absurd in the music video that borrows from it. Perhaps no music-video imagery can be truly radical, because no image has the power to break the continuity of the musical texture and undermine the authority of the soundtrack.[15]

A less than benign example of the Kuleshov effect can be found in Whitney Houston's "Step by Step." In a standard, rather abstract and generic music-video set, Houston stands on what looks like some sort of platform or catwalk, behind which walls (of indeterminate material) slope back strangely. Surrounding the star is a group of putatively average, dancing youths who wear casual, everyday clothing. Houston, wearing a trench coat, rhymes with the intermittent outdoor footage of people dressed in working-class uniforms: firemen put out fires, and volunteers help with such "points-of-light" activities as food banks and house building. It is not at first apparent why the performance and the exterior spaces should be linked in the video; they share only simple features such as clothing and movement. But as Houston keeps singing "step by step" and her lyrics inch us metaphorically out of one space and into the other, the video seems thereby to argue that the work of celebrating the music is related to the volunteerism of the inset narrative. (The hortatory power of the lyrics confirms the link between performance and work spaces.) Thus, "Step by Step" might be capable of raising consciousness, of encouraging us to engage in acts of greater social responsibility. (I realize that this is not very likely. I am sitting on the couch—not going anywhere. In the music video's moment, however, I feel I have done the necessary social work.)

Toward progressive ends, directors sometimes use the Kuleshov effect to showcase the interests and needs of disempowered groups. A video can depict individuals and spaces in a city—several shots of people on the street, a few wide overhead pans of the city, and some performance studio footage which shares ground with the cinema verité footage. Suddenly, the city's secrets—the ways time and space ought to be inhabited—belong to these people.

The Kuleshov effect takes place not just across settings but also across shots of performers and supporting characters' bodies. Often we are drawn into a body that is rendered in fragments, each part possessing a different disposition. We must imagine what type of body and what sort of person might own all these modes of deportment; we do so in part by constructing an image of the body through the music. Mariah Carey's "Honey" features a variety of shots of the star: a sultry low-angle view of her breasts inside a tent; a provocative machismo come-on of her thighs and legs on a desert island; a close-up of her face pouting like a sex kitten. We see her also frolicking on the beach, and bumping and grinding, on the prowl, on the deck of a boat. What kind of body can possess all these shifts of mood and tone? Our experience of moving over the surfaces of bodies, as well as over the landscape of the music, may result in a loosening of our sexual inhibitions as well as our allegiance to a particular gender identity, and we may slide into what Freud called a state of polymorphous perversity. By the end, our sexual identity is almost always restored, but the interior of the video can be quite free.

Music video's exploration of space does not just reveal the terrain of body, but also a heightened relation of body and space. Distributed across a music video, several close-ups of faces might be set in iconic expressions, and parts of bodies could be twisted into stylized poses. This variety of physical dispositions sometimes speaks against and sometimes imitates the music; a pose sometimes resonates with something local, and sometimes with something broader in the music. One might imagine that the emotional tone of these shots lingers over a section of the video. (Kuleshov's experiments suggest as much, as do the ways film theorists talk about film.[16]) The viewer might take hold of and carry forth these dispositions, along with its complementary musical material, into the future as the video unfolds. Often, the subsequent shots reveal a strange space—a strangely dressed set shot through a distorted lens, irregular camera movement and speed, a lurid use of color, and so on—and one might imagine that the viewer would play at performing the feelings and physical dispositions that they are presently carrying into this present space.

Music video's pleasure stems from catching a way of feeling (in a physical representation and in the sound), and performing that in a new environment. Yet the phenomenon that I have been describing only carries through for three to seven shots. Quickly, the video turns to other concerns. The fact that music-video space is fragmented and unstable may render the autonomy of the music video less secure: even the best-made production can seem fragile. When an image that foregrounds musical structure loses its autonomy, each shot becomes a single item, separate from those preceding and following. Often a shot does not fit quite as easily as others into the video's texture. It may be the flying batboy at the beginning of Smashing Pumpkins' "Tonight, Tonight," the dark image of Madonna buttoning a dress in "Take a Bow," the dogs circling one another in Peter Gabriel's "Mercy St.," or the bouncing balls in Biggie Smalls's "Hypnotize." Such images can disrupt the video's harmonious surface. In Madonna's "Cherish," for example, the merchild threatens to run out of the video, which would mean the loss of the song's raison d'être. These moments either hint at a structure that can never be made whole or realize a complicated work, enriched through the director's ability to incorporate disparate materials.

A CLOSER LOOK AT THE POTENTIAL OF
SPACE TO SERVE PARTICULAR MUSICAL ENDS

A director's use of space can highlight musical structure in ways that help to signal a song's beginning, middle, and end: a performer may cross a threshold in the beginning, move to a higher or lower position as the action progresses, and then, as the video draws to a close, work her way back to a location similar to that of the beginning.

Space also draws the viewer's attention to the scale of the song. The expansive spaces in a video like Boyz II Men's "Water Runs Dry," shot on the dunes of New Mexico, give the illusion of an openness that should provide a means for the melodic lines of the string quartet and the voice to run unimpeded. The song would sound different if the video's imagery were shot in a small studio.[17]

The intimate setting is used most often when a musician, typically a female guitar player, performs in a folk idiom. Examples include Lisa Loeb's "Stay," which consists of only a single tracking shot in a small empty apartment, and Jewel's "You Were Meant for Me," which takes place in a poster-painted studio set with a single bed and a toy boat. In Alanis Morissette's "Ironic," as additional instruments are included in the chorus, Morissette crawls out of the tiny confines of her car. The density and activity of the music—the number of instruments and the song's tempo—usually correspond to the packing of figures within the frame. Celebratory up-tempo tunes might feature more figures, as in the chorus of Coolio's "1, 2, 3, 4," which shows fifty partygoers crammed into a ten-by-twelve, luridly painted miniature of a living room.

There are exceptions, however, to the generality that large, cavernous spaces go with full, open, and resonant musical arrangements, while intimate spaces go with smaller, sparser ones. For example, U2's "With or Without You," a ballad, is set to blue-green tones and rear-screen projection. The song is intimate, but the space seems slightly smaller, making the viewer feel claustrophobic. Madonna's "Cherish" is a moderately arranged song, yet the space for the video is larger, giving to the viewer and performers a sense of room; with a larger space, the song even appears to take on a bit more class.

A significant number of videos use spatial deformations: the walls come in too close or are pushed too far back; the ceiling is too low, too high, or canted; the walls slant in at the center or bulge out like a partially collapsed or expanded balloon. Because we associate sound closely with space, we hear the song as if it were sounding within this deformed landscape and itself distorted as a result. We judge a sound according to its source of emanation as well as its degree of echo or reverberation. When the space is strange, we may listen even more closely for aural clues, examining both music and space to figure out the relation between them. A pop song creates a manifold space that the image may echo and/or extend. The section in Coolio's "1, 2, 3, 4," when the older white

DJ appears, sounds much more closely miked than we would expect, considering the flatness of the video's space. The same is true of Robert Palmer's "Addicted to Love," which places the performers in a shallow space against a painted backdrop. Even more subtly, the low ceiling in Solo's "Where Do You Want Me to Put It" draws our attention to the interlocking construction of the quartet's vocal parts.

In his thoroughgoing treatment of popular music's recording and production practices, *The Poetics of Rock: Cutting Tracks, Making Records*, Albin Zak describes how records create sonic spaces unlike anything in the real world.[18] Producers achieve these effects through the recording site, the placement of the musicians within the space, miking, and all of the manipulations that occur during and after recording, such as multitracking, overdubbing, reverb, compression, equalization, flanging and punching in, and placement within the mix and stereo field. Zak describes the techniques Phil Spector employed while at the Goldstar Studios in Los Angeles between 1958 and 1966. Parts were commonly doubled and tripled, and large numbers of musicians—four keyboardists, three acoustic guitarists, two drummers, and so forth—were placed in a relatively small recording space to create a wash of reverberant sound. This musical soup was then fed through a loudspeaker to one of Goldstar's ambient chambers, really a converted bathroom. This was picked up by another microphone and mixed back in with other tracks. Though Spector's music came before the era of music video as a satellite service, we can look to the Thompson Twins, who pay homage to Spector in their song "Hold Me Now." The video honors the band's tribute: during the verses, as instruments are brought in one at a time, close-ups on different types of percussion appear, but during the big chorus, the image showcases a gigantic, broad, overarching space, with the musicians placed on terraces. Such a space suits the song's sonic world.

Sometimes the revelation of space in a music video is orderly enough that the viewer can follow and even predict the camera's course. Here the unfolding of space becomes a metaphor for the song's structure—whether we follow a spiral or a straight trajectory. The final chorus of "Like a Prayer" borrows the bass line from the bridge, giving the sense that the form returns to itself. Similarly, there is backtracking in the imagery: the movement out and around a building to a large semicircle of performers, a smaller circle of soloists, and then a point made up of the two lead performers. Madonna's "Cherish," by contrast, incorporates new musical material in the middle of the song. It makes sense, then, that the image continually moves stage right without turning back.[19]

The type of space and the disposition of figures in the frame can underscore the changes in individual parameters, particularly by providing a sense of distance—the harmonic reach of the song, the ambitus of the melody. In "He'll Be Coming Back to You," Amy Grant's climb to the rooftop of a house reflects the song's chord progression. Some music videos, like Busta Rhymes's "Woo

Hah" and Tori Amos's "Caught a Lite Sneeze," have a number of spaces that echo one another. In "Woo Hah," we see the lurid neon lights of Times Square at night, while the rapper and his homey drive down the boulevard. Next, Busta Rhymes raps in front of a square array of yellow light bulbs that seems like both a part of and a reduction of the earlier space. Perhaps the videomaker is speaking here about the plethora of materials that are repeated or varied within a pop song, even as the song continues to move forward.

A large number of videos depict free movement from one space to another through a juncture—orifices of the body (often the mouth or the ear), pipes, a window or keyhole, a computer screen or television set, or a picture frame. Such effects have some phenomenological justification: sound permeates walls, whereas light does not; and breaking boundaries in this way lends authority to the soundtrack. This traversal of boundaries also reflects elements of both change and continuity in the music. (For example, the crossing may underscore both the delineation of song sections and the continuity of the rhythm arrangement.) Moreover, it can suggest a psychological element, proposing that the shifts from section to section derive from the all-powerful will of the performer. In Mariah Carey's "Fantasy," a seamless shift from day to night, established by the camera's passing through the mouth of a clown, reflects both musical features and the continuity of Carey's desire for her imprisoned lover.

Although the space can reflect musical features, it does not always do so in a sensitive way. The trick is puzzling out whether the space is reflecting the song or serving other aims. Because objects on a gigantic scale can evoke the numinous, sublime, or simply grand, painters, sculptors, and graphic designers favor the technique—the same stratagem used to sell tires sells music videos.

SPACE IN THE SERVICE OF STARS, DIRECTORS, AND GENRE

A pop star will often inhibit space in a consistent way from video to video; videomakers, like advertisers, may find it advantageous to hold onto a familiar image or trademark, even as they accommodate changes in setting, narrative, genre, musical style, or costume. Green Day is likely to be shunted into the corner of a room, while Janet Jackson is commonly given a wide berth. Madonna is usually centered and set back, as if she were a statue wheeled out onto the stage, whereas the camera moves much more freely and easily with Mariah Carey. Prince's diminutive stature may contribute to the fact that he often stands on a podium. Toni Braxton is typically placed in liminal situations, on porches, garden trellises, verandas, and elevators. For some reason, Boyz II Men and Guns N' Roses are treated as deserving an enormous amount of terrain.

Some directors create strongly personal realizations of space. Randee St. Nicholas takes the viewer through an entrance and into a rounded and safe area, suggestive of a womb. (Toni Braxton's "Breathe Again," Donna Lewis's "I

Love You, Always Forever," Prince's "Gett Off," and Baby Face's "When Can I See You Again" are all examples.) In David Fincher's boxy style, figures are typically dwarfed by their environment, and they seem to move stiffly from mark to mark (see Madonna's "Express Yourself" and "Oh, Father," and George Michael's "Freedom"). The monumentality of Marcus Nispel's videos gives viewers the sensation of crossing gracefully between canyon walls that slope gently on either side, almost like being perched in the control seats of a biplane. Matt Mahurin uses indistinct, shallow space that never achieves equilibrium—even with a variety of settings—as if he wished to retain some of the flatness of two-dimensional drawing.

The ways that space is revealed in music video pose a special challenge for directors: how to explore the possibilities of space while providing the viewer with a sense of ground. Director Francis Lawrence has developed a style well tailored to music video. His videos often open with the star entering or waking up to a somewhat surreal environment. Soon, a performer tests the possibilities of the space—playfully flicking on and off a light or brushing her hair back so that birds fly off (as in Janet Jackson's "Son of a Gun" or Nelly Furtado's "Like a Bird"). A corner of hospitable space will then be revealed—handprints might mark a wall, or a finely drawn sheet of a Japanese calligraphy might hang by a doorway; a small bowl of water with a bonsai may sit on a shelf, or a plump cat may crouch on a dresser. Before the video's midpoint, the musician—and therefore the viewer—will move freely out into a larger space. Furtado rises up and soars through the branches of redwood trees. Jackson heads down conference halls and basement kitchen corridors of a gothic hotel with wide, authoritative strides. In "Jaded," an adolescent girl chucks a book, and it is carried fifty feet across a room. One way of constructing music videos is to chart a path through an interesting space; the director could then fill this space with unusual objects or tableaux vivants.

Mark Romanek, one of the most subtle architects of video space, is worthy of special note. As a rule, the general outlines of his constructed space are well defined—strangely sloping or stiffly standing backdrops possess surfaces that evoke a particular color or texture, such as warm and soft or cool and hard—and their qualities reflect our understanding of the songs they accompany. The set, props, background figures, and star seem disposed in exactly the right way, so that even when the set is large, the image as a whole has the ambiguous quality of being simultaneously in miniature as well as monumental. We may feel we are looking in on a special, privileged, enclosed space, sometimes boxy, more often rounded and womblike. Toward the back of the space might stand a large and enigmatic sculpture (like the obelisk in *2001*) or a projective surface (a movie screen). The star usually occupies the center of the space. As the music begins, everything seems resonant, as if the voice or odalisque initiates the sounds and then the walls reflect sound waves back and forth until they finally reach the audience. Or the listener may feel that she is inside a wonderful musical instrument.

A discussion of genre and space appears in chapter 4. One might assume that when a particular type of space reappears in the same configuration within a home genre, it becomes familiar and adopts some qualities of place.

SPACE: CONCLUSION

Music-video space resembles but is not equivalent to narrative film space or lived space. Its air has a different weight—either thick like corn syrup, or extremely thin, as if from a high altitude. The music video's empty spaces resemble ether, and directors often work to enhance this quality, shooting with colored gels, diffusion, and smoke or fog. Drawing on what we have learned about musical multimedia and metaphor from the chapters discussing modes of connection and props (chapters 5 and 9), we know that music transforms the image and vice versa: the music parses the space, helping to mark out the distances among people and objects. Music, of course, is transformed as well, acquiring a bit more dimensionality, as if we wanted to reach inside a hologram and touch the surfaces. If the spatial coordinates in music video matter so much, it is essential that the cinematographer have a sensitivity to the music. If the figure within the frame is to work, it must fall within its own well-judged proportions in relation to the frame, as well as in right proportions in relation to the song. With poor framing, the video falls flat; bad music-video framing is more deadly to the medium than a poorly composed image in a Hollywood film. Does this make music video closer to painting and still photography than film? In a good photograph (I am thinking of the work of Irving Penn), every bit of negative space is palpable. So should it be in music video. This chapter, as with the chapters on other parameters, claims that music video reduces to its raw essentials—props, spaces, gestures, color, rhythm, melodic motives, and so on. Moving through music video space is perhaps the genre's greatest pleasure, even if we only move down hallways, through exits, and toward dead ends. When we watch music video, we may be seeking a body that can exist with a right disposition. Really, it is a wish to live gracefully in time.

COLOR

Even before we recognize the figures in videos, we often see fields of color, then perhaps a predominant texture—soft, fuzzy, metallic, rough, or jagged. The image is a moving painting, and its materials become wet paint, oozing and shimmering. Music video directors trumpet their allegiance to lime green, magenta, and cobalt blue—or, less often, more earthbound tones like burnt sienna. Directors frequently spread color, rather than emphasize line (except in videos featuring black and white), drawing the work closer to Titian and Rubens than to Ingres and Raphael. This downplaying of linear form—avoiding hard outlines in favor of a sensuous surface—makes the director's job easier in several respects. By means of soft focus and similar devices—aureoles of light, shallow depth of field, swish pans, and weather effects like rain and fog—the camera can wander both within and beyond the set, and the editing can be less precise.

In contrast to feature films, videos can be memorable for the way their color relates to the music: a viewer will remember Brandy's "I Wanna Be Down" as purple, Pearl Jam's "Jeremy" as red, and Weezer's "Buddy Holly" as pale yellow. In a form without narrative or dialogue, the connotations of color can immediately create affect: the red in Henry Rollins's "Liar" instantly connotes rage, the blues and greens in U2's "With or Without You" grief, and the yellow in Weezer's "Buddy Holly" innocence. It can sometimes seem as if music video's attractiveness stems almost entirely from its depiction of space and color. (This, and perhaps the hint of the possibility of a narrative, and some interesting props.)

Color and music may be correlated at a very deep structural level. In the evolutionary history of *Homo sapiens*, the ability to make out shapes in both image and sound occurred first, while the ability to discern color and timbre were later secondary systems. (Most animals do not see color or hear timbre.) Kant proposed that while weight and mass are inherent properties of objects, colors are attributable to them only momentarily; the transitory, fleeting nature of color complements that of sound. Colors are shifty in that they do not permanently adhere to objects. An object's color appears duller or brighter depending on whether it stands in bright light, shadow, or dusk.[20] The color of an object looks warmer or cooler in relation to adjacent colors; for example, gray next to green adopts an orange cast. In addition, an object's color shifts hue in response to reflected light: a field of grass will color human skin green, and a restaurant's red lighting will turn a plate of lettuce black. Though sound may not be quite as volatile as color, both are more contextual than a stationary object's mass.[21]

Concepts of dissonance and consonance apply to both color and pitch. Whereas fully saturated complements (imagine these colors in their most intense and pure), such as red and green, yellow and violet, or blue and orange, are jarring to the eye, so-called analogous colors—those close to one another on the color spectrum, such as yellow, yellow-orange, and orange (with yellow dominant)—are found to be soothing. The presence of all three primaries, when muted (mixed down with a little white or black), produces a sense of equilibrium. The imagery for Rob Zombie's videos looks as if it was composed of a color salad—hue, saturation, and value are applied freely and irreverently. The frenetic and jarring color combinations within shots and across edits complement the sonic onslaught. Early hip-hop videos ratcheted up the complementary saturated colors on the background chromakey that contained graphics of twirling flowers, and jumping checks, squiggles, and stripes. This was an inexpensive way to create a sense of instability and excitement and to show off the new and somewhat brittle synth and drum sounds. Janet Jackson's song "That's the Way Love Goes," on the other hand, aims for Marvin Gaye at his most relaxed. Correspondingly, the video's image works within a carefully modulated range of golds and browns.

Can painting be useful for analyzing music video image? In a painting, blues and greens tend to recede in the frame, while reds and oranges come to the fore. Blues and greens seem emotionally cool, and reds and oranges are warmer. Within the video image, colors also elicit emotions and move to the fore or the background. A deep metallic blue that tints the entire frame and is paired with slow motion most often seems to push the figures farther back in the frame, to suggest a slower speed, and to become solemn or subdued. A reddish-orange shot placed within the image's flow often suggests a movement forward and a moment of emotional intensity. A golden hue tends to sedate the image, but not to slow it down as much as blue. Images that feature tonal themes such as half red and half green can suggest passage. Complex applications of color can be achieved by adding additional effects, as in Lenny Kravitz's "Black Velveteen Girl," in which the image sports both a deep blue hue (which imparts a slowed down feel), with flashing strobe lights (which lend the video some speed) and patches of deep red. In Kravitz's video, the mixing of different discourses within the same shot creates a sense of disequilibrium. Patches of color within the frame, when edited together as a series of shots, can also suggest both a visual and a musical line. In Sting's "Desert Rose," the blues that move across women's shirts and into the background of the set function as visual stepping-stones, drawing our attention toward the recesses of the set, all the while holding onto a sense of the song's momentum. The silver tones from the car, Sting's video camera, and some of the actors' hats, both at the beginning and end of the video, serve to frame the blue. By modulating colors over the course of a video—bringing up a dull, blackish red to a more saturated ruby red and then bringing it back down again—a director can suggest a sense of heightening and falling away; these moments of visual intensification and release (the application of blues and reds in Brandy's "Blue Moon" video, for example) speak against moments of intensification and release in the song.

Color and sound have some even more fine grained applications for music video. Both color and pitch can be modulated along a gradient or as a series of intervals (in the case of color, via three separate parameters—hue, saturation, and value). We could imagine a song with a glissando that can be accompanied by a color scheme that shifts in a consistent way—for example, smoothly along a gradient or evenly as a series of intervals.[22] The fact that music and sound enter such felicitous relations may stem from the fact that color and sound comprise similar materials: both color and pitch are waves that vary in length.

Timbre and hue (the level of pure color) have analogies. Each of their values can be reduced, leaving a schematic outline. With just luminous values (no hue—only the gray scale), information remains concerning an object's shape and perspective, and with a timbral reduction (for example, a piano realization), aspects of the song's form stand out. When a music video is shot in black and white, the timbre can appear less vivid. Think of the way Tone Loc's black and white "Wild Thing" possesses less timbral presence than his luridly saturated blue, green, and purple "Funky Cold Medina" or Robert Palmer's brassy red "Addicted to Love."

This leads us to the point that aspects of hue (the color), saturation (intensity), and luminosity (the amount of black or white), can serve different functions in relation to the music. One aspect of color—that of hue—is strongly linked to emotions, and this relation may be hard to piece out in terms of culture or biology. When color practitioners point to the cultural bias of colors, they often cite the example that white signifies mourning in India, while in Western cultures it suggests purity and virginity. Colors that had at one time formal symbolic meanings may lose the original symbolism over time, but the association of color and idea persist. Which came first—the Western association of yellow with cowardice and treachery, or the medieval convention of painting Judas in a yellow robe?[23]

Picasso once claimed that while luminosity reveals structure, color was only a cultural symbol. We might note that the blue hue from the painter's blue period suggests for European audiences a mood of youthful moroseness. Aesthetic theory has characterized both music and color as languages of emotion. The symbolic and affective impact of a video's hue works similarly; performing the thought experiment of changing a video's hue will help make this clear. Imagine U2's gently melancholic green-tinged video "With or Without You" in blues. With this change, the video seems bleak and detached, while complementary colors like tangerine orange and hot pink make the song sound as if it were a primal howl. The emerald and more muted greens are depressing but approachable. A closer consideration of our responses to "With or Without You" reveals that even though our visceral response to color is immediate; color, sound, and the disposition of the figures in the frame are also most likely heavily influenced by culture. Both the color and sound seems bound up in how men should mourn in our culture—a soft pink would never be appropriate here.

Yet some scientific evidence suggests that our responses to music, color, and emotion are physiological (or that culture is so all-encompassing that our responses are written into the body). Research has shown that the color red will momentarily raise blood pressure, while blue lowers it. A bubblegum pink has been shown to reduce violent tendencies.[24] Mozart has been touted as producing a momentary calming effect. When a subject listens to music, testosterone in the saliva drops, and when the opiate centers of the brain are inhibited, a listener feels less pleasure.[25]

It can be difficult to tell whether the relation between color and music works in a video because of biological response, or a well-learned cultural association. Relations can also reflect current notions linked to the genre, technology, or a fad. Directors seem partial to certain colors simply because a new technology—

a faster film—makes a certain shade of green, say, look appealing. Some colors are associated with eras—the neon of the 1990s versus the pastel of the 1980s— and other colors with musical genres. For a long time, alternative rock videos featured very saturated greens and blues. Film theorist Richard Dyer has documented the ways film stock and lighting equipment is keyed to Caucasian skin and how African American film directors have had to jerry-rig equipment and film to produce flattering or true results of their subjects.[26] Many R&B and rap videos feature browns and golds, most likely because these tones are complimentary to African American skin (thereby establishing an analogous color scale across the image.) However, it may also reflect a historical trend (a remembrance of the gold-toned films of the black action era), or simply a making good use of the equipment available on hand. As a corollary, of course, Caucasian skin would tend to different shades for a related set of reasons. It is interesting to wonder whether songwriters might subconsciously shape their compositions to fit colors that appear in videos within their home genre.

One common argument for a link between biology and color involves synesthesia. Synesthetic relations involve a person's receiving visual impressions from aural stimuli because of a genetic predisposition. Many musicians, composers, and visual artists have reported experiencing synesthetic relations between color and sound—most famously Wassily Kandinsky and Alexander Scriabin. (Kandinsky reported seeing yellow when he heard a high-pitched flute. Scriabin wrote an organ concerto accompanied by colors projected on a screen: the colors reflected ones that he envisioned accompanying sounds that he heard while he composed.) Analogously, music-video directors connect particular colors with timbres and harmonic schemes with such regularity that one might think they were experiencing a form of synesthesia—for example, reds and oranges are placed most commonly with brassy or percussive sounds (as in Prince's "Gett Off") and blues and greens with flute- or bell-like sounds (as in U2's "With or Without You"). As suggested previously, whether biologically determined or the result of enculturation, our responses to color and music happen so quickly that they can feel natural: Institutional walls are painted certain colors to calm or excite the people who inhabit them; melodies with specific contours, like lullabies, are soothing to adults as well as young children; and certain jingles are designed to make one start. Yet it is true also that a taste for color can be acquired: the orange and pink tones of Matisse's *Odalisque* may be appreciated most by the connoisseur. Insofar as color in music video is likewise an acquired taste, those who have not watched many of them might assume that what is before them is needlessly garish.

Yet most contemporary theorists argue that true synesthesia is rare. Nicholas Cook notes that no media intermingling occurs in synesthesia because "real sound cannot interact with imaginary colors."[27] No "universal system of vibration" can be mapped between sound and color.[28] Here, Cook dispels the biological model with its accompanying spiritual overlays; however, once he has done so, the question of how music may relate to color in a multimedia work still lingers, needing further exploration. The claims made for multimedia and synesthesia are no different from those for music proper.[29] If we broaden our scope to include quasi-synesthesia—color/music relations that are influenced by biology, culture, and formal considerations—striking and peculiar relations come to the fore. What kinds of mechanisms are at play, I wonder, when, after spinning a pop song for my students, we find that we can make a good prediction about the look of an upcoming video? A bad color choice feels palpable, almost as if the director has heard poorly, is out of tune. The music-video industry rewards its most valued color timers with lavish salaries, and the newest working method leaves both local and large-scale decisions for post-production, when the color can be optimally aligned with the music. A description of the relations among image, music, lyrics, and color can illuminate a video such as Madonna's "Material Girl": here, the pink and red work against other media to reflect shared notions about femininity and danger, raise questions about biological links between timbre and color frequency, and shape formal considerations, for example, white in the beginning, middle, and end frames the video.

COLOR AS A STRUCTURAL DEVICE

The use of color as a structural means is exemplified by videos like Lisa Loeb's "Stay," which stages the action in a neutral, beige loft. The sequential placement of a gray cat on a gray wrought-iron chair, a gray-blue curtain in a closet, and the cat on a windowsill help give the piece a beginning, middle, and end. In R. Kelly's and Hype Williams's "Down Low," a video drawn from gangster films such as Brian De Palma's *Scarface,* color assists the narrative and highlights arrangement and tempo. When the lead singer R. Kelly and his lover Lila proceed with their secret affair, their clothes shift from black to white, while those of Mr. Big, the head Mafioso, remain in a murky darkness. Yellow roses placed on the dining table of a party recall the blond hair of Mr. Big's white girlfriend.[30] The color continues into the next shot as an out-of-focus pool of yellow placed next to Kelly's face. Later, cool purple and blue flowers wrapped in tissue paper, presented by Kelly to Lila on a date and then placed on a table, resemble the colors of an abstract painting (similar to the work of Sam Francis) that hangs over the lovers' bed; it is also a strange echo of the deep blue pajamas Kelly wears under the sheets, attire that comes into view as the mobsters descend on them. The smeared colors in the painting foreshadow the pulp that will be beaten out of both after they are discovered in bed. The extension of color across both frames and across scenes seems like the long tremolos in the song's arrangement.

As a means to underscore musical form, color figures prominently in Smashing Pumpkins' "Tonight, Tonight," following singer/songwriter Billy Corgan's melodic line farther and farther. While the string arrangement thickens and ascends, an increasing number of ghostly, pudgy men dressed in sheets and playing violins perch on clouds that stretch into the distance. (The band members have their own clouds, on which they play folk stringed instruments.) Both the bottom of the clouds and the ridges on the pasty moon are at first rimmed by a soft pink, which deepens gradually to a rosy hue flooding the screen; near the end of the video, we see a purplish giant octopus with pink shells and a pink Poseidon. Here, even as it connotes the ripening of the song, color suggests the fulfillment of the journey for the couple embarked on a trip to the moon.

The differences between musical sections are marked by color in Toni Braxton's "You're Making Me High," in which the image shifts gradually from a baby blue to a soft brown to a garish pink. Similarly, the music moves from a quiet beginning to an upbeat verse and chorus to a bridge that is full-throated and raw, suggestive of heartrending desire. The deep pink color at the bridge fits both the lyrics and the music's development.

A video that stays within a restricted color scheme maintains visual consistency as well as uniformity of mood. When a complementary color migrates to the foreground and takes on primary importance, it becomes a means to alter the video's focus. Marcus Nispel's blue-toned video for Changing Faces "G.H.E.T.T.O.U.T." and his gold-toned video for Lil' Kim's "No Time" shift for a moment to pink. In the former case the change signifies the sharpening of desire and in the latter a cooling down into quietude.

There are instances when color simply helps to divide a video into sections—a beginning, middle, and end—and does not relate strongly to the music. In extreme cases the use of color suppresses the narrative thrust altogether, appearing to constitute a thing in itself. This can work to advantage in differentiating dramatic events from the reality of everyday existence, but, when the color seems chosen more for its flash than for its sensitivity to the music, the relation is quite likely wrong. If the color is too insensitive to the music, the video will likely fail to garner a wide audience.

TEXTURE

Music videos use texture to elicit a visceral response—to the softness of fur, the smoothness of glass, the roughness of stucco, the sharpness of metal spikes. This physical response helps to draw our attention to elements in the song's mix, while the music can direct us to things within the frame, suggesting in part a sense of drawing near to or keeping away from surfaces. Musical timbres are often described as having tactile qualities. The waveforms of sounds produced by the vibraphone and the flute are said to be smooth, while the waveforms of instruments like the electric guitar and saxophone are called rough. Like color, texture seems to work well in music video because by producing a visceral response it can substitute for a story. Scenes that imply a time of day or story can be placed in sequence. Different scenes with textures do not imply a sequence. The temporal indeterminacy of texture serves to allow additional space for the music.

TIME

A rich description of time or musical time is more the province of philosophers than the scope of this book—as St. Augustine remarked, "What, then, is time? If no one asks me, I know; but, if I want to explain it to a questioner, I do not know." *The Oxford English Dictionary* offers a ten-page entry for time and twenty-seven different definitions for the noun, including "a limited stretch or space of continued existence, as the interval between two successive events or acts, or the period through which an action, condition, or state continues," and the "indefinite continuous duration regarded as that in which the sequence of events takes place." Musical time is also difficult to define. Jonathon Kramer has stated that "time and music can be many different things," and Gerard Grisey has remarked that "real musical time is only a place of exchange and coincidence between an infinite number of different times."[31] Musical time is often associated with specific temporal features of music: accent, beat, meter, period, rhythm, and tempo. This view of musical time can be broadened to include everything that pertains to the temporal structure of music (such as musical form, for instance), clock time (an objectively measurably duration), and the listener's subjective experience of the music's temporal unfolding.

Philosophers such as Henri Bergson and Maurice Merleau-Ponty have stressed the ways that an individual's lived time differs from social or clock time. Time spent in engaging, pleasurable, purposive activity moves more quickly than when one is waiting, bored, or depressed. Pop songs can draw our attention to a range of experiential time: one of its great pleasures is the way we can shift our sense of time away from where we are to match our time with that of the music. Two examples of a song's ability to offer the listener a particular type of experienced time are Madonna's "Borderline" and R. Kelly's "Down Low." In the opening of Madonna's "Borderline," the shrill synthesizer patch suggests a succession of instantaneous moments perhaps poorly valued, happily and immediately consumed. R. Kelly's "Down Low," on the other hand, with its Isley Brothers sample, slow trills, bird sounds, sparse arrangement, and mellow mid-tempo ballad, implies a time that stretches closer to infinity. Even if Madonna's "Borderline's" "temporal window" (the ways that the past and future are suggested within the immediate moment) is much more compressed that that of "Down Low," both songs possess qualities that music philosophers highly value—music's ability to suggest a fluid sense of time where time is not broken up and discrete, but rather where the past appears to flow seamlessly into the present, and the present into the future: "hearing a melody is hearing, having heard, and being about to hear, all at once."[32]

When images are placed against the music in a video, other layers of time are evoked, some establishing connections between the music and image and some held by the images alone.[33] In the following section, I demonstrate a range of temporalities for music video, beginning with the simpler and moving toward the complex. One simple example is when the music is consistently faster than the image, or vice versa. Mentioned elsewhere in the book is Green Day's "Jaded/Brain Stew," in which grayed-out images of the band on a couch, moving across a city dump in a slow tractor, suggest a time even slower than the music's tempo. Madonna's "Take a Bow" suggests music for a piña colada time out, while the characters in the video are stuck doing manual labor. In Brian McKnight's "Miss You," the couple moves more and more slowly against a song about McKnight's depression after his lover has left. The viewer gazes down, unwilling to drop into McKnight's dark sea. That the characters move even more slowly than the song makes them heroic and unfathomable.

But pop songs tend to convey more than one type of time. Richard Middleton has written about the ways that time can switch in a pop song from that of the lyric to the epic.[34] In addition, strata within the song can suggest different senses of time—that reiterating cymbal on the sixteenth note differs from the mellow pad or frisky bass line. In a music video, particular individual shots can reflect various strata of the music.[35] A director can also create complexity by taking a patch of music, claiming it as some sort of (shifting) ground or constant, and then cutting among imagery possessing two or more different temporalities— jumpy, rapidly cut footage, footage at a moderate pace and footage that is meandering and slo-mo. The contrasting footage against a consistent musical background helps us become aware that lives are experienced in pockets of time, that our attention can shift quickly.

Music videos can heighten our awareness to the fact that lived time can be personal and subjective, different from the rhythms of the environment and that of other people. Like other art forms, music video provides opportunities for the viewer to choose where to place her identification. If the viewer identifies with the music, or with the performer's experience of the music, the environment can seem to fall out of sync with subjective experience. A hyped-up jungle accompaniment against a slo-mo POV shot of a camera winding down a hallway, or a slo-mo camera pan over an audience caught in the throes of adulation, can suggest that personal time does not belong to that of the outside world. Of course, the viewer's identification can shift, with the image drawing the viewer's attention and the music standing outside. We most often follow such occurrences when the image contains something very attractive, for example, a wide arcing trajectory of a figure or object as it jumps or floats across the screen—we identify with that moving form and look out. (Such is the case with Janet Jackson's "Runaway," in which she leapfrogs among the Seven Wonders of the World.)

A very strange aspect of music video is the way that each medium can distort our experience of the other media. Because human time is a function of lived experience, we can imagine how the music might serve as a ground or as clock time, and that the image would then cut a path against it, acting in a purposeful way, picking up some of the music's activity and putting it to use; and then suddenly the image will go on holiday. Imagine a motor-rhythmic techno groove against imagery of people running, wheels turning, and the like. Next, the image takes a breather, meandering in an empty room, and then fading to black while the music continues. And, of course, our point of focus can switch. Our attention can be drawn to the media with the strongest profile, which can be, at this moment, the music, and it will build up energy, to go momentarily slack against a relatively stable visual scape. With these moments of dilation and contraction (and, of course, other distractions along the way, including lyrics and star shenanigans), we lose our sense of an accurate experience of clock time. So many types of depicted time, both layered and changing, takes some virtuosity to track. Let me give two examples of the media's ability to create a sense of temporal distortion, one drawn from film and the other from a music video.

In one of the most famous film sequences—the shower scene in Hitchcock's *Psycho*—music changes our perception of time. The opening sequence with Janet Leigh drawing the shower and Anthony Perkins standing behind the curtain with a knife seems long because the viewer does not know if and how a murder will occur. The music adds more rather than less confusion to the situation—the music is so painful and strange: Bernard Herrmann's elongated, falling electronic and birdlike sounds correspond to what in the frame? Conversely, the music speeds up both the shot of Leigh's collapse to the floor and the slow camera move to the drain and her eye. The moaning bass, as it drops lower and lower, focuses our attention on the drain and suggests that her life is trickling out of her body. Without the music, in the opening of the scene, when Perkins walks up to the curtain, draws it aside and stabs Leigh, time seems experientially fast; with Leigh's collapse to the bottom of the tub, it seems incredibly slow. That music can attach itself to screen objects and provide them with a new type of volition can be seen with our perceptions of Perkins's knife. In *Psycho*, the weapon does not actually strike Leigh's skin: intercut within the stream of images are still frames with the knife held parallel to Leigh's ribs that, viewed silently, quickly become obvious and almost hokey. However, when the soundtrack is added, the shrieking violin strokes possess such directional force that the viewer infers real stabs.

En Vogue's video "Never Gonna Get It" shows that music can alter our sense of visual duration. The sequence of shots begins in a living room lit in the deep blue of retro film noir, with the appropriate slashes of light from off screen Venetian blinds. We see a man's back as he approaches a woman who faces him with her back to a wall. As he moves closer, shots are intercut of individual band members singing lines like "not this time" and "never gonna get it" while shaking their fingers. The woman slaps the man and he falls to the ground. A low-angle shot reveals her high-heeled shoe poised to kick the fallen body. When we listen to the music, the man's path across the floor seems swift, while the subsequent fall to the ground seems interminably long, as if in slow motion. Here, in the case of the music with the image, the singer's re-monstrations frequently fall at the beginnings of phrases and along with the thrust of the music, carry us forward, giving the viewer as much momentum as the man who approaches. When the fall happens to the floor, the verse has nearly run its course, and the singers have stopped singing. No musical or visual target focuses the viewer's attention, so the man's drop seems intermi-nable. Viewed silently, without the music to serve as a guide, the converse seems true: the man's approach takes up a lot of time and the fall happens quickly (fig. 6.1).

I have discussed how a pop song can contain a high degree of temporal complexity—both within strata and across sections of the song. What contri-bution does the listener's time play here? Claude Lévi-Strauss claims that each song contains a silent part written for the heart. The heartbeat, breath, blood, nerves, feet, or hands in motion all suggest different temporal orientations. I have long been fascinated by the fact that my physical rhythms can match pace with, or serve as a counterpoint to a video's visual rhythms—the flicking of spangles or light, waving fabric, performer's gestures, edits—as well as, of course, the song's musical rhythms. Even more strange is the way that, when watching music video, I have the illusion that I know the characters' temporal orientation. As I hum along, tied in with the music, I come across a close-up of a face, or a torso with a different rhythm—perhaps more solemn or animated than I. Perhaps the performer is locked into another of the song's rhythmic strata, or she is following her own personal clock. A heightened awareness of the gap between me and the person dawns, and I am able to study her with an unabashed clinical curiosity. Why do I experience the other performer's rhythms in such a clear way? Do my rhythms, locked in with the music, become a clock against which I can gauge the other person's speed? (I may well judge her speed because I am set at a pace with the music; the camera also supplies me with a tempo. It may be easier gauging the speed of another person from a moving vantage point rather than from a stationary one. If I am running, I can better guess how much exertion is required to match another person's gait than if I am standing still.) Perhaps it is also that I do not watch her as I would if I were engaged in a film narrative—if I do not expect the character to speak or to act purposively—why might I treat the figure as a person? (Imagine if the music

FIGURE 6.1 (A–D) En Vogue's "Never Gonna Get It." Music changes the viewer's experience of time.

suddenly dropped out and the close-up of a face happily moving to music turned suddenly and started hurling invectives at me.)

Throughout this book I call the people who appear in music videos automata. Why do they seem mechanical, and what sorts of temporality does this imply? The forces of music, editing, and framing make music become more spatialized, while the temporal qualities of space also come to the fore. These forces of space and time can be imagined as casting a grid across the video's frame. As performers fall on this grid, so do they move in and out of sync with the music, and to and from a balanced position in the frame. In this way they flicker between human and mechanical. (The attraction may resemble that of wind up dolls, marionettes, and the actors in Elizabethan masques. What is alive, and what is not?) Sound structures music video's world, determining the paths of its characters. Stanley Cavell claims that sounds "are warnings, or calls; it is why our access to another world is normally through voices from it; and why a man can be spoken to by God and survive, but not if he sees God, in which case he is no longer in this world."[36] Free from the risks of being found out and punished for our viewing, we can watch music video's characters with intense scrutiny. These characters also become automata through the ways that they exist in a heightened state. Singing and dancing, they are placed on display. Song and dance can be thought of as extreme forms of everyday talking and walking: in music video speech is song and all movement becomes dance. The incisive probing of the camera, as well as the work of editing and framing, capture the most performerly gestures and construct phantasmagorical bodies.

Such unusual forms of depiction encourage a kind of voyeurism. Cavell claims that the cinema's greatest pleasures derive from our invisibility to the screen and our ability to look at the world without changing its features in any way. Even more than cinema, music video gives us permission to watch with impunity. Sound's power over the image, the spatial and temporalizing of the image and the theatricalization of the characters, makes music video a distant cousin to cinema. Videos do not always present views on the world. They can even refuse to suggest a world beyond the frame; what lies in the frame often remains mysterious. Yet even as we viewers gaze at figures who are more allegorical than human, the music reveals something personal—the characters' insides, what their bodies are sensing. Film suggests at a further remove how to understand a character's situation. During music video's heightened moments, I have the illusion that I directly perceive the rhythms of the body before me, the contours of that body's affective life. Skilled directors, such as Mark Romanek, David Fincher, or Francis Lawrence, reward our efforts to follow the lines of the camera and the music as they trace paths through and across bodies and empty space.

Time in music video is undoubtedly strange. Narrative films, sitcoms, and commercials, even when they are layered with wall-to-wall music, reflect our sense of lived time. Even if the music is lush and busy—foreshadowing something or cueing us as to what the characters should feel—the protagonist still seems recognizable and whole. Though the music helps to make the two-dimensional image more lifelike, we can do quite well without it. Most music-video images, however, do not possess a speed similar to that of ordinary lived time, and we cannot do without the music. All of the qualities of the image—the way it is shot out of focus, at odd angles, through distorting lenses, at different speeds, lurid colors, with strangely textured and constructed sets, where editing occurs between gestures, and figures are facsimiles of people—serve to form an image that makes room for, matches, or plays against the music's sense of time. Some videos use imagery with a wide range of temporal markers—both full and empty—some with spaces that suggest time, such as kitchens that are laid out carefully with bric-a-brac, and some that are devoid of temporality, like the empty, blank sets with one person in the frame. Often, if the temporality of the image is different from that of the music, the viewer's must work to make the video whole. Music-video directors can even create two senses of time within a single image, as in Dido's "Best Day of My Life," in which movers carry away Dido's possessions in the background, while she sings as if in a different realm.

CREATING A SENSE OF TIME

If music videos wish to depict a time period, how do they do it? Often music video will present a multilayered representation of time, and the viewer must piece together different temporal strands in order to make the object whole. Without access to many of the traditional temporal markers available in narrative film—meeting times, sound foleyed in from the real-world environment—music videos possess other devices for suggesting temporal processes.

Though the music of the pop song can delineate the shifts in thought and feeling of the performer, it cannot describe an exact expanse of time (fifteen minutes, a week, or a year). Pop lyrics are equally vague, and the image can only suggest time's passing through references to certain types of light, or a type of clothing or prop that suggests an era. Videos that suggest a narrative compel us to put the video's depictions into temporal order, however. A comparison of two rather similar videos can show what we discover when we draw upon cues in the music, image and lyrics. The videos for Madonna's "Papa, Don't Preach" and No Doubt's "Don't Speak" each deal with the singer's boyfriend problems, but the women's responses differ. The viewer can decipher each character's emotional state. In "Papa, Don't Preach," new song sections appear unpredictably without much preparation. This leaves the viewer with the sense that thoughts and sentiments seem to rush in on the singer as she moves across the song's sectional divisions. On the other hand, in "Don't Speak," Gwen Stefani has enough time to catch her thoughts and pull herself out of the slightly mournful verse into the much more emphatic, almost angry chorus. In both songs, the lyrics provide some information about the time-scale of the song's plot. Lines like "you and me together" or "I can't believe I'm losing my best friend" suggest a past tense that stretches a ways back. How far, we are not sure. Names that are tagged to performers and actions are very generic ("You and Me Together" or "I'm Keeping My Baby"). The images also show a number of different settings, participants and activities, often differentiated according to the song's sectional divisions, yet temporal markers are few. "Papa Don't Preach" does not say for how long or how often Madonna dated, or when she became sexual with or fully committed to her boyfriend, but perhaps the tightly cropped blonde haircut provides a clue. (The viewers who remember Jean Seberg's role in Jean-Luc Godard's *Breathless* will assume that it is a quick, heated affair.) Similarly, for how long Gwen Stefani in "Don't Speak" had a relationship with a member of the band and when she developed troubles is also uncertain. (Her long granny dress, droopy, straight hair, and bare feet may suggest long enough to feel as oppressed as our grandmothers.) The listener/viewer must ask how much time must have elapsed for the character to grow into the kinds of thoughts and feelings that the music suggests. He must ask how the video compensates for the fact that each medium describes the event using a different scale: most often, each medium can vacillate in terms of mode of representation, for example, the lyrics may seem symbolic, the image iconic, and the music affective. It takes a type of readjustment between music, image, and lyrics—how long a patch might have come before this event, and later, when a significant exchange of glances takes place, a reassessment (fig. 6.2).

FIGURE 6.2 (A–B)
No Doubt's "Don't Speak" and Madonna's "Papa Don't Preach." Music, lyrics, and images offer imprecise evocations of time: the viewer fills the gap.

Music videos can suggest a temporal shift by depicting the passage of time or a change in the weather—the sky darkens or dawn approaches, rain starts to fall. Because the video shows these changes incompletely, we look to the music to help explain these temporal cues. A video that encompasses a stretch of time—from mid-afternoon to post-sunset—helps to make the claim that the song possesses a wide scope.

Music videos most commonly illustrate a sense of the past through a shift in color or a move to black and white, greater diffusion, slo-mo, Super-8 or grainy film, as well as expressive props and settings—photographs and lockets, period dress and so on.[37] One video especially noteworthy for its use of emblematic props and setting is Simply Red's "Holding Back the Years": a train comes into town and billows black smoke; the singer walks across the heath with a cane; children throw paper airplanes in a classroom, while one child (most likely the singer as a young boy) stares off in reverie.

Yet, just as often, the images simply go there. The mechanisms most used to establish a flashback in narrative film are often not employed in music video—the actor reflects back alongside overlapping sound or dialogue, or the image turns hazy—because the song provides the video's most important temporal cues. In No Doubt's "Don't Speak" the song shifts from a generic, alternative, anthemic chorus, to a Spanish-flavored verse, then to a retro-'70s bridge. In the bridge, the band happily rehearses in what seems like the past, as the image shifts from warm pastels to a nostalgic, faded gray-brown. The time elapsed may be a year or just as likely seven years. We do not know precisely, but we can tell it has been significant enough to cause a psychic change in all of the band members.

Just as the image can freely shift temporal domain, it can also traverse spatial, physical, and cognitive boundaries. A video can suddenly make a performer's thoughts physically manifest—almost like the film *Harvey*, which involves an imaginary rabbit. Because these thoughts can suddenly and unaccountably appear in music video, the viewer has to guess their relation to ordinary life by judging the thoughts and sentiments expressed in the music. In TLC's "Waterfalls," suddenly a man and a woman gaze at a framed photo on a bureau, and the photograph begins changing rapidly within the frame, replaying images of the woman's lovers. In Green Day's "Basketcase," fish suddenly start swimming around the performer, and we are meant to take it as his everyday hallucination. Interestingly, film music, as Anahid Kassabian claims, can just as fluidly traverse such boundaries—switching effortlessly from source to diagetic to nondiagetic sound.[38]

Film theorist Michel Chion points out that moving images without sound possess an ambiguous temporality.[39] If we see an image of a picket-fenced suburban house, we cannot judge how quickly time passes unless we hear a soundtrack—birds, cars, wind, kids playing across the street. Without the soundtrack, the house can have a mute quality, as if it has lost its voice. The soundtrack of a music video imposes a new temporality upon the images. However, this temporality does not match what we expect of figures and objects in ordinary life. Strangest is the performance music video shot in a stadium arena with a song that was recorded in a small studio space. If the viewer looks closely, he can catch a type of mute silence creeping in at the edges of the frame. So there is a palpable discrepancy that we can measure, something hard to believe about the relation between the music and the images.

TIME: CONCLUSION

I would like to close with a consideration of music video's sense of time in relation to that of other art forms. Music resembles a carpet unfurling before us, and rolling up afterward: in any instance, sounds have already passed us by, and the rest of the music is yet to appear, and this aspect of music, more than for any other medium, draws our attention to the transitory nature of time. The music-video images attempt to keep pace with the music—its speed, volubility, transitoriness. They are instantly gone, like cotton candy or dry ice, they immediately dissolve away; we had held them briefly and cannot know them in a similar way until we watch again. Painting can seem to open up to us for our endless contemplation, and narrative film most often occurs at a pace close to our ability to comprehend. The viewer's relation to music video can be more vexed. Henri Bergson describes the present not as a sliver but as a saddle within which the disappearing past and the now approaching future coexist.[40] Music video can offer long stretches that are in the flow, where we feel fully present within both the music and the image. All of a sudden there is an edit or a musical shift, and we have the frightening sensation that we cannot access the past, and that the future is uncertain. So a music video oscillates between presence and dissociation.

Successful music-video directors develop trademark styles that work well with music video's effects, its transitoriness, incomprehensibility, and speed. Marcus Nispel's figures tend to be monumental and simple, smoothly surfaced, perfectly sculpted, and slow moving. They seem enormous and heavy, and the viewer has the illusion that he can reach forward and grasp these sturdy forms against the onward unceasing rush of the music. On the other hand, some of Matt Mahurin's imagery is so blurred, fuzzy, and weightless that we feel we do not have to possess the image. We let it stand away from us, a bit inscrutable and intractable.

Paradoxically, while music video is constantly disappearing, it also has its firm materiality; it seems clearly bounded with a highly marked beginning, middle, and end. With such a small scale, yet such grand themes, a video often seems like a miniature, a memento forever encased and out of reach in amber, a lively overpopulated flea circus forever locked under glass.

The musical track is both a priori and a stern master unto which the image must bend. Soon into the song, the listener can gauge the scale of the song—how long it will be until the phrase ends and the verse closes, how soon the next chorus will arrive and the song as a whole will drive to a close. The image can tarry, match, or run ahead of the music, but at some level, it must subject itself to the steadfastness of the track. We feel the need for the image to assist in the process of closing sections, of finding an end that will be approaching soon, almost certainly on the first or third beat four or five measures from now. If the image and music in the first verse had ended with a striking build-up or fade away, we hope for the same or even more in the next. The video director's ultimate goal is to keep the tape spinning well (almost like a group of twirling plates) until the song's end. I wonder if it is because of the unyielding, onrushing undercurrent of music, which forces the image into frenzy. There is a need to make jokes, to run away, to try to obliterate and transcend what one is irrevocably yoked to.

7

Lyrics

AS WE STEP BACK from the surfaces of music videos, the twitches and turns of bodies, the melting colors, dazzling camera work, and fleeting edits, we might wonder what the lyrics are doing.

This chapter attempts to address this question, discussing such aspects of the topic as (1) How important are the lyrics of music video in relation to their image and music? (2) How do viewers receive a music video's lyrics, and how does this reception differ from that of lyrics when the song is heard alone? (3) Do music-video lyrics function similarly to pop-song lyrics, poetry, or dialogue in movies, or do they function differently, as a new entity? (4) Do music-video lyrics transform music and image, and vice versa? (5) What structural role do lyrics play? (6) How do lyrics contribute to a video's sense of time? (7) Do lyrics differ based on musical genre, gender, ethnicity, or era?

THE IMPORTANCE OF MUSIC-VIDEO LYRICS

Throughout this chapter, I argue that lyrics rarely take on a superordinate function, instead jostling with music and image for a moment in the limelight. Among the three media, lyrics most commonly play a subservient role. They may almost become like film music, essential but often unheard and only sporadically capable of occupying the viewer's attention.[1] Claudia Gorbman's description of unheard and unremembered film music sounds similar to the role lyrics play. She provides an early example that shows how music had to give way to the dialogue: "In the United States, the practice of lowering the volume of music behind the dialogue, rather than eliminating it, was already *de rigueur*. A machine nicknamed the 'up-and-downer,' developed as early as 1934, had as its purpose to regulate music automatically. When dialogue signals entered the soundtrack, the up-and-downer reduced the music signal."[2]

Like film music, music-video lyrics frequently make way for materials with sharper contours—an interesting timbre, a dancer's gesture, a dramatic edit. The lyrics' broken continuity and uncertain effects may stem from their genesis.

With pop songs, music is most commonly composed first and the lyrics second. (Of course, as we consider the importance of lyrics in relation to music, we find significant differences from genre to genre, song to song, and band to band. One notable exception is hip-hop, in which the rapper and DJ often work in isolation, and then bring beats and rhyme together.) A song that developed as music first, lyrics second is "Rocket" by Def Leppard, whose members noted that the lyrics were chosen primarily for their timbres; the hook line "skin on skin" may work because the consonantal cluster *sk* fits with the timbre of the snare drum. Historically, song lyrics and music have often been composed separately, as in Tin Pan Alley, where songwriters and lyricists worked in teams and sometimes received separate compensation. Charles Hamm describes the way Berlin would sometimes take a tune and add lyrics, or write music and deliver it to a lyricist. Hamm cites a contemporary description of Berlin's songwriting process, in which he plays both roles, but writes the music first: "A musician sat at the piano. Mr. Berlin began to hum and to sway in the motion of ragtime. Round and round the room he went while the pianist jotted down the notes. Mr. Berlin stopped occasionally: 'That's wrong, we will begin again'. . . . The actual melody took him an hour. Then he began on the words. While he swayed with the pianist playing the humming gave way to a jumble of words sung softly. And out of the jumble came the final composition."[3] Music-video directors seem also to replicate the songwriting process, turning first to music, then to lyrics. Music-video directors I have interviewed (including David Fincher, Kevin Kerslake, Francis Lawrence, Marcus Nispel, and Floria Sigismondi) report that they listen to the music first, wondering to what kind of place this music might go, how the camera might move, how it makes him or her feel.

When we watch music videos, lyrics rarely maintain the upper hand. Even when at first glance a music video seems to orient itself toward the lyrics, on closer inspection, other relations take precedence. In Soul Asylum's "Runaway Train," the image is less about a runaway train, real or figurative, than about the inexorable drive of the melody and the reckless way that it heads into an abyss. And in House of Pain's "On Point," the line "When it's time to rock a funky joint—I'm on point" seems designed to reflect an enthusiasm for a very short, prominent, and funky melodic hook accompanying the voice. This hook, not the words, wins out at conveying the working-class environment and the image's dirty quality.

Andrew Goodwin has noted that music videos rarely point to the lyrics; typically they serve to set a mood.[4] The hook line of a song is represented most often in an indirect way. In Madonna's "Cherish," the imagery is focused on expressing an imperative—cherish—but it is not clear how or to whom. Prince's "Gett Off" expresses an image of community and an experience of flux and movement, rather than the satisfaction of sexual desire. In both these cases, the hook line is taken up, only to be left behind. Its sole function is to get the video started.

VIEWERS' RECEPTION OF LYRICS

The viewer's attention to the lyrics of a music video most likely bears some similarity to the ways an audience attends to pop song lyrics generally: some listen closely, many casually, and some not at all. Although some scholars have found that few people remember a song's lyrics,[5] one often finds that, in concerts especially, fans can recite considerable portions of the words. (I find it interesting that a small proportion of my students persist in claiming that their primary focus remains on the words, but the rest of us often find our attention wandering from them.) It is true also that a viewer's attention shifts within each song and from song to song; with images and without, the words can come to the fore and then recede. In general, however, words work less directly in music videos. If the song's lyrics are opaque or enigmatic, the video makes us experience them through a mirror even more darkly; the words appear as fragments, the most foregrounded words seem simultaneously near and far, and others inaccessible.

Two videos by Alanis Morissette will show that lyrics can be experienced differently in different videos, and that they tend to become more opaque in videos than in songs. The first example is "Ironic," which seems at first to be an instance in which lyrics come to the fore. For most of the video, the camera is placed in the front passenger seat, eyeing Morissette as she drives a junky car along a snow-covered highway. That the singer wears mittens and places a cup of coffee beside her gives the video a sense of intimacy. Because she occasionally looks sleepy, we may feel obliged to help keep her awake. The song bears so close a resemblance to chitchat (being about funny things that have happened to her and to the people she has met), and our role as guardian is so familiar, that we are disposed to feel a connection to the music. The singing is clear and the lyrics close at hand, but how much does a viewer actually attend to the words? Perhaps we are only drawing on the pleasures of sitting next to a good storyteller, with the low-key responsibilities of a companion. Here, we are interpolated into a familiar role, but the words no longer fit the old context. Written with wit as well as flow and rhyme—"a man who has too many spoons but no wife"—the narrative of the song may be crucial, but the delivery comes too quickly or slowly. Despite this presumed relevance to the singer, which is argued for visually throughout the video, a gloss seems to exist on the video's surface: just as its images and musical flow cast a spell, its words become distanced, vague, and extraneous. Does the viewer string the fragmented text into a coherent line? And can the words be replaced by others, say, an homage to Milk Duds or *Mr. Rogers' Neighborhood?* What matters here is the *perceived* availability of the lyrics.

While the lyrics for Morissette's "Ironic" seem at once close at hand and opaque, those for "You Ought to Know," similarly crucial, are almost impossible to follow. The second video looks heavily processed, in terms of both color and grain. Morissette's singing is throaty and garbled, the musical accompaniment raucous and grainy, and the soft Super-8 footage of the setting—most often of her wandering in the desert with a suitcase—bears only remotely on the lyrics and encourages little curiosity about a possible narrative. The difficulties of extracting textual meaning from unlinked, opaque layers encourage viewers to shift their focus toward primary functions like contour, movement, and color instead. Though the lyrics are racy—students who can recite them most likely garnered them from the CD booklet rather than the CD or the music video—and phrases like "you ought to know" and "since you went away and left me" occasionally come to the fore, it is hard to make out anything else, nor is there any point in trying. The lyrics may impel focused listening, but as a part of the video they require so much of the viewer's attention that they become inaccessible and impotent.

"Ironic" serves as a limit case for how inaccessible lyrics can become once they are heard as music television. Listening to the lyrics of a song alone is difficult enough—to develop a trademark style yet fit within a genre's performance practices, a singer will often garble her words. Words also become less accessible as the vocal line becomes musical. Pop singers modulate their performance through numerous means, such as changing volume and tempo, shifting the points of stress employed in ordinary diction, and adding timbral inflections. These touches serve to mimic and even speak against other instrumental lines in the musical texture. While watching music video, we may have trouble following the words simply because of poor television speakers. Music-video directors, most likely in an attempt to sell the song, appeal to both those listeners who are musically inclined and those who hear words first: they refuse to locate our attention in any one place. The image shifts rapidly, in part to match the energy, emotional intensity, and semiotic richness of the song.

There are rare instances when music-video lyrics are clearer than those of the song alone. I can think of one example. In Sinead O'Connor's "Nothing Compares 2 U," the singer's vocal performance is tinged with an Irish dialect, and her voice is flanged and reverbed, making the words inaccessible to most U.S. listeners; however, the video showcases the singer's large, sad, almond-shaped eyes; pale, trembling lips; and shaved head, which emerges from a limitless black background. The simplicity and emotional urgency of the image focuses our attention on the words.

A SONG AS A PREEXISTING MULTIMEDIA TEXT

Lyrics wrestle with music and image for a claim to the foreground. But we should note that even before the advent of music video, music and text formed an interdependent and frequently volatile multimedia work. The types of relation possible between music and lyrics are of interest to numerous scholars, with some contending for mutuality—for taking up what the other cannot do—and others arguing for transformation, engulfment, or antagonism.[6] According to Lawrence Kramer, text and music can coexist, but the problem of bridging the two disparate media never disappears. Text and music wear each other down in a song because, although music and lyrics have points of connection—music has a syntagmatic aspect, and words have a musical side—the difference in media remains too great. Each medium has too many of its own particular properties to meld fully with another. In addition, words and music will always have different cultural resonances, and as Kramer points out in *Music and Poetry,* each undercuts or eats away at the other's authority. Think of Bob Dylan's "Like a Rolling Stone" or Lesley Gore's "Look of Love." In both songs, the lyrics' focus might be described as depressing, yet the choruses are unquestionably upbeat, and the viewer may need to make up a complicated story that requires identification with the narrator and the subject of the song.

This uncertainty of perspective is writ large in music video. The music video functions simultaneously on various levels: lyrics and accompaniment suggest one vantage point, lyrics and image another, and the image and song a third, with a gap in meaning needing to be broached by the viewer. In The Cardigans' "Love Fool," the lyrics, following a short, simple pattern, assert over and over "love me, love me, say that you love me," yet the arrangement and vocals resemble a Tin Pan Alley tune played through an old radio, and they lack weight. The video, on the contrary, heads off in numerous directions, sometimes sporting a nautical theme. The image nods to the music with scuba divers holding old cameras, and then to the lyrics, undermining them with clichéd imagery of a message in a bottle bobbing on the surface of the water—are the scuba divers supposed to recover the bottle?—and *then* to the director's visual fancy or his need to showcase the star, presenting the lead singer against a soft focus background, suggestive of a fairytale setting.

Kobena Mercer's analysis of Michael Jackson's "Thriller" is a second case in point.[7] Mercer explains how various elements in the music video create a complicated portrait. Jackson's falsetto hoots and hollers and the funky bass line convey sexuality, the lyrics suggest menace, while Vincent Price's voice-over is pure camp. The viewer's attention vacillates among all three media. After each long visual section and musical vamp, Jackson's date finds herself at the turn of a path with the chameleon Jackson possibly giving her a sexy kiss, the touch of death, or a launch into a Broadway-musical dance sequence. Music and lyrics are often at odds: there will always be a moment, perhaps once the voice stops singing, when the music suggests, "no, you love him more than that" or "you should have your mind on other things." The music-video image often offers an additional suggestion the song does not consider.

Yet one can also say that lyrics are well suited to music because each medium takes on what the other cannot; the problem of overcoming the gap between music and text resembles that of music, image, and lyrics in music video, and suggests that a song (lyrics and music) is a preexisting form of multimedia. To understand how image and lyrics can fill in for what music cannot do, we need first to consider music's capacity for representation. The question of how much and in what ways music can depict things has a long history. On one side are strong claims that music possesses its own language or internal coherence, that it does not need to maintain connections with the world.[8] By this definition, music is "only for itself." Few take up the diametrically opposite side of the argument: that music describes things in the world such as chairs, tables, or full-fledged stories with characters and plots the way language and pictures can. Between these two poles most theorists maintain a middle position; they would allow that, in a trivial sense, music can represent mechanical and natural sounds such as trains and birds.[9] They would also acknowledge the possibility of word painting: stylized depictions of specific textual elements such as laughing or crying. Occasionally, the composer even uses music, lyrics, and the listener's previous understanding of a context to suggest a character and setting— for instance, Bach's G-minor Mass, in which a descending melody is suggestive of sinners descending into hell. Some scholars have argued the power of music to represent social organization through an iconic resemblance. Hip-hop, for example, with its horizontal organization and call-and-response among parts, suggests a communally based, African American social structure. Western classical and romantic art music, by contrast—emphasizing large-scale structure, novelistic design, and massive physical spaces—suggests a unified bourgeois subject.

Apart from these limited representations of natural and mechanical sounds, stylized affects, characters in specialized contexts, and social structures, music has been thought to represent physical processes of motion, chaos, balance, weight and height, continuity, succession, motivation, and impulsion. Some theorists have claimed that music can mimic the ways that feelings ebb and flow.[10] Music can express emotion, but only in an ill-defined way. For example, when we hear music, we may have difficulty deciding whether it is truly happy or sad, or exactly what kind of happiness or sadness the music suggests. There are those for whom music describes such finely nuanced colors of emotion that language cannot name it, while others hold that music conveys only the gross emotions without the nuance. Most agree that music cannot represent emotions that must take specific objects such as is the case with envy or pride.

Given these limitations, it remains for lyrics and images to define the social organization whose basic contours the music traces, or the object whose weight, size, or affect the music suggests. When image is added to a song as the third term, the subject becomes clearer in many ways—we know more about what kind of people own this music, where it should be played, and how it might be used—yet new layers of ambiguity are also added: who are these characters, why do they do the things they do, where had they been before the video began and where will they go after it has ended? Why is this so? Roland Barthes has argued that in a relation between textual captions and photographs, each element works to constrain meaning.[11] Hollywood film features a bundle of three media—sound, image, and text—and each, in general, serves to promote clarity and a narrative end. With music video, however, we seem to be dealing with a much higher degree of uncertainty.

Perhaps music video keeps all three terms ambiguous because videos need to sell the song. For listeners to want to buy the song, they need to learn its attractive features. Embedding a conundrum, problem, or confusing detail that cannot be resolved is a good way for directors to encourage the repeated viewings frequently needed for such learning. Other ambiguous features of music video—the short form, nonnarrative structure, and busy interaction among elements—support a space where the ambiguity of text can be explored. Pop-song lyrics typically fail fully to specify what their music suggests. For example, we rarely know whether the singer is singing to us, to a particular hypothetical person, or to himself. The lyrics might be subbed in by others: "If I were only your woman" could be interchanged with "I would like to rest awhile under a tree." Music-video directors keep this vagueness in play; with schematic sets and blank human figures rather than what we would call characters, they usually opt to keep the musical and verbal connotations open, especially when they are at odds.

Whatever role lyrics, music, and image play in a music video, it is important to remember that the lyrics' functions can shift over the course of the video to encompass a number of relations with the other media. According to Richard Middleton, lyrics can be shaped to music in three ways: (1) Words can function as expressive objects. They merge with the melody and the voice generates feeling—for example, in ballads. (2) Words can adopt a narrative function. They govern the rhythmic and harmonic flow, and the voice generates speech— as in rap or in Bob Dylan's early work. (3) Words can act like sounds. Music absorbs those words that function as musical effects and as rhymes, and the voice becomes an instrument. Examples are nonsense language ("awopbopa-loobop alopbamboom") and the organization of inconsequential verbal phrases into rhyming musical parallelisms ("Rock to the east, rock to the west, she's the girl that I love best"; "Got a girl, her name's Daisy, she almost drives me crazy").[12] Here, depending on their function, lyrics can draw attention to musical parameters such as phrase, rhythm, and timbre.

In music video, not only lyrics but also image and music shift roles. There are moments when the music seems like pure timbre and flow, when it evokes a sentiment or crystallizes into a style. The image, too, can suggest color and form, evoke an emotion, or refer to a style or a period. If all three media shift rapidly, we can have a very complex texture. In addition, lyrics are transformed in the process of responding to the music. Antoine Hennion discusses the ways that the hook of a song takes on strange features within the song's context: "Certain key words . . . [that] function as pure signifiers . . . are selected for the way they ring, for the expressive power [that] gives them their opacity; they have to engage the imagination of the listener, and at the same time effect a sort of disengagement from the everyday words of the text, so that the role of dream can be given full play. These unexpected metaphorical turns of phrase interrupt the unfolding of the text, giving one a shiver of pleasure, in a way very similar to the effect of the musical gimmick."[13]

As in songs alone, a word or part of a phrase in a video will break apart from the texture and carry an unforgettable, chimerical charm. Such moments include Jay-Z singing "hah hah" alongside the fragments from Foxy Brown's extended wordplay "menanies, nine eyes, ballies and mammies" in "Ain't No Nigger like the One I Got"; Salt of Salt-N-Pepa rapping "Can I have a scoop? Let me take a ride in the coupe" in "Shoop"; Snoop Doggy Dogg's "One, eight, seven, undercover" in "What's My Name?"; Madonna's "Let's get unconscious," from "Bedtime Stories"; Onyx's "slam" from the song of the same title; and Janet Jackson's scat singing of "da da da" in "That's the Way Love Goes." These fragments of music-video lyrics differ from those of songs alone in that they are extremely short, even shorter than a hook line from a song or a commercial jingle; the fragment is attractive not just for the sound but for the way the artist performs it. These moments confirm the notion that the quantity of lyrics that can be remembered from a music video is very small, no more than a few words. Two factors—the unceasing momentum of music and image, along with the way the image directs our attention to many different features within the video—serve to fragment the lyrics; by creating a pocket where a word momentarily comes to the fore, the videos link such a moment to other isolated moments that occur earlier or later in the video, but are now set off in time and space. Insofar as lyrics fail to sustain continuity, they are functionally no more important than a dance step or the close-up of the star, and the casual viewer finds that what has made these words attractive remains out of reach.[14]

I have just argued that in music video, the lyrics' thread becomes broken. Yet its fragments can also take on new power and emphasis. Any word carries a constellation of affective qualities: "claim," "surrender," "soil," and "star" all possess different colors of mood. Both songs and music videos reaffirm old and claim new territory for words. In Aerosmith's music video "Jaded," each medium—music, image, and text—contributes to a shared pool of attributes: the word "jaded" gives a sense of decadence, ennui, and sexuality; the southern rock inflections connote music possessing power, headiness, male authority, and transgression; the image lends brightness, play, and perhaps something naughty. These attributes mingle, transforming the meanings of music, image, and lyrics respectively. The sonic qualities of the word "jaded" itself chips in. The "*j*" suggests something hip, swinging, and African American—jingle, juke joint, jazz. The long "*a*" suggests freedom of movement and space—*day, may, hay, play, say,* and *way* (a vowel frequently used for melismatic elongation in a song's hook line). Another word, like "faded" or "icy," would not contribute quite the same colors.

In general, the sporadic application of images to lyrics may derive from the impossibility of representing any large amount of the lyrics directly. When pop lyrics employ generalities of the type "You Are My Everything," or "I Only Want to Be with You," any one-to-one mapping between word and visual reference cannot help but be a visual cliché. Images following lyrics that describe a series of particular events or items may be so disparate that the video will lack a unified tone. The Fugees' song "Ready or Not," for example, has lines that seem almost impossible to connect: "I'll be Nina Simone and defecating on your microphone," "Guantanamo Bay," "My girl pinched my hips to see if I still exist," and "Rap orgies with Porgie and Bess," "I wanna play with pelicans from here to Baghdad." Rather than regarding lyrics as the primary determinant, most directors respond to them quite flexibly, using them as only one source of inspiration among many, relying just as much on the sounds of the music, the album cover, the name of the band, conversations with the artists, and the appearance, temperament, and image of the artists themselves. When lyrics are used to shape the image, it is often that a single line is drawn from the deepest recesses of the verse, as in Dido's "Thank You," in which the line, "And even if my house falls down now, I wouldn't have a clue" shapes the video's theme: a wrecking crew comes and destroys Dido's house as she looks on.[15]

LYRICS AS FORMAL ELEMENTS: THE HOOK

Before considering the entirety of a song's lyrics, we should examine its hook line, whose functions are distinctly different from those of the remaining words. More likely to be reflected in the image, the hook line often states a generalized truth or a crystallized point of view. (Examples include "You Mean the World to Me" and "Don't Go Chasing Waterfalls.") Because the hook line is placed in relief—set off both verbally and musically—its importance is already underscored. A literal visual setting of this musical and visual hook becomes an easy way to make both the song and the video memorable and therefore marketable.

Hook lines that describe simple physical actions like "Everybody Dance Now," "Jump," "Scream," "Freak Me," or "On Bended Knee" are most commonly set explicitly in music videos. Even in these cases, however, we do not know how high a person might jump or how loud she might scream or when and why she might choose to do so. Some of the play comes from the questions the video poses: "When is everyone dancing?" What does "on bended knee" mean? Is it more or less than a physical enactment? Ludwig Wittgenstein, J. L. Austin, and other philosophers have claimed that many of our words are understood contextually. Austin describes how word like "real" can mean different things depending on in what context it is used: "Other members of this group, on the affirmative side, are, for example, 'proper,' 'genuine,' 'live,' 'true,' 'authentic,' 'natural'; and on the negative side, 'artificial,' 'fake,' 'false,' 'bogus,' 'makeshift,' 'dummy,' 'synthetic,' 'toy'—and such nouns such as 'dream,' 'illusion,' 'mirage,' 'hallucination' belong here as well."[16] In the case of a song in which there are so few words to constrain one another, interpretation is wide open.

While simple hook lines can receive straightforward visual realizations, those that express complex thoughts, feelings, or relations (such as those in "You Don't Know How It Feels to Be Real," "Losing My Religion," or "Devil's Haircut in My Mind") are rarely depicted literally. Such verbal precision may tax music video's capacity for representation. Like dance, music videos do not readily signify relationships that are a product more of language and culture than of nature; lacking the visual symbols to accompany them, dance and music cannot be expected to render concepts such as "mother-in-law" or "deceased elder brother." In music video, the devices used to point to these cultural concepts can be quite oblique and can take the whole of the video to unfold. For example, toward the close of Beck's "Devil's Haircut in My Mind," we discover that secret agents may be stalking the singer, but that only he can perceive this; the stalking occurs in another temporal domain, outside the perception of most of the people on the street, and it takes a long time to guess that these images are his private obsession. (The video is homage to *La Jetée*, by Chris Marker.)

The lyrics for R.E.M.'s "Losing My Religion" deal with either a loss of faith or of a homosexual romance. Either or both would be hard to realize in music-video, so the director takes a different tack, illustrating the gap between a rural man and great works of art. For most viewers, the meaning of these images— why they have been modified or juxtaposed—remains unclear. However, one can sense that the artworks take on a weight similar to that which cannot be shown or spoken about, and so can serve as a proxy for the video's serious subjects.

A large number of videos paint their visual world much larger than the hook line implies, thereby claiming a greater authority for the music and image and, in the process, complicating the relations among the three media: in "Come to My Window," by Melissa Etheridge, the window pane becomes the largest object in the set, dwarfing both a house and the female figure; in Janet Jackson's "Runaway," Jackson literally runs around the world; in Ozzy Osbourne's "No More Tears," the room fills with water; in TLC's "Waterfalls," water stretches as far as the eye can see; in Madonna's "Take a Bow," a cape cascades through the frame, while the matador bends forward from the hips with his arm raised before him. His gesture seems to be one of the most theatrical in Western culture.

With a paucity of means to construct a thick narrative context, music-video directors frequently attempt to provide satisfactory results through other means. To create a sense of drama, they place the image in an abject relation to the hook line—we note the disjunction between image and lyrics and wait to see whether a character's lack can be filled. In her "Private Dancer," Tina Turner works as a paid companion. In Lenny Kravitz's "Again," the philandering singer never gets the woman of upright virtue, even though he earnestly sings the hook line "All of my life where have you been? I wonder if I'll ever see you again." In Travis's "Laugh," the lead singer exhorts the main character in the story, a woman of the British upper crust, to let loose, singing "laugh, laugh";

however, she seems too enmeshed in her social role to benefit much from his encouragement.

Some visual settings for hook lines take the metaphorical possibilities of the text and extend them to remarkable lengths, as in David Bowie's "Let's Dance." Here the term *dancing* describes the encounter between two cultures—white and aboriginal—in Australia. In Ginuwine's "What's So Different," the director hijacks the lyrics about creeping on a boyfriend to develop a critique of the alienation of blue- and white-collar labor. Some videos disregard the words altogether. Hootie and the Blowfish's "I Only Wanna Be with You" includes lyrics of heterosexual courtship ("wear my ring"), but the band goes out and plays basketball and golf without much of a homosocial or homoerotic payoff. (Similarly, U2's "With or Without You" and Oasis' "Wonderwall" are homages to a lover, but the final sense of the videos is with or without the band.)

The lyrics can pique listeners' curiosity, encouraging them to seek out additional information in the music and image. In Jackson's "Runaway," the hook line ("The only thing missing was you") invites viewers to search for a missing lover among the people she meets, as well as to attend to a musical texture that borrows from other musical cultures. In fact, any video that makes mention of a lover prompts the viewer to look through the image and await that person's arrival. Words that suggest activities viewers can participate in—such as looking for or listening to lost objects—encourage them to respond similarly. For example, the hook line "looking for Mercy St." in Peter Gabriel's "Mercy St." video is our cue to search for some landmark as we move across the city and then pass over the water in a boat. In Creed's "Higher," the viewer may wonder how far the video can extend, judging from limited visual effects such as a 360-degree swish pan with figures frozen in midair and huge over-the-head crane shots. Lyrics can direct our attention within and/or out of the frame.

Repetitions of the hook line draw our attention to repetitions in the music or the image. In George Michael's "Freedom," every time the hook line "freedom" appears, an object—coat, guitar case, or jukebox—blows up or bursts into flames, and a cymbal crash comes to the fore along with a short piano motif. From this and other examples, it is obvious that there exists an enormous variety of connections between hook line and music. There is no set distance between lyrics and other media, and relationships can change over time. Part of the challenge of hook lines in music video lies in the degree to which these few words extend into the rest of the video—does the hook influence the bridge or the verse, and to what extent? When George Michael sings about freedom, is he referring to everything that occurs in the video or only the pyrotechnics?

LYRICS AS FORMAL ELEMENTS: THE BODY OF THE TEXT

The foregoing discussion has illustrated how the hook line can have a powerful influence over a music video—a range of whose boundaries we are unsure about. But the rest of the lyrics are typically not rendered so faithfully. Because the lyrics provide more material than a video can include, most of the text is left behind. Most often, the connections among word, music and text are one-to-one—an image, a sound, and a few words that separate themselves from the rest of the video. When one-to-one connections occur, they do *not* have to be temporally contiguous. (An image might link to a phrase or to a melodic fragment that occurred much earlier or later.) Most commonly, however, the joined elements are simultaneous or adjacent. When these elements are slightly offset, rhythmic sophistication, ambiguous meaning, and questions of cause and effect can come into play. These elements form simple blocklike structures, glacial entities yoked together with slender threads that might otherwise slip apart and head off on their own way. In Vanilla Ice's "Ice, Ice Baby," the rapper sings the hook line "ice, ice, baby," and a moment later we see a young, attractive woman licking an ice cream cone. The video presents an example wherein lyrics correspond to an image that lags behind it. Even with this temporal displacement, the two elements remain connected.

Lyrics that have a tangential or poetic connection to image and music tend to stand out. In Bush's "Swallowed," the performer sings "fishhook, you're the wave" as he walks down an aisle surrounded by elderly businessmen; the executives are brought in and out of focus continually, almost as if they were in the process of being transported onto the starship *Enterprise.* Enigmatic connections between text and image can encourage the viewer to search through the frame to uncover the meaning of the text; they also encourage consideration of the image in relation to the audio track. In this video, the viewer is encouraged to search for a sound.

Yet lyrics can also be set boldly. A name provides a way for a prop, location, character, figure, or sound to take on a greater sense of definition. Among the most powerful one-to-one relations between word and image are those of places and proper names: Ireland, Tennessee, or Brooklyn; "Dear *Mamma*" or "Luka." When lyrics are denotative, the realization is likely to be more profound than crude because any word suggests many possibilities; any visual setting is only one in an infinity of realizations.

The lyrics can foreshadow activity in the music and image, or provide the context for what has already occurred. In Metallica's "Enter Sandman," James Hetfield sings the words "off to never never land." Next, the guitar solo comes forward and proposes a musical equivalent, sweeping the viewer along into another section of the video—and another nightmare. Conversely, the lyrics may enter last, describing earlier events, as in No Doubt's "Spider Web," which changes from major to minor at the bridge. The image shifts almost immediately thereafter from a stately wedding banquet, shot in color, to a hailstorm of flying telephones that attack the guests, shot in black and white. The line "my dreams become nightmares" thereby frames the foregoing musical and visual events as a function of the singer's fantasies. Not only lyrics but also narrative or graphic elements seem to exist in flux, crystallize momentarily, and then flare out again.

Similarly, lyrics may echo one or two images that occurred earlier, or they may point to images that will appear later in the video. At the outset of Madonna's "Take a Bow," both the star and her lover lay out their clothing for the day. Gingerly, Madonna pulls her glove up above the elbow, while the lover's glove remains on the table. Halfway into the video, Madonna sings the words "all the world loves a clown," while the lover wears a fatuous expression. He holds his gloves and we now know what he is made of and who owns whom. After a beginning that shows the long preparation for a bullfight as well as a seduction, the story of possession and fame comes into focus.

A literal depiction of a phrase in the lyrics might well give the viewer a sense of being drawn momentarily into the video, even pasted against it. An example is "Crash into Me," in which Dave Matthews sings, "Hike up your skirt a little more," and we see twin geishas slowly pulling up their dresses. In such cases, the moments of synchronization among music, image, and lyrics begin to form a pattern that complement patterns in single domains. The videomaker may have set a number of patterns in motion. For example, there may be sequences in which the rhythm of the song is predominant: the lead performer articulates the beat through one part of the body (hand, foot, torso, or head) or many figures bob up and down in the frame, while at other times rhythmic features are of less concern. Or there may be periods when the performer's face appears in close-up and points when the camera centers on scenery and figures in the background. Sometimes the lyrics acquire the greatest importance—and they will come to the fore, fade away and then move in again. Each one of these elements—rhythm, close-ups, lyrics—as well as parameters such as timbre, harmony, and camera placement and movement become individual threads that comprise the weave of the video.

Images can do much to widen the interpretive possibilities of the lyrics. When, in "Take a Bow," Madonna sings "I've always been in love with you," she appears to be sometimes adolescent, sometimes middle-aged. It is not clear whether we should take the song's lyrics literally or figuratively, as embodying a lasting affection, as separate parts of Madonna's psyche, or as the exaggerated claims of a groupie. When Madonna sings "do you feel it" and pricks herself with a needle, her relation to the matador becomes more ambiguous rather than less so. Another example, Nine Inch Nails' "Closer," shows that each of the three media can be so opaque as to create meaning only when placed in a metaphorical relation with the others. Here, an aggressive male sexuality is generated from a combination of studio-based music using industrial-sounding samples and images of salamanders and eels plus the line "I want to feel you from the inside." Remove one component and the meaning of the video disappears.

Music, camera, and lyrics work in tandem to create some of the most striking moments in music video. The first chorus in Lisa Loeb's "Stay" begins with the singer's multitracked voice rising in pitch and dynamics. At the same time, the camera tracks away from the artist while she sings lyrics like "distance" and "I'm only here in negative." The three media together suggest a mixed message of closeness and distance—a message appropriate to the video's theme: the singer's ambivalence toward a difficult lover.

Lyrics can converse with other musical materials—the lyrics can subdue other elements within the musical texture or force them to listen, instruments can seem to encourage the lyrics to adopt one direction over another. In her "All about Our Love," Sade repeatedly sings, "After all this time, after all is said and done, it's all about our love." Toward the end of the second verse, she claims, "We have seen some suffering baby. It has not always been perfect." A masculine guitar solo moves forward in the texture, and seems to compel her to reconsider and sing "Darling, we know it. Whatever may come, we can get through it as if it's just begun." Madonna, in the "Don't Tell Me" video, also sounds distressed, singing "Don't tell me to stop. Tell the rain not to drop. Tell the wind not to blow. 'Cause he said so. Tell the sun not to shine, not to get up this time." The consistent string arrangement that weighs heavily at the top of the arrangement suggests a sense of equilibrium and resignation in the face of a loss that the singer does not possess. If the singer cannot be comforted by this instrumental line, other parts of the arrangement and the video image take up the slack and offer solace: the multitracking of the voice and a small vocoder line that comes in toward the end of the song lends the singer greater solidity. Two-thirds into the video, two flanks of dancing cowboys and the lively mechanical horse Madonna rides give her some weight. The final shot of the video closes with a mythic rodeo cowboy falling off his horse as the graceful strings descend. This contemporary Icarus and string section suggest that courage and patience are available on an earthly plane. Whether or not the singer will assimilate these cues remains uncertain; nevertheless, we sense that she and we can surmount our travails through commonplace perseverance.

Lyrics that are acted out through the bodies of the performers warrant special attention. As with all other music video parameters, there are many possible relations between gestures and sounds, including one-to-one connections, obfuscation, and a stance of complete disregard. A star's saying "I feel love" as a hand moves across her chest and pats the place over her heart (as in Britney Spears's "Oops, I Did It Again") would constitute a rather literal relation. A looser relation is seen in Keith Sweat's "Twisted," in which the lyrics ask a woman to lie down, and the video shows a woman sitting down on a couch. As an example of lyrics being purposely ignored or obscured, one might point to Tboz's holding up four fingers as she sings the number three in "Creep." Yet even when lyrics are set—for example, Da Brat's dropping bills from a car as she sings "I've got five G's"—the relations still seem tangential or accidental. This is partly because the world of the lyrics will always be slightly removed from that of the images. The lyrics exist in another type of space and time; nevertheless, the markers of their origin—different from those of music and image—still exist somewhere in the music video.

Lyrics can appear to gain magical properties in music video. I would like to return to Hennion's suggestion that lyrics shimmer. Videos allow them to exert a special influence on music and image. For example, in "Don't Tell Me," Madonna sings "pull the black off the crow." Earlier images had featured black: a truck rolled behind her, blowing black smoke; later she smears fistfuls of brown sand on her black pants. Her blonde hair is streaked with deep brown, and she sports a brown and beige raccoon tail. As the video progresses, the sky and mountains behind her become lighter. Madonna's invocation seems to encourage her and the setting to strip themselves of their blacks so that both can move toward a more joyful plane. Music theorists, including Nicholas Cook, have written extensively about the ways that music's open-endedness affords listeners an opportunity to place their own associations and readings upon the music.[17] Music-video lyrics may work similarly.

In Sheryl Crow's "Every Day Is a Winding Road," the lyrics exist in an enigmatic relationship to the music and image and take on greater weight as the video progresses: when Crow sings "every day is a winding road," she rides down a curving slide in a playground; when she sings the title phrase of the song, she approaches an anonymous person on the street, and her face is reflected in his sunglasses; when she sings "why I'm a stranger in my on life," she sits on an abandoned couch in an alley; when finally she sings "I've been swimming in a sea of anarchy," the alley turns watery. Here the periodic elliptical connection between image and lyrics forms a pattern, and it seems as if Crow's lyrics and music have the power to create images from her dreamscape. It is almost as though the lyrics change the image into the transfigured state of poetry. (These transformations are mysterious: for no apparent cause, a bottle of liquid soap sitting on a windowsill tips over, the soap hits the jet stream of the fan, and the alley fills with bubbles. In this magical world, words and music can serve as causal agents.)

"Every Day Is a Winding Road" exhibits a phenomenon common in music video—lyrics becoming so tangential that they break away from the flow of image and text to create a momentary musical and visual pun. In Aerosmith's "Crazy," Steven Tyler sings "I'll pull down the shades." In the context of the song's lyrics, this line suggests lowering a window shade, but in the video the female star playfully mugs by raising a pair of novelty sunglasses over her eyebrows instead. In the Cars' "You Might Think," Ric Ocasek sings "hanging around with you," and in the video, he transforms into a clothes hanger. In Madonna's "Ray of Light," she sings "she's got a silver universe, she's falling," and when the word "silver" occurs, the image picks up the gray color—we see asphalt or chrome. (If she sang, "she's got a golden universe," we might see golden imagery; in a blue universe, we might see something different again.)

The connections between music and image can be so fragile that we wonder how they work: does a lyric lie below our level of reflection, does it register at all, or is it only the private realization of a director who has listened to the song many more times than we? In Jamiroquai's "Virtual Insanity," the lead singer dances in a cold, metallic, boxlike room. A glance at the lyric sheet might lead to the conclusion that the line "we all live underground" has suggested a bomb shelter. Many of the visual clues, however, such as the singer's Dr. Seuss hat and prancing step, the ready-for-sale plastic covered furniture that slides along a conveyer belt, a centipede and a crow, create other possibilities. Surely, an earlier mention of test-tube babies is so far from the video's final image of blood seeping along the floor that any definitive connection is difficult to make. Perhaps this is only another non sequitur—the dye serves to create a sense of drama at the end of the video, an incitement to watch the video again.

Examining the lyric sheet can be a useful technique for understanding a music video.[18] Kobena Mercer has mentioned that music videos are crypto-grams; they seem to possess some buried secret.[19] A consideration of the lyrics does not solve the mystery. Rather, the now-heard text presents a hovering trace of what the director left behind or could not include. Perhaps we can now understand a bit more why some of the images that we see are there, but we also have one more tale of absence, one more shadowy aspect of the music video. This missing element is similar to the unanswerable questions about supporting characters—are they actors, models, or friends of the band? It can affect us like questions concerning the production—did anyone really intend that eighties drum sample, mixed in so prominently against that scratchy acoustic guitar?

The description I have provided of music video lyrics thus far—fragmentary and elliptical—holds true for many of the ways that music videos respond to the large-scale unfolding of song lyrics. Occasionally there is a culmination that coincides with the lyrics. The visual denouement usually occurs before or after the denouement of the text. In Pearl Jam's "Jeremy," the revelation comes when the video is over, with the child protagonist wielding a gun; Alicia Keys's "Fallin'" has the singer wave goodbye to her imprisoned lover only after the last chorus has trailed off. Our sense then is that the moment of truth in text and music lies buried earlier in the song, and we must turn back toward it. Sometimes both music and text reach points of fruition, but these moments are presented as separate processes on different tracks. In Smashing Pumpkins' "Tonight, Tonight," the lead singer sings about a lover and himself turning the world upside-down through a transfigured understanding of the present moment. The video depicts a Victorian couple watching a show of swimming mermaids and assorted sea creatures as flash pots go off.

Sometimes an ending can seem to be structured around condensation and displacement. In U2's "Beautiful Day," some of the most striking lyrics are in the third verse:

> See the world in green and blue
> See China right in front of you
> See the canyons broken by cloud
> See the tuna fleets clearing the sea out
> See the Bedouin fires at night
> See the oil fields at first light

See the bird with a leaf in her mouth
After the flood all the colours came out.

The imagery here is largely left aside, but the penultimate image of the video reveals the band playing on oriental rugs stretched out on a flight runway. It is hard to ascertain how much this image resonates with earlier text.

Music videos quickly communicate how closely the lyrics are tied to the music and image, and in what ways we should attend to them.[20] Yet even when a music video suggests an overarching vantage point, we may still find a range of types of multimedia relations. In Maxwell's "Fortunate," the hook line "fortunate to have you, girl, I'm so glad you're in my world" seeps over most of the video—he is clearly singing about a loved one. Some settings of lyrics are direct. Maxwell sings "I never felt a love so strong," and he straightens up and raises a fist overhead. Some are enigmatic. A close-up reveals nail polish dripping from a bottle, and the words are "never seen a waterfall so bright." By the end of the video, words and image have gone their own way. The woman seems to fade away, even as Maxwell keeps singing how fortunate he is to have her.

LYRICS, TIME, AND THE VIEWER'S ATTENTION

A song's lyrics may appear sporadically and influence a video unevenly, but they do much of the work of establishing a sense of time in a video. At one level, lyrics work on an equal plane with other media. Music, image, and lyrics seem both interdependent and independent in music video: while each exerts a shaping force upon the other, each also possesses its own arc or teleology. For example, if the lyrics state, "by the time I get to Memphis," we can surmise what might be involved. There are questions to answer, however: How far should we imagine into the future of the tape? The music might seem to be slinky and stealthy, to rush onward like a never-ceasing train, to come on with the explosive fury of a fireball, or to meander, trip, and fall. The image will cue us as well; but of the three elements, the image is often what slows momentum the most. Stuck in the space of what we see right before us, we stay put until the next cut. The phrase "by the time I get to Memphis" calls forth a meaning out of its own history within language, yet it also impresses on us by virtue of the voice's expressiveness, the song's rhythm arrangement, and by the expectation the image conveys of this not-yet-present city.

The rate at which the lyrics unfold, and the duration of time they describe—which are not the same thing, of course—also form important components in the video's creation of meaning. Sometimes the lyrics, even more than the music and the images, seem to suggest that something has already happened, when in fact it has not. In Metallica's "Unforgiven" and LL Cool J's "Doin' It," for example, the music and image press onward while the words take us back, thereby sending our attention in two directions. R.E.M.'s "Losing My Religion" works in the opposite fashion. The folk-tinged music and the log cabin suggest a retrospective view, though most of the lyrics are in the present tense. The confusing sense of temporality places us on uncertain ground, which makes sense because the video is "in code."

Yet even though the influence of lyrics spreads unevenly, they, more than other media, serve to ground us temporally. The silent image is often so bereft of information that we cannot tell whether it refers to past, present or future. A performer may walk through a doorway into a room in slo-mo, the camera cuts to a close-up, and the performer lowers his head. (A melancholy figure might imply the past tense, just as upbeat music might predict a turn toward the future, but we cannot be sure.) Although inferences about the experience of time can be drawn from music, specific durations and time frames are less certain. Often, we can discern past or future only by whether words possess an "-ed" suffix. Not uncommonly, lyrics, music, and image depict an event that happens as the tape unfolds, and we experience a sense of possibility, as if we were watching an expanding soap bubble. Whatever fragile creation the supernova in Soundgarden's "Blackhole Sun" might turn out to be, we feel it emerging into its own as we watch.

A video in which the image, music, and lyrics each adopt different senses of time is Aerosmith's "Janie's Got a Gun." In a tale of incest, the daughter guns down her father and is captured by police. The lyrics make it perfectly clear at the outset that the daughter, Janie, is a doomed heroine: "Janie's got a gun, dog's day just begun, whole world's come undone." Nevertheless, the music refuses to foreclose on the event, continuing to spin and gain momentum across song sections. When the verse begins, the music returns to equilibrium, but the mayhem of the chorus and bridge remain vibrant and unresolved, making any prospect of balance tenuous. The image waffles, denying the point of view of either the music or the words. At first there is a sense of great but ominous possibility: in the introduction, the band members, bathed in darkness, sing beautifully held tones, sounds that increase in dynamics as the lights shine with greater intensity. The verses begin in a pastoral mode, with a family on the grass enjoying a sunny day, and the father sitting before a window. At the close of sections, doom is the price for culmination: the police stand guard, suggesting that the video will arrive at a dead end. Only at the song's outchorus, as a cheesy synthesizer enters and we get musical closure, does the video provide an answer. (It has the unsatisfying resolution of a *Looney Tunes* cartoon— "That's All, Folks"—and the director, David Fincher, is subtle enough to use an overhead crane shot to pull out from the scene before the musical fillip begins.) In "Janie's Got a Gun," the image portends the end more quickly than the music does but more dimly than do the lyrics.

How do gender, ethnicity, genre, and era play into the role of lyrics? My sense is that whereas listeners do not attend to women when they speak, they take women seriously as singers. Perhaps it is because we assume that a woman sings for more than the pleasure of hanging out with the guys in the band. If a woman is going to take the trouble to sing, she has something to say. I have noticed that my African American students tend to listen more closely to lyrics than do my European American students. This may be, in part, because they find forms of media such as television and film less trustworthy. Some genres place greater weight on the lyrics. Rap music, with lyrics that are closer to speech, are more or less accessible based on the community of listeners. Some of my African American students can recite the complete lyrics to almost any rap tune that I can name. Those who are not in the practice of listening to rap music or are uninterested in the lyrics may hear little. R&B singers often make promises concerning a sexual or romantic commitment. These claims can give the words added power. Pop songs are famous for trite lyrics, and we might expect more literal and simple kinds of word/image treatments, different, perhaps, from the treatment for types of college rock that rock critics like. How much attention directors draw to lyrics may also have to do with where the genre is in its life cycle. When heavy metal attempts to reassert itself, there may be special claims visually or lyrically.

CONCLUSION

In this chapter, I have discussed the ways that lyrics fragment and shimmer, cast a narrow or wide net, and relate closely or distantly to music and image. Most commonly, the image does not follow the progress of the lyrics, nor does it respond with the same intensity at the lyrics' moment of culmination. More commonly, we see a ripple effect. As with lip-sync, the entrances of media are offset, released from relations of cause and effect: the lyrics are written as a response to the music; during the recording session, the musicians provide an answer to the lyrics; the video director adds his own interpretation; the editor adds touches as well. We are left with a sense of completion, but we do not know how we got here.

Music-video lyrics can take on an oracular function. They name and point, but they do not describe. Words seem to concretize into things. They separate from and hover over the music and image. Perhaps because lyrics are backed by such strong forces (a bed of music fit to their contours), they seem capable of *doing something*. Perhaps it is the craft within the lines themselves, the sense of poetry or verbal play, which makes them seem more about affect than meaning. Music and image seem to color words, and vice versa. Surely, in music video, words are changed.

8

Musical Parameters

ALMOST ANY musical feature can be reflected in the music-video image. The image often directs our attention to different musical elements one by one, like a tour guide. By the end of the song, the video has revealed many musical features. A single image can also underscore several musical parameters simultaneously. When music, image, and lyrics are placed in relation, questions of cause and effect arise—is the music generating the visual dimension, or does the image somehow transform the lyrics and the music? The people and objects depicted in videos seem to inhabit a strange world, somewhere between the real and the imaginary. Within this shadowy landscape, correspondences between song and image can become as solid as anything else. Music videos therefore seek to establish many sorts of connection among media. Through many examples, this chapter discusses the ways that videos respond to musical features.

MUSICAL MOTIVES AND HOOKS

When a musical figure stands out from its context in a song, a music video can draw attention to it in many ways. A song's hooks are most likely to receive emphasis, but any gesture or technique a song contains can become noticeable to the director, set designer, cinematographer, editor, or performer and be brought to the fore.[1] What traditional music theory calls a *motive*—a recognizable melodic/rhythmic shape—can gain meaning and distinctiveness through visual underscoring. Sometimes a strong image can work in tandem with a feature of the song to create a musical-visual hook. These can possess charm and power and seem to hold some secret about the tape. Pearl Jam's "Jeremy" begins with the image of a slab of burnished metal hanging before a luminous, red background, as we hear a guitar playing harmonics. The bell-like sound of the harmonics might suggest the ringing of a metal sheet, even though nothing touches the slab's surface. In cases like this, when the image does not disclose a sound's source, the viewer can be drawn into the tape as into a mystery. The absence of a sound's visual depiction lends greater authority to the song. Here, the slab makes a musical connection immediately, but its thematic function becomes clear only later. By the end of the tape, it rhymes with the image of a chalkboard, with life-size photographs that the protagonist, Jeremy, encounters in the forest, and with the window that encases a giant image of a closed eye. (The plucked harmonics continue to ring through these scenes.) We realize finally that the slab is not only a metallic surface but also a metaphor for Jeremy, who is written on by everyone yet remains locked within his own private world (fig. 8.1).

In "Jeremy," the music/image connection relies not only on their shared metallic quality but also on their simultaneity. A connection between a musical element and a visual one can be discerned even when the two do not occur in sync, however. Metallica's "Until It Bleeds" contains a recurring guitar melody that has a convoluted shape; within the frame are people and objects contorted into gnarled forms that sometimes remain shut and sometimes unwind. The repetition of these visual and musical materials tells the viewer that an isomorphic similarity exists between them.

A very small musical detail that is submerged in the mix in conjunction with a costuming touch can shape the meaning of a video. In Madonna's "Take a Bow," the star plays the role of a wealthy blonde who has a brief affair with a matador. In the bullring, her lover slays the bull, and in bed he ravishes her both physically and emotionally. The song contains a quiet bell-like pentatonic cluster that might be heard as Asian, and Madonna wears a kimono. Although the costume and melody echo Puccini's *Madame Butterfly*, the video inverts the opera's plot. "Take a Bow" depicts a foreigner who takes a lover in a strange country, yet here it is she who is ravished and left behind. Madonna, in her kimono and in a room empty of all but a single, bare light bulb, also echoes Glenn Close's role in *Fatal Attraction*, suggesting that the character is perhaps mad. Through subtle elements like the barely heard pentatonic motive and one costuming detail, allusions to colonialism, insanity, and tragedy complicate the video (see fig. 1.3).

Madonna's "Vogue" also demonstrates that a small musical detail combined

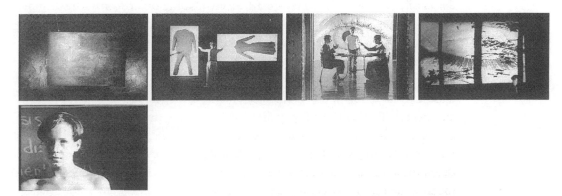

FIGURE 8.1 (A–E) Pearl Jam's "Jeremy." Visual and musical motives and the question of the sound's authority.

with a visual touch can help to define the music video's world. In the bridge, the camera tracks from right to left, and we see close-ups of the performer getting a beauty treatment. Augmenting the camera's movement, photographic flashbulbs are firing and trumpets hit a high note twice. The trumpets suggest the mechanism of a still camera going off, perhaps a foot or two behind the lens. Suddenly the viewer begins to construct a new diagetic space that encompasses both in front of and behind the camera: the sound/image relation assists the viewer in imagining a wider musical and visual terrain.

David Bowie's "Little Wonder" challenges our recognition of the kinds of sounds things make. A funny synthesizer glissando ascends; at the same time, a Bowie look-alike stirs his coffee with a spoon faster and faster until he pulls out an eye. The glissando seems to mimic the way that the spoon moves in tighter, more concentric circles. As the music becomes up-tempo—the drums start counting four on the floor—he jams himself into a crowded and speeding subway train. Sitting across from him are a number of strange characters, including a woman who holds something that looks rather like a baby. When its stuffed head falls off, the synthesizer makes a "beep-beep" sound, which is just the right cry for the baby doll.

A video that establishes greater momentum by focusing on the rhythm of the singer is No Doubt's "Sunday Morning." The video shows the band making a spaghetti lunch in a California bungalow, as singer Gwen Stefani chops onions to the beat. Whether because of the sound, her careless handling of the knife or her performerly exuberance, she nicks her finger and draws blood. The video begins to unravel; the music breaks into a much slower section, and the camera creates showy effects like simultaneous zooming in and tracking out.

In TLC's "Waterfalls," the snare drum on beat four is gated and played backward. This novel sound functions as a hook, and the song's texture thins out to showcase it. In the context of the video, this hook begins to suggest a spirit passing through space as well as to foreshadow ominous events, concepts that are difficult to render. In the former case, the camera speeds across the sky, and as it passes through a patch of clouds, it pairs with the ripping sound of the gated snare. (We assume that the sound describes the flight of the ghostly female stars.) In the latter case, the gated snare appears immediately before the death of two male characters—one from AIDS, the other from drug dealing. The viewer must make a judgment about the proximity of spirit and death because the two are linked through a common sound.

Bone Thugs-N-Harmony is a hip-hop group famous for incorporating a stutter. In "The First of the Month," the performers, blurred intermittently, appear to jump forward and fall back in time to the edits. The extent to which the camera flutters, shifts out of focus, jogs and reframes serves as an index of the performers' vocal nuances. In this video as well as in the Red Hot Chili Peppers' "Give It Away" and Shaggy's "Boombastic," the camera jerks or glides along the z-axis to emphasize the hook of each song: "boom," "give it away," or "f-f-f-first of the month," respectively.

A musical hook underscored by an image can carry weight within the context of a video's form. When such a moment occurs near a video's close, a viewer can often remember a related moment at the tape's beginning. In this way, music videos create structure and infuse a video with meaning. In Smashing Pumpkins "1979," a tiny vocal sample that sounds like "do-do-do" corresponds to the image of wheels turning—first, kids playing with a giant rolling tire, and soon after, the front wheels of a car as it turns a bend in the Hollywood Hills. This hook, which establishes a gentle, melancholy mood, marks where we are in the piece and helps to tell a story. The musical fragment returns toward the end of the song, and at this moment we see a car, at night, swerving to turn down a road in the distance. Although a lot has happened, the viewer can still remember the imagery and music from the beginning of the tape and may experience a sense of history and nostalgia. Another moment of connection between image and music is the "sssh" sound that accompanies the Slushie machine in the convenience store. The seemingly offhanded ways that the melodic materials are incorporated into the song fit nicely with the video's theme of the twilight of adolescence in suburbia.

It would be hard to explain how Bon Jovi's comical leaps in "Livin' on a Prayer" fit the song's main instrumental hook, a four-note bass riff played with a wah-wah pedal. The hook underscores the performers' physicality and allows for a joke on ethnicity and musical genre. The image and sound are humorous here partly because the sound is funky and these young men are decidedly white. The sound seems simultaneously risky and nostalgic, and the men, bouncing off the ground like Peter Pan, reveal a wish for a physicality and a freedom that they can only play at possessing. (Are the members of Bon Jovi funk's true heirs? I don't think so.) By contrast, Michael Jackson's spin alongside the bouncing balls in "Scream" is crisp and light, matching the twangy accompaniment, which has a shorter decay and sounds a bit more pointed. Jackson's movements, consonant with the motivic materials in his song, would not suit those of Bon Jovi.

THE MUSIC'S SENSE OF CONTINUITY

Musical time is not discrete, a song's past flows into its present and its present into the future.[2] Music derives its temporal flexibility in part through its continual change and momentum, even as it repeats itself. Richard Middleton has pointed to the repetition in pop music and how it might return us to some sort of pre-oedipal bliss.[3] How does the image relate to the music's continuity? One way is simply by repeating and varying a set of materials. This visual repetition, along with a moving camera, and rapid editing, creates a sense of visual continuity that matches the song's flow.

Videomakers often use a fixed set of materials throughout a tape to create continuity across frames. These visual connections match the frequent repetition of musical materials within the pop song. Peter Gabriel's "Shock the Monkey" includes both circular shapes (film reels, coins, and mannequin, animal, and human heads) and linear forms (Venetian blinds, slashes of light, and cages) as unifying elements. Madonna's "Like a Prayer" is peppered with crosses, while embedded in "Take a Bow" is imagery of the Virgin Mary.

Incubus's "Warning" features a postapocalyptic landscape where all of the people in a city suddenly disappear (the video may comment on 9/11). "Warning" makes use of repetition and variation—what might be called visual rhymes. This device is common in music video: it may complement the wealth of repetition across a song's many parameters. In "Warning," repetition and variation blend seamlessly into the visual texture: a chalkboard in the office space on which someone has drawn wispy shapes resembles the sky. There are also figures on a chalkboard in the classroom that resemble the office building and the sun. Chalk dust blows past the child/druid's bedroom window, and something similar to the obsessive notes pasted to her wall reappear tacked to the walls of the classroom. The spaces—the office, hallway, grocery store, church, and classroom—resemble the bus. We also see the rhyming of office workers, car drivers, and performers. Little druids even appear in the background (fig. 8.2).

CONTOUR

A melody's contour—the shape it traces as it rises and falls—often relates to movement within the frame.[4] "Take a Bow" presents images of the matador's

FIGURE 8.2 (A–J) Incubus's "Warning." Repetition and variation of visual material when placed against the music can create a visual rhyme.

pink cape swirling up and down in the bullring followed by Madonna's hand moving higher and lower as it caresses a television screen. These patterns trace the repeated melodic contour of the chorus. As our eyes travel toward the bottom of the frame, and as we approach the end of the melody we find ourselves led to Madonna's crotch. The question of who occupies the high point of the frame and the peak of the melodic line—matador or Madonna—corresponds to the ultimate question of who is on top. While Madonna peers down from her box seat during the bullfight (verse two), the matador is on top during sex in the second chorus; in addition, he has managed to seize control of a second musical parameter: the rhythm, particularly on downbeats. At the beginning of the video, Madonna has control of one element (the downbeat), and she both narrates the story and sings to the television set; by the third chorus, however, the matador has taken control—his head and sword fill the frame at the beginning of every measure. After her musical and visual domination, Madonna loses ground; she crouches dejectedly in the corner at the bottom of the stairs (fig. 8.3).

A relation between a moving line in the image and melodic contour can be established at a local level in subtle ways, as when Bono glances down in the video "One" while the melody drops a whole step. In Biggie Smalls's "Hypnotize," Puff Daddy falls to his knees as the phrase ends and the pitch descends. So important is this gesture that the camera jerks in and out to foreground it. Or a video may at first present an image of the performer in a still or withdrawn position and then show the body opening up. Thus Toni Braxton's "You Mean the World to Me" starts quietly with the protagonist sitting at the piano and then reclining by the pool. While the melody rises and the song builds, Braxton's body becomes more upright until, at the high point, she stands with her arms raised above her head. The same strategy is employed in "Unbreak My Heart": the melodic apex features Braxton standing with arms outstretched; the end of the phrase leaves her collapsed in a corridor.

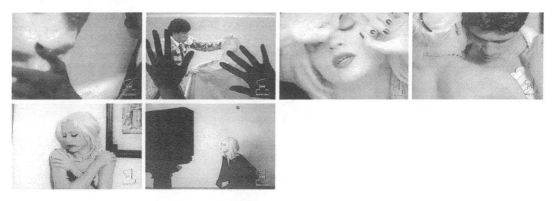

FIGURE 8.3 (A–F) Madonna's "Take a Bow." Movement and placement of objects within the frame follow musical contours. Power struggles between a man and a woman for the downbeat; Madonna no longer possesses beat one.

In a medium that does not employ many traditional narrative devices, the gradual disclosure of the body can create a sense of suspense. The first frame of "Vogue" shows a head shot of Madonna looking away, followed by a shot of her turning toward the camera, revealing more and more of her body. In an interview with me in spring 1998, David Fincher, the director, claimed that he started with a shot from the back so that he would have somewhere to build from. Videomakers exploit such techniques to build arch or A-B-A structures; they even make use of them when a video has little teleological drive. In "Bedtime Stories," Madonna begins recumbent on a white disk, then sits in a pool of water, stands before a larger pool of water, and finally, in a long tracking shot, floats down a hall. The slow disclosure of the body in order to articulate the song's form seems gender-driven; women's bodies are used more commonly in this manner than are men's.

Whitesnake's "Here I Go Again" places the lead singer's body against the song's melodic contour to express the struggle for power between the sexes. In the verses a woman climbs over the lead singer, who has his hands on the steering wheel of a car; she then goes out through the window and onto the hood. At the apex of the melody, the woman has made her way onto the car's roof; the lead singer is way ahead of her, however, performing on stage with phallic microphones lifted high overhead, exploding fireworks, and band members running along the crest of a steeply canted stage. In a comparable example, Van Halen's "Jump," singer David Lee Roth leaps when the word jump occurs, but his highest leap (lovingly shot in very slow motion) comes when the keyboard player ascends to the highest note of his solo, two octaves above the tonic.

Videos can also follow the contours of bass lines or inner voices. In "Scream," Janet Jackson raises an outstretched palm toward the camera and her fingers curl into a clenched fist: this gesture of her fingers rolling up draws our attention to the bass line's contour. The same is true in the Bell Biv DeVoe video, which presents the group raising their arms toward a passing woman's legs, having spied her from within an elevator shaft. Forms within the frame do not need to follow the song's contours exactly in order to establish a link between the music and image. In Toni Braxton's "Unbreak My Heart," the vocal line drops and then gradually rises to a peak before falling back. The image features a stark white background with graphic volumes that press forward from the recesses of the space: Braxton is shown in an elegant mansion with white walls surrounded by beautiful green and blue open spaces. She and her beau swim together, play Twister, and snuggle in the shower. The shapes that these intertwined figures form become a lilting visual line that rises and falls against the melody.

PHRASING

That images can support the shape of the song's phrases is borne out in U2's "With or Without You"; as phrases draw to a close, the image will fade to black, or a figure will become more still, or slip to the bottom of the frame. In some videos, at the highest peak of the melodic phrase, the camera, placed at a low angle, might reveal the star standing before a high vaulted ceiling (as in Tevin Campbell's "I'm Still in Love with You") or the performers wrapped in halos against the sky (as in New Edition's "I'm Still in Love with You"). At the peak of the phrases in the verses of Michael Jackson's "Earthsong," we see the protagonist before the silhouetted frame of an abandoned doorway, making us aware of a new sense of height.

Often the treatment of a verse or chorus is varied or repeated in such a way that the viewer comes to expect a pattern. For example, the most engaging part of the verse in TLC's "Waterfalls" is the conclusion: gradually the voice and guitar trail off to reveal an ominous gated and reversed snare. The first time we reach the verse's end, we encounter an image of death: the young drug dealer meets a bigger criminal eye to eye and is fatally shot in the chest. We expect a similar or even more dramatic build-up in the second verse, and we get it as a young couple practices unsafe sex. The young man turns from his lover to watch his approaching demise described poetically in rapidly changing photographs on the bureau; like Dorian Grey, his portrait fades out.

At the end of phrases in Michael Jackson's video for the film *Free Willy*, there is often a moment of friendly contact between whale and boy—a pat on the back, a quick piggyback whale ride, a mammal-to-mammal kiss. The song is meant to be hopeful, tender, and reassuring, so we should not be surprised that these touching encounters occur at phrase endings with great regularity. (A side note: When the song modulates up a whole step, Willy dives over the jetty and becomes a free whale.)

The image may possess its own phrase structure apart from the music, and, in consequence, can suggest another line of counterpoint to the song. This creates a lovely tension between music and image. In Janet Jackson's "Runaway," the points when Jackson lands on monuments around the world—the Great Wall of China, Christ of the Andes—differs from that of musical expectations. The rebarring against the music (often in cut time) creates a feeling of freedom. Similarly, in the concert version of No Doubt's "Don't Speak," the editing features footage of band members jumping and stomping up and down shot in slow motion. The music has been rephrased by the image to emphasize a triplet feel.

THE SONG'S SECTIONAL DIVISIONS

Pop songs commonly divide into clearly demarcated sections. A video will often draw attention to a song's sectional divisions in order to help the viewer remember the song and its structure. The music-video image can boldly set off sectional divisions—through a dramatic shift in location or color, for example—but it can also do so more subtly.

The value of assigning visual highlights to the sectional divisions of a song can be seen in an early 1980s rap video by Bell Biv DeVoe titled "Do Me." Here, lyrics like "hip, hop with a smooth R&B tip" draw attention to the song's large-scale structure. The images underscore the sectional divisions by showcasing models who hold up cards announcing "Biv's Rap," "chorus," and "remix."

Imagery for a chorus is likely to be schematic and iconic in order to show off the most successful or saleable feature of the song—the main musical or verbal hook. Some videos use a new location to show off the chorus. In this section of Duran Duran's "Rio," all the band members appear on the bow of a swift sailboat as it cuts across a harbor. TLC's "Waterfalls" features the three group members singing in front of a huge expanse of water. In The Cars' "You Might Think," the Lilliputian band members perform on a gigantic bar of soap, while Toto's "Africa" shows the band playing on top of a monumental book. In Salt-N-Pepa's "Shoop," the women occupy a composite set somewhere between gym, girlie bar, and stage; in Nine Inch Nails' "Head Like a Hole," the band performs in a pit; and in Nirvana's "Heart-Shaped Box," the band performs around silvery trees. Some videos, on the other hand, set off the chorus with a new activity. In Madonna's "Vogue," both she and the household servants break into a dance. In the Spice Girls' "Wannabe," the girls sing and dance in formation on various staircases and within rooms in a hotel, while George Michael's "Father Figure" shows the couple engaging in steamy sex play while a corresponding dash of red spices up the frame. Madonna's "Take a Bow" reveals the star engaging in erotic play with a sheet, or Madonna and the matador having sex with a cape.

Sectional divisions can be underscored in creative ways. For example, Soundgarden's "Blackhole Sun" crowds a lot of visual information into the chorus: an elderly woman in a nightgown puts on red lipstick while being exercised by a vibrating buttocks machine in the back of her bedroom; a golden Adonis does push-ups on the floor in the extreme foreground; a giant Dalmatian watches from the midground with an expression of disdain. The imagery of the verses is much less active, featuring only one or two objects in the frame, such as a boy eyeing a bug through a magnifying glass or a man feeding a lamb with a bottle. Images that accomplish what Arnold Schoenberg describes as the "liquidation" of material, like the butterflies that float above a couple watching television—which liquidates the three-note ascending motive—guide the viewer from the frenetic chorus to the sedate verse.

Subtle changes in the background can help cue sectional changes. During the chorus of Tori Amos's "Caught in a Lite Sneeze," sky, water, and clouds fill the frame. In Janet Jackson's "Runaway," the clouds shift from white, streaky cirrus formations to puffy, golden pink, cumulus ones. It is not unusual for one song section to possess its own trajectory; in the first chorus of Brandy's "In My Room," the star is up off her bed and standing upright, in the second she is dressed and ready to go to an event, in the third she is dancing with others at a party. There are many variations on verse material moving into what is traditionally a more active chorus. In "I Know," Dionne Ferris makes tiny stepwise motions with her feet, shoulders, and neck that lead us to the energetic chorus and bridge in which the camera spins around the room. (The camera complements the song's harmonic modulation upward a whole step.) In Hole's "Violet," the figures punch and slap one another, generating enough energy to move the video into a raucous chorus, where, not surprisingly, the performers jump around and create mayhem. Sometimes the chorus is marked by the close-up of the star, often during the hook line. The viewer learns to expect the close-up and to take pleasure in the ways that material is varied: videos can present the close-up too soon or too late, or they can place the star farther away or nearer than a close-up ought to be. The Divinyls' "I Touch Myself" and Faith No More's "Epic" are such examples. Certain videos make the movement toward the final chorus more important than the transitions across other sectional divisions. Peter Gabriel's "Sledgehammer" is a case in which sectional divisions appear to play a significant role; what seems most relevant in the video, however, is arriving at a room with a green grid on the floor.

Junctures between song sections are another element that merit scrutiny. During every join between song sections in Smashing Pumpkins' "1979," a low-angle shot reveals the legs of kids running up hills or into suburban houses. Similarly, in "Take a Bow," a light pans across the room or the camera encircles an embracing couple at these moments. The bridge is often figured as a place outside the video, as a possibility for another way of being, beyond the verse and chorus. In both Green Day's "When I Come Around" and Red Hot Chili Peppers' "Under the Bridge," the camera speeds down a road with accompanying colored lights; in Michael Jackson's "Black or White," the star walks away from still-life tableaus and into projected imagery of the Ku Klux Klan; these same burning crosses form a backdrop for dance in Madonna's "Like a Prayer." In the B section of Live's "I Alone," the setting turns to night and the figures hold candles; in Mariah Carey's "Fantasy," the star sings in front of a fake starlit backdrop; in Stone Temple Pilots' "Big Bang Baby," the bridge fills with cartoon psychedelia; and in Peter Gabriel's "Sledgehammer," two lonely chicken carcasses line dance on a purple-curtained stage.

Commonly, at least at the beginning of a verse, the lead performer is set alone, often against a large barren space. Don Henley's "Boys of Summer," Madonna's "Express Yourself," and U2's "With or Without You" all begin the verse with the performers standing in isolation.

QUALITY OF SOUND: TIMBRE, TEXTURE, INSTRUMENTATION, AND ARRANGEMENT

One way to draw our attention to the song's timbres is to depict the instruments as enormous. In Steve Winwood's "Roll with It," the huge bell of a trumpet draws our attention to the presence of brass arrangement. Among other videos that work similarly, Smashing Pumpkins' "Disarm" focuses on strings and timpani, and the Dave Matthews Band's "Eat Too Much" gives prominence to the saxophone. Simply foregrounding instruments or a background singer within a shot can highlight an instrumental line or a vocal countermelody, especially if its performer (or performer and instrument) fill the entirety of the frame. This gambit is especially popular when the video can draw attention to a violin, viola, cello, or bass. Particularly appealing is the weighty cello; neither diminutive like the violin nor oversized like the bass, it is an instrument to scale with the human body. (Videos with cellos include Smashing Pumpkins' "Tonight, Tonight" and Guns N' Roses' "November Rain.")

Heightened activity in the frame is often associated with a dense arrangement. One video with an upbeat noisy song and many figures in the frame is "Ride the Train" by Quad City DJs. Sparse arrangements like that of U2's "With or Without You" may be set visually by only one or two figures in the frame. Other determinants of instrumentation include the qualities of sound and color. Fittingly, the music for Michael Jackson's video entitled "Scream"— which takes place in a hermetically sealed spaceship—is sharp and brittle. Madonna's "Bedtime Stories," by contrast, is set in a reverberant environment made of wood, paper, and water. The synthesizer's ostinatos have long delays that complement the wet, earthy textures and cool hues. Similarly, the blue-green imagery of U2's "With or Without You" matches the pure, flutelike tones that Brian Eno realized for the song. And in TLC's "Digging on You," when the horn section kicks in, the camera shows off a red mural, a giant rendition of the album cover.

Des'ree's "You Gotta Be" shows that the image can direct the viewer's attention toward shifts in instrumentation and arrangement. It begins with an acoustic guitar and voice, while the singer, dressed in black, stands against a plain white field. When the arrangement opens up to include electric guitar, bass, and drums, we suddenly see five multiples of Des'ree. In U2's "Where the Streets Have No Name," the beginning of the song is paired with an image of the band walking down an alleyway. The image shifts from black and white to color as the arrangement fills in. Similarly, as Madonna sings "Love Don't Live Here Anymore" in the middle of an empty suite in an abandoned posh hotel, the camera moves aimlessly; with the entrance of the basic beat there commences a slow dolly shot toward Madonna that continues for the rest of the tape.

Melissa Etheridge's "I'm the Only One" sounds like a down-and-dirty rock-and-roll anthem. The grainy look showcases the raunchy sound. Notwithstanding the artistic conceit, however, the muted colors and raw video quality simply reaffirm our cultural associations with the music. (The visuals could be said to evoke a thousand and one beer commercials.) Garbage's "Stupid Girl" also has a raspy sound, but the image has been scratched and colorized, then smeared with paint. Because of its associations with alternative culture, experimental film-making, and early-seventies fashion, "Stupid Girl" prompts questions about its historical links, and it proves to be much more engaging than Etheridge's video.

Both Madonna's "Human Nature" and Des'ree's "You Gotta Be" place their star in a black dress against a plain white background. The concept works well, but the snare drum, which corresponds to nothing in the imagery, seems to float above the soundtrack. An important moment in the latter video occurs when the singing becomes raspy and nasal and we see a close-up of Des'ree wrinkling her nose. The singer's crinkled nose gives the sound a source: finally, there is a connection between the grain of the song and the image.

In the first verse of Michael's Jackson's "Thriller," the performer walks alongside his date in a contemporary urban setting; the bass line, played on a keyboard, has attacks that are imprecise and mechanical. (They lack the nuance and variety attainable on an electric or acoustic bass.) In the second verse, zombies emerge from the grave, line dance with Jackson, and terrify the girl-friend. Here, with a live bass player and a guitar, the music becomes exceptionally "warm-blooded." Some of the "thrill" of "Thriller" comes from the fact that its zombies are cold on the outside yet passionate on the inside. On the contrary, the first verse shows Jackson, though warm-blooded (as a vibrant, breathing person), to be cold-blooded at heart. In other words, the sound quality tells us that it is the *zombies* who know the groove. If the arrangement of the song were inverted, the video would lose much of its charm. It is interesting that, during the stretches of the song that look contemporary, Jackson remains a bit cold and aloof, but when a horn figure recalling Earth, Wind and Fire enters in the third chorus, all of the sudden he and his ensemble of zombies break into a joyous dance. Suddenly, all of the dancers are dressed in red, shiny costumes that look somewhat seventies.

RHYTHM

Images can match or play against the speed of the music's beat. While images can be set at a consistent speed that departs from the song's tempo, they can also exhibit varying speeds against a song's various rhythmic elements. Music video is orchestrated to showcase the most arresting features of a song. If the song is notable for a sprightly rhythmic feel or a languorous one, the images will often seem to move at a speed even faster or slower than the music's.

Green Day's "Jaded/Brain Stew" provides a good example because it is really two short songs spliced together, one slow and one fast. To match the slow tempo, the first song is accompanied by gray-green slo-mo images of a tractor dragging a couch across a landfill. The driver is an old man whose expression suggests that he is working hard for a living; the band members, who sit on the couch tethered to the tractor, remain completely unengaged. When the music turns up-tempo, the room becomes tiny, the colors turn lurid, and we spot women in grass hula skirts and tops and toy airplanes that spin through a kaleidoscopic, fly-eyed camera lens (see fig. 2.18).

But the image can be set at any speed in relation to the music—closely matched, slightly divergent, or at a great distance. Videos that seem precisely synched include The Pet Shop Boys' "West End Girls," Bob Seger's "Breakdown," and U2's "With or Without You." The image for Al B. Sure's "Night and Day" creates an interesting tension with movement slightly more up-tempo than the music, while the opposite is true of Brandy's video "I Want to Be Down." Rocking back and forth dreamily on a swing, or lazily holding a telephone receiver, she moves slightly more slowly than the music, producing an effect that is hypnotic and seductive.

Examples of up-tempo songs in which the image goes much faster than the music include Wang Chung's "Everybody Wang Chung Tonight" and Sting's "Set Them Free." The former song—with its strobed images—was banned in England because authorities thought that a viewer might suffer an epileptic fit.[5] Videos in which the image moves notably more slowly than the music include R. Kelly's "Down Low" and LL Cool J's "Hey Lover."[6] When a string of images differs markedly in tempo from the song's in this way, the viewer will sometimes experience a sense of alignment with the music. One may then reach out for a different tempo in the image, almost like trying to grasp the brass ring on a carousel.

The individual images in a music video can possess a variety of tempi. In such a context, the viewer will likely judge each image as reflecting a particular rhythmic stratum in the song. For example, in Living Colour's "Cult of Personality," the images reflect several speeds: still masks, a slowed-down shot of a dumbstruck girl who watches television, teeming masses of people, and finally, Corey Glover's stage performance made up of sharply angled gestures. The characters seem to speak to each layer of rhythmic activity. Other examples include Steve Winwood's "Higher Love," Green Day's "Basketcase," and Snoop Doggy Dogg's "What's My Name." In the last, some images are quite sped up (like the dogcatchers who eventually break up the barbecue) and some are much slowed down (like Snoop's running with his pack of dogs).

The image and music of Biggie Smalls's and Puff Daddy's "Hypnotize" contain many rhythmic layers. A car speeds down tunnels and freeways, while a yacht skims along the ocean under a fleet of helicopters taking aim at it. Chased by a line of cars, a nervous Puffy climbs out of a convertible. A chorus line of women in flouncy miniskirts dance around Smalls with an easy spring to their hips and knees. A ball bounces above the lyrics at the bottom of the screen. The shifting elements that we attend to in the music are alternately nervous and fast, playful and bouncy, and broad and slow. (The slower stratum of activity appears when a door opens slowly and mermaids swim in a giant aquarium; later, a sultry woman runs her finger languorously along the edge of a martini glass and even more slowly sucks an olive while slightly widening her eyes.)

A song's rhythmic features are most often underscored visually by movement within the frame and by editing, but other visual techniques can serve to highlight the characters' rhythm as well. There is something satisfying when a performer takes a prop and uses it to articulate the beat. Think of Annie Lennox striking a riding crop on the surface of a boardroom table in the beginning of "Sweet Dreams."[7] The satisfaction derives from multiple sources. First, in the strange world of music video, many of the sights and sounds fail to do what we expect of them to in everyday life; we no longer have a sense of exactly what sounds and images mean. By wielding a prop to mark the beat, the performer fills in the gap, telling us how to feel the weight and quality of the percussion.

Second, we do not have enough information about the characters in a music video—what animates them, what drives them forward, remains unclear. We see people who may be intended as emblematic or realistic depictions or as an elaborate projection of the performer's or videomaker's psyche. Thus, when the performer takes up the prop within the setting, the character within that context becomes less abstruse. (This is especially true when the musician's implement could make a noise like that of everyday objects.) Earlier, I have spoken about the ways that image, music and lyrics fail to mesh into a whole. The moment that the sound, setting, and performer belong to one another, a distance has been broached. The performer has found a way to negotiate this difficult terrain and perhaps acquires the status of a hero.[8]

Third, our relation to the prop changes. While a broom or a clothes hanger in a Hollywood musical can become a dancing partner and then return to normal,[9] the relation among setting, prop, and person remains more ominous and uncertain. When the actor and the prop are brought into play with the music, the prop—backed up by strange sounds—seems more potent.

Last, the synchronization of performers, music, and props is a triumph for the director and for the video itself. Music rarely represents real things in the world—with few exceptions like cuckoo clocks, trains, and ringing telephones. The pleasure of music video, therefore, derives in part from the ways that the performer can negotiate two worlds—one like ours, and the other a parallel musical universe in which the performer becomes a musician who moves through a musical landscape. Wielding a prop, a star functions as an actor as well as a musician. The question is, for how long can the performer straddle both roles well, or will he lapse into only one?

Some effective accentuations made by supporting figures on the beat:

- The matador kicks the table, and a riding crop whacks the side of a wall, as the bull runs out to the ring in Madonna's "Take a Bow."
- The kids throw plastic lawn chairs into the pool while a cymbal crashes in Smashing Pumpkins' "1979."
- When the synthesizer enters the mix for the first time in Sheryl Crow's "Every Day Is a Winding Road," a pail of water hits a man holding a ball (lyrics: "jump back, let's go").
- At the beginning of Nine Inch Nails' "Closer," a heart impaled on a chair expires steam on the second and fourth beat of each measure.

■ As Naughty by Nature's "Hip Hop Hurray" opens, the lead singer whacks a trashcan with what looks like a gumball stuffed inside a sock on the beat. (The metallic sound on the can might fit the rim shot of the snare.) Perhaps the gesture is charming because "Hip Hop Hurray" is a community-based video, the sentiment being that anyone can make music with whatever tools are on hand. A subtle visual thematic rhyme occurs a few shots later, when we see a performer who wears a beanie with a pom-pom drooping over his eyes—a form that resembles the shillelagh wielded earlier. The potential for music making is thus made more immediate and personal, a way of being that might extend throughout the tape.

■ In the opening sequence of Green Day's "Basketcase," a video in which we assume the band members are locked down in an asylum, the drummer hits the drum from his wheelchair, and we cheer his accomplishment. In TLC's "Baby-Baby-Baby," while Left Eye carries a load of laundry, Chili swats her butt with a book—a swat that serves multiple purposes: besides articulating the beat and advancing the story, it describes a type of camaraderie between band members.

Some videos' treatment of rhythm is more thoroughgoing. Smashing Pumpkins' "Tonight, Tonight," a song containing a constant pulse on the eighth note articulated by the rim shot on the snare, sounds like a clock marking time with a "tick-tock, tick-tock." The video is a homage to Georges Méliès's black-and-white silent film *Trip to the Moon*; because the video narrates a children's story, it is not surprising that so much occurs on the beat. Music and image are presented in a simple, straightforward, one-to-one relationship: the moon men jump out of craters, and the European travelers clunk them on the head with umbrellas; Poseidon's "Mighty Trident" releases a puff of smoke and the couple tumbles through space, to be saved by umbrellas that pop open into parachutes; the plane touches down on the surface of the water, then crashes to the ocean floor.

Where "Tonight, Tonight" works with simple rhythmic structures, Prince's "Gett Off" is highly ornate. The arrangement has many layers of rhythmic patterning, setting up a dense texture of sound. The image is similarly unpredictable in what falls on and off the beat. A video for grownups—a play on Caligula's orgies—its complicated movements and intertwinings of bodies draw our attention not only to the rhythm arrangement but also to the far recesses of the physical space.

One subtle way that videomakers keep the image responsive to the beat is to have a band member pat his hand on his thigh. This happens often enough, and in a studied enough manner, that the gesture seems to acquire a musical function, as in Nirvana's "Heart-Shaped Box" and Mista's "Blackberry Molasses."[10] In hip-hop videos, a passenger in the rapper's car will bob his head, shrug his shoulders, or cross his hands to elucidate the beat, as in Busta

Rhymes's "Woo Hah," Biggie Smalls's and Puff Daddy's "Hypnotize" and LL Cool J's "Doin' It." Some of the pleasure of these moments comes from the fact that although the companion *might* be listening to the radio, he is not. It is a role that *might* be ascribed to a second banana—but not quite.

On a large scale, the video often moves between stretches where the beat is heavily articulated by the image and stretches when the image does not draw attention to the beat. This kind of alternation can last throughout a tape and can give the viewer a sense of being grounded and set free, lost and found again. A case in point is Biggie Smalls's "Big Pappa," where the rapper is alone on a bed or on the staircase, and then we see a high-angle shot of a room full of people moving in rhythm.

Syncopation and rubato are considered to be aspects of performance central to many forms of musical practice. (Syncopations are accented offbeats, and rubato denotes "time slackened or hastened for the purposes of expression" while preserving a sense of the basic tempo—*tempo rubato* translates as robbed or stolen time.) Clock time, by contrast, is understood as unmusical. Even drum machines are commonly designed to approach the subtle temporal irregularities of human performance. This kind of musicality can be established in music video through the ways that the image deviates from the music's patterning, coming before and after the beat, or ahead or behind the flow of the music. Chapters 11, 12, and 13 each attempt to capture those moments when syncopation or rubato and music image relations come into play in a heightened form.

Paula Abdul's "Straight Up" shows a way that a video can draw attention to rhythm. This video creates a pattern that sweeps across the entire video. At the song's opening, music and image are closely synchronized. Toward the middle, the two diverge, and at the end of the song, image and music return to sync. Equally significant is the simple fact that a rhythm moves from the foreground to the background and then forward again. In the first halves of both Boyz II Men's "On Bended Knee" and Tom Petty's "You Don't Know What It Means," the performers articulate the beat carefully; later in these videos, such articulations move toward the edge of perception. The rhythm of "On Bended Knee" is simple, and the matches between the image and music are fairly blatant: right on the beat, the lover of one of the group members cracks a record in two. Yet, at the end of the video, firecrackers go off on beats two and four. Similarly, in "You Don't Know What It Means," a wrecking ball threatens to destroy a building right on the beat, but toward the video's end, the flare of popguns accentuate two and four as they hit a field of paper targets in the far recesses of the background.

A performer simply tapping, clapping, stomping, raising an arm, or blinking emphatically in a way that emphasizes the beat can also work powerfully. Through body slaps, the following women performers provide both moments of sexual titillation and suggestions for feeling the beat: Chilli of TLC's "Waterfalls" smacks her hip, with her belly dancer's pantalets draped over her hips helping to accentuate the rhythm; Janet Jackson hits her buttocks at the end of "Scream" (and raises her fingers to her lips as a kiss-off); in "In My Room," Brandy places both palms on her lower abdomen and taps as she leans back. Men seldom enact the rhythm with so much sexuality. (The sexist adage that a woman's body is a drum holds true for music video.) Men typically brandish their fists and elbows to articulate the rhythm: In "Twisted," Keith Sweat slams both elbows on the hood of a car; and in "The World Is Mine," Ice Cube pumps his fists in the air. The Eurythmics perform much freer gender roles. Their video "Sweet Dreams" creates a sync between music and image at many different rhythmic levels. While singer Annie Lennox strikes an office desk with her riding crop on the beat, the male keyboardist taps away on a homemade composite of typewriter and analog synthesizer in a way that articulates the eighth-note pulse of a sequenced keyboard part. A cow chews its cud on two and four.

Images of gender and power (or ethnicity, sexuality, class, and so on) can be encoded at any structural level—the beginnings and ends of a song, its sections, phrases, measures, and so on. Let me give an example in the case of the measure. Most pop songs have four beats to a measure, and the first beat can provide an organizing force or authority over the rest of the beats. In a crowded upscale house party, the rapper Jay-Z and his male troop in "Just Want to Love You" pick up one woman after another and lead them to different parts of the house where they might have sex. Unfortunately, all of the closets, bathrooms, and other potential sites are occupied. Sometimes Jay-Z bumps into an old flame and risks trouble. "Just Want to Love You" opens with some play concerning who possesses beat one, but soon the female characters start falling off the beat, and Jay-Z and the other men demonstratively control it. (They raise their fists or jab their elbows outward on the downbeat.) Even the middle-aged gardener, who wears a phallic chain saw slung on hips, bounces up and down and gets the one. Men control the sexual scenario here.

Herbie Hancock's "Rockit" uses rhythm to raise questions concerning social role and ethnicity. How do live and dead things move to a beat? The video features Hancock, an African American jazz musician, next to a middle-class house inhabited by white dummies. Almost none of the animatronics moves in sync with the music. For example, the chorus line of stuffed, stubby legs kick a bit behind the beat, and their movements seem repetitive and stiff.[11] Hancock, on the contrary, moves in sync with the beat, with his hands gracefully flickering over two turntables, as is the head of an animatronic quacking duck. The musician has greater poise than the duck, because while he remains in sync with his own gestures the duck can stay on the beat only thanks to a series of jump cuts. Both Hancock and the duck provide the sort of ground on which the viewer can return after drifting freely along with the awkward yet improvisatory movements of the mechanical dummies. It is not the white automatons but rather the natural (the duck) and the human (Hancock) who possess the rhythm and by extension the music as a whole.

HARMONY

Videos can reflect changes in harmony. Guns N' Roses' "November Rain" shifts from major to minor. The first shot, before the song begins, reveals singer Axl Rose suffering from a nightmare in a gothic bedroom flooded with blue light. The song begins in major, and the video matches this with a golden hue. Two-thirds of the rest of the video remains gold-toned until the song shifts to the relative minor and returns to the original shade of blue. The scene before the shift contains patches of blue, anticipating the entry of the new song section; all of the wedding guests wear something blue. As the key changes, rain falls, the wedding guests duck for cover, and a spilled bottle of wine runs red. The scene cuts to the bride's funeral, where blue lilacs flow over the coffin's lid; from now on, the video will stay with the minor key and blue tones. Very few videos kill off their characters, but "November Rain" creates a semblance of the process of death: the loss of the body, and grief over the deceased's absence. It can do so, in part, by intercutting a gold-toned flashback of the bride throwing her wreath, which contrasts with the final section's blue cast. The woman no longer belongs in the realm of the video or the living. Music videos often establish relations among several musical and visual parameters in order to underscore the overall theme. The harmony for "November Rain" stands on the tonic for an unusually long time and gives the song a ponderous tone, a tone that works well with the overwrought imagery.

Unlike "November Rain," Madonna's "Bedtime Stories," based on trance music, is harmonically static: the harmony sits on a single chord. There are no strong sectional divisions within the song, and correspondingly, the camera floats from tableau to tableau, with no scene set off dramatically from another.

The most common key change in pop music is the move up a whole step, which usually occurs two-thirds into the song. It is an easy modulation to hear; the physical sensation might be like taking a step onto a platform, and the emotional rhetoric of the move can be articulated as having moved through problems and being now on a higher plane. Singers in music videos often throw their hands over their heads and into the air at this moment—for example, in Boyz II Men's "On Bended Knee." In "Just Another Day Without You," John Secada throws open the doors of a church, and the outdoors bathes him and the structure in white light. In Amy Grant's "House of Love," the song modulates up, and the camera and Grant gradually make their way up to the second floor and then up to the rooftop of a Victorian home at first seen from a distance across a long expanse of lawn.

In contrast to the shift up of a whole step and the visual sensation of rising, Janet Jackson's "Runaway" is a song that modulates downward as the performer tilts backward. Jackson looks as if she might fall off the wing of the airplane on which she dances; the tug of the harmonic progression, along with the immense distance below Jackson, feels palpable.

This chapter has stressed the most obvious one-to-one type connections among music, image, and lyrics. For example, we might assume the rhythm in the music might be picked up by the visual editing or movement in the frame. But a parameter in one domain can cross into any number of other parameters in another medium's realm: we can imagine the way the musical rhythm can be reflected through a shift in color, texture, or set design in the image.

9

Connections Among Music, Image, and Lyrics

THIS CHAPTER examines the ways that music, image, and lyrics exist in relation. Directors can establish connections across media through a number of devices: the image can be shaped so that it mimics the experiential qualities of sound; an image can be chosen that has drifted away from its sound source but is still linked to it through a syncretic relationship[1]; an image may match a sound through a symbolic, indexical, or iconic resemblance; sound, image, and lyrics can be placed in a metaphorical relation. In addition, any highly marked image, if repeated, can create a sync point, especially if it is linked to a recurring musical feature. The first part of this chapter catalogs types of local connection among music, image, and lyrics. The second considers how these connections accrue into larger shapes, and the third examines higher-level connections and the creation of beginnings, middles, and ends. The chapter closes with a discussion of methods for analyzing music video.

SOUND AND IMAGE AS EXPERIENCED IN MUSIC VIDEO

The first formal element I will discuss concerns a video's attempt to match a song's shape, texture, and flow. Music video accomplishes this goal by approximating the experiential qualities of sound. To understand what an image must abandon and take up in order to transform itself into an object that resembles sound, it is helpful to spend some time considering the experiential properties of sound and image.

People seem to process sound differently from image, and this may be reflective of both biology and culture.[2] Walter Ong has argued, "Sight isolates, sound incorporates. Whereas sight situates the observer outside what he views, at a distance, sound pours into the hearer. Vision dissects. . . . When I hear, however, I gather sound simultaneously from every direction at once: I am at the center of my auditory world, which envelopes me, establishing me at a kind of core of sensation and existence. . . . By contrast with vision, the dissecting sense, sound is thus a unifying sense. A typical visual ideal is clarity and distinctness, a taking apart. . . . The auditory ideal, by contrast, is harmony, a putting together."[3] Words that describe image take precedence in all human societies over those that characterize sound. In the act of seeing, people think of an image in ways similar to how we think of grammatical nouns; that is, objects of sight seem to be something that can be owned, procured, possessed (my book, the car, my tree). In content, sight objects seem to be primarily static and consistent. We imagine images more as occupying space and as being clearly bounded than as changing through time, and we usually assume that images are both nontransforming and existing even when we are gone. (The book remains in the room even when the light is turned off and I have left the room.) Images have a strong specificity (my father's felt hat is different from mine even though they are of the same style); therefore images seen in the world are not fully capable of being notated into representational images. A schematic line drawing (an ideogram) represents an image, but leaves out much of the object's specificity. Images, however, although they prove to be rather nonnotational, can be described with great linguistic accuracy ("I see a brown dusty 24-caliber colt revolver, with one point of black grease near the pin").

In contrast to the act of sight, in the act of hearing we think of sound as being more akin to a verb or adjectival form than to a noun form. Sound usually describes a process belonging or referring to an object rather than an actual object "I hear the babbling *of* the brook." We also have fewer linguistic terms with which to describe and define a sound. We also never feel we can own or possess a sound; we cannot control and limit its boundaries, as we feel we can an image. Sound is process-oriented. It ebbs and flows, and it begins and ends. Secondarily, while sound unfolds in both time and space, we seem most attuned to its temporal features. The spatial qualities of a sound often seem fuzzy and nondeterminate (even the sound of the speakers in a room, or of a person's voice seem to lack fixity or spatial boundaries), but we keep a strong sense of sound constantly changing. We feel sound upon and within our bodies (loud sounds even produce reverberations within the body), and we feel music pulsing through us,[4] as opposed to images that we feel as primarily external to us. Sound often cannot be linguistically transcribed fully (try describing one room with many types of sounds or a piece of music), but it can be surprisingly well notated through the communally agreed upon methods of music and graphic notation. We have also different means of regulating the content of image and sound. We have a direct, intermittent control over image (control of eye movement and eyelids), but not of sound. (No earlids: sound reaches us from whatever direction we turn.)

The boundaries between how we think and feel about sound and about image are not impenetrable. A better way to think about the experience of sound and image is of falling somewhere toward ends on a continuum—we tend to have certain types of experiences with each medium. The statement,

"Honey, they're playing our song," and the popular motive of Beethoven's Fifth Symphony show how we grant sounds the attributions of objecthood. The beam of light from a lighthouse and the way that it shifts and passes often seems ephemeral, blurring into qualities that we attribute to sound. Our culture has the potential to experience sound and images in a larger way than we have to this point. For example, we could become sensitive to the processes belonging to objects, and the immediate and fixed spatial qualities of sound. (This sound is here, at this location, and I can precisely describe it.) We can imagine a culture where sounds are thought of and experienced more as grammatically focused nouns, and objects as processual verbs.

To share ground with or showcase features of a song, images must often relinquish qualities associated with objects and adopt those of sounds. Music-video image, like sound, tends to surround and engulf us. Both music-video image and sound—unlike objects seen in everyday life—tend to be processual and transitory rather than static, and to project permeable and indefinite rather than clearly defined boundaries. The music-video image, like sound, foregrounds the experience of movement and of passing time. It attempts to pull us in with an address to the body, with a flooding of the senses, thus eliciting a sense of experience as internally felt rather than externally understood. My argument will be that, in music videos, images can work with music by adopting the phenomenological qualities of sound: these images, like sound, come to the fore and fade away, "stream," surround us, and even reverberate within us, and mimic timbral qualities.

A video does not need to incorporate all of these sonic properties to be musical; however, most videos will foreground at least one parameter on this list. It has become increasingly common for videos to work with a number of these parameters within the same image, and even to use increased activity in several of these domains as a way of building toward climactic points in the video. Live's video "Selling the Drama" is a case in point, with its morphed and distorted imagery, intense color, fog, mottled trees, sometimes diffused light, and projected patterns that move over subjects in a constant stream. Offspring's "Come Out and Play (Keep 'm Separated)," on the other hand, showcases smoke, billowing plastic, superimpositions, and polarizing and tinting effects (fig. 9.1).

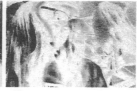

FIGURE 9.1 (A–B)
Offspring's "Come Out and Play (Keep 'm Separated)." The image reflects music's experiential properties.

Film-sound theorist Michel Chion's descriptions of sound's features can prove helpful to our examination of musical multimedia. Chion notes that whereas images have a static aspect, sounds present a trajectory: "All sounds consist of an attack and a slight fading resonance, a finite story, oriented in time in a precise and irreversible manner."[5] In a similar fashion, music does not show, but rather takes us through an experience. We listen by following the movement from note to note. Music is propulsive; it seems continually to flow onward. Videos that foreground a continual tracking motion as well as slo-mo draw attention to the ways sound unfolds in time in a precise and irreversible manner. In videos such as Domino's "Sweet Potato Pie," Pink Floyd's "Take It Back," and Smashing Pumpkins' "In Arms," the motion within the image attempts to match the sense of flow in the music. Videos utilizing tracking and slo-mo often seem imbued with nostalgia, as they make us aware that, even if our perceptions reside in the present, past events are irretrievably slipping away. In all three tapes, the images move at a pace quick enough to create the sense of following the music. This sense of constant tracking matches the progress of the song.

Chion refines the comparison, and considers both sound and image as following a kind of trajectory. He offers that sound might be thought of as having properties like those of a gas, while image might be compared to directed lines. Sound is characterized by gradual diffusion, by a progressive loss of clarity and grip.[6] Video image can reflect this property: in videos such as "Don't Walk Away," by Ace of Base, the band members, particularly the blond singer, are shot in aureoles of diffused light, so that their borders are soft, and their bodies appear to spread outward. Madonna's "Express Yourself" and Janet Jackson's "Anytime, Anyplace" are examples of videos where intense color and heavily diffused light are adopted to mimic the diffusion of sound.

The inevitable diffusion of sounds and the irreversible manner of their trajectory, can be taken together to suggest their ephemerality. In videos such as Eurythmics' "Missionary Man," Radiohead's "Creep," and U2's "With or Without You," the strobe effects and the image's murky quality create the impression that the tapes are fragile and ephemeral, like the fleeting sounds that continually pass across us, swell, diminish, and then move past the image in these videos. The objects depicted in these videos become unlike the objects in film, in their dependence upon movement and process, upon the environment in which they are seen, and upon the camera's point of view.

The dependence of sounds upon their environment—much greater than that of images, according to Chion—means that a sound cannot be separated from the field in which it exists.[7] The sense of demarcation and boundary that we attribute to images is less true of sound. Images also in music video do not seem isolated, but rather exist in a state of relation—for example, in Collective Soul's "Shine" the trees in the video seem eerily responsive to the performers. Often figures and objects in music video appear to be placed in tableaux—for example, we can sense the distance from, but also the connection between, the human figures and the water in Peter Gabriel's "Mercy St.," even though the figures are separated in time and are shot from a number of locations.

The fact that sounds cannot be made distinct from their environments gives them the power to take over these environments; this phenomenon might be compared, again, to the image of a gas filling a room. Videos can work in a similar way. Examples of videos that create the sense of filling up or flooding the space with movement and color are Ace of Base's "I Saw the Sign" and Deee-Lite's "Groove Is in the Heart." Much as sound does, these videos attempt not to reach us from a single point, but rather to surround us from all directions to create an overload rather than to tell a story.

Along with this power to take control of or flood an environment, sounds can occupy the body. Some videos possess a kind of tactility that can mimic the effect of loud sound vibrating within the body. In Nenah Cherry' s "Under My Skin," the image and music seem to press forward, on the beat, as if they could reach out of the frame and knock or rub up against the flesh of the viewer. The video actually contains imagery of vibrating speaker cones and bodies clothed in a clinging plastic material. Both of these images are shot in metallic shades, thereby establishing a connection between sonic vibration and the body instead of suggesting interchangeability.

MODES OF FORMAL CONNECTION: IMMEDIATE CONNECTIONS

Theorists of music video, when they talk about how music and image can be put into relation, tend to focus on the potential for moments of synchronization between music and image. Film theorist John Anderson speaks about the way that music and image are connected through rhythmic verticality—simply put, he wants to say that images are cut to the beat.[8] In such an approach, it is assumed that (1) music video works by establishing one-to-one correspondences between music and image, and (2) every moment of connection carries equal weight. This notion of music video leaves out the complex ways that image and music can begin to work together to create a form. A simultaneity functions like one type of join used to construct a building, but it does not describe the different types of material that can be used, nor does it suggest how a structure can be put together using these materials. Simultaneously, music video's qualities of speed and flux make its structure difficult to pin down. Nevertheless, the concept of a join is a good place to begin a description of music video.

SIMULTANEITIES AND MICRORHYTHMS

Perhaps because he has been a composer and sound designer, Chion calls the fine patterns that can occur in the images for narrative films—the mottling of light, the smoke from a candle—visual microrhythms.[9] The music-video image can also contain such fine patterns, and these can reflect patterns in the music.

For example, in Madonna's "Cherish," the play of foam and spray in the image constitutes a microrhythm against the broad planes of the beach and the ocean. Fine spots of light projected on a rear screen form a microrhythm in U2's "With or Without You." In both cases, the microrhythm draws attention to fine details and slight imperfections in the timbres of the song. The arrangement for "Cherish" sounds quite cool and restrained, partly because all of the sounds are synthesized or sampled and then (with the exception of the bass line) played via sequencer; what the microrhythm in the image does is to bring out the subtle graininess of the synthesized bass and sampled tambourine, and to naturalize the amateurish singing of Madonna. Similarly, the vague flickering of light in the U2 video reflects the subtleties of Brian Eno's production, a production style known for its use of ambient sound as a ground for the band's playing.

SYNCHRESIS: VISUAL/AURAL DISTANCES

Music and image can appear to exist at various distances of relation from one another even at the instance of the sync point. Music video accomplishes this through a phenomenon that Chion identifies in film.[10] When we listen to sounds, we can be indifferent as to their singularity, for example, to what makes this collection of refrigerator sounds different from all the sounds of refrigerators in general. We often tend to listen within types. Even with sounds that we are intimate with, such as footsteps or voices, we often make errors about who created them. It often takes a half of a verse before we can identify one guitarist over another or one saxophonist over another, and quite often all we hear is the sound of a saxophone playing in a jazz idiom. Film often exploits this indifference toward the particularity of sounds. For example, the sound of the crushing of a skull can be foleyed in with the sound of a melon being crushed, and the sound of footsteps in snow can be achieved by fingers moving through cornstarch. Film may be able to make use of this generic approach toward sounds because sounds change when they feel phenomenologically close to us. (The sound of dropping pencils, when we are upset, can sound overwhelmingly loud.) Music video is a medium in which sounds can sometimes be closely linked to their sources, but can at other times differ or be separated from them.

The degree of correspondence between the music and the image at a given moment, and the way that this moment stands in relation to the video as a whole, gives authority to the music video. The freedom of sound sources in the video "Gett Off" is a good example of how casual connection between sound and image can be severed—here performers lip-sync and play instruments different from those that occurred on the recording. Let me give an example of one type of dramatic sync point. In film, when a sound is made to break through the tapestry because of its distance from others, Chion calls it a punctuation of sound.[11] (Examples might include the sound of footsteps or the puff of a cigarette that suddenly leaps out from the audio track.) Music videos can create moments of punctuation through both music and image. In these moments, a seemingly unworkable sound/image pair can exist in relation as long as a few parameters are related—contour, timbre, and the like. In Onyx's "Let the Boys Be Boys," when the rapper sings "slam," his whole face fills the frame. The moment exists in a state of both emphasis and suspension. The moment is bracketed by the rest of the surrounding imagery, and thereby connected to other such heightened moments in the video. These points seem to break apart from the video's texture. More tangential aural/visual connections raise questions about whether the viewer should attribute a relationship at all. The serendipitous link between the "ch-ch-ch" of the 7–11 Slurpee machine and the snare fill on Smashing Pumpkins' "Tonight, Tonight" is one example.

AN INVERSION OF ROLES

Sounds are often described in terms of an envelope: an initial attack, and then a pattern of decay. If you place a cup on a table, you will hear a sharp articulation and then a diffusion of the sound. Sound designer Walter Murch says that sounds tend to trail after objects and calls sounds the shadows of objects. If you clap your hands and then notice what happens to the sound, you will sense that the sound will seem to come an instant after when the hands meet. In music video, the music can seem responsible for the attack of the sound, and the image can seem responsible for the subsequent pattern of decay. At one level, sound is responsible for setting objects in motion: the singer who lip-syncs trails after the music, the dancers move in response to the music, the rate of the ripple in the moving cloth, the reflections of water, and the designs on the set are all set in motion in response to the sound. This creates a slight shift in the viewer, which lends authority to the music video. A heightened instance of this occurs in Peter Gabriel's "Mercy St." Here the music and image create the illusion that an isolated flute melody sets the imagery of circling hands in motion. In Madonna's "Cherish," the bass line appears to move the figures forward. In both of these videos, the image seems responsible for the sound's decay. The image and music can switch roles because we only see a part of the body; and what propels the body forward is unclear. The music's agency affects not only bodies but objects as well. In Melanie C's "Things Will Never Be the Same Again," Venetian blinds open upon a photo of a lake, mountains and sky, and then snap shut after a prominent snare fill. The dreamlike setting makes more plausible the possibility of the music's new powers.

CONNECTIONS BASED ON A CONTINUUM RATHER THAN A BINARY OPPOSITION

Musical parameters, as Richard Middleton points out, exist either as a binary opposition or as a continuum.[12] Such features as dynamics and gradual tempo shifts are examples of the latter. In a video like Janet Jackson's "Anytime, Anyplace" there is a gradual unfolding in both media—the color gradually intensifies as the arrangement thickens. Here we have a connection that might more accurately be called a smear than a sync point. These types of connection speak to musical parameters that wax and wane. They are helpful in creating continuity and building toward key points in the video.

OTHER SYNC POINTS BASED ON REPETITION AND ABSENCE

Sync points can be created simply through the repetition of a striking feature. If objects and people are shot mostly in close-up, and then an object suddenly appears within the extreme background a few times, the background objects with the accompanying text and music will become linked. In "The Stakes Is High" by De La Soul and Prince's "Dinner with Dolores," depth cues are used to poetic effect. The former shows us an object placed far back in the frame— a basketball in a court, a tractor on a field of grass, a train coming into the station. Set off in time, these objects nonetheless remain mysteriously connected in the context of the rest of the video. In "Dinner with Dolores," a hand reaches into the front of the frame first with a note and later with a condom. Again, these two moments seem both highlighted and linked in time, with each object or figure holding its own weight against the music. Connections can also be created based on similar color, texture, shape, or the like. These moments become more potent when linked to a recurring musical feature.

Sync points can also occur through an absence of a join. Sometimes elements in the frame or in the soundtrack are not answered for by the other media. These loose elements hang, seeming to float above the multimedia texture. A video with a white cyclorama backdrop and only a few people or objects in the frame, like Madonna's "Human Nature," might leave the snare drum without anything to connect to: each attack seems to linger over the image. Sometimes a visual element in the frame is so apart from the rest of the visual surface and the song that it also floats. In Smashing Pumpkins' "Tonight, Tonight" an animation of a batboy suddenly enters and moves across the frame, against a background containing real objects and people. In the "Rite of Spring" sequence in *Fantasia*, the baby dinosaurs (inserted by Disney's animators as a plug for family values) seem unrepresented by the music.

Connections are not just perceived vertically. The singer may sing the word "purse," and the viewer will see the image of a purse. Here the link between lyric and image is slightly offset. The relations among music and image can also set off a chase across the tape. Madonna's "Material Girl" contains the high-pitched sound of the triangle, and a number of sparkling objects, among them chandeliers and jewelry. Audiovisual sync among these items loosens as the video progresses. Late in the video, Madonna starts emptying out the contents of men's pockets, and the viewer starts measuring the gap between sparkling sounds and visuals.

When images imitate sonic qualities, they can approach sound's quality of diffusion, transformation, continuity, and motion. An example of these processes found in a song might be when we hear a voice singing, and then an electric violin or guitar takes it up, and we then hear some of the material of the voice carried through into the new section. In Prodigy's music video "Breathe," the most exciting element is an alligator who wanders on and off beds and across floors. Band members mimic aspects of the alligator—one wiggles and twists, another opens and shuts his jaws, another flaunts his tattooed stripes, and another displays his knotted hair and ridged metal jewelry. The bass line suggests the alligator's writhing; the human voice, the snarl; and the abrupt silences, the reptile's bite. The alligator's essence permeates the tape. Another example can be found in Eminem's "Without Me," in which the genital/scatological humor seems to extend much further than the instances when we directly confront it.

ICONIC, INDEXICAL, AND SYMBOLIC LINKS

The semiotic categories of icon, symbol, and index can be useful for understanding the relations among sound, image, and lyrics. To appreciate this approach to video aesthetics, the reader is asked to anticipate that a visual gesture will be mirrored by an aural one. Many music/image correspondences in commercials and films bear this out; for example, in the *Roadrunner* cartoons, Wile E. Coyote falls from the precipice to the bottom of a canyon, and the pitch drops. In the opera-house sequence in *Citizen Kane,* the camera rises up and the pitch moves higher as well. Moreover, there are sound, size, and shape correlates in many common creatures and objects: a small bird makes a high-pitched sound, a heavy mammal emits a low roar. The most noticeable frequencies of an electric toothbrush are higher and softer than those of an electric blender. Most notably, our familiarity with dance sensitizes us to other connections between music and the body. Adolescents turned out in polyester pants with ornamented jackets, stomping to a Sousa march seem to establish a natural musical/visual correspondence, as do excitable kindergarten children in tutus pitter-pattering to "The Song of the Bumblebee." The Sousa march is a very good example of how an image can be tied to music through a number of different types of connections—symbolic, indexical, and iconic. For example, the body/music connections of the marchers are at one level iconic: sharp, severe physical gestures match a crisp 2/4 meter; at another level indexical: when I hear marches, I think of marchers because I have seen and heard them this way before; and at the same time symbolic: brocade and marches suggest pomp and status simply because we say that they do. A filmed version of the Sousa march might possess more robust music/image links than a live experience of the event because the image is rendered partially: in the filmed example, we may draw upon musical cues to determine spatial relations and to provide the image's affect.

METAPHOR

Until recently, discussions of musical multimedia have focused on the ways that media can be put into relation based on parallelism and counterpoint. Nicholas Cook, in *Analyzing Musical Multimedia,* proposes a more volatile model. Cook uses the trope of metaphor: the attributes of one medium transfers to another, and the yoking together of two concepts from different semantic realms creates a new meaning. Earlier theorists have assumed that music in the film simply represents a meaning already inherent in each medium, rather than participating in the construction of that meaning.[13] Instead, Cook argues, multimedia has a dynamic, processive character. "The result is qualitatively distinguishable from each component element viewed separately."[14]

For Cook, a metaphorical relation begins when two elements and two media become linked simply by virtue of being placed in relation. This "enabling similarity" allows for the transfer of attributes from one term to the other: meaning now inheres not in similarity, but in the difference that similarity articulates.[15] For example, the commonplace saying "Love is war" puts many values into play: it allows us to consider the similarities and differences in both terms. Cook's analysis of a Citroen commercial is useful for showing how this works. The television advertisement shows a car speeding down a highway to the accompaniment of the beginning of the overture to *Le Nozze de Figaro.* The camera then cuts to a series of shots of amateur artists doing paintings of ocean, hillside, and car, all the while accompanied by a subdued soundtrack composed of natural sounds. Most of the rest of the commercial crosscuts between the car with Mozart and the landscape painters with nature sounds. Our understanding of this advertisement derives from our ability to decipher a number of codes. We tend to match music with a simultaneity, rather than an adjacency, especially if there is some correlation in terms of scale, based on what appears in the frame and on the soundtrack. Crosscutting usually infers some sort of comparison. Our cultural associations cue us that Mozart's music is precise and inspired, and the car possesses similar features—technological savvy and detail-mindedness. While car and Mozart accrue meaning based on related qualities, the Sunday painters and their nature sounds pull together through more scrappy attributes—they seem humble and serene. Cook points out that not only do the car plus Mozart and painters plus nature become linked, the meaning of the linked pairs changes as well. While Mozart in light of the car becomes crisper and more technologically sophisticated, the car becomes more pristine, classy, and authoritative. Cook suggests "that the vivacity, power, and cultural prestige of the music (its activity, potency, and evaluative properties, if you like) are transferred wholesale to the product."[16] Cook notes that when music is alone we can often have difficulty describing its meanings, but we rarely experience music alone: we experience it in relation to other media—album covers, conversation, fan magazines—and in the context of specific sites—the car, the film theater, the symphony hall. These elements color our musical understanding in significant ways. In the Citroen commercial, Mozart means something specific.

Is our tendency to experience phenomenon metaphorically a function of culture or biology? George Lakoff and Mark Johnson argue that such thinking is intrinsic to us: small children conflate notions that certain attributes are linked to others, for example, up is good, or powerful is big, and, as we grow older, these ways of thinking spread to other domains where they become more entrenched.[17] Although some of our tendency to think metaphorically is cultural (our language is embedded with metaphorical links; for example, the statement "I see things clearly" reveals our preference for vision over sound; looking is synonymous with conceptual understanding), Lakoff and Johnson claim that such modes of thinking are also a function of genetics. Is metaphorical listening a function of genetics and/or culture? Our interpretation of the Citroen commercial suggests that culture plays a role. Only because we have a story about Mozart and the Citroen's value do we transfer qualities of prestige or savvy from one to the other. Yet I also wonder whether our tendency to transfer the sounds' and images' attributes can also be traced to deeply rooted biological processes. When we hear a sound that puzzles us, we may try to locate its source. If the reverberating object is at a distance, sonic and visual cues will help determine the object's character. If we dimly see a saber-tooth tiger and hear a loud roar, we will believe the saber-tooth tiger is more powerful and imposing than if we hear a meow. The sound fills in the image and vice versa. Filmed images are two-dimensional and bereft of cues in terms of size and depth; hence, we may be more dependent on sound to piece out the nature of images than in the real world. When we watch a music video or film, we may even wish to parse out the music and determine what part belongs to the characters and what part to the background. Citing Bernard Herrmann on movie soundtracks, Cook notes that the music seems to "seek out and intensify the inner thoughts of the characters" as well as "invest a scene with terror, grandeur, gaiety, or misery," and this seeking facilitates the metaphorical relationship.[18]

This discussion leads us to some of the strangest aspects of musical multimedia relations: the viewer's experience of the fracture and reconfiguration of the multimedia object's components. Music, lyrics, or image may jut out. When my students write music-video analyses without much coaching, or after they have been snoozing during lectures, they will gravitate—as students do—to what feels most familiar, and they will write about music videos as if they were silent movies with the visual imagery signifying in full regalia. In "Whenever, Wherever" Shakira rolls around in the mud, signifying that she is a seductress who is willing to get dirty during sex; as a young woman emerging shyly onto a rock, she is Botticelli's Venus; diving into the ocean, she is Hans Christian Anderson's mermaid. In Garbage's "Breaking up the Girl," a red rose encased in glass symbolizes singer Shirley Manson's virginity, and the case fracturing represents her sexual liberation. I do not deny that these analyses have value. Flickering in and out, at some semiconscious level, the images must, at some points, stand for us in their isolation, unreeling like a silent movie. Similarly, with the music-video soundtrack, there are moments when the music seems to lie below the image, flowing underground, so to speak, and we must fill in the song's contours. The viewer also forges connections between music and image. These connections are Golem-like creations in which music animates people and objects so that their dispositions, implied power, and directionality have shifted into new configurations. Similarly, physical spaces become newly inflected so that they appear warm or cool, inviting or dangerous.[19]

Other relations emerge as well. Some elements fracture and then pair through a top-down relationship—such as when an element in one medium supersedes another and the two become linked. An upbeat motive in the soundtrack, a snare fill perhaps, links up with something even more hyper in the image—the sparkles at the back of the set. Opposites also bond, leaving the rest of the mix aside. The more pliant and melancholic singer links to music that sounds angrier and more defiant. The two media do not mesh, and the music stands as a shadow to the performer. There are also relations of connotation and denotation, gapmaking, and so forth, soon to be discussed.

These last descriptions have focused largely on pairings within a music video, but multimedia relations can color the whole surface as well. Music, image, and text could be described as existing in a relationship similar to those that people have. Almost any kind of transference or projection among people or within the psyche seems possible. U2's video "With or Without You" might be seen as a case study in melancholia. Worn down by a sense of loss, the image reels back from the music. Sometimes images can seem to repress or cloak musical materials. Madonna's "Material Girl" and Cindy Lauper's "Girls Just Want to Have Fun" are very different songs. Yet they could be heard to share some common ground in terms of vocal production and a sense of working-class, raucous, female adolescence. Lauper's video seems truer to the song, catching the jerky, bouncy movements, celebratory romp, and playful zaniness. The imagery for Madonna's "Material Girl" could be heard to constrain the music with its silken surfaces, baby-pink colors, ludicrous bow ties, costume jewelry, and world of men. We almost have to hear those musical elements that are rebellious and loose as separate from our viewing experience, somewhere outside of the tape.

We can take these audiovisual relations a step farther to leave more room for the viewer's experience. When the mind forges a metaphor, a third term may arise. The difference between the two terms that are brought into relation creates a space where a surplus value comes into play. A statement such as "What is black and white and read all over? (a newspaper)" is funny. "My boss treats me like a punching bag" provokes anger. "Work is freedom" or "Freedom is slavery" produces a disconnection. Because music-video image is so often chained to music to which it does not belong, for the viewer, an excess of affect rarely abates. A good example is the Super Furry Animals' "It's Not the End of the World?" which features a series of exploding atomic bombs. Many kinds of iconic and indexical connections link the bombs to the music. Guitar strums and the bass drum occur an instant before the bombs explode, seeming to trigger the weapons. The fuzzy and distorted production of "It's Not the End of the World?" matches the rough and fluffy texture of the mushroom cloud's ever-expanding debris of steam, smoke, and radiation, and the music's pace matches that of the appropriately sped up or down explosions. The song's anthemic style—it is very much within the tradition of Electric Light Orchestra's simple songs with ornate production values—fits the grandeur of the explosions. The song has a classic power-pop exultation—it makes me happy. Yet my response to the bombs is the same as to many horror films— I get an overwhelming urge to shrink back in my chair, or even better, to make a full-out break for it. The image and music together produce these two emotions oscillating rapidly with a third—a sense of disbelief and mild nausea.

SYNC POINTS CREATE LARGER FORMS

Though incomplete, the model of a music video as an array of points is a useful preliminary description for many videos. Are all of these joins—metaphorical, syncretic, indexical, symbolic, and iconic, those based on repetition and absence, and those responsive to sound—experienced differently by the viewer?[20] I believe that each type of point has its own flavor and provokes its own kind of response. We should talk about the ways that points prick, rub, or glide, seem near or distant, big or small, or even loud or soft.[21] Yet, even as each point has its particular nuance, all points seem equivalent at a higher structural level. At one level, music video transforms itself into momentary articulation— differences are erased as the song's melodic hook, a drum hit, an edit, or jab of the elbow comes forward in the mix. Within the musical context, all points become linked to pleasure. Points of connection in music videos resemble Lacan's *objet petit a's,* tiny desirable moments for which we yearn and which are distributed like a constellation.[22]

The last has been a discussion of how one-to-one connections can be established in music video. How do these connections begin to coalesce into larger units? The relations among music, image, and lyrics can unfold in a manner analogous to music's varied repetitions of a core set of materials. For example, in the case of music video image, modulating visual microrhythms— dappled light, smoke, water, fluttering cloth—provide variation in one domain. In U2's "With or Without You," we anticipate lead singer Bono's shifts in physical presentation: throughout most of the verse he carries himself with restraint, but at each verse's end, he offers an expressive gesture—a sudden collapse, a raising of his arms, a lean to the side, or a twist of the hip.

MUSIC VIDEO'S POETRY: VISUAL RHYME AS ENDLESS REPETITION

We now shift to a discussion of how patterns emerge over time and in space. In lyric poetry, words can be wrested from their ordinary context and made strange. What holds the words together in a lyric poem is often formal—similar sounds, rhythmic values, placement within the line. Such formal patterning contributes to what we recognize as art's heightened effects, wherein the object seems separate from ordinary lived time and space—sublime, even transcendent. Similarly, in music video, an image's apt reappearance against the musical line, and a well-judged change in its internal structure, creates patternings. By providing a mnemonic device, music's formal grid contributes to the structure. We can connect an earlier image that rhymes or relates thematically to an image we are now seeing, partly because the current sound and/or image echoes what took place two measures ago or in the previous verse; we will also learn to anticipate the image's placement in the near future—at the end of a melodic line or apex of a phrase.

Building subtle connections across a string of images is one of videomaker Mark Romanek's strengths. In the director's and Michael Jackson's "Scream," triangular plastic objects gradually morph into the roundness of Janet Jackson's breasts; the bungee balls that bounce down a corridor change into Michael Jackson's ponytail and then into the rounded branches of the bonsai that sits in the back of the meditation room. The Jackson Pollock action painting at the end of another aisle is an amalgam of earlier material—breaking glass, Michael Jackson's face contorted into a scream, and the wild blonde hair of the Andy Warhol litho. The transformation and culmination of these materials most often occurs at the ends of phrases.

Of course, other forms of art can reflect a similar structure. Comedy often relies on a tightly constructed form with temporal, spatial, and rhythmic elements. For example, at the end of each scene in *Bringing up Baby*, Cary Grant calls out, "I'll be with you in a minute, Mr. Peabody," which always gets a laugh. This recurring phrase dovetails with the film's references to children's games such as pin the tail on the donkey, hide-and-seek, and musical chairs. But music video, like poetry and song, presents its formal permutations in such a compressed way that the nature of the image's placement and internal deportment carries great weight.[23] Such transformations of material resemble that of motives in music, which resurface in new ways, with transactions occurring in the interim becoming mysterious. Much like musical motives, a series of images, separated in time, can seem well proportioned and linked together: both can be similar to a series of ripples created by a stone skipping off the surface of the water. If a varied image reappears, we can be encouraged to think it has undergone some change in its absence; perhaps the music has somehow changed the nature of this image. In Nine Inch Nails' "Closer," new images force a reconsideration of the links among many of the previous images. The video creates particularly elaborate chains of iconic connections: the black "door-man" blows dust off his hat—perhaps a reaction to something that caused the film to melt earlier; the juror's eye echoes a paper eye pasted on the arm of a metronome (à la Man Ray), and these eyes rhyme with the image of Trent Reznor's eye popping open in a still-life tableau; the salamanders hatching from eggs grow into eels that seem to stand in for the singer's genitalia while he hangs from the ceiling bound and gagged; the eviscerated heart nailed to a chair in the opening shot suggests the monkey stretched out on a surface (pos-sibly for vivisection) and the medical drawings of arms with tendons splayed out; Reznor's microphone looks like a breast with a nipple, and his tongue seems phallic. This string of imagery culminates in the image of the doorman holding a cow's tongue in one hand.

Repetitions can happen as frequently as in Nine Inch Nails' "Closer," but they can also occur less often. Through imagery separated in time but linked through similar small physical gestures, Michael Jackson's "Earth Song" asks viewers to save the planet. On beat four of the last measure of each verse, a tree is felled or a seal bludgeoned by a club. All living things seem endangered. In the choruses, indigenous people claw the earth, and in the bridge, a dolphin, trapped in a fisherman's net, rubs its snout against the knotted ropes. Though these two moments are separated temporally, and the actions are different—digging to get in, scratching to get out—musical codes connect man and animal.

As with Jackson's "Earth Song," audio/visual patterns can congeal to make a larger point, and they can do so through heterogeneous materials. In LL Cool J's "Doin' It," a video celebrating sex, a string of connections drawn from lyrics, image, and music unfolds in what feels like a type of metric order (with sync points occurring most frequently on 2 and 4): LL passes a hotel called "rock-dale." He then eats an apple while he ogles a woman at a strip joint. She swishes her skirt appreciatively to the rapper's gesture of raising his hands in the air and holding the apple in his mouth like a stuffed pig. (A few shots later we see a policeman—a pig.) Walking toward LL's car, the stripper opens her coat, flashing the viewer, and we see the word *cock-tails*. As she climbs onto his lap, he pulls a straw out of his mouth and sings, "Baby, you can bounce me back." The sex play then builds to a fever pitch, and the straw, paired slyly with the rim shot of the snare drum, suggests that the male member will rise to the occasion.[24]

MORE ON REPETITION IN PATTERN BUILDING

Exploiting the viewer's familiarity with music video's codes, directors can forge numerous iconic, indexical, and symbolic connections across different visual and musical parameters—beat, contour, dynamics, harmony, timbre, arrange-ment, color, space, setting, prop, and types of shot. These connections can help directors construct larger forms. Such connections are possible in part because particular associations occur so frequently that they start to make up a language. A camera pulling out from a crane shot underscores a swell in the arrangement (as in Creed's "With Arms Wide Open"); a camera tilt up with the performer's arms raised overhead matches a modulation up a whole step (as in John Secada's "Just Another Day without You"); a bell-like pentatonic melody is reflected by a performer wearing a kimono, while jangly guitar music is accompanied by ripped T-shirts and jeans (as in Madonna's "Take a Bow" and Blur's "Song 2"); a thin vertical flash of light two-thirds from the left-hand margin of the frame brings the snare to the fore (as in Maxwell's "Fortunate"). These articulations differ from one another, but they all serve to accentuate the music. These many ways of linking music with image can be shaped into larger patterns, each iteration creating expectations about both the music and the image: the unfolding of a visual pattern prompts us to wonder whether the music will carry on accordingly—or if one medium is more prescient, foreshadowing some transformation that will soon occur in the other.

Within such a richly articulated skein, one particular type of connection serves to establish music video's continuity. It is formed by iconic shapes: musical shapes, through contour, dynamics, or rhythm, or visual shapes, by means of camera movement, editing, or physical gestures. In such cases the music and image become reducible to a few strokes, such as glide, glide, glide, hold, dip, hold, something that could be heard or visualized as a few curves and dashes. Though there is a lot of variety in the ways a basic shape like glide, glide, glide, hold, dip, hold can be realized, its simplicity allows viewers to recognize the norm and departures from it. Such variations upon a theme might include a series of visual glides suggested through a beam of light passing across the frame, a camera panning momentarily, and the back wheel of a bicycle turning forward, a musical one through a held tone on a saxophone, a drum roll, and a sustained note on a guitar. With the addition of hold, dip, hold, such a pattern can be extensively manipulated—one medium can put the pattern into retrograde, diminution, or augmentation, as well as permute or offset it slightly from another's.

Such patterning does limit possible readings, but there is a considerable gain in a type of focused viewing. Let us look at a common example of this kind of pattern: the glide and hold realized through a long tracking shot followed by a big close-up of the star. The video seems to say, "Lie back for awhile. Now look at the hook. Let's try it again!" Though this type of articulation is simplistic if not brutish, it offers different vantage points on the music. We might first hear the music as a wash, even if we sometimes notice particulars, and next we focus more intently on an immediate thing, at this moment in time. Such a pattern offers the viewer a sense of prowess, of being able to traverse the distance from the broadest structural landmarks to the smallest details. When the pattern repeats—three types of tracking shots with three different objects within the frame—the viewer senses how to experience a section and how to hold onto a visual line against the music. Of course, a musical pattern can also constrain the ways our eyes move within the frame, drawing our attention to what is cluttered or empty, high or low within the frame, and to what moves or stays still. So which medium's pattern takes precedence? Most frequently, it is the one with the sharpest contours. A deft director can delineate the contours of the image in this manner at points when the music needs underscoring. Because recorded popular music is a multiparametric practice open to numerous interpretations, the visual scaffolding can lead us to adopt one type of listening over another, but this is often a musical one. In Hype Williams's treatment of Macy Gray's "Do Something," as the song moves from the verse into the chorus, the camera pulls back as Gray makes the basketball signal for traveling, rolling her forearms one over another. Such a gesture directs us to move past the end of the verse and head straight for the chorus; a fade to black, for example, might suggest that the verse and chorus are separated off from one another. We could choose to hear the song in either way; a director's interpretation will need to show us the merits of a particular way of listening, most likely by establishing a link between one moment and another. Perhaps, in the case of Gray's "Do Something," it will be through the grand outchorus waiting in the wings.

LARGER-SCALE STRUCTURES

We have focused on moment-to-moment connections among music, image, and lyrics, and considered how they form larger patterns. Now let us shift to a different structural level. What about swatches of music or image? The notion of the topos is helpful here. Musical materials tend to possess cultural associations. We can recognize music that is sexy, rowdy, angry at adults, particularly good for parties, or gloomy about everything. We also recognize music that is coded as reflecting a specific race, class, age, gender, or sexuality, as well as belonging within one musical genre more than another. A string of images also possesses a cultural and social content. When music and image are placed together, the image can mimic, play against, mock, or even ignore the song. Our understandings of musical codes can play with and against what we know about visual codes. The question of how such topics are linked to genre, race, gender, and so on is well covered in the chapter on settings, so I will only give a few examples here.

Music videos are obliged to advertise their home genres (much as record covers have long done), yet at the same time, they need to exhibit the new. This is lastly because they must withstand multiple viewings and appeal to a wide range of viewing audiences. We all know the core ingredients for one strand of rap video: expensive cars, money, champagne, scantily clad women, pools, and Jacuzzis. What is interesting is when the representation takes two steps to the left, as in Puff Daddy's "Mo Money, Mo Problems," in which some of the self-aggrandizement can be displaced onto flashpots, Puffy's pretending he is Tiger Woods, and the stars' maneuvering a Sputnik-type spacecraft. A sense of play can then be created through such devices as bug-eyed glasses, puffy clothes, and some nice joshing in front of the wide-angle lens against Diana Ross's thin, vocal sample. The odd combination of the too-tough men, the woman's breathy voice, and expanding rows of show lights suggests a sense of self-reflexivity and even humility.

The image can construct a home genre for a song. For Gloria Estefan's remake of "Turn the Beat Around," director Marcus Nispel placed the singer on the roof of a cylindrical glass building at night, encircled by helicopters with beams of lights flashing on and off and the twinkling city lights below. Nispel told me in an interview of spring 1997 that he felt that such a setting might remind the viewer of the disco dance floor, complete with the mirror ball and multicolored lights. What does disco share with metropolitan centers and corporate capitalism? And how do these relate to this version of the song?

In Eminem's "Without Me," imagery of Jews and Muslims suddenly allow us to hear the source for the vocal adlibs as ethnic folk music. Perhaps the realm of rap music and Eminem's and Dre's musical world stretch wider than we assumed. What do vaudeville and rap share in common?

To gauge the meaning of a music or image, viewers can draw upon a large reservoir of cultural associations; these connections have sources like opera, church hymns, radio, vaudeville, pulp magazines, film posters, magazine ads, and so forth. When a variety of visual and musical materials are brought into play in one video, these materials can seem to enter into conversation with one another, offering commentary, calling one another into question, and even, through placement and underscoring, one or several deriding or discrediting the others.

In LL Cool J's "Six Minutes of Pleasure," the video's music and image possess a hypnotic quality that occasionally slips into the deranged. The joke of the video is that the music—performed in the video on a tiny toy piano—wins out. LL, the protagonist, taunts a young woman flirtatiously in a gigantic playpen; all of the toys are adult-sized, and he chases her around with enormous hobbyhorses and tricycles. LL's slow, seductive, repetitive vocals against a sleepy trancelike musical accompaniment might lead one to wonder whether the star's intent is on hypnotizing and then seducing the woman, or whether his libido is more free-floating. He likes the adult-sized Fisher-Price bicycles, and the video sometimes cuts to children's versions of the couple wearing child-sized rap accoutrements of furs and jewelry, and playing with toys cut to their scale. LL sometimes abandons his manly chase, because a toy piano becomes much more mesmerizing. He will occasionally turn his attention toward it and play a toy piano melody—here the video switches to a close-up with a miniature piano and his enormous hand and face swelling to fill the frame, while the accompaniment thins to foreground the piano—it becomes clear that the melody is more crazed than anything we have witnessed thus far. It is strange that the music should be able to comment on materials used earlier in the video, and even be able to up the ante. The irony is that a little toy-piano melody is more authorial and perverse than the video's heavily Freudian setting, and more knowing than the buff, muscle-bound superstar and his attractive partner. Suddenly, the relations among gender, sexuality, childhood and adulthood seem called into question.

In Robert Palmer's "Addicted to Love," elements in the image and music provide a take on the song in an unusually sophisticated way. The director exploits a feature of film music that Bernard Herrmann understood, that musical materials seek out elements within the frame. Here, parts of the song are distributed across the image, ultimately to critique our notions of gender and power. The song possesses a hard-hitting bass drum alongside the power chords on the guitars, all of which are rounded out by the entrance of the horns; together, they give the music a great deal of frontality and power; however, very little reverb is added to the mix, and the ends of phrases seem to be cut short. It might seem that the "breaking-ball" quality of the music would not have any visual equivalent, but here it does: the video possesses musical and visual correspondences based on size, shape, color, and movement. Both Palmer and a group of models, who look like mannequins carefully disposed in the background, stand rooted to their marks. The women claim our allegiance more than Palmer does; we sense that the video's authority resides with them, not with him. Although the models do not sing, their high-heeled steps and swinging hips carry great weight. Their clinging dresses—a pastiche of prison, schoolmarm, and Gestapo uniforms—grow longer and more severe as we read from left to right. Color and movement organize the frame. The colors of the women—pale white skin, black dress, red lips—are echoed by the painted backdrop of ominous, unfurling storm clouds of red, black, and white. Palmer is color-coordinated as well, dressed in black and white, with a trace of red ringing his microphone stand. In addition to their black dresses, the braless women wear slicked-back hair, silver waistbands, black tights, and fire-red, high-gloss lipstick. Their breasts roll, exhibiting the motion and power that we would associate with the images of the clouds; here is our first moment of strange redistribution. Both clouds and women thrust forward, but the clouds are a static image, which leaves the women with a greater degree of agency. A flat, frontal light, almost like a car headlight, trains on the figures and freezes Palmer like a deer in its tracks. This gesture breaks the momentum a bit and holds the video in abeyance. While Palmer gets stuck, the women keep moving, nonplussed. *He* risks falling outside of the song's flow. (An early medium close-up reveals the singer pumping his arm off the beat, and his singing is more constrained than the arrangement as a whole.) The women, on the other hand, may become linked with an element in the mix that continues to resonate— the noisy, even bawdy guitar lick in the upper register. Our desire for a visual correlate to the voracious musical elements makes us circulate within the image. These musical elements do not bind to Palmer, who seems overlit and washed-out, nor to the static storm clouds. Finally, we must choose the women, or at least their accessories—the metal jewelry, lip gloss, and stilettos. These women cannot be addicted to love. Perhaps Palmer (or the viewer) is the fall guy.

This contradiction of cause and effect is a key feature of the "Addicted to Love" video. Containing the same qualities of force held under restraint as the music, the imagery distributes the materials in a surprising way; the pleasure of the video stems from the fact that power comes not from the expected sources, like the male lead singer and the storm clouds, but from breasts and flowing hemlines. The confusing roles played by light, sound, color, and mobility provide an opportunity for the women and the song to take on greater authority (fig. 9.2).

FIGURE 9.2 Robert Palmer's "Addicted to Love." Subverting the dominant discourse through musical multimedia relations; to what parts of the image do the song's various materials belong?

CONFORMANCE, COMPLEMENT, AND CONTEST

Nicholas Cook offers descriptions of a range of musical multimedia connections that can be used for our discussion of music video. He enumerates types of connections, from conformance (based on similarity and congruence, but not metaphoric play—a rare occurrence, he claims), to complementarity (exhibiting neither consistency nor contradiction), to contest (foregrounding collision). Cook does not make clear whether these terms work best for describing momentary sync points or larger sections of material, or whether they should be understood as generalized analytic techniques; while I believe they can serve all of these functions, they seem best suited to a discussion of larger formal sections of music video because such relations are understood within a context. An example of conformance might include the moments in Walt Disney's *Fantasia* that contain line animations and color solely. In the "Mercy St." analysis (Chapter 13), I claim that the ghostly qualities of music and image are conformant: at one level, music and image say the same things, are synonymous. Multimedia makers, however, often like to work somewhere in the felicitous middle, where each medium does what the other cannot; this would represent complement, in which, as Lawrence Kramer says, the media "confront each other across the locked gate of semiotic difference." though the transfer of attributes can still take place.[25] For example, in film music or opera, the image and words may adopt a denotative function, the music, a connotative one; in such cases, the music informs the viewer of the image's social import or context. In music video, the situation is reverse: in order to showcase the music, the image connotes, providing a gloss upon the music. In Madonna's "Cherish," the image informs us of the music's timelessness, in "Gett Off," the music's ornate exoticism, and in "Mercy St.," the music's ability to carry a secret. Here, the image interprets the music; it even frequently oversteps its complementary role and begins to act as a tour guide: "attend to this rhythm, now listen to this timbre, now back to that rhythm." Cook also describes a special instance of complementary relation known as "gapmaking." In film music, some registers of the music are left empty to make room for the voice track. To make way for the music in opera, singers are rendered more as archetypes than as richly drawn characters. Music video's bare settings and schematic characters can function similarly. Yet, music videos rarely stay in a complementary relationship, often lapsing into contest. The voice supersedes the lyrics to become pure utterance and then takes over the arrangement, the image suddenly draws our attention away from the voice, encouraging us to think about it in a narrative fashion. Such examples highlight the transitory, processual nature of most multimedia relations. As Cook notes, "the idea of complementation easily turns into an assumption of primacy."[26] Sometimes the image in music video can seem to boss around the song. The image in Madonna's "Material Girl," for example, forecloses the possibility of critique by settling for an easy ironic stance toward the video's kitsch sources. Cook suggests that the image in "Material Girl" often works through contest, because it superimposes a complete diegesis upon the song.

MODES OF FORMAL CONNECTION: BEGINNINGS, MIDDLES, AND ENDS

Music videos work to establish a sense of a wholeness through the creation of beginnings, middles, and ends. Though there are many ways to create beginnings, middles and ends, the following is one common method that videos use to create a sense of closure. Many videos open by attempting to convince us that we are moving into a special realm by presenting imagery of boundaries or thresholds. In Prince's "Gett Off," once Diamond and Pearl (the female protagonists) have been allowed entrance into the hall for their "audition," huge double doors are opened, and they are invited to pass through. The space that they find beyond this threshold is the studio in which the band performs the song (which begins immediately), but more important, this space functions as a kaleidoscope of settings—a bachelor pad, a harem, a nightclub, a warehouse.

Close synchronization between music and image occurs much more frequently near the beginnings of videos, perhaps to impress the viewer with a sense that the two realms are more than arbitrarily related. The clarity of close synchronization can be used to suggest the presence of deeper, less obvious music-image connections. At the beginning of Peter Gabriel's "Mercy St.," there is a group of shots in which the camera pans upward on various houses. This upward panning creates the effect of the houses falling through space, and thereby reflects the falling contours of the melodic line. This close synchronization rarely lasts through the whole of the video. More typically, the video will relax into a looser mode of connection with the music, underscoring this change by a movement into a more open space. Even though the mode of connection between music and image becomes less obvious, the connection is not therefore dissolved: freed from the requirement of close synchronization, the editing of the image, and the imagery itself, can draw attention to musical features other than the rhythms in the foreground of the song, in particular, the song's structures—the character of a chord progression, or the movement from one section into another. For example, in "Cherish," a large section of music and a group of images, work together to form a slow ritard that takes us into a new section of the song. As the bass line moves downward, our eyes sweep through the frame from high to low, and this sweep takes us from the shore into the water where the mermen reside. The final section of a video will often allow the connections between music and image to become even more tenuous. Rather than the close synchronization typical of openings or the careful delineation of larger musical structures that characterizes many middles of videos, the endings of videos present very simple but broadly spaced connections between music and image—the points of synchronization will be very clear and simple, but they will appear only infrequently. These more casual kinds of connection rely upon the trust that the rest of the video has created in the viewer by means of its more obvious music/image connections. Without a belief in the depth of the relation between music and image in the video, the closing sections of videos will seem simply to have dissolved the music-image connection. In "Mercy St.," oars from a rowboat dip into the water on the first beat of every measure, and then the image tracks down a long hallway. As the music continues, we have a sense of hovering over it.

Music videos have other strategies to create beginnings, middles, and ends. Although one common beginning is an image of transition, such as a doorway or a passageway, another is a moment of liminality—the performer wakes up from a dream and falls into a reverie. Sometimes we may not recognize that what we are seeing is transitional until the song kicks in. In Janet Jackson's "Love Will Never Do," we see Jackson dancing, as it were, a maypole around her lover, as if accompanied by plucked harp sounds and a synthesizer. The song kicks in with a hard rock backbeat, and we see Janet Jackson in the middle of a desert, shot with more high-contrast black-and-white film. We realize the previous moment exists within a type of twilight or border state.

Many videos often have a longer, more fully developed middle-section. In the midsection of LL Cool J's "Ain't Nobody," the underwater camera repeatedly returns to a extended shot of a woman swimming underwater in a pool, while in Madonna's "Cherish" a group of male mermen swim in arc formation underwater. In New Edition's "Hit Me Off," Wu Tang's "Ghost Face Killer," and The Presidents of the United States of America's "Peaches," ninjas stage elaborate martial arts fights against the performers in each band. All of these videos build to a larger set piece.

Sometimes music videos are organized less around the principle of beginnings, middles, and ends than one of "slow disclosure."[27] Here, the video's context is offered piecemeal, thereby enticing the viewer to watch the entirety of the video to make sense of the whole. In Blackstreet's "No Diggity," elliptical references to film noir and early black action films, early southern blues performance, and contemporary song and dance must be put into relation: a group of dancers works a concrete highway; the group "Blackstreet" raps in overalls on a sandy beach at night; behind them stands a strangely lit shack carved with Chinese insignia; a miniature animated doll, like the Penny Hardaway look-alike in the Nike commercials, accompanies himself on a banjo or an old rundown piano; a woman rapper slithers and speaks like Betty Boop; dancers raise their hands into doggy poses and slap their hands on the concrete. Even though the song contains a number of early blues references, it is only when we see the dancers perform a certain type of strut (reminiscent of the old black-and-white Warner Bros. cartoons with, for example, a line of decked out, trucking, lascivious wolves) do we see the depth of the video's historical references and are able to place the more modern elements of the song within a context.

Prince's "1999" works similarly. The video opens with band members standing on a severely canted stage adorned by pink neon hearts. All are shown in silhouette and then briefly illuminated by a searchlight. The revelation of shots follows instrumental entrances, first the drums, bass, keyboard, female backup singers, and finally Prince, who runs out from back to center stage, grabbing the mike to sing, "Sky was all purple, people were everywhere." The camera then stays with no more than groups of two or three performers, leaving the disclosure of space incomplete. At the second chorus, the back-up singers, framed by heart-shaped cutouts above the star, provocatively sing, "before I let it happen I'll dance my life away," doubling Prince at the octave. Finally, the camera cuts to a long shot with all of the band members in the same space. Not only do we now know the space, but we also have a greater sense of how instrumental parts fit within the song as a whole.

PHYSICAL DESCRIPTION

Yet the descriptions thus far do not seem fully to encapsulate the large-scale structure of music video. Though of limited use, imagery drawn from the physical world can help illustrate the ways music video looks and feels. For example, music video's three media—sound, image, and lyrics—can seem similar to the merging of three rivers, when some of each river's basic outlines remain discernible. We can make out the contours of each medium, yet some elements become erased. A question arises: When media combine, do elements placed in the foreground (and background) shift? In the case of a still or moving image, the elements frequently do not coexist equally in the foreground. We may not see some of the background—it may be submerged in shadow or as parts of the bric-a-brac on the wall—and in a pop song we might not be able to hear all of the inner voices, yet we sense these elements' presence. Do some of the spatial, temporal, and narrative elements in the music video's song or image move to the background solely to contribute a bit of depth and sheen?

A conflicting model would suggest that depth drops out. Are music videos just scaffolding, suggestive only of essential structures, like a book's table of contents? Recent cognitive science supports this view.[28] In either case—a structure with only partially revealed content, or a sketchy grid—do media combine into something that is a new whole but also unstable and flickery—a substance like Jell-O? What holds together the composite is tenuous, and the viewer may struggle to conceive of the work as a whole—much the same as trying simultaneously to see both sides of Wittgenstein's duck-rabbit. Perhaps music video triggers a surprising species of viewer synesthesia, where attributes of one medium transfer to the other. Some of the spatialization connected with visualization may infuse the music, making the audio track seem as if it were a three-dimensional object. (Elsewhere, I draw on the image of reaching into a hologram and touching a sound's edge.) The image may change as well, becoming more active and present, possessing a more measurable, charged space, as if space could be placed within a grid.

Because music videos are experienced temporally, we may want to create a more dynamic model. A director who brings elements to the fore and back, may still need to account for the course that a viewer's perception follows. Does the image come to the fore at the edit, and only then—as the visual material within the frame becomes redundant—do the sounds and lyrics take on their own weight? Because the media shift quickly from the fore to the background, the viewer may not fully grasp any of them, leaving an aftertaste.

Can we begin to develop a kind of background-to-foreground model for music video, as has been done for the Viennese classical style in music?[29] Or should we remain on the surface of music videos? A depth-model for music video might look quite different from one for music alone. A visual fundamental line might include a narrative or a process-driven structure—for example, the distance we must cover to get to the party, the interval required for the fireman to climb up onto the roof and catch the cat, or the time it takes the image to find something witty within the section in which he plays out his drama. The music of a video might reveal a few descending pitches or a basic harmonic movement—elements that may be patchy to make room for image and lyrics. With this as a background, the middleground distinguishes itself through the kind of broad matching shapes just discussed involving music, image, and lyrics. The extreme foreground might include the smallest details—the image's microrhythms, the music's timbres, and the words' sonic qualities.

10

Analytical Methods

FOR MONTHS, when I worked on Prince's "Gett Off" video, I could not find a way in. All I could do was admire a number of its features: its ability to seem warm and forthcoming, yet reactionary; its ability to embody so much detail. In this case, I learned a new way of attending to subtle inflections in the background of the image, and I became interested in holding off the analytic method until I had found a way to be sensitive to the demands of the video before me. But when materials run dry, I consider the video by means of the issues discussed in the previous chapters. Often, I will take a single musical or visual parameter—harmony, motivic transformation, rhythm, phrasing, settings, editing—and consider the entirety of the video in its light. By the close of the analytic process, I will have considered the tape in terms of all of the parameters I have listed. I find it useful as well to turn off the image and study the music alone, or to focus on the image without the sound or with the sound turned very loud or very soft. I watch the tape in slow motion, or I go over small sections of the video.

I have not found a quick or easy method for analyzing music video. From my experience, what a video has to say is located in the relation of all of its parts as it plays out in time—in a play between both the visual and musical codes. This is found in the figure's gesture or facial expression in one section, and its relation to another in another section, in what the music is doing in one location and elsewhere, in what the videomaker finds musically worthy of emphasis and in what she chooses to downplay. An approach such as this, which centers on formal concerns, can take one deep into these processes. But this approach is slow—it calls for learning all of the music, image, and lyrics, and the relations among all three. I will propose a method for accomplishing this in the chapters that follow. My analyses suggest paths of attending to music video.

Although I have stressed the notion that music video works as a processual form, its character is determined as well by moments that change or break the flow. Such moments include not only surprises and anomalies but also shots that contain especially pointed messages or depictions, and even shots that establish a peak in some visual domain—brightest or darkest, clearest or murkiest, closest or most distant, and so on. How can we both attend to the disruptive force of these moments and preserve the importance of changing relations? (This question demands negotiations similar to those required by the economy of videos that include reflections of musical structure, use of narrative techniques, and borrowing from advertising.) Perhaps the best way to answer the question might be to see what might be added to an analysis of a video that treats only these moments.

Kobena Mercer's "Monster Metaphors: Notes on Michael Jackson's 'Thriller'" contains sensitive discussion of the multiple ways that Jackson is depicted in the video—as "fictional boyfriend," "real superstar," and monster. Mercer focuses explicitly upon two moments in the video: when he becomes a monster, and when he becomes a zombie. He uses the multiple characterization of Jackson as a way of discussing these transformations, calling them not only metamorphoses, but also metaphors for "the sexual and racial ambiguity of his image and for the *aesthetic reconstruction of Michael Jackson's face.*"[1] The video's theme of transformation can be brought into relation with its more processual features, the dance sequence in particular.

Like so many of Jackson's videos—"Bad," "Smooth Criminal," "Beat It," and so on—the dance sequences form a major part of "Thriller," and in these Jackson is one member of a collective group. There are two important features of these dance sequences. One is where the dancers move at a slower pace than, move in sync with, and then seem to supersede the music, thereby incorporating an almost overwhelming momentary sense of power and presence. The other is where Michael Jackson gains, loses, and regains his identity within these sequences. These sequences point to music and image as responsible for very large processes of transformation, and for larger questions about who Michael Jackson is as both a public and private persona. These dance sequences must now be put into relation with the moments of physical transformation. This will begin the process of a music-video analysis.

I have found that music-video analysis brings forth a wealth of material, some of it useful for providing insights into the concerns of the videomaker. A music-video director works in a state of self-denial: the illusion is that the power comes from the music. But by the end of the analytical process, I will become so familiar with the inner workings of a video that I will have a sense of a directorial voice speaking in the video. A well-made video can exhibit musical kinds of expressive nuance, through variations in phrasing, rhythm, and pacing. It can have qualities reminiscent of a painter's brush stroke—one can sense how the director met the material, how he or she feels about different parts of the music; one can detect a pattern of thought. But because these patterns blend into the texture of the video, these traces can be hard to sense.

The process of analysis can bring forth an awareness of the ways music videos present images of the world that have fragility and beauty. For example, Aerosmith's video "Crazy" can be seen as a commentary on the Ridley Scott film *Thelma and Louise*. The video seems to elide some of the film's more progressive aspects; for example, the exploits of the two girls in "Crazy" become more clearly sexual than political. Similarly, though the progressive image of homosexuality is drawn more sharply, it may serve simply to make us feel better about objectifying the characters as desirable objects. Nevertheless, the video is able to maintain a sense of daring, pleasure, and deviance that *Thelma and Louise* only supports sporadically. The video creates this sense through a subtle play of visual and musical codes. The "Cherish" video, which I analyze in chapter 11, puts forth the image of a new social configuration: here, women are strong enough to hold up the social structure; gay men can exist in their own community in peace; and children can have a kind of autonomy to move as they like. This image goes against the grain of patriarchy. In "Cherish," this fragile worldview is held up by the harmonic structure, which acts like pillars to hold up the ephemeral images. In this music video, such an image is held up with a great deal of generosity, grace, and restraint.

I do not want to say that all videos are progressive, nor do I want to deny that the forces of capital, vertical corporate structures, and a somewhat unengaged public create huge restraints on the medium. However, I think that a number of videos are indeed progressive, and that some of this progressive spirit can be traced to interpersonal dynamics—videomakers tend to pride themselves on working with music that they care about and to which they feel committed. Many videos are expressions of relations: the videomaker, the band, the locations, and the music can all be brought into play. Music is one thing that people in our culture can still care deeply about, and we should not be surprised by the fact that many videos are strongly felt. Angus Fletcher, speaking about the role of the author in literature, may be useful in reminding us of the author's role in many media, including music video:

Often in recent criticism we have seen a pretense that no author is doing the thinking; there is only a text. Critics personify the textual as if each text could write itself or as if each text were the automatic product of some magical, corporate, cultural machine known as ideology. Furthermore, these personifications mutate and reproduce, anything at all can be text, or be so called. The net effect of pantextualism has been to weaken the last saving remnant of individual style and wit. It is not always remembered that great works of literature require style and intelligence, which belong to an author. An impersonal critique claiming the automatic production of texts, tends to enfeeble the reader's awareness that authors may seek to be thoughtful and mindful. To be able to study such relationships requires that we use superordinate terms for the activity of mind, namely "thought" and "thinking." Postmodern critical subtlety cannot supersede such terms.[2]

My belief is that videos can have authors. This is argued for in the analyses that follow.

Let me suggest a way of opening up an understanding of music video. Watch a video that is engaging, and attend to moments that are the most evocative. Seize a moment and play it in the imagination. This moment, when committed to memory, may be a bit transformed: the music, in particular, will sound a bit different. (Chion discusses how our audiovisual memories often change when we reflect upon them, pointing to films such as *Blade Runner* and *Touch of Evil*.[3]) Still in the imagination, learn the features of the moment, its feel and affect. Upon return to the video, most likely, the image and music will seem more familiar, and it will be possible to work toward seeing how the video builds toward this moment and moves away from it.

I have learned that the moments I value tend to be those of the figure in a moment seemingly of grace and meaning in suspension against the larger flow and movement of the music. Once I have chosen to attend to these moments, they acquire a kind of permanence. This sense is similar to the way that people speak about their relation to music, its repeatability, its permanence. I have been thinking about Aerosmith's "Crazy," and particularly the scene in which one of the girls is singing in the bar, and the image suddenly turns a very deep blood red. The way that this image works so well on me is still, for all of my justifications, a bit inscrutable, but I can feel its weight against the music, and can move into the moment and out of it, *with* the video.

OTHER METHODS OF ANALYSIS

The previous chapters provide numerous ways of considering music videos. Before moving to the close analyses, I would like to provide a couple more. The technique of commutation can be helpful for considering music videos. Here, we take an object and imagine changing one of its cultural parameters, such as race, class, gender, sexuality.[4] We might also substitute a formal feature, such as color, setting, or sense of time, and then see how it reads. Such an approach can also be used with popular music.[5] For example, we might consider how a song works with a Klezmer accompaniment, a male rather than a female singer, different tempi or lyrics. What types of new meanings emerge? Using such an approach with music video would mean imagining different types of music against visuals. One can also do the opposite experiment—keep the music as a constant and change the visual parameters. In the case of the latter trial, one might imagine imagery that would be the least surprising— that falls along the grain of the song—then move into more unpredictable realms. Madonna's "Music," which features a vocoder as part of a house ar-rangement, could conceivably involve robots clad in aluminum foil–covered cardboard boxes dancing before a white cyclorama or within a disco environ-ment. This imagery would bring forth not only the dance and mechanical elements of the song but also its homemade qualities. Next, we might try imagery from Jonas Akerlund's music video (screened in high rotation on MTV). The video features imagery of a disco combined with a 1970s black action theme. While Akerlund's setting in a disco environment feels right, the 1970s black action theme seems like surplus, almost a tag-on. At a still greater remove from the music would be a concatenation of the numerous sundry images from Madonna's oeuvre—geisha, polar bear, Tide detergent packaging, green turf, and the court of Louis XIV. With this fantastical arrangement, the synthesizer pad sounds busy and thin, and the lack of detail in the song comes to the fore. The experiment with placing different types of imagery against a pop song shows us that music-video directors rarely choose to use material that replicates our cultural and biological understanding of the song. Rather, the imagery and lyrics stray a bit from the music, teasing our perceived conceptions of the music's uses. Many of Madonna's music videos extend the song's possibilities through a transgression along the lines of race, culture, and class. Is Madonna rich, white, cheap, or highbrow? Is the music working class, black, classy, or tawdry? (Think of the provocative yet tongue-in-cheek "Like a Prayer," "Material Girl," and "Express Yourself.")

Attending to moments of disjunction or contradiction among media is helpful. Directors who work against the grain, challenging a conventional understanding of a song, share something in common with those who create commercials for print and television. Both exploit the trick question "What's wrong with this picture?" In a print ad there is often something to catch the viewer's eye—a fish growing out of a person's ear à la René Magritte, for example. Even brand names like Sunkist, Brill-o, and Tasty Cake possess disparate elements—sun-kissed reveals a taste for the poetic, and the abbreviated misspelling shows an interest in American no-nonsense practical speed.[6] The visual discrepancies in advertising can serve several purposes, first functioning as a stop sign, catching and holding the viewer's gaze rather than letting it swim within the stream of ongoing advertising. They then force the viewer to make sense of the gaps within the image as well as among other visual images and other experiences. These disjunctions can even provoke reflections about the status of the product, its history, value, and place in the culture. (Think of the enigmatic slogans for ads by Volkswagen—"Drivers Wanted"—and Apple Computer's "Think Different.") In music video, arresting the viewer's eye and ear accomplishes this and other goals as well. The gap between the music and the highly compressed, concatenated images creates a sense of speed and energy. The image has a variety and depth to equal the music's bite, thus enabling it to establish its own trajectory.

The comparison with television ads may provoke the familiar argument that music videos are themselves advertisements. Although this argument would not carry us very far, it is important to attend to those *moments* in a video that look like advertisements, that borrow techniques from advertising or that bring music videos closer to advertising. It might be argued that music videos function as advertisements no more than do pop songs or films.[7] Let me provide a few examples of how advertising can play a role in music video.

Videos designed to promote movies and their soundtracks with their straight incorporation of movie footage that might already be recognizable from trailers and ads are the most frankly like ads. From my experiences with talking with fans, I have learned that these videos are seen as manipulative and too easy, and are not "true" videos. Warren G's and Nate Dogg's "Regulate" forms an exception. The video held the Number 1 spot in the MTV Top 20 Countdown throughout the summer of 1994. This may be because the director chose un-dramatic, everyday footage from the film *Above the Rim,* and this footage bears an elliptical relation to the footage of the members of the band. The film footage is not material that would be used in trailers, and is related to themes as well as the visual style of the video. The film does not seem like a pretext for the video, and Tupac Shakur, who appears in this film footage, is a rapper himself.

Videos that emphasize performance footage can also work as ads, but there is a great deal of variation in the way this is articulated. Metallica's video "Noth-ing Else Matters," shot in a small rehearsal studio in warm tones, seems like a very clear attempt on the part of the record company to show a more intimate side of the band.[8] Unlike their other videos, "Everywhere I Roam" is a perfor-mance tape compiled from footage taken from an entire tour. The tape does not point to any particular concert, but rather seems intent on creating an entire effect. The lyrics talk about being on the road and thereby place the song in a well-established subgenre with representatives from southern rock, hard rock, and heavy metal, such as Lynyrd Skynyrd's "Freebird" and Bob Seger's "Turn the Page."

The notion of a video as advertising is compatible with the ideas and func-tion of a musical hook. The main vocal hook of the song already functions as a technique to increase both visibility and memorability. The device of under-scoring the musical hook appears most frequently in rap: rap songs often set off the vocal hook from the rest of the song by assigning it to the whole crew, by repeating it within the chorus, and by complementing it with a memorable sample or instrumental lick. This is frequently matched by a catchy physical gesture. The hook for Naughty by Nature's "Hip Hop Hooray" is accompanied with hands waving in the air. The hook for A Tribe Called Quest's "Oh My God" is set by a man enthusiastically rapping "Oh, my God!" while he stands on top of a building wearing a yellow coat. Here the hook is underscored, as it were, by a yellow highlighter.

The video can advertise the song by showing the pride that the band has in the hook. In Tag Team's "Whoomp, There It Is!" and Naughty by Nature's "OPP," the rappers and their crews seem excited by the hook, and this excite-ment becomes contagious. The image suggests a way to experience a hook that might be considered as a communal endeavor.

For the last examples of analytic approaches, we can turn to Nicholas Cook's work *Analyzing Musical Multimedia.* Cook suggests ways of working that would serve music video well: "analyzing multimedia requires a sensitivity to what might be termed degenerate or decayed hierarchies—hierarchies, in other words, whose internal connections have begun to unravel, resulting in flattened, network-like structures or associative chains" (145). He provides a number of useful questions to consider: "Do there appear to be constant relationships between the various media … or are these relationships variable and contextual? How far does the IMM [an instance of multimedia] correspond to discrete stages in the production process … and to what might be called the hierarchy of authorship?" (133–34). He offers good plans of action: "listen to or look at each contributory medium on its own" (133–34). Invert the "natural relationship" (135); for example, in opera, "ask not how the music expresses the staged drama, but how the staged drama expresses the music" (136). Watch for "patterns of openness and closure, of implication and realization" (134). Look for "significant distributions of oppositions across media" (142); with a Prudential commercial, for example, one might consider "Apollonian values that rise above the sometimes Dionysian qualities" (133). Cook suggests that analysis may begin with the "pairing of each medium category with every other," but he acknowledges that such an approach quickly becomes interminable because "the number of pairs increases so rapidly with each new identification as to quickly become unmanageable." He encourages the theorist not to panic because "before long, any IMM is likely to suggest its own way of continuing" (146).

Cook would agree with me that even with several analytic tools at hand, music video's incommensurable structures may foreclose the possibility of a thorough analysis across media. Some processes in music video unfold in a temporal domain, whereas others occur in a spatial one. Should some processes be interpreted more as a simultaneity, as a single temporal strand, or as ones that cross parameters, and how much weight should be assigned to each of these? For example, in a particular music video, a song may suggest one musical practice, while the image reflects a style from another era. All media can suggest different senses of time (relaxed and lethargic or frantic and compressed, directed toward the past or to the future) and different rates of unfolding. The lyrics can point toward an occurrence several measures back or in the future, and they can contradict what the characters in the frame are doing. An element of the arrangement can suggest the nature of the space, perhaps warm and inviting or ominous. The song can suggest a sonic space that conflicts with or diverges slightly from the video's setting. There may be tight or loose types of synchronization (including variation and transformation) among musical, verbal, and visual parameters: for example, the textures and timbres of the song can speak with and against the texture and color of the space. Words can also convey a type of energy and speed.

The viewer's interpretive share in multimedia relations demands attention as well. Cook himself attributes agency to one medium in relation to others when he suggests that a medium may contribute "activity, potency, and evaluation" (97) in a multimedia work. In the absence of narrative drive in music video, viewers may project dramatic content onto the relationship among different media. Because music, lyrics, and image are relational, it may be fruitful to explore psychoanalytic and sociological models—repression, condensation, and hegemony. Phenomenological models can become useful when music seems to color a setting much as a scent might. We may need a different way to account for videos in which causality and origin are hazy. For example, in recent R&B, the music and the sinuous tracking camera can seem to warm up the cold, austere hotel lobbies. And while the camera may seem to guide the viewer through the video, the music may also seem to buffet the figures in the frame, holding them aloft or pushing them forward.

Last, a change in one medium often forces a reevaluation of the others,[9] and this must be worked through analytically with regard to particular texts. We should pay special attention to shifts in cultural position. In Carlos Santana's "Maria," for example, a hip-hop beat is juxtaposed against what sounds like clichés of Spanish songs, and the performers in the video move alternately with more assertiveness and gentleness than we have previously seen with this music. The relations among Spanish, Latin American, and African American cultural approaches are tested and transformed. The British singer Sonique's "It Feels So Good," a retro-house song, appears in the video against visuals that raise questions about cultural geography. The video seems to ask of the song what one should do and how one should be at work, at home, and at the club. As Cook suggests, a multimedia relation does not only "engender meanings of its own" (20); "the coupling of image and sound contextualizes, clarifies, and in a sense analyses the music" (74). And, of course, as Cook would also argue, music acts similarly upon the other media.

11

The Aesthetics of Music Video: An Analysis of Madonna's "Cherish"

WHEN WE BECOME engaged with a music video, what draws us in? What constitutes craft or artistry in the genre? Theorists of music video have usually addressed these questions from the perspective of sociology, film theory, or popular cultural studies. Film theory, in particular, has had a tremendous influence on the analysis of music video, because of the two genres' apparently similar structuring of sound and image. But by the criteria of film, music videos tend to come off as failed narratives; the genre's effectiveness eludes explanation.

Much has been written about the ways that advertising, film, television sitcoms, and newscasts have borrowed from the rhetoric of music video. However, there has yet to be a detailed analysis of any one video, an analysis that can describe how particular moments are set up and departed from and why some moments seem important and others less so.[1] This absence of close readings results in part from the difficulties associated with analyzing music, particularly popular music. Nor are there adequate theories of how music and image might work together to create a hybrid form. A number of theorists, including Alf Björnberg, John Fiske, Dick Hebdige, and Susan McClary, have emphasized the need for such a theory. Andrew Goodwin is the most outspoken in his call for a reading that would reflect musical concerns: "In the study of music television a number of major lacunae are evident, but underlying many of them is the neglect of the music itself. This deafening silence in the corridors of the academy combines with an overestimation of the power of the visual to disfigure the study of music television."[2] As Goodwin suggests, no one has attempted an analysis that takes musical codes, processes, and techniques as providing means by which video image can be structured.

This chapter attempts to accomplish such goals. It provides both a description of the ways that musical and visual codes operate in a music video, and an in-depth analysis that shows these operations at work in a temporal flow. These two modes, one largely taxonomical and the other more processual, work together to inform us about music video as an artistic practice and as an ideological apparatus. If we attend to the particular features of a single video, we can begin to understand how music video works as a distinct medium. It is by attending to these features—many of which would be called aesthetic features—that we can learn about music video's modes of representing race, gender, and sexuality. The first section of this chapter looks at aspects of "Cherish" in order to develop the analytical tools for reading music video, drawing from music theory and popular music studies. The second section provides a chronological reading of the entire video, as well as close analyses of two particular sections. The final section takes up more fully the video's representations of race, gender, and sexuality.

THE "CHERISH" VIDEO

As a clip from Madonna's *Immaculate Collection*, "Cherish" is one of the most widely available music videos. The video is set on the beach. Madonna lip-syncs from the shoreline, wearing a dark, wet, form-fitting dress. A group of mermen swims farther out, in formations reminiscent of Busby Berkeley. A boy/merchild moves between Madonna and the mermen. Critics saw "Cherish" as designed in part to provide an opportunity for Madonna to display her newly muscle-bound physique; but it was at the same time undeniably arty, in the whimsical mythmaking of the mermen, and through being shot in black and white.

The video is directed by photographer Herb Ritts, and reflects the same impulses as Ritts's still photography: as Allen Ellenzweig says about Ritts's photographs, the video exaggerates the heroic statuesque, yet also gives a sense of weightlessness and transparency.[3] Ritts might be described as a video artist with a "classical" impulse: in "Cherish" all musical parameters are reflected in the image with a sense of clarity and balance. It can therefore serve as a model for describing the issues encountered in many music videos. Other videos place greater emphasis on tension and contrast; nevertheless, "Cherish" makes a useful text for showing the nature of correspondence generally, its evenhandedness notwithstanding. Though other videos do not achieve, or even attempt, the balanced structure of "Cherish," they use many of the same techniques.

"Cherish" is remarkable for the way that it reflects both local musical features and larger sections. One of the video's most unusual aspects is the strong, clean contours that it traces across edited images. The clarity of these lines enables Ritts to make the video into a large form that responds to a viewer's changing experience of the song. Ritts's classicism can also be discerned in the grace and self-restraint with which he treats both the figure of Madonna and the imagery of gay desire.

Because a music video must—above all—sell the artist and a particular song, the degree of self-restraint demanded of its director can be considerable. A director must usually abandon hope of creating a traditional narrative, even one that the song's lyrics relate. Moreover, he or she will find often that the pressure exerted by the song prevents the accurate representation of fixed objects: objects in music video will tend to shimmer, change continually, and threaten to fade away. Some directors, including Ritts, have developed strategies better suited to the conventional requirements of music video. What Ritts's work on "Cherish" suggests, and what is shown by other videos, is that music-video image can relinquish qualities traditionally associated with vision and adopt those that resemble the experiential qualities of sound. Walter Ong's characterization of the differences between sonic and visual perception can provide a useful basis for comparison: "Sight isolates, sound incorporates. Whereas sight situates the observer outside what he views, at a distance, sound pours into the hearer. Vision dissects. . . . When I hear, however, I gather sound simultaneously from every direction at once: I am at the center of my auditory world, which envelops me, establishing me at a kind of core of sensation and existence. . . . By contrast with vision, the dissecting sense, sound is thus a unifying sense. . . . The auditory ideal, by contrast, is harmony, a putting together."[4]

Ong's description of sound reveals perfectly the qualities of the image in a music video like "Cherish." In "Cherish," the image reflects sonic properties through its continuity of motion, most clearly in the imagery of the ocean. The permeability of the water's surface and the force of the waves set the tone for the video, helping us to notice that the boundary between natural and mythic, or human and animal, has also become permeable in the figure of the boy/merchild. The dynamic nature of sound is also reflected through editing, as shots lose their sense of focus as they move toward the edit point. The inevitable decay of sounds shows in the way that figures move away from us, and in a natural process like the approach of dusk.

FLOW

The muscular movement of the huge figures in slow motion, almost pulling themselves through the space, along with the waves rushing to and fro, gives the "Cherish" video a particular feel, which might be called a capacity to carry the viewer through the video (fig. 11.1). This parallels the way that the propulsive

FIGURE 11.1 (A–E) Flow. The muscular movement of the figures carries the viewer through the video.

elements in the music—the bass line, the rolling drum tracks, the harmonic motion—create and maintain the song's momentum.

This sense of pull characterizes the feel of many videos and helps to distance the feel of music video from that of most narrative film. David Bordwell argues that narrative films place viewers in a position of mastery.[5] These films, he says, are edited in such a way as to create the illusion that the viewer owns a secure position in the space, from which he can judge the action objectively. In "Cherish," as in many videos, the viewer is drawn through the space by the constant motion within the frame. The searching eye of the camera moves too much to provide the viewer with a stable position. This kind of camera movement exists in a give-and-take with the figures, as they lead us through the space, and with the waves, as they rush forward and back. The song's groove—the rhythmic figures whose momentum continues across sectional divisions—works with the image's continuous motion to encourage the viewer to give up her secure position and go along for the ride.

Another way that the image helps to pull us through the video is in the passage from shot to shot. First there is the edit, then a gradual establishment of motion, and then a lunge into a state of right proportion—the perfect photographic moment. Conventional film editing is designed to make the connections between images appear seamless except during periods of crosscutting and accelerated montage. Issues of repetition and variation within edits are played down. In "Cherish," as in many music videos, the edit and the movement within the shot are highlighted for their ability to establish a characteristic rhythm—which in this instance can be bluntly stated as a three-part structure of catch, pull, and hold.

There are several rhythmic strata of the music: the slower harmonic rhythm, the basic pulse in the drums, and the quicker tambourine articulations. We can also sense a similar rhythmic stratification in the image: the momentum of the waves; the movement of the camera—hand-held by Ritts himself; the pace established through editing; the athletic movements of Madonna and the mermen; and the fine visual articulations created through reflected light off sand and surf, the spikiness of the figure's hair, and the spray and foam from the ocean. These structures support one another, helping the viewer appreciate a level of detail that might well be overlooked in the song. Similarly, the rhythmic organization of the song gives focus to the image.

CONTINUITY

Traditional theory describes melodies as growing outward by preserving certain features and varying others. Part of the way that a sense of line is created is through a quality of self-similarity among the materials of a video. Here, some parameters stay constant across a series of shots—for example, the side flank of a merman, and a side flank of Madonna; the mermen pop up, and Madonna pops up and puts her hands on her head; Madonna sashays back, and the fishtail correspondingly slinks back into the water (fig. 11.2). In traditional Hollywood narrative, the editing techniques work to suggest the viewer's mastery of the space (through shot/reverse shot, 180-degree rule, eyeline match, and point of view.[6] Music videos forgo such mastery in order to create the sense of a continuous line. The editing attempts to keep the eye moving fluently through the space in a way that supports the directionality of the song.

CONTOUR

The musical lines in a piece of music—the melody, the bass, the inner voices—have contours; composers often talk about these musical lines as visual shapes.[7] In music video, the shape of the musical line can correlate to the shape of the visual image. There may be a few reasons for this. We have, perhaps, a culturally learned disposition to categorize movement by high-low relationships. Register often correlates to a sky and ground orientation. For an example, think of the cartoon figure of Wile E. Coyote falling, as the high pitch drops, and conversely of Orson Welles's famous opera-house scene in *Citizen Kane,* in which the voice "soars" higher and higher as the camera moves up towards, and then through, the ceiling of the opera house. (Imagine the opposite effect—the coyote falling and the pitch rising.) We also have a disposition to scan photos and paintings, as we read, from left to right. Many music videos assist in our desire to scan the image by moving from left to right, including "Cherish," Metallica's "Everywhere I Roam," and U2's "With or Without You." (One rare exception, Metallica's "Unforgiven," moves from right to left, but here movement signifies disintegration and disillusionment.) Spatial and aural shapes can also correlate to emotional affects.

Musicologists have noted that within a piece of music, melodic contours relate closely to the affect we perceive in the music.[8] Jagged lines produce music that seems anxious and intense. Lines with a narrow ambitus seem more meditative. The contours of an image have qualities similarly suggestive of certain affects: tall is courageous; flat or near the ground is safe; off angle is unstable.[9] We respond to imagery and music that work together to reflect these spatial relationships. At the high points of phrases, hard rock and heavy metal artists will jump toward the top of the screen and fireworks will go off. Bon Jovi's

FIGURE 11.2 (A–D) Musical continuity. In a series of shots, the figures' heads pop up. The images support a vertical orientation.

"Livin' on a Prayer" provides one good example. At the ends of musical sections, the image often seems to darken, to slow down and collapse into itself. In the first verse of the "Cherish" video, the highest pitch in the voice (D4) is accompanied by the image of a cresting merman. The verse closes with a shot of Madonna on the sand, which provides balance, followed by a fade to black. The undulation of the melodic line is supported by the curved shapes traced by the figures within the frame. Images of height, depth, and balance correspond, respectively, to high points, low points, and moments of stability in the vocal line (fig. 11.3). A more precise description of the musical and visual contours is included later in this chapter.

FORM

The video traces many large-scale structures: a gradual shift from day to evening, an implied maturation of the boy—being born, growing up, and separating from Madonna; and a tracing of the human body—there are more shots of heads in the beginning, more torsos and hips in the middle, and more legs and feet toward the end of the video.

Music videos often sketch a large-scale formal design that matches the large scale musical structure; for example, in Madonna's "Like a Prayer" and "Open Your Heart" videos, the sections of the music continually return in their original form, and the space can be seen as built upon a spiral. "Cherish" seems more continuous, less repetitive,[10] and the image's sense of motion from left to right and of continual branching outward matches this aspect of the song. In "Cherish," both music and image create large sectional divisions in the music

FIGURE 11.3 (A–G) Contours. In support of the song's primary contrapuntal lines, there are images of height, depth, and balance. (a) Madonna dips as the melody drops a tone and returns. Lyrics: "broken hearts." (b) Madonna bends forward as the melody drops a major third. Lyrics: "before I start this dance." (c) Madonna crouches as the melody drops a fifth at the end of the period. Lyrics: "more than just a romance." (d) Madonna stands erect as the melody centers itself at a fifth above the opening pitch. Lyrics: "you are my destiny." (e) Madonna drops her hands to her hips as the melody drops a fifth. Lyrics: "can't you see." (f) The mermen crest underwater as the melody reaches its highpoint. Lyrics: "Cupid, please." (g) The image of Madonna's head, following the shot of the merman, appears balanced. The melody rests a fifth above the opening pitch. Lyrics: "take your aim at me."

video. These sectional divisions can be seen in the shot-by-shot description of the video. I have also included a brief video "narrative," inasmuch as the analysis often refers to specific points in the song (see appendix). Most importantly, over the course of the video, music and image shift from a state of close interdependence, to a greater degree of freedom, to a return to synchronization in the closing section.[11]

BASIC SHAPE

Many music theorists argue that a primary musical motive changes continually throughout a piece, providing a key to the piece's structure.[12] The most obvious example might be the first eight notes from Beethoven's Fifth Symphony. This is the basic building block that informs the whole of the first movement. Music video image often works similarly by presenting a recurrent shape. In "Cherish," an arch shape occurs at several different formal/temporal levels.[13] There is a secondary emphasis on spiral motion, which functions as a transformation of this basic shape (fig. 11.4).

There are arching contours in the song, but their perceptibility is hard to ascertain. The melody of the verse forms an arch as it sweeps up an octave and then drops a fourth. The bass line, too, has a wide ambitus. The song's smallest identifiable group of pitches—a leap followed by a step in the opposite direction—forms an arch, and some of the transformations of this cell—through addition of another step—continue to retain the arch shape. Similarly, one can hear spiral shapes in some of the melodic materials. In any case, the idea of a basic shape remains a useful analytical concept for music-video image, even in cases in which the song's melodic materials do not reflect this shape. Pop songs, of course, are not written according to the logic of motivic development, and hooks—a related analytical concept that is more useful here—can be rhythmic, timbral, harmonic, or verbal, as they can be melodic. Connections between

FIGURE 11.4 (A–F) Basic shape. An arch shape appears throughout the video. Note that two-thirds into the video, the arch begins to stretch across edited images.

visual motives and the song's hooks, therefore, will often come down to a question of affective resemblance across media.

MOTIVE

In the "Cherish" video, some of the song's most prominent melodic shapes are linked to visual motives. In the chorus, the melodic gesture F♯-G-A-D, which has a quick moving harmonic background, is often associated with Madonna's assertively taking three steps forward. When, in the verse, the synthesizer rises above the voice to hit a high D, a wave or a hand crowns Madonna's head. When she then sings a high D, we see her coming forward in a state of suspension, or with a merman swimming above us in an arc. In both the chorus and the verse, a shot of Madonna's half-moon face is often associated with an ebb in the melodic line. These last examples help to delineate the phrase structure of the music. For example, Madonna's round face carries an inertial force that slows down the visual material so that it is able to keep in sync with the music. The repeated image of her half-moon face—most often occurring at a point two-thirds into the verse—becomes a marker that the verse will soon end.

PHRASE

The image in "Cherish" forms small sections closely related to the phrases of the music. In the first verse and chorus, the image parallels the music by beginning with a strong articulation and ending with a movement toward a closing lilt that leads us into the next phrase.[14] In "Cherish," the most clearly articulated moments are those that serve to emphasize the beginnings and endings of musical sections. At the opening of every section, the image begins with a sharp visual attack. As the energy of the musical section is used up, so is that of the image. Fade-outs help further to close sections (fig. 11.5).

LYRICS

Lyrics, in "Cherish" as in most videos, provide only one among many kinds of material to attend to. As might be expected, the hook line or word in "Cherish"

FIGURE 11.5 (A–C) Phrasing. Beginnings and ends of musical phrases are articulated in the image, as are the internal contours of a phrase. (a) The beginnings of phrases and sections. (b) The ends of phrases and sections. (c) The internal contours of phrases.

is strongly underscored—the imagery is focused on expressing an imperative ("cherish!"). The pseudo-high diction that marks much of the song (in phrases like "I'll perish the thought"), along with the references to Cupid and to *Romeo and Juliet,* contribute to both the nostalgic character of the music and the whimsical mythmaking of the video. Lyrics that have a strongly performative or theatrical dimension in Madonna's vocal performance ("Who? You!") receive confirmation of this quality in her deliberately stagy turn toward the camera followed by her and the merboy's playful mouthing of the word "you!" One might also suggest that the line "can't get away, I won't let you" might have encouraged the director to let the boy make a run for it.

Direct word painting—we hear the word "bell" and see the image of a bell— is less common, however. More frequent is a linking of image, word, and music that is more tenuous and enigmatic. For example, there may be a lag between the delivery of a lyric and the appearance of a corresponding image. There may also be a confusion over what the lyrics point to. For example, the phrase "Cupid, please take your aim at me," in the context of the video's opening— the shot of Madonna's hips, followed by an undulating merman—might be read as a wish for closer connections among the figures, or even, in the larger context of the video, for impregnation. This reading might inspire the viewer to reconsider all of the lyrics, the image, and the music that has come before.

TIMBRE AND TEXTURE

Frequently, the sound world of the song provides stronger associations for the videomaker than do the lyrics, and can exert a greater influence upon the video. In "Cherish," though no lyrics refer to mermen or to water, the snare and tambourine, the voice, or the multilayered chorus accompanied by its glittery synthesized timbres, the sibilants *ch* and *sh* all have a white-noise component that we might associate with foaming, rushing water and the prismatic light reflected off the ocean and the sand. Each character corresponds by association to one of the song's countermelodies, and these correspondences—built upon a familiar connection between physical size and registral placement—reflect gender and power stereotypes. The mermen are associated with a synthesized saxophone in its lower register, Madonna with a sassy synthesized trumpet in the middle register, and the merboy with a slightly comic synthesizer patch in the high register.[15] Later in the analysis, we will see that the video questions the primacy of Madonna relative to the mermen and the boy—on this hierarchical plane, all of the figures have an opportunity to move into the foreground.

The bass line, with the bass drum, gives the image its impetus for movement. In a successful music video, the video can trick the viewer into believing that the image and the music are so closely intertwined that the image is spurred on by the propulsiveness of the sound, or conversely, that the image sparks activity in the music. In "Cherish," what animates the figures is mysterious. We almost never see the fins and feet as they animate the figures. Instead, it seems that it is the bass line, as it moves toward and then over the crest of its line, that propels the images onward. When the bass line takes on a different type of musical authority, we have a different type of motion. For example, in the bridge, when the bass arpeggiates two root-position triads, Madonna skips sideways through the water. When the bass line drops out—at the end of bridge 1, there is a long, held chord without the bass—the figures seem to lack momentum: here, there is the sustained image of a dragging fishtail. Similarly, at the end of bridge 2, when there is a repeated chordal guitar riff, with a reduced accompaniment, Madonna slinks back into the water.[16]

Other, more tenuous sound/image connections include the imagery of the clinging wet cloth on Madonna's body, the snugly fitting costumes on the mermen, and the water flowing against her flesh and her dress, any or all of which might stand in for the synthesizer line that wraps around and closely tracks the voice. By contrast, the finer rhythmic articulations might be carried by the spikiness of Madonna's hair and the fine detail of the foaming water.

The song is mixed in such a way that none of the backing tracks are brought to fore. The prominent bass line commands more attention because it moves more actively, not because of any emphasis in the mix; the goal of the production must have been to create a wall of sound that places all of the backing tracks on an equal plane. To complement this approach, the images of Madonna, the mermen, and the child are correspondingly huge and engulfing. Nevertheless, the arrangement varies as percussion, bass, and backing vocals are added or drop out, and, more subtly, as the reverberation effects on Madonna's voice change through the song. Similarly, the video makes an issue of how Madonna and the mermen move closer to or farther away from us within our field of vision. For example, when she sings the words "who" and "you," her voice comes to the front of the mix and she advances toward the viewer. The beginning and end of the song are produced to sound distant, and it follows that the figures appear small and move away from us.

These local sound/image connections play a large part in shaping the video. What I can only call the nostalgic quality of the video originates in various aspects of the song. Besides the archaic touches of the lyrics, there is the swing rhythm (perhaps always nostalgic), the finger snaps, Madonna's chirpy, child-like voice, the girl-group backing vocals, and the hook line taken from The Association's 1966 hit "Cherish," all of which allude to earlier pop music. It is important to recognize as well that the song's arrangement scheme, production values, and performance styles had been in place for at least five years before the release of "Cherish" in the summer of 1989.[17] These conservative qualities, along with the song's pop acumen, help to bring its retrospective dimension to the fore.

HARMONY

The song's harmonic language emphasizes smooth, sometimes almost elliptical motion, using a large number of first- and second-inversion chords, and moving through the bVII and the II as it wends its way to the subdominant or dominant. This aspect of the song, too, shows the balance and restraint that bring out what I have termed Ritts's classicism.[18] Yet within this narrow range, the video makes a subtle response to harmonic changes. For example, in the verses, the beginning and end rest on or near the tonic, D. Here we see stable images of Madonna, or the mermen and Madonna, as if these figures stood for arrival points, or places of stability. Within the verse, as the harmony begins to shift away from and then toward the tonic, Madonna starts to turn away from us and shift her focus toward the ocean.

The chorus is more active than the verses in this song: here, the harmonic rhythm moves at a faster rate than in the verse, the harmony oscillates between the subdominant and the dominant without much tonic, the orchestration opens slightly to include a clavinet and guitar, the melodic sequences become shorter, and the drums accentuate the pulse—many of these features contribute to a more marchlike or anthemic quality to the chorus. (Although the song is in a shuffle groove, the chorus has a more "square" feel, because of the quarter note harmonic rhythm.) The images in the chorus respond to these features with a more lively set of paired two-bar phrases. Unlike the verses, in which beginnings and ends of sections regularly feature Madonna, the chorus creates a sense of uncertainty as to whether Madonna or the mermen will appear first—sometimes Madonna takes up the first half of a sequence, and sometimes the mermen do.

At the bridge, the harmony implied by the bass line conflicts with that of the keyboard pad, with the bass line really defining the harmony. The motion of the bass line moves toward the dominant, unfolding a III-IV-V progression: F♯-A-C♯, G-B-D, A. In response to this, Madonna steps sideways for the first time in the video, as if drawing us toward something new. When the bridge returns, the bass line reiterates its movement toward V. This time, we do find ourselves in "another region," with imagery of Madonna and the little boy beached on the sand.

Much of what we know about the disposition of the figures in "Cherish" is defined through the harmony. For example, the child commonly appears at the same time as the subdominant in second inversion. This chord is pulled in two directions: it is often subsumed by the tonic, while it also resists the dominant. This harmonic pull might contribute to the way that the child is volleyed back and forth between the mermen and Madonna. The mermen tend to land on the relatively stable chords of I, IV, and V, and the way they seem to float suspended in space, performing a slight acrobatic twist, suggests their freedom from the influence of the song's harmonic motion. Madonna's appearances, on the other hand, coincide with passing chords; these correspondences make her seem somewhat hemmed in by the harmony. In each section of the video, she forges a winding path toward us, yet monumental harmonic forces toward the end of the section pull her back toward the water's edge. (The most pronounced instances occur in the first and second verses.) Later in the video, Madonna breaks free of these constraints, affecting the video as a whole.

RHYTHM

"Cherish" has a strong triplet feel, but the drums count a standard pattern with the bass drum accentuating beats one and three, and the snare, beats two and four. At important points in the video, the editing and the broad physical gestures within the shot (like the shrugging of shoulders) fall squarely within the beat pattern, emphasizing, for example, beats one and three, one and four, or simply one. This accentuation of the beat pulls us back in whenever we start to drift along with the flowing imagery. Perhaps to compensate for the absence of a live rhythm section, the mostly sequenced rhythm arrangement fills in nearly every eighth note in a number of instrumental parts (fig. 11.1). This rolling pattern might have helped to suggest the carriage of the characters, the setting on the ocean and the figure of the mermen. Against these more general rhythmic qualities, each section of the video displays its own particular pattern. In verse 2, the move toward the downbeat of the measure carries the metaphor of wave and flow into another domain.

A CLOSE READING OF TWO SECTIONS

I will now look closely at two particular sections of the video. In music video, the images frequently divide into sections according to the song's sectional divisions. The image can highlight differences among musical sections through shifts in color, pacing, gesture, or topic.[19] Often the image exhibits a character particular to a section of the music. In "Cherish," as in other videos, the image for the verse features constrained or restrained imagery, typically a solitary artist in a barren landscape. The imagery of the bridge often points away from that of the rest of the video. The chorus, on the other hand, can usually be characterized as communal, and will be set with imagery of freedom (running, jumping, flying), of fusion (between a couple or among a group), of plenitude (crowds, a large group of objects), of paradise (fields of grass).

I will first discuss the second verse. As I have mentioned, the chorus is more marchlike, more public and extroverted, while the verse is more reflective. We have already seen the first verse. The image traced the winding and sinuous quality of the line, closely following local inflections, and the high D4 was matched by the image of a merman seeming to soar under water. Now, in verse 2, the image encourages us to listen no longer to small articulations, but to hear one broad line.[20]

In verse 2, the image focuses on a larger form—the overall contour of the melodic line (fig. 11.6, table 11.1). This focus is established through a use of space similar to that of dance. Dance theorist Rudolf von Laban speaks of a "kinosphere" of the body: a center of gravity and an implied larger sphere that the limbs can move into.[21] In music video, one can speak of a larger kinosphere established through camera placement and disposition of the figures—a series of shots creates the illusion of a center and defines a space around it. In verse 2, a point in the water is fixed as the center. As we begin to move in different directions away from this center, we feel the breadth of the melodic line. Yet, simultaneously, the image also plays with our sense of time. Because we have already heard the first verse, we know the length of the second verse. In the second verse, the implied visual center has been established, and soon, there seems to be nowhere to go. Yet the verse is not over. The voice continues searching for the higher register, which leaves us with a sense of constriction.

Our anxiety breaks as we see the image of Madonna crossing a boundary. She rises out of the water and moves toward us, like the first amphibian emerging from the ocean to walk upon land.[22] As Madonna continues to approach, the music hangs on the tonic before finally moving to the dominant. Both image and music continue to linger, raising the question as to whether the music or the image will spark the next section of the video. Music video often works by scrambling effects and causes, making it hard to remember that the song is ontologically prior to the image. A characteristic power relation is thus established, in which nothing is taken for granted, and in which each medium must work with and against the other. The possibility exists that either song or image will dominate, forcing the other's hand.

My next example comes from the third verse, at the moment when the mermen swim underwater in formation. A long visual and musical slowing

FIGURE 11.6 Kinospheres. The exploration and closing off of visual space correlate to the song's sectional divisions.

TABLE 11.1

VERSE 1	CHORUS	VERSE 2	CHORUS 2—BRIDGE 1	VERSE FRAGMENT	BRIDGE 2—OUTCHORUS
merman swimming underwater		kinosphere: figures exchange glances		mermen swimming within a kinosphere	
visual material		*sense of space*		*visual material from verse 1, sense of space from verse 2*	

takes us into this section. This is the only section in which the music departs from the structure of the conventional pop song.[23] First, the beginning of the third verse sounds more like an extension of the previous section (bridge 1) than like the downbeat of a new section. The voice elides this sectional division: it draws out the end of its phrase as the rhythm section begins the third verse. (Madonna sings, "love. Together, you're giving it to me boy.") We may think, for a moment, that we are still in the bridge. The first half of this verse functions as an instrumental with prominent vocal ad-libs. The "Steve Winwood" synthesizer patch enters the texture with a solo line supported by the rhythm arrangement of the verse. Madonna, drawing attention away from the synthesizer solo, sings, not material from the verse, but new material that seems more appropriate to the bridge because of its improvisatory character and shorter phrase lengths. If it were not for the voice, these eight measures would seem like part of a conventional instrumental. Interrupting the synthesizer solo and vocal ad-libs, the second half of this verse suddenly returns to the arrangement scheme and vocal melody of the previous verses, as if it had been just another verse all along. Only at measure 58 does it become clear that this is the third verse.

This fifth "extra" song section works strangely. Besides the conflicting tendencies of its first half, its surprising split down the middle, and its elided beginning, its middle verse fragment is preceded and followed by appearances of the bridge. Because this fragment seems both isolated and out of context, we will recognize the melody as familiar, but we may be unable to remember whence exactly it comes and why it has suddenly reappeared. The song's complications of conventional song form here encourage us to think back over all of the music that we have heard thus far. The image assists in the process of reconstruction, as it draws from and condenses visual material from the earlier verses. The imagery in this sequence combines material from the culmination of verse one (the image of the merman swimming underwater) with the spatial arrangement at the close of verse two (the kinosphere established by Madonna and the mermen). Here, the imagery *with the music* recalls the earlier half of the video, and we experience a moment of very potent recollection (see again fig. 11.7).

Herb Ritts is known for his homoerotic photography, Madonna for her close ties to the gay community. Hinted at throughout the video is the possibility that some desirable being resides in the depths of the water. We assume, as Madonna continually backs into the ocean, that it is she who is our object of desire. Yet, in this musically isolated fragment, veiled by the murky water, Ritts is able to express the possibility that our primary interest in the depths includes an erotic attraction to the mermen.

As I have suggested, music video suppresses some important facets of the music in order to draw our attention toward others. A beautiful moment in the song occurs eight measures earlier where Madonna steps back into the water, and the fishtail is dragged along the water's edge. The long-held IV chord serves as an extended suspension to the tonic. In the video, the held IV is subsumed under a long visual ritard that leads into the close of the third verse.[24] This ritard is established through a descending contour in both the image and the music. Our attention sweeps across the musical texture: the image of the child reflects the high-pitched synthesizer melody; the image of Madonna holding the child connects with Madonna's voice in the midrange; and the image of the watery depths and the merman placed at the bottom of the frame is linked to the low register of the synthesized bass.[25]

In the extended sequence that features the mermen, their visibility is obscured, and one might think that their power is therefore muted. Yet, in a large part of the gay community, the politics of concealment and revelation is a complicated, richly inflected phenomenon. Like Michelangelo's *The Holy Family*, in which the artist may have chosen to paint a group of nude men into the recesses of the painting for his own desire and enjoyment, Ritts may have partially obscured his mermen for personally defined erotic reasons. Gay colleagues of mine talk about the titillation of seeing adventure or nature films of foreign lands, because one knows that one might see gorgeous naked men in the background—the most recent filmed version of *Last of the Mohicans* is a case in point. For those who are willing to take time with the "Cherish" video, the obscurity of the mermen works to good effect. Viewers who watch the video only a few times, and who have little contact with gay culture, may lose an opportunity.

I have discussed these two sections in some detail, before moving on to a chronological reading of the entire video, partly because they have an internal coherence that makes them worth studying independently. More important, these sections form the locus of certain themes that I will bring out further in the final third of this chapter, particularly themes of gay desire. I will return to the end of verse 3, which features underwater footage of the mermen, as it constitutes a nodal point in the video.

A CHRONOLOGICAL READING

A central claim of this chapter has been that music-video image creates its meanings within the flow of the song. The clarity and stability of these meanings remain subject to the song's temporal unfolding. I will give an abbreviated account of the overall flow of the video, picking up what has been left out thus far, and pointing to the aspects of the video that will be discussed in the sections of the chapter that follow. A chronological account of the video will prove helpful as a way of describing the relations among sections and the progress of many long-term processes. Because this chronological reading differs from most close analyses of film, it will be worth explaining quickly how it is organized. Close analyses of film usually use the shot or the scene as the fundamental unit of analysis, and close readings of music video have tended to do the same. Here, the method of detailed, sequential description is similar, but the fundamental unit is the musical section, rather than the scene or the shot. The use of the musical section as the fundamental unit places an emphasis upon varied repetition of materials over linear development of plot. Treating the form of the song as the analytical ground for the video better reflects its semantic and formal structure.

Introduction We are frequently led into the world of a music video across a threshold or through a liminal state. "Cherish" achieves this effect through a shot of the child running along the shoreline, with sounds of the ocean, before the song begins. The somewhat dreamlike character of this shot confirms its liminal function. In this shot, it is not clear whether the child is running away from or toward Madonna's breast, and whether he imagines Madonna or she imagines him. Similarly, the sound of the ocean may seem to suggest a lack in the song, and vice versa. When the song begins, Madonna's repeated "cherish" sounds like an echo or a call heard across a great distance, either in space or in consciousness.

In the opening of the video, the disposition of the figures seems to conflict with the contour of the bass line and the voice. The figures move laterally. The music here, on the other hand, is made up of falling gestures in the synthesizer and bass. The weight of this introductory musical material is not taken up by the image, but rather is deferred or carried over into the first verse. The image of Madonna's gradual descent toward the sand in verse one is suggested by the dramatic falling gestures of the song's introduction.

Verse 1 The outer voices move in contrary motion, first outward, and then inward.[26] As a complement to this motion, the video presents images of increasing height (Madonna's head, the crest of the wave, and, as the high point, the mermen cresting at the surface of the water) interspersed with images of increasing depth (Madonna crouching and rolling on the sand). The images that follow reflect the balance between the bass and the melodic lines above it, especially the voice (Madonna turning with her arms spread out, and the paired images of a merman soaring and Madonna's head on the sand).

Chorus 1 The chorus begins with one of the simplest and most functional relations in music video: the arrangement thickens as the frame fills with more figures. The music in the chorus more clearly articulates the quarter note pulse, and the metallic synthesizer doubles the voice, with the background vocals further emphasizing the punctuated style of Madonna's vocal delivery. The melody in the chorus is made up of shorter, more regular phrases than is the verse. Chorus 1 loses some of its iterative, terse quality as it moves into verse 2.

Verse 2 As mentioned, in verse 2, the imagery has a quality of line and extension.

Chorus 2 This section distills earlier aspects of the song. As verse 2 intensifies and simplifies the linear quality of verse 1, so does chorus 2 intensify and simplify the clipped, marchlike character of chorus 1. Images of upward motion are even more prevalent here than in chorus 1. The emphasis on the breadth of the figures and their high placement in the frame helps to create a visual arch, as it were, that spans the length of the tape. Chorus 2 contains imagery that foreshadows that which we will see later in the video. For example, the image of the child held in the merman's outstretched arms, and the mermen's and Madonna's broad shoulders prepare for Madonna's movement from left to right in the first bridge. The image of Madonna placing a frond of seaweed on her shoulder (a makeshift feather boa), and of her reaching toward her ankles, prepares for the "vamp" section in the second bridge. In retrospect, we will be able to look back upon the first bridge as a section in which energy is concentrated. This section returns to the questions of identity hinted at in chorus 1 (who is it that we see, Madonna or the mermen?), but here these questions become more pointedly about *difference* (what do you have, fins or legs?). The issue of sexual or gender difference will be revisited in bridge 2, when Madonna and the merboy playfully flex their muscles. The imagery of three mermen moving into the frame after the end of the second chorus preceded by a lengthy fade to black can be seen as a culmination of a section.

Bridge 1 Musically, the bridge is quirky. It contains a new element, a varied form of the "cherish" motive from the introduction: G-F♯-D (bar 1) becomes F♯-G-B. It also combines musical fragments drawn from both the verse and the chorus. In response to this construction, the first half, like the chorus, reflects a celebratory "surf's up" attitude. A closer reading of this section shows that it goes far in creating the video's clear sense of nostalgia. The lead synthesizer patch seems rather kitschy and outdated, and, in tandem with the image, may conjure up memories of old beach movies. The placement and movement of the figures point to early—and inexpensive—modes of visual entertainment, like the spinning top, the carousel, the zoetrope, and Disneyland's (now dismantled) "Circle of Progress": here the mermen and Madonna move from left to right along the seashore, simultaneously but at different rates, and it seems as if someone were dragging a painted backdrop behind Madonna while she moves toward and then away from us.

Verse 3 (with Instrumental and Vocal Ad-libs) This verse contains an interesting formal conceit. Its first half is an instrumental over the rhythm arrangement of the verse (which is typical for an instrumental), with the synthesizer taking the solo. This synthesizer line, however, is dominated by vocal ad-libs which Madonna sings over it (and which return counterpointed to vocal material from the chorus in the outchorus). More strikingly, the second half of this verse abruptly returns to the vocal melody of the previous verses, abandoning the synthesizer lead and the vocal ad-libs and proceeding as a "regular" verse. The first half of verse 3 is composed of music and images that slow down gradually, and that move toward the second half of the verse (when the vocal line from the earlier verses returns). The visual material comes from the more restrained, tender imagery of the first two verses. The second half of this section features the mermen swimming in formation. The underwater choreography echoes Busby Berkeley's famous waterfall sequence in the movie *Footlight Parade*.[27]

Bridge 2 In the second bridge, a varied repetition of bridge 1, Madonna and the merboy loll on the beach. It is the only section that makes a feature of being edited off the beat. Because it is edited in this way, this section seems rhythmically out of step with the rest of the video. The fact that it takes place on the sand, unusual for this video, further helps to set it apart. The merboy shows off his muscles; Madonna picks up on this gesture in the break, when she adopts bodybuilders' poses. A two-shot of Madonna's feet and the merboy's tail foreshadows the set of oppositions that end the video. At the end of this bridge, Madonna backs into the water.

Break Madonna vamps for the camera in a section that reminds one of old home movies. The break does more than create a nostalgic flavor, however. For all of Madonna's activity, this section has a strange sense of emptiness. The propulsive elements of the music—the bass and the snare and bass drums— have dropped out. The space behind Madonna is open and still. At first, it is not clear, in the quick editing, whether Madonna is moving to the music, or whether the music is dragging her around as if she were a marionette. The attempts at close synchronization here sharply contrast with the rhythmic freedom of the first bridge. Throughout the video, Madonna has seemed constrained by the harmony. However, by the end of the break, she is depicted as no longer having to struggle with the harmonic structure, but, like Atlas himself, as being capable of upholding it.

The way that the harmony is realized in the "Cherish" video relates to the way that liberal corporate culture tends to picture social obligations. We speak of the "smaller, more intimate domestic sphere" and the "glass ceiling of the workplace," and we can notice the way that the harmonic structure constrains Madonna. In this video, both harmony and social obligations are figured as reassuring, but also palpably constraining, sets of boundaries. Because they are treated similarly, one could be considered as a figure for the other. By the close of the break, however, the video reveals something new: we begin to know more about the mermen, the boy and Madonna, and what they aspire to.

In the break, Madonna adopts a triumphant stance. For the first time, she steps assertively into the emphatic *ch!* of "cherish." Her squared-off arms and torso condense the kinospheres of verse two and the second half of verse three into a single form. As she adopts a bodybuilder's pose, showcasing her biceps, a second vocal line, drawn from the first half of verse 3, enters in counterpoint to the vocal line of the chorus. This second line, made up of shorter phrases and fragments from earlier in the song, has an insistent quality that lends Madonna additional authority.

There is a shift across the video in the representations of the characters. For the first half of the video, the mermen move assertively, propelling themselves out of the water. In the second half of verse 3, however, they move with restraint and poise. Here in the break, and in the sections that follow, Madonna's compact, precise gestures dominate. There are shifts in the arrangement that correspond to these changes of character: in the second half of verse 3, the nearly static synthesizer pad becomes the most prominent instrumental voice, thereby underscoring the mermen's timeless existence. In the break, the bright trumpet patch cuts through the texture, emphasizing Madonna's assertiveness. By giving the mermen and Madonna these actions at these particular points in the song, Ritts can make use of the cultural associations of the song's timbres in order to play with traditional notions of gender.

For the first half of the break, the image emphasizes episodic, rather than teleological, features of the song. A strength of this approach lies in its not conferring greater authority upon either Madonna or the mermen. In the second half of the break, the snare and bass drum return, and the backing vocals from the chorus enter behind Madonna's ad-libs, anticipating the outchorus.

Outchorus By the time that the outchorus appears, the video establishes a variety of connections between music and image. We can therefore hover over the image, waiting for a moment of engagement between it and the music. At this point, we may be waiting for the grounding images of feet to return, as well as for the completion of a spiral that is traced out across many edits. The second vocal line seems to match the prismatic late-afternoon light on the ocean, through both its kaleidoscopic construction and its use of echoes from earlier in the song. The return of the synthesizer lead (the "Steve Winwood" patch) works likewise to a similar effect. Typically for an outchorus, this section brings in all of the timbres we have heard in the song. The image, for its part, creates the sense of an ending through similarly conventional means: the mermen ride off into the sunset, Madonna and the boy share a final embrace before he runs away, and she lies down on the sand.

The video closes with Madonna and the child facing off against each other—the image of the child seems, strangely, to be composed of adult legs and a child's head. Popular-culture theorist Philip Hayward reads this image as a sign of patriarchal authority.[28] He argues that Madonna's freedom is reined in at the end of the video. The legs, torso, and heads, however, function most importantly on a formal level. As a pair of bookends, the images serve to stop the flow of the video, to slow down the image so that it can close in sync with the music. The merman's legs remain topped by a child's head (so that the phallic presence is not that impressive), and Madonna assumes a siren's pose, a mythic image of great power. The boy's legs and Madonna's torso come at the moment that the song is over, and function as a frame for the song.[29] Madonna lands on beat one, a position of power within the song.

The ending works through a compression of thematic oppositions. All of the video's dualistic imagery—adult and child, female and male, human and animal, myth and camp—is squeezed into the closing shots. This kind of an ending is common in music video.[30] It achieves its effect partly by providing a thematic payoff in the absence of any conclusion to the narrative. The enigmatic character of the final series of shots asks the viewer to return to the beginning and watch one more time, in order to see how the video could have arrived at this ending.

REPRESENTATIONS OF RACE, GENDER, AND SEXUALITY

This chapter, thus far, has focused on music/image relations that would be called formal. I have argued that the logic of these relations established a ground for an investigation of race, gender, and sexuality. Here I will explore these issues, beginning with one example that shows the interdependence of formal and depictive modes. In the remainder of this final section, I will discuss other parameters—narrative and emblematic modes, affect and self-reflexivity, and musical and visual space. This discussion forms the necessary complement to the explication of formal modes of continuity.

The video for "Cherish" contains three kinds of figures: Madonna, a group of mermen, and a boy/merchild who moves between Madonna and the mermen. Madonna and the mermen are clearly European American, while the boy is clearly not—although his specific ethnicity is unknown, he is pointedly "other" to the rest of the figures in the video. One might well wonder about the boy's ethnicity and its role in "Cherish." The imagery of a young child of color being passed between Madonna and the mermen is not innocent when one considers that the depiction of adult black men and women passing around a single white child is rarely seen in popular culture. In the current critical climate, it might be acceptable to note this as an instance of aestheticized racism and terminate the analysis there.

Yet, on a more formal level, a darker figure as an object of exchange creates a strong degree of separation between the white figures of Madonna and the mermen. The video is shot entirely in black and white, and, because of the way that tones are developed gradually over the course of the video—dark black dress, black roots, a merman in the water with very black hair and white skin as opposed Madonna's *blonde* hair and *black* dress, gray water, medium gray and white mermen, and a very white-skinned Madonna—the young boy of color is almost argued for on formal grounds, as one shade within a gray scale. The young boy's color in this context is a transitional tone.

But neither can we stop here: we must acknowledge that this formal device reflects a racialist way of viewing skin color. We could imagine a tape produced in a culture where such differences do not mean the same thing, such as in Brazil, Puerto Rico, or North Africa. The decision to emphasize these differences so strongly relies implicitly on the fact that skin color, and race, mean a great deal to us as Americans.

Yet it is also important that the boy's color in this context is a transitional tone. Imagine the video with everyone of the same skin tone: the figures would lack separation. The image of the child of color is, at one level, offensive, at another, progressive. The child's skin tone subverts the viewer's projections concerning the nuclear family, allowing for both the imagery of gay desire and the imagery of Madonna's independence.

This kind of interdependence of aesthetic and ideological aspects shows that, ultimately, we cannot look to any one place for an understanding of music video, but must rather deal with the relations among a video's narrative, formal, and sociocultural aspects, particularly as they are complicated by the tensions between music and image. The ways that music and image combine cannot simply be taken as natural; styles of performance footage change from year to year, and the construction of a music video always requires effort. Videomakers have developed a set of practices for putting image to music in which the image must give up its autonomy and abandon some of its representational modes. In exchange, the image gains in flexibility and play, as well as in polyvalence of meaning. Many of the meanings of music video lie in this give-and-take between sound and image, and in the relations among their various modes of continuity.

QUESTIONS OF NARRATIVE

The first wave of academic writing about music video concerned itself with music video's ability (or inability) to sustain a narrative. More recently, however, there have been attempts to put narrative in its proper place, as but one of several ways to establish continuity. Music videos suppress narrative direction for various reasons. The fact that the figures cannot speak and seem preternaturally animated by the music may work against narrative clarity. The brevity of the medium contributes as well. Pop songs, usually, are sectional forms (verse, chorus, bridge), and it is difficult for an image track to maintain a strong narrative drive against this sectional differentiation and repetition. But most important, it may be in a video's interest to point only vaguely to a narrative. If the image were overly narrative in orientation, we might be drawn to the image as we are in a traditional film. The music for the video would most likely resemble film music—usually unacknowledged, almost unheard.

David Bordwell defines narrative as having (1) an agent with identifiable goals and distinct characteristics, and (2) obstacles to this agent's success.[31] This definition shows immediately why music video might limit the role of narrative. If we were to engage with the figures in music videos as if they were people with clear traits and identifiable goals, who were approaching difficult or dangerous encounters, we might try to predict upcoming events. That kind of engagement would pull us outside of the here and now of the video, its moment-to-moment flow, and we might well lose the detail in both the music and the image. Videos draw heavily, but schematically, from traditional forms—for their familiarity as much as for their novelty.

"Cherish" is similar to many videos of a certain type, in which there are moments that suggest a storyline. In such videos, these moments function more like "hooks" than like parts of a story. We are carried between these narrative moments by the ultimately more important play of movement and texture. With this understanding of narrative in mind, one can suggest several possible plotlines for the "Cherish" video: (1) a community gives birth to a child, and turns him over to a woman for instruction about culture; the child is later returned to the nurturing community (this inverts the Lacanian notion of a society in which men teach the "law of the father"); (2) Madonna and the mermen give birth to and raise a male child; (3) Madonna imagines a love affair with a merman, and transforms one into a child whom she can love and nurture; (4) The child is Madonna's son and the mermen are merely imagined; (5) The child is a member of a family that will not shield him from adult expressions of sexuality; (6) Madonna steals both power and a child from the gay community; (7) The child cannot fit into human society: "Cherish" is a kind of "coming out" story, and the mother is supportive.

For these narratives to exist, the viewer must infer or find them by "connecting the dots" between particular charged moments in the video, and he or she must pay close attention to the music and the image between these events. Because no parameter comes to the fore to the annihilation of another (although features become submerged or move to the background), multiple storylines can seem to exist simultaneously in the video. The viewer must consider all the visual gestures and all the musical codes in order to understand the connections among these moments. The vagueness of "Cherish" may serve it well. It gives a committed viewer enough space to imagine what might be the relations among the figures.

SPACE

One way that music video substitutes for a lack in the narrative is through a focus on a set of relations. In music video, the disposition of figures and their movement on a ground often takes the place of plot and character development in a traditional sense. In "Cherish," one simple way that this is played out is in the sense of scale between musical and visual space. The musical "field" of the song seems smaller than that of the image for the video. As I have mentioned, the musical field for "Cherish" seems narrow, even thin—it contains very few dramatic rhythmic, harmonic, melodic, or timbral changes. By contrast, the visuals for "Cherish" seem to occupy a broader realm. Though the visual field is filmed entirely in black and white, and is set exclusively on the beach, it has a quality of great expansiveness—the distance from sea to land, from the surface of the water to its depths, or from one point along the shoreline to another, seems quite wide. In this instance, the larger expanse of imagery, against a more narrowly constructed band of music, gives the viewer the sense that the figures are highly individuated yet only loosely bound to one another.

Of all of the figures, the mermen are particularly well defined through the use of space. They possess their own realm, and act as if they have always been and will forever be in the ocean. Some elements of the music, perhaps the sectional changes, seem to become *real* barriers—like the rock formations that we see in the water—but the mermen seem to communicate across this distance through a secret code. The mermen seem comfortably placed in the musical and visual materials of the video.

The sense of space also helps to define Madonna. An approach that focuses on the imagery without sufficient attention to musical time and space might suggest a deeply sexualized text: Madonna is a siren who lures us into the video with a sexuality that moves from chastity to naughtiness to polymorphous perversity. The viewer may desire the child. Yet the appearance of the fishtail dragged along the water's edge provokes a moment of anxiety at the sight of the uncanny. The mermen remain remote, deaf to our interest. At the video's close, the child realizes his own desirability. Madonna drops her social graces and threatens to consume us.

Yet this story leaves out much of what is important in the video. What might seem frightening in the image is safely marked off as separate space—through the clear delineation of ocean and sky, and water and sand. Only when we are underwater do we deal with the presence or absence of male genitalia, or with male sexuality in general. When we are on land, both the little boy and Madonna seem quite comfortable. The membranes of separation—the surface of the water, the shoreline—are very gently elided. The time and distance that separates the appearance of those visual hooks that carry narrative charge also provides a sense of security.

The music also works hard to repress what might be frightening about the images. Madonna is held within the harmony; similarly, the fishtail is held within the long sweep of verse 3's first half; the merboy and Madonna stand as a pair of balanced closing images. These images remain detached from one another. A reading that attends to both music and image will draw attention away from these moments and toward other features such as the process of the figures' individuation and their relation with one another. Neither the song nor the video is committed to an ending. Both are nonteleological in nature.

This does not mean that the video is free of emotional complexity. Rather, those elements that are more sharply edged appear on another level and are safely submerged. The characters' actions and expressions, which sometimes seem to reflect a sense of anger or hostility, provide one way that the figures in "Cherish" are given voice. These moments do not determine the video's tone; rather, they provide contrast in a circumscribed way. Because one knows that they will not overwhelm the video, they can function well as ornament and texture.[32]

One must not exaggerate, however, the extent to which the characters are in fact given voice. Of all of the figures in "Cherish," the young boy is the most short-changed. More than any other figure in the video, he fills the role of a structural device—he is both a powerful figure of exchange and an agent of disruption. Through his attempts to both run out of the video's bounds and to disrupt internal boundaries, he holds the integrity or the disintegration of the video within his frame. For dramatic charge, music videos often have a figure that threatens the video's surface. Yet the video's point of view can be said to be structured for him. Aspects of the "Cherish" video are meant to evoke feelings associated with childhood. Large sections of the image engender feelings of being rocked, bounced on a knee, thrown up in the air, and twirled around. The sections of music that accompany this imagery match this physical movement. For example, the chorus has a bouncier, more anthemic quality, and there is a gentler, rocking motion to the verse. Much of the imagery revolves around the child's expressions of fear, distance, and pleasure, though the video works to suppress this fact.

Though all of the figures are limited by the conventions of music video, "Cherish" remains committed to expressing the roles of the characters within a set of relations: Madonna is powerful enough to uphold the whole social structure; the mermen constitute a community of men who are playful, noncompetitive, and free; the child becomes so autonomous that he almost seems like an adult. These relationships can be seen as a proposal for a new social order.

THE STAR PERFORMER

Madonna appears throughout the video, and her role as "star" is clearly important. Ritts treats her as he treats Janet Jackson in the video "Love Will Never Do." The infectiousness of the singer's smile functions as a hook that carries the viewer into the video. As the video progresses, this approach is modified in order to work more with spatial relations and with the body as form.

Most of what we know about Madonna derives from her facial expressions and physical gestures as she switches between coyness and exuberance. These moments highlight musical structure. Madonna's flirtatious, sweet invitation in verse 1 helps us to hear the contours of the melodic lines, partly because, with a tilt of her head, she continually beckons downward, and the camera follows the lines of her body. The flat, deadpan expressions in verse 2 (with mouths drawn into straight lines), help us to hear the breadth of that section. It is hard to argue, though easy to sense, that the sparkle in Madonna's eyes and her joyous expression give a buoyant levity to the image that seems to match a playful element in the music. Yet the video is more complicated than this. The video was shot in the winter, and the water was extremely cold. To keep warm, Madonna was wrapped in blankets between takes. A trace of athletic stoicism may be present in the video that exists in tension, rather than harmony, with the song.[33]

SELF-REFLEXIVITY

Against Madonna's buoyancy, hard work, and flirtation, the song and video sustain a critique of Madonna. The song has a naive, untutored quality because of Madonna's vocal delivery and the thin orchestration of its two-voice structure. The impulsiveness of the jump from D_1 to D_2 in the second half of the verse's vocal line seem to highlight this naiveté—it does not proceed according to traditional formal rules.[34] However, if one listens to the synthesizer break, in the middle and at the end of verse 1, one might find it a bit too sarcastic or mocking, in its relation to the voice, since it is articulated as even, measured half notes. When Madonna's voice is chorused, the image shows her alone on the beach flexing her muscles. This image renders Madonna's autoeroticism, self-determination, and self-absorption ironic.

The image also comments upon itself and refers to its relation with the music. For example, the fluke is often used as a foil to the vocal line. At the bridge, the music starts with an instrumental lick rather than with Madonna singing, and we see the mermen, not Madonna, propelled upward by their flukes. The mermen with their flukes have gotten a taste for stardom, and later in the bridge, the flukes impertinently appear in small gaps between the singing.

A reading of the song with the image can broaden our understanding of Madonna's work. Critics claim that Madonna merely affects a series of poses or masks, and that her work is therefore fragmentary—that it relies upon the most superficial of associations. Yet attention to the "Cherish" video, in a way that is respectful of the song's role in shaping it, can offer this vision: that the youthful, girl-next-door vocal delivery in the song is connected to, not detached from, the video's more direct, sexualized modes of expression.

If I remember the song, it is for Madonna's singing, which flows in tandem with, but is not given over to, a charismatic bass line and a minimally differentiated arrangement. I think of Herb Ritts's supportive vision of Madonna, and of the long lines of his images, which seem to radiate like spokes across the surface of the video. All of these features, through their attentiveness, clarity, and directness, give a sense of integrity and commitment, qualities not acknowledged in the scholarly community, either for Madonna's work or for Ritts's.

HOMOEROTIC CONFIGURATIONS

The mermen are native to the place of the video, and Madonna is but a visitor. The video hints that they may be Madonna's, and our, real object of attention:

it was built around the mermen—they were shot separately, with a great deal of concern lavished on the mechanics of the tails. (Does this make the men in this video merely "pieces of tail"?) The second half of verse 3, which features these tails, is a critical moment in both song and video. If we look more closely, it becomes clear that the mermen reflect a homoerotic perspective.

The mermen exist in a self-contained world, a world without women, and they procreate their own kind, not biologically, but socially. It is true that the mermen do not seem to possess genitalia, but the men in Herb Ritts's other work—more clearly marked as homoerotic—show a similar tendency toward becoming sculptural forms without genitalia. The prominent tails, however, call forth numerous associations, including sexual ones. The mermen's flukes can evoke Christian symbolism, Hans Christian Andersen's "The Little Mermaid," the mythography of dolphins and their noble rescues of people, the birth of Venus, and the TV series *Flipper*,[35] but also sperm and phalluses.

Philip Hayward reminds us that images of mermen are quite rare—we are much more familiar with mermaids.[36] If their origin is unclear, this lack of clarity might itself be read as a gay image—gays are sometimes called "fairies," perhaps partly because we do not know how they come to be. The mermen's mysteriousness and elusiveness play a crucial role in defining them. They never address the camera, and are often shown disappearing from view. Invisibility is a central theme in the gay experience. It is linked to oppression, but also to desire—to watch and not be seen; to be seen but not to acknowledge being seen.

From a homoerotic angle, the elusiveness of the mermen makes them, if anything, more powerful. It creates a context in which their every appearance carries meaning. Some sequences wittily upstage Madonna, making the mermen into the real stars: the image of Madonna's opening her blouse, possibly to reveal her breasts, interrupted by a shot of the merman's bare chest instead; or, perhaps, the moment when Madonna sings "makes me feel so good," and the merman rubs noses with the merboy.

A homoerotic perspective allows us to sense the force of figures that would seem, at first, to add no more than a whimsical touch to a video dominated by the presence of Madonna. Like many figures in the backgrounds of videos, the mermen take on an enigmatic character partly because the conventions of music video do not allow them to speak. In "Cherish," however, the mermen's muteness seems, not merely conventional, but a matter of will or nature. Their silent presence and the way of life it suggests become integral to the video.

▬▬▬▬

This chapter was written to provide a means for analyzing music video. "Cherish" shows that a video can reflect a multitude of musical parameters. It argues for the sheer complexity of the relation between music and image: it reveals that correspondences between music and image can range from the strictest to the most subtle or enigmatic—and that the most fragile may be the most engaging. The "Cherish" video shimmers between the most traditional of texts—the topos of mother and child—and the most radical—a social order in which gays, women and children can live with independence.

I do not want to claim that connections between music and image are natural, or that we have an innate capacity to see these connections, or even that all or most people do see them.[37] More than proving what people do with music videos, I want rather to show what videos and videomakers can offer us. I might say, paraphrasing Wittgenstein, that learning the *language* of music video means learning a *form of life.*[38]

APPENDIX: "CHERISH" VIDEO NARRATIVE

- Introduction: The boy runs along the shoreline.
- Verse 1: Madonna sings while the waves crest behind her.
- Chorus 1: Three mermen swim away from the camera. The section cuts rapidly among Madonna, the mermen, and the boy, now a merboy.
- Verse 2: Water runs up Madonna's legs. Madonna and the mermen spy on each other.
- Chorus 2: Madonna spirals away from the camera. The figures of Madonna, the mermen, and the merboy are placed high in the frame.
- Bridge 1: With their arms reaching upward, three mermen fill the frame; Madonna moves from left to right at the water's edge. Madonna remains at the shoreline while the mermen remain at sea.
- Verse 3 (instrumental): The camera travels a path out to sea, passing Madonna as she cradles the merboy. The mermen swim in formation under water.
- Bridge 2: Madonna turns toward the camera. She frolics with the merboy on the sand.
- Break: A merman dives backward into the ocean, revealing his chest. Madonna flexes her muscles at the water's edge.
- Outchorus: A merman twists away from us, pulling himself out of the water. The boy, human again, runs toward the mermen as they swim out to sea. Madonna remains on the sand. The boy (now older?) returns to face her.

12

Desire, Opulence, and Musical Authority: The Relation of Music and Image in Prince's "Gett Off"

IN PRINCE'S "Gett Off," two women calling themselves "Diamond" and "Pearl" gain admittance to a huge performance space. The space is extremely ornate, disposed with the band members, many extras, and a vast number of props. As Diamond and Pearl move toward the back of the space as a locus of fulfillment, they encounter Prince at various points and in various guises. All three figures tease each other in what amounts to a complex courtship ritual. The video ends with the scene of a mock orgy. Reflecting the song, the video alludes to many visual and musical styles. This allusive quality and the density of the image operate almost independently of the sexual teleology of the video.

My analysis of "Gett Off" is organized as a movement from general features to particular moments of the video. Such an approach attempts to reproduce the changing sense of engagement that the video creates with multiple viewings. Let me begin with a general account of the look of the image and how it speaks with the music in "Gett Off." This video looks so strikingly different from all other videos largely because it is a panoramic image. Much of the video is in long shot. There are very few close-ups or extreme close-ups. Many figures remain in midscale, and most remain extremely small. What in the music relates to this sense of panorama? Unlike most popular songs, the solo voice is not the focus of "Gett Off"; the song does not have one "center." Instead, the song comprises an ensemble of forces: in terms of vocal performance, there are the backing tracks of primarily male singers, and in the foreground there are rapper Tony M. and singer Rosie Gaines who, together, sing as often as does Prince. In fact, Prince is largely absent from the choruses, and even in the verses, his voice is not the song's center. This may be in part because Prince is a virtuoso who does not need to place his voice front and center to assert his authority. He composes and produces his own music, sings, and plays many instruments. Members of his band, The New Power Generation, report that at the time of the making of *Diamonds and Pearls,* Prince's main interest was in building up, erasing, and then rebuilding the rich mixes for the album. "Gett Off" is unusual as a popular song in that the backing tracks of the mix are as present as is the voice. The backing tracks counterbalance the voice, partly because these tracks have their own rhythmic identity, forcing the listener's attention to move between the backing tracks and the voice. The panoramic quality of the image therefore points to the decentered, broad nature of the music.

Many elements of the music besides Prince's voice help to define the nature of the space in the "Gett Off" video. The main timbral hooks of the song—the scream, the bass, and the bass drum—all have a long resonance that calls forth a cavernous space. The highest harmonics of the scream and the reiterating cymbal may call forth a vaulted ceiling. I would also suggest that the most important of these hooks, the bass drum, is represented by the most expensive item in the set, the inlaid emerald and gold faux-marble floor.

Now, let me propose a surprising notion. Music video, through its use of scale, can speak about musical proportions. If the space of the "Gett Off" video is large, bottom-heavy, and redolent with figures, then the musical lines that cut across the musical texture like a knife—the bass, voice, and cymbal—can seem to account for the ways that the human figures are bifurcated. In videos, a song can seem to control and direct a character's movements (and only more rarely the other way around.) The song's close weave of voices could appear to restrain some of the human figures, rooting them to the floor. The many sudden stops and starts, the sharp *vocalises,* the exclamations ("get off!"), and the huge percussive booms might transform others into automatons that perform repetitive gestures on demand.

For me, however, the most important large-scale relation between music and image is the relation between the background of the image and the background of the musical texture. In the video, the foreground is coarse and comedic. The background, I will later show, is delicately inflected, both reflecting foreground gesture and owning a shape in its own right. Similarly, the background of the "Gett Off" song—the rhythmically complex patterns of the woodblock and the actual pitches of the electric bass, for example—is so subtly articulated that it is barely audible without equalization or a superb stereo system. However, if one listens attentively, one hears the musical operations of diminution and augmentation in both the music and the image. The characters of Diamond and Pearl—like the camera's eye—probe toward the background in an attempt to discover its recesses. This should tell us that the music is neither flat nor one-dimensional. We are told, rather, that we should listen more deeply, that we should attend more carefully than our initial responses to the music might encourage.

One aspect that I will only point to is the fact that, unlike most videos, "Gett Off" acknowledges the song's debts to other musical cultures. The image is nonchalant in its footnoting—we see a "North African" woman playing a soprano sax, and we hear an "Indian" flute melody—but, if we are drawn into this video, this mismatching may encourage us to attend even more carefully to the music than we would if the image were perfectly synchronized. We may feel tempted to tease out the displacements. And the energy of both the music and video derive from transgression and pastiche. Both throw styles together, juxtapose the old and the new, the valuable and the commonplace. In the music there are allusions to James Brown, Arabic melodies, Depression-era pop songs, and Jimi Hendrix. There is also the everyday—the banal "get off" and the tambourine sample. The image similarly reveals moments of obsessive detail and deliberate haphazardness (fig. 12.1).

FIGURE 12.1 The opulent set of "Gett Off."

Another surface connection between the music and the video is that both seem racy and sexy, or racist and sexist. The music seems at first to reflect this coarseness: what could be blunter than the song's heavy kick and snare? However, the more we begin to listen to the mix, the more we will find complexities, rich inflections, instances of gender bending and expanded identities.[1] Similarly, the lyrics on first glance seem sexist, but perhaps they are in some way chivalrous: "23 positions in a one-night stand. *I'll only call you after if you say I can.*"[2] Similarly, the image is not as sexist and pornographic as it may seem on the surface.

Let us consider the image. Here are two possible readings:

1. Two women come for an audition and find a casting couch. They enter a site of ultimate male power—a fusion of the impresario's rehearsal studio, the bachelor pad, and the harem. In their baby-doll dresses, these women appear to be playing roles of women who are underage, and who, as the common—and painful—story goes, arrive looking for validation, knowledge, power, love, sex. An older, promiscuous, predatory man holds power over these women, because with more life history behind him he knows what the odds are: these women will not obtain what they are searching for—wisdom or an enlarged view of the world—but rather what *he* wants, which is simply sex. We watch as sensual and courageous Diamond crosses a boundary into the lascivious, and as virginal and frightened Pearl becomes jaded. Sexual relations are not equal here. It is the women who are pointed at, ogled over, pushed around, and undressed. Prince remains unapproachable, his clothes are unzippable, and, unlike the women, he is almost never given over to or made vulnerable by sex.[3]

2. Two suburban women are slumming at the nightclub. Prince plays the role of the "tragic mulatto" who starts fights with everyone, and who picks up and pushes around the white women. We watch to see whether and how he will be made to pay for these transgressions.[4]

Yet I do not want to stop with these two readings. There is something about this music video that encourages us to listen further. The invocations of James Brown and Jimi Hendrix, in the song, should tell us that we cannot rest with these two readings. As I mentioned, the way to understand how race, sexuality, and gender speak in a video is through attending to both the music and the image. We need to attend to the music video's structure, to hear how each charged moment in the musical-visual context speaks, and to attend carefully to the nature of performance and to the tone and affect.

At the close of the video, Prince invokes the musical and visual codes of Jimi Hendrix—and here either sidesteps or answers the question of transgression through allying himself with one of the most important black-white crossover artists of our era. Similarly, the scene of Prince unzipping Pearl's dress is not as upsetting as we might assume it to be, because this scene, in the video, is troped as a historical moment, as one type of courtship among many. In both of these moments we must attend to both the music and the image.

In terms of tone and affect, it is important that, unlike most sexist work, the tone of the "Gett Off" song and the video is not mean-spirited. Rather, both works are warm, forthcoming, reflective, and expressive. The fact that I am so deeply drawn to this piece, that it is directed by a woman—and that it deals with race, power, and sexuality, all provoke me to consider this piece with a great deal of care. I am going to read the video through the lens of a number of musical and visual parameters. Only by pointing to these parameters will the piece start to open up for us.

FORM

The "Gett Off" video seems complete, in that Diamond and Pearl come in, explore, and leave the space. They move toward the background and seduction, and then toward the foreground and an orgy. The video narrates their falling into sex. (By verse 2, Diamond and we as viewers have fallen under the spell of seduction.) Key points in the music and in the video mark where we are in the piece. For example, when Pearl crowns the top of a pile of human figures, we know the piece will turn toward closure (fig. 12.2). We have a similar sense about the music—at this point one thread of musical material has been liquidated (the "get off" calls recede towards a vanishing point, and the bird-like scream has vanished) and the song is two-thirds over. In retrospect, within the larger process of intertwining figures, climbing over and pushing beyond

FIGURE 12.2 As Pearl crowns the group of entwined figures, the piece begins to turn toward closure.

one another towards the background, the image of Diamond putting her leg on Prince's shoulder is a preparation for this ascent. Though these images do not speak to a world of cooperation, they might be considered feminist in that they speak about a woman's desire to take male power, sometimes to be ascendant, to be king of the hill. Yet we have something even more richly textured than this. The image of ascent is problematized in both the music and the image. In the music, perhaps in an attempt to meet the opening flute melody, the vocal line raises its pitch center.

However, the stationary aspects of the voice, the bass, and the cymbal, and the stasis of the harmony, make the song feel nonteleological, and the ascent may be more felt than acknowledged. Similarly, in the image, the space appears so distorted that we may feel unsure about whether or not, as the stage doors open, we descend into and then ascend to the background. Because of this issue of an ascent, it is important that the image inverts the classic placement of objects within a frame. The image of transcendence that our culture usually strives toward and places highest in value is a thin, willowy, white, blonde female. Yet this figure is placed lowest on the floor, and we move up toward a heavy, dark piece of statuary—a fertility goddess.

The second half of the video loses momentum, I believe. The video's final third reveals several shots of Prince and his male band members clowning around. After the numerous scenes that suggest heightened forms of sexuality, this comes as a bit of a let down. One could say that the video fails to keep true to its promise always to offer transgressive imagery. This loss of directionality begins when the image becomes multilayered and Prince directs Pearl to "Do it with her feet in the drawers," and takes full effect when he claims "Grab the eight ball stick," and ambles around, shaking his hands with an imaginary pool stick. I will argue that the video picks up its thread later. To explain how the video falls away, it is helpful to return to the discussion of individual musical and visual parameters.

SECTIONS

In "Gett Off," director Randee St. Nicholas establishes sectional divisions by having her lead characters Prince, Diamond, and Pearl mark a site, and then establish a sphere of influence around this site through a strongly delineated style of movement and behavior (fig. 12.3). The magic of this technique lies in its creation of the sense that the music, too, defines the outer boundaries of these sites. We may be able to perceive the outer edges of this imaginary sphere in part through a rough estimate of the proportions of the "Gett Off" song— the length of the verse, the harmonic movement, the melodic ambitus. Both the first verse and the first site of "Gett Off" are heavily underscored as Prince roots himself to a particular location on the floor. As is common in music video, the sections in the image correlate to sections in the music. The verses tend to be rather solitary and narrative (Prince seduces here); the choruses are more timeless, philosophical and communal ("23 positions in a one-night stand," muses rapper Tony M); and the time of the bridge remains outside both of these realms, in a world of limbo and pure dance. Much of the activity of the figures in "Gett Off" is about moving towards and then away from the three states embodied by verse, chorus, and bridge.

FIGURE 12.3 Prince and Pearl mark a site. Pearl rises above Prince as she heads toward the background of the set.

RHYTHM

Frequently, the sole acknowledgement that critics make of the musicality of music video is that "It's cut to the beat." This is almost never true. Most videos move between periods of synchronization and disjunction. But "Gett Off" is highly unusual in that it is almost never cut to the beat. This is because the image can peg itself to the finer rhythms of the claves and the voice, and because the edited image can ground itself in the movement of a body as it approaches and then marks the beat. St. Nicholas makes a political decision when she decides to highlight the domain of rhythm, and specifically African American rhythms. Here she carves out a space of her own; she claims the right to inflect the image in the ways that she chooses. She becomes the guide to a personal but culturally inflected sexuality that would be otherwise unapproachable.

Beat structure in music video can take on representational features. In "Gett Off," every beat is marked as important and so there is great room for play. The fourth beat is the most strongly highlighted. It is often emphasized by a pattern that occurs at the ends of certain phrases: a drop in the contour of the voice on beat three and then silence on beat four. This gesture is literalized in the video. A music video character performs a drop, and then the extension of a drop. In the video, this fall is figured as a moment when the figure seems stunned—a freeze—or when the figure appears to risk falling into a frightening abyss. This abyss is figured as a place of wanton sex, vulnerability, embarrassing disclosure, and even death. But it is also a place of power, because it is the one place where a response to Prince's voice can be made, where things can suddenly happen or shift, where power is more diffuse and up for grabs. The visual drop, with the musical drop, is a key motive in "Gett Off." As a motive, it is carried through the video until the end, when everyone finally drops to the floor.

Continuing the examination of the beat, I would point out that, during the courtship, Prince hangs on the more suave two and four, snapping his fingers with one raised arm. When Prince finally takes control, when he begins really to push Pearl around and direct her movements, we know that he is in a position of authority and directorship: for the first time in the video, he articulates the downbeat of the measure. He even threatens to hit Pearl once. This is a harsh gesture, perhaps called for by the music, but also unprepared for—misogynistic, or more than the video can assimilate. (I have mentioned earlier that the video begins to lose steam at this point.) In numerous music videos, as is true for "Gett Off," beat one is the position of greatest control and authority. It is often figured as patriarchal.

KEY MOMENTS IN "GETT OFF"

Now that we have some sense of the video's larger processes, its sectional divisions, and its rhythm, we can look at key moments in the video. What image can match the transgressiveness of the song's opening scream? It seems as if the video were so struck with that sound that the whole first third desired solely to serve as a prolongation of that scream. One image in our culture that can serve as a match to that level of transgression is sodomy. If the women are screwed, so is Prince. "Gett Off" argues for not one type, but rather for the possibility of many erotic positionings—and this one is homoerotic and homosocial (the boys in the band). If Prince is a manipulator, the video lays out a whole social mechanism: we see Prince's multiple lovers, including men, feared and revered figures of authority (those gigantic, archetypal men and women, singer Rosie Gaines, drummer Michael B., and the mythic reed-player), and the social group within which he exists, who stand as responsive, attentive witnesses. The video emphasizes a system of relations over the star quality of Prince himself.

The subsequent image of rapper Tony M. pointing with a black leather glove toward the woman's buttocks is not as offensive as it might immediately appear to be. It is pulled so much outside of the immediate flow and texture of the image that it speaks of the larger scale of the piece. It answers a question that we may have had about the transgressiveness of the tape and places it at a pitch such that St. Nicholas can move quickly to where she wants to be (the later threesomes in the back of the space at verses 5 and 6). As an image in itself, it is almost a dead end. It is presented quickly and quickly discarded. Unlike all of the other images in the video, it contains almost no forward momentum. It is static, safely folded into the rest of the material of the chorus, closed off by Rosie Gaines's turn of the head. (She will later pump a male guard's arm: both sexes practice some form of objectification.) Nor is the argument necessarily reflective of Prince's point of view or of his actions. The video depicts Tony

M.'s lines as one theory, one philosophy. As continually happens in the video, we "Gett Off" it and move on.

Three instances set up a limit, a threshold, before crossing into the realm of sexuality. Verses 5 and 6 describe two forms of courting, one more contemporary (a quarrel over dinner and a moment of gender bending—the scream), one more classic and old school (James Brown, and a way of talking and sleeping with big-assed women). The latter mode of courtship succeeds at seduction.

Verse 5 (during Prince's discussion of whether or not there are ribs in his crib) is elegant because St. Nicholas listens very deeply into the mix, and her response to the music is an extremely subtle one (fig. 12.4). In verse 5, there is a lovely steel drum melody buried in the lower register. Because this melody is placed low in the mix, the image is weighted more toward the ground (Prince leans down, the figures rest as bottom-heavy furniture, the floor is heavily underscored). The contour of this line is smooth and undulating, "rounded" rather than short and spiky as in the upcoming James Brown section. Hence Prince "rounds" the figure, and the circle in the Prince symbol is strategically placed here. In addition, placed farther in the background and in the right hand side of the frame, a second circle—composed of one upright and many seated figures—underscores the circle motif.

FIGURE 12.4 The steel drum melody buried in the lower register corresponds to the color and shape of the insignia on the marble floor.

The steel drums that I have just mentioned contain more pure sine tones than the rest of the song's material, and consequently, for the first time, the image turns purple. (It is a simple equation. In our culture, sawtooth-type envelopes are traditionally associated with warm tones, sine tones with cool ones—so we have purple imagery.) Notice the dancer, placed back stage left, whose downward pointing arms help lead the viewer's eye to the marble floor.

Next, we cross the boundary from verse 5 into verse 6, and into an older form of music and courtship. We also move, in the mix, from something both subtle and buried low in the musical texture to something both high and frontal (the trumpets and the surface noise of the James Brown sample). The image of the woman holding the phonograph is enigmatic. She looks Native American and appears to take the role of a gatekeeper. bell hooks argues in her recent book *Black Looks* that for African Americans, Native Americans bring gladness to the heart because of a shared history of cultural practices and of oppression.[5]

So, this figure might stand for a crossing from the present moment into the depth of cultural history, solidarity, and affection. (The soundtrack becomes more richly nuanced, with sounds appropriate for tap dancing as well as vocal pops.)

The next section answers the question of why it matters that this video was directed by a woman. This is the point at which sex happens. Here, in the music, that nagging tambourine sound finally drops out, and Prince finally starts speaking slowly, rather than keeping up that annoying patter. The video may argue that a woman may choose sex simply because she wants a moment of quiet, privacy, and intimacy. It seems to argue as well that a woman's sexuality may always be homosocially and homoerotically linked to that of other women. Note the ways Diamond and Pearl move in concert and finally walk off together.

In the next bridge, when Pearl becomes an automaton, or a musical instrument, she is brought into relation with the background. The video raises this question: If foreground figures can become mechanical, could not all those rigid figures, and the statuary of the background, become animate?

The image looks the way that it does in verse 7, at the moment of these dense overlays, perhaps because for much of the length of the video, St. Nicholas has been very carefully tracing out single melodic lines in the music. In order to avoid redundancy, she must shift our attention to another scale, she must now take a new tack, and she wants to move to euphoria, to go beyond the bounds of the video. Yet, although Pearl may be able to see Prince's promises for sexual activities, we cannot see, even much less imagine them, because multiple superimposed images of the set pass before our view.[6] The viewer may feel left out, and his attention may begin to wane. So, this video may contain a flaw, even as it is held together by its richness, contradictions, and complexity.

I have suggested that "Gett Off" spins in the wrong direction, and the sexual charge dissipates in the last third of the video. However, it is important to point out that, since many music videos *do* work as wholes, the fact that we can point to the failure of *this* video argues for the integrity of music video as a genre. Music videos, like lyric poetry, can be full of allusions and moments of intra-textuality. They require the perfect balance of gestures placed at exactly the right time. One poorly gauged or mistimed decision and the piece suffers.

What fails?[7] The video seems to succeed in that it does what we might expect it to do, which is to track the music with care. In the second half of the "Gett Off" song, the music, for the most part, "thins out." Similarly, the image in the video, after the momentary dance overlays, becomes sparser—we see fewer wide shots of the dense background and fewer framing devices such as picture frames, pillars, and bodies marking off the frame. So the image closely tracks musical processes. However, the video does come up short in that it is unable to hold true to its promise of never ending novelty and change—even Prince's rapping about twenty-three positions in a one-night stand suggest as much.

"Gett Off" makes a promise that anything can happen, beginning with the opening scene of absolute transgression—Prince and his male entourage enacting the primal scene.[8] The viewer may begin to try to figure out what is happening here, and therefore may try to parse out the setting and form parts of bodies into wholes. She may soon begin to wonder what will happen to Diamond and Pearl. Perhaps the two women will become interested in each other. Perhaps they will force Prince to perform sex. Perhaps they will dance the dance of the seven veils. Perhaps they will run away from home and join the carnivalesque figures in the background. (Pearl knows who these figures are and seems to belong to them. Her dress contains a microcosm of the set.)

Both music and image set the stage for a heady concoction of sex and transgression. The "boom cha-ka-la-ka" recalls a slowed down version of a dimly remembered tune heard in old cartoons and black and white films of cannibals from the dark continent dancing around missionaries boiling in a pot. The video's main concern may be not sex, but human sacrifice. (A fertility goddess stands over a giant statue of a hand holding a flaming plate, as well as a steaming Jacuzzi around which are placed sacrificial offerings. The drummer sits as the head, with maidens fanning him. Some of the guards look like the officiary that will carry out the sacrifice. Diamond and Pearl have wandered into the wrong place. This scene can awaken an old forgotten thrill.) Several other musical elements continue the thread of danger and exoticism. The snare drum is so loud and bright that it seems to crack the viewer so hard alongside the head that she forgets what she has heard. The scream is displaced and free-floating—a call of hysteria located in no single place. (Is it a bird's cry, a man's or another woman's?) The snake-charmer melody, rhythmically displaced, pulls the listener into the sonic fabric, threatening to transfix and seduce her. The tambourine jingle suggests falling jewelry and the loosening of clothes. The claves and wood blocks sound like creatures rustling in the background. The later "oo's" that enter around verse 7 and 8 sound like the soothing chorus of women from the South Seas.

The image alone demands that we watch closely. Many of the double entendres stem from repetitions of visual rhymes: a woman grabs her crotch, a forearm, and a hand (upon which is tattooed a curling snake), then turns and ignites in flame. Drummer Michael B.'s lips drop lewdly, and the woman behind him pulls forward her pants. Hands drape over shoulders and then heads fall back. The image is so thick that the best way to watch it is to break the frame into six quadrants—and view one section at a time. We watch closely as Prince makes a number of strange faces: is he a pixie, a Svengali, too immature for the activities unfolding around him, or too mature—completely above it? Perhaps he is harmless when he skips and twirls, but sometimes his movements are brusque. Diamond and Pearl are sometimes languid and sometimes stiff. What do these gestures mean?[9]

By the two-thirds point the video's imagery might be taking up these tantalizing details. When we as listeners experience the repetition of a musical section, we hear it differently. We are in a different place. We may feel deepened by the music. Most music videos break out of their orbit two-thirds in as a way of acknowledging the changing experience of the listener, even though the music may remain more or less the same. Perhaps, if "Gett Off" had shifted in the second half, becoming either more narcotic, or more pornographic, the video might have seemed more structurally consistent.

The video seems to lose it when Prince hunts around with the pool cue and his sidemen twirl on pedestals. The section only lasts for fifteen seconds, but that is enough to lose the line. Perhaps it is because what was so bewildering in the video's opening has been normalized. Here, Prince and his male friends hang out together after sex and swap tales about their exploits. The straight couple embracing in the background affirms heterocentrist norms. Perhaps if "Gett Off" contained one or two gay couples making out, or if Diamond and Pearl had not disappeared, our engagement in the tape might remain more intense.[10]

We can find value in the way that the video thins out in its second half. Prince and Randee St. Nicholas may have been moved to draw a story about the world of the sexual entrepreneur—a story that necessarily includes the moment when the women are gone and the viewer lacks an object of desire, and faces a moment of emptiness. In this moment, earlier fears of overwhelming women may surface. Hence, in the last third of the "Gett Off" video, we see images of loneliness and of monumental women.

This moral point is made at a cost, however. Some attractive aspects of the song cannot be underscored. A listener attending to the song alone may decide that the most powerful moment is in its second half when Rosie Gaines jubilantly sings, "Let a woman be a woman" (with her voice chorused, and with the pitches C and E♭ completing a long-range pattern). To match this moment of celebration, the image might need to become opulent (more opulent even than the dense overlays that we see in verse seven). We do see the rather charged image of the fertility goddess in the background and that of Prince in Rosie Gaines lap (with Prince wiping snot from his nose, a mother-child image), but these last moments are more ones of solitude than of celebration (watch for the moment when the two figures take leave of one another).

The last series of events—Prince pretending to hit Pearl, the men dancing by themselves, and the monumental figures of Gaines and the fertility goddess—all have equivalence within the song. Every image fits its musical weight as the video unfolds in time. However, the objects and events within the music video also carry a kind of cultural and ontological weight. To move across these events and objects, including Prince's intent on hitting Pearl, the desexualized images of the gigantic motherly woman, Rosie Gaines, and the mythic flute player, to the floor, that is, to the orgy, would demand a longer stretch of music or an abrupt musical change (fig. 12.5).

FIGURE 12.5 The monumental figures of Gaines and the fertility goddess.

Yet a music-video viewer can chart her own path through a tape—especially in the case of "Gett Off" where the eye can wander through the image and select any of a number of figures to attend to. Beginning with Prince's use of a pool cue, I must hunt through the music and image in search of my own erotic payoff. I hold onto the almost mythical image of Rosie Gaines. I take pleasure in the ways the male servants stroke her inner thigh, and she taunts them with a handkerchief. I like her unworldly laugh at the close of the tape. The video's last gestures possess ethical weight. What may be wonderful about "Gett Off" is that St. Nicholas adopts so many responses to the music—slavish attentiveness, willful disobedience, frontal aggression, generous pliancy, and playfulness. The director's responses to the music are wide reaching, and the song seems so big that it may never be compassed. Some aspects of "Gett Off" that make it look dated—for example, the makeshift set with scaffolding in the background—may distract the viewer from what is one of the richest videos in the music-video canon. This is unfortunate. I cannot think of another video that offers such a surfeit of sound and movement.

TIMBRE AND GESTURE

Often, in "Gett Off," the amount of detail seems to be more than the eye can assimilate. Let me describe some of the ways that detail is used in the video.

In "Gett Off," musical motives are often clearly linked to visual motives, for example, the "rip" of the tambourine sample, and the snapping cloth that fills the frame for a moment; or the jumping and swirling movements of Prince and Pearl against the words "get off." (Both Prince's and Pearl's dance movements and the musical motive have the same rhythmic articulation, short-long.)

Visual activity in the foreground is commented upon in the background. For example, while Prince seduces in verse 1, Tony M. performs an array of movements—he steps up to and down from the podium, rolls legs alongside his chest, pulls his arms together and apart, claps, and kisses a woman. Tony M's movements make sense in their own right—they form coherent phrases against the music—yet they also fill out Prince's movements. Together, Prince's and Tony M.'s gestures function much in the same manner as that of a Bach melody (two streams of musical activity that make a coherent whole). The independence of the backing tracks from the voice in the song provides a supportive environment for this phenomenon.

Gestures seem to traverse the surface of the space. They move from one side to another. They also seem to leap across edits. For example, the prominent percussion melody in the song's center drops in pitch and moves to the front of the mix. Similarly, in the image, performers seem to carry the gesture from the background to the foreground. Another example is when the rhythmic motive associated with the lyric "get off" moves from an identifiable dance movement made by Diamond and Pearl, to a charismatic camera movement, to a snakelike pattern on a piece of clothing and a tattoo, to a striking dance movement made by Tony M. and a woman. (This last instance is an inversion and augmentation of the previous material.)

In many of the above examples, boundaries between domains become porous. As at the moment when the viewer encounters the Native American woman and crosses into the James Brown section, the viewer senses, in these instances, both the boundary and its momentary dissolution. Of particular interest is when one term in the equation seems to lie almost out of perceptible range (for example, the image or music might be deeply embedded in the background, or might point to something subtle in the mix). Hence we experience a moment of emergence, of something's coming into being. The "Gett Off" video demands a great deal of the viewer's attention. Any movement, within the space of a single beat, may become a gesture that furthers a narrative, or that functions as ordinary lived experience, or as dance.

What are the implications of gesture in the "Gett Off" video? First, the figures in "Gett Off" may create a state of heightened ambivalence on the part of the viewer. On one hand, the figures are frightening. They are like automatons; they are inhuman. (One wonders if we are simply watching the mechanism of an impressive clock. The figures seem warmed up and animated by the floor, as if the floor might be a hot skillet.) However, on another level, they are more human than we are. Many of the gestures belong to all members of the band. (Notice the way that almost all of the band members lip-sync parts of the lyrics, regardless of who was responsible for the originating sound.) Gestures pass from figure to figure as if they were messages moving along a series of relays: in the process, commentary is added on, and the message is changed. This creates the sense that we are watching a closely knit community that shares a kind of wisdom and knowledge that we do not, and may never possess. When confronted with the figures in the video, the viewer may feel a sense of awe. In "Gett Off," band members and dancers move in a state of sublime excess—they seem infused with a sense of play, humor, archness, and camp that carries them beyond whatever they might be doing at the moment. Through the high level of craft of the video and its commitment to what functions as a kind of consistent worldview, "Gett Off" poses questions that can be deeply felt. "Why not celebrate sex in the post-AIDS era?" "Why am I so in favor of monogamy?" "What is appropriate sexual play?" "How is this community, how are these relationships, like or unlike my own?" In terms of how to live, how to be responsive to the moment, how to move with a sense of flow and to move on, the "Gett Off" video provides a way to move from the panorama of the video to the realms of action and thought.

13

Peter Gabriel's Elegy for Anne Sexton: Image and Music in "Mercy St."

THE VIDEO for Peter Gabriel's "Mercy St." begins with a man taking a boat out onto the water. He carries some unidentified cargo that might be a person—alive or dead. A woman, possibly institutionalized, prepares for death through the practices of Catholic faith. The connection between these two strands is never made clear, partly because the two stories move at different paces. At the end of the video, the man remains on the boat, but the status of the woman is unknown. The figures become more purely iconic as the video progresses; they change in some degree, but it is hard to say whether some transformative event has actually taken place.

The song's subject is the poet Anne Sexton, and the "Mercy St." video can be described as a composition, in roughly equal parts, of, homage, elegy, pastiche, and biography. Sexton was an untutored housewife and mother, who, on the advice of her psychiatrist, began to write poetry at the age of twenty-eight, and quickly achieved renown. (In her lifetime, she wrote ten books of poetry and was awarded a Pulitzer Prize.) Her poems are most admired for their powerful and surprising metaphors. In 1974, at the age of forty-six, she committed suicide.

Appreciated by music-video directors and industry personnel, Gabriel fans and music video aficionados, yet screened only a handful of times on MTV, Gabriel and director Matt Mahurin's "Mercy St." is hardly typical of commercial music video: it was not tied to a hit single or the appearance of the star. Moreover, it deals with serious themes, contains frequent temporal disjunctions, and makes an unusually broad range of music/image connections.[1] The video's obscurity and complexity notwithstanding, "Mercy St." is a good choice for close analysis. Many of the devices that structure "Mercy St." fall within the traditional codes of the genre, and in the hands of director Mahurin, seem not only to illuminate the genre, but also to hint at what music video has the potential to become.[2]

This chapter attempts to provide a close analysis of a single music video, and to account for why some moments in the multimedia object seem important and others less so. It describes the ways that musical and visual codes operate in a music video, and shows these operations in a temporal flow. Although music video is a pervasive presence in contemporary culture, few such attempts have been made. In addition, adequate theories of the ways that music, lyrics, and image might work together to create this hybrid form are lacking. The chapter divides into three parts. The first section provides a chronological reading of the video interspersed with fuller descriptions of music/image relations. The second section considers questions of large-scale form. The final section investigates issues of gender and authorial voice.

The first section moves among a sequential narrative of the video, a discussion of musical parameters, and fragments from Anne Sexton's poetry. These two modes of description and Sexton's poetry place the material in an accessible form and reproduce some of a music video experience. When watching music videos, we often multitask: following a narrative or processual trajectory, piecing together music/image relations, and placing lyrics, we work to make sense of the whole. The individual descriptions of musical parameters can be used as an analytical tool for reading music video in general. Sexton's poems may encourage the reader to find out more about her life and work.[3]

READING "MERCY ST."

Before embarking on a detailed description and analysis, it might be useful to point out that the video's multivalency makes any streamlined approach or summary difficult. Without a body of literature describing music video genres, styles, historical trends, and directors, or providing methodology or close analyses, it seems hard to characterize "Mercy St."[4] The video is elliptical. "Mercy St." narrates a woman's experiences as she struggles with mental institutions, the memory of incest, and the threat of suicide or being drowned; the story is told out of sequence and in fragments, and the viewer must struggle to learn the piece. The viewer may search for a large-scale structure, yet she may come up empty-handed. The song itself is unpredictable, based upon a drone that allows for materials to be brought in and out of the mix, and containing irregular section lengths. In addition, Mahurin's imagery and Gabriel's music share an affinity of tone and affect, allowing space for any individual element or image to depart from the norm. The sporadic appearance of a boat going out on the water provides one thread of continuity. Without much to serve as a guide, however, the viewer must crawl from one shot to the next: each shot must be interpreted in light of musical and visual cues. Moment by moment, relations among music, image, and lyrics shift. This shifting ground creates an unstable subject position for the viewer, who is alternately left out and given clues, pushed away and drawn in, asked to look ahead, reflect back or simply wait. In the final analysis, the video may concern itself less with revealing anything for the viewer than with its own "blanking out" or withdrawal.

The shot-by-shot description highlights how the video creates these shifts in subject position by moving from an emphasis on one musical parameter to an emphasis on another.[5] It is important to note that not only the emphasized *parameters* but also the *nature* and *degree* of emphasis change. Moreover, although the images often seem to follow the music, the reverse is frequently the case as well; music and image possess different kinds of power over one another. The individual descriptions of musical parameters, which appear in italics, can be used as an analytical tool for reading music video in general.

Introduction As with many music videos, the introductory section of "Mercy St." displays the most precise relations between image and music. The song quickly establishes itself as "other" to Anglo-American pop through its modal harmonic materials and Brazilian percussion. Hushed, solemn, and vaguely religious are good descriptors for the introduction's affect. The video's first shot contains a thin man or woman in half light, with a flowing garment and bare feet, walking on sand. Taken with the music of the introduction, this image suggests a mystical figure in a desert setting. Upon closer examination, however, other elements complicate such an impression. The figure, for instance, wears two Band-Aids, and this puzzling detail limits any idealized reading—what type of wounds along the edge of the feet might need covering? Are they stigmata, or do they suggest ritual or aestheticism? Are they a reference to Oedipus (fig. 13.1)?[6]

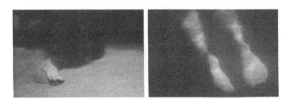

FIGURE 13.1 (A–B)

Subsequent viewings of the video suggest that the Band-Aids serve not only a narrative and depictive function, but a graphic one as well. The director's manipulations of shape suggest a concern less with people and events than with a form that empties out. Narratively, the video first adopts a distanced stance toward the world, and then absents itself completely.[7]

In the second shot, we see the lower half of someone's legs. As the legs rise in the frame, they stop moving, perhaps suggesting a loss of consciousness. At the moment that the motion ceases, however, the surdo enters, sounding almost like a heartbeat. This seeming contradiction in affect—the music asserting vitality as the image shows death—raises several questions: which figures are animate, and which inanimate? Is it the image or the music that provides the video's impetus? The heartbeat alongside the dead body may suggest the spirit's release from the body, allowing it to wander across the landscape of the video. Such a ghostly cinematic point of view is reinforced in shots 13, 23, and 33–37. Yet almost every shot raises questions of point of view. Does it belong to a ghost, a youthful or older Anne Sexton, Peter Gabriel, the spiritual guide, the boat rower, a father, the viewer, or some combination of these figures?

CONTOUR

"Mercy St." uses the movement of objects within the frame for more than incidental or coloristic effects. In fact, by tracing the contour of this movement across a number of edits, one can gain a greater appreciation for the song's melodic materials and their affective characteristics.[8] The song's introduction presents a four-note "cambiata" motive several times in different registers. The objects in the frame trace the up-and-down contour of the cambiata. The rise and fall of the shadow in the first image of the foot follows the contour of this motive, sometimes appearing a bit before or behind the melody, but still responsive to it. A second synthesizer part enters, playing the same cambiata figure in a lower register. Similarly, the line of the shadow crosses the foot and repeats its rise and fall. The low bass note is matched by the feet hitting the sand. Just as the foot's next step launches the following image, the bass "pushes off" into the body of the song.

A related example lies in the melody of the verses' "a" section. Although this melody begins with a rising skip of a third, its overall contour emphasizes downward motion. It is repeated three times before the "b" section appears. The image draws our attention to the melody's gradual descent by presenting three shots of objects falling slowly through the frame.

> my real dream,
> I'm walking up and down Beacon Hill
> searching for a street sign—
> namely MERCY STREET.
> Not there.

Verse 1—Shots 1, 2 Verse 1 begins by establishing a fragile connection between music and image. The vocal line is doubled at the octave. Similarly, images of houses have a pale border both above and below, and these parallel lines slowly fall through the frame. Aspects of the ghostly houses serve more than musical functions. The houses are shot through a mirror or puddle, and this mirror image raises questions of both the identity and the position of the viewer. The lyrics ("Looking back on everything, all she could see") also lead one to imagine a subject and the town or city that surrounds her. Because the second falling house is older and less distinct than the first, it may suggest the memory of an earlier house, perhaps evocative of childhood (fig. 13.2).

FIGURE 13.2

Verse 1—Shots 5, 6 The next shot, of a woman's head low in the frame, plays on the video's first shot. In the first shot, the foot creates a hole in the sand, and its corresponding sound—the bass's initial attack—a kind of sonic pothole. Here, the sound seems to flood over the woman's head, suggesting the inverse shape, a dome. Following this shot is one of a woman praying as she falls through the frame, yet we do not know if she is the same one who traversed the sand, died in the water, or looked onto the city streets; this is so in part because her body is turned away from us and her features are indistinct. We may be reluctant to consider her the main character of the video.

Bridge Fragment Images of feet stepping in sand and hands pushing the boat (shots 7 and 8) set the "b" section of the verse. This section exists as a fragment inserted between repetitions of the verse and can be heard as the kernel from which the more substantial bridge grows. Because Gabriel's hushed, semi-spoken singing sounds tender and conspiratorial, one might guess that Sexton remembers a moment from her childhood or a secret wish: she and her brother steal away to take a boat out to sea. Since this small section will grow over the course of the song, something illicit yet beloved develops in the video. Perhaps this is one reason why the video does not have a completely dark tone, despite its focus on suicide (fig. 13.3).

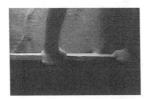

FIGURE 13.3

A woman's half-lit face (shot 9) closes the section. The face is shown in three-quarter shadow—a shocking effect. The image, here, seems to run ahead of the song.

The image-music connections also become more like puns. The whistling sound might fit the wind blowing across the woman's face. The strong attack and nasal vowel of the word "comes" recall the feet stepping on sand and the surdo's "heartbeat," respectively (fig. 13.4).

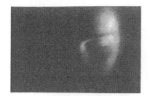

FIGURE 13.4

We are fishermen in a flat scene.
All day long we are in love with water.
The fish are naked.
The fish are always awake.
They are the color of old spoons
and caramels.
The sun reached down
but the floor is not in sight.
Only the rocks are white and green.
Who knows what goes on in the halls below?

CONTINUITY

In "Mercy St.," repeated or varied visual patterns create a subtle mode of continuity that compensates for the video's narrative lacunae and more drastic visual transformations: it does not rely on character or plot to create stability. The video establishes continuity from one shot to the next using a variety of techniques—graphic matches, repetition of visual patterns and schemes, preservation of tonal values. For instance, a sense of continuity is established in the opening series of shots through an unbroken line across edited images.[9]

The first shot is of a foot stepping on sand. Toward the end of this shot, the foot and its shadow fill the lower right-hand corner of the frame. Next, a shot of feet drifting in water begins in the lower right of the frame and moves toward and exits from the upper left. Next, a series of shots contains objects dropping from the upper left-hand corner, each object starting a little lower than the previous one. The last image, of the crown of the woman's head, is planted at the bottom of the frame.

In the middle of verse 1, a sense of continuity is preserved no longer through an unbroken line that leads the eye, but through number and light. Two falling spheres—which turn out to be a head and clasped hands—are followed by two shins and then two arms (shots 6–8). Shadows pass over and cover these images until the sequence ends with a woman's head in three-quarter shadow. In the chorus, the lace on the girl's hat blends into the crest of a wave. The final images all contain a vertical band of light in the center of the frame.[10]

Verse 1—Shot 10 For the first time, the lyrics come to the fore, yet just as suddenly they recede into the mix. The image responds to the line "Nowhere in the corridors," particularly the emphasized word "nowhere": a hand searches upward against a black background with lace streaming from the fingertips, before image and text fade away. As the second hand takes the lead, a countermelody in the synthesizer comes to the fore. The phrase "There in the distance" follows the image of the boat going out, and the word "there" and the boat's bow seem to pierce the darkness. The coming forward and fading away of the text "nowhere in the corridors of pale green and gray," and "nowhere in the . . ." suggests a treacherous journey or an unreliable guide. The boat holds what appears to be a severed head. The lyrics "like stone," though barely audible, reflect the image of a granite-like head.

> In north light, my smile is held in place,
> the shadow marks my bone.
> What could I have been dreaming as I sat there,
> all of me waiting in the eyes, the zone
> of the smile

Verse 1—Shot 12; Chorus 1—Shots 13–17 The face of a woman who may represent Sexton becomes an unyielding mask, a dead end. The close-up of the ocean provides a surprising moment of renewal, suggesting the fullness and breadth of the self, the bounty of nature. It is hard to tell to whom the point of view belongs, or even why this shot should appear, inasmuch as the image reveals the water's surface solely. Half a measure later, the synthesizer plays a four-note flourish that suggests running water. The flourish confirms the sense that this pure image of water provides a respite from the video's largely ominous tone. (This is so despite water's dark connotations in the rest of the video; see fig. 13.5.) The video soon returns to its former tone, however. The shot of the mysterious man in a large black coat throwing a rope into the boat gives a sense of foreboding: his return to the boat seems to discourage any hope of a positive outcome. An earlier shot reveals a human figure in the back of the boat, but does not adequately explain the severed head in the boat's bottom and the corpse tethered to the board. The music assists in creating this sense of foreboding. Though the chorus is livelier and fuller than the verse, the movements just described—of the father and the boat—serve to bracket a segment of the melody. Here, effort is needed to keep the melodic line moving upward and the weariness of the voice reflects this difficulty. This musical "snapshot" connects this moment to other points of weariness and labor in the verse.

FIGURE 13.5

The music for the chorus as a whole is lilting and soothing, yet the image leaves us to our own devices, as the instances of close synchronization between music and image become much more sporadic.[11] Despite the lack of direct music/image pairings, a more subtle kind of connection derives from the repetition of simple shapes. Three breaking waves correspond to the fully orchestrated chorus while isolated pairs—two houses, two hands, two feet, balled head and hand—match the thinly textured verse. As in many music videos, this repetition of small numbers of objects in successive images helps us to chart the flow of the song's form.

Chorus 1 closes with a long shot of the father pushing the boat with his daughter in it. The last image of this sequence is worthy of close attention. Because this cut to a long shot is so abrupt, we do not know what is happening. Within the rhetoric of narrative film, a long shot at the end of a section typically suggests that the viewer possesses some insight and is prepared to move on to the next sequence; here, however, we have no idea what the man is doing or why. The image might show a pastoral scene with a father spending an afternoon with his child just as easily as a suicide or murder. Perhaps the man is the spiritual guide in shot 1, or the rower who carries a drowned body tethered to the bow in shot 2. The viewer must watch, without knowing the meaning of the scene and yet sensing that the song's chorus is drawing to a close. This produces a sense of anxiety, even impotence (fig. 13.6).

FIGURE 13.6

And what of the dead? They lie without shoes
in their stone boats. They are more like stone
than the sea would be if it stopped. They refuse
to be blessed, throat, eye and knucklebone.

SECTIONAL DIVISIONS

One way that music-video image can establish connections with a song is by acknowledging the song's sectional divisions and reflecting the varied characters of individual sections. With repeated viewings of "Mercy St.," one can see that its verses are oriented toward the individual, the intimate, the secret and the illicit; those in the chorus explore personal relations and provide the narrative; and the music and image of the instrumentals are objective and resolute. This represents an unusual rhetorical structure for a music video. In most videos, the verse traces the plot and the chorus presents a more general observation. In this video, the chorus carries the burden of the narrative. In the first chorus, the father takes the girl out to sea. They acknowledge and confront each other in the second chorus. The third chorus shows the father abandoning the daughter or assisting in her death. Though the verse shows the effects of Sexton's grief—her prayers, her writing, as well as her shock treatments—these images tell of a general truth more than a particular story. We know that the heroine is doomed, in part, because the placement of the imagery against the song departs so far from most pop songs.

Individual sections of the song grow and diminish. The verse becomes shorter each time it appears. By contrast, the chorus seems to grow out of the "b" section of the verse. In response to the stretching and shrinking of sections, the video plays with the length of time occupied by sequences of images. Most shots last about five seconds, but a few last much longer. In verse 2, the shot of the hand fills the frame for twelve seconds—the total amount of time taken by three shots from the previous verse. This shot suggests that the materials of the video might ultimately be pared down to a single image.

Each kind of section—chorus, verse, and instrumental—can be understood to have its own affective character. The final chorus gains in strength through greater expressivity and grain while the verses gradually seem to wane. By contrast, the instrumentals hold fast. They maintain a consistent length and seem isolated from other sections. When slight changes occur in the final instrumental, they function simply as a means of enhancing the instrumental's already resolute character: the Andean flute melody becomes more emphatic and the percussion more prominent. The instrumentals hint that a sense of extreme distance, of being "beyond" things is a necessary state one must experience. Both sections feature high-angle shots that look down upon rote activities.

The beginnings of musical sections are marked by threshold imagery (a hand pulling out a drawer) and the ends of sections are matched with images of closure (the father leaving). An instance of the precise internal structuring of sections might be helpful. The woman's head appears frequently, and indicates where we are within a section and how we ought to experience this section's mode of continuity. Partial views—the crown of her head or her half-seen face—occur in the middles of sections. The ends of sections are announced by her face filling the frame. The position of her head suggests the mode of continuity: when it faces the camera, as at the end of verse 1, there is a sharp break between verse and chorus. A less frontal head, as in the third "a" section of verse 1 and the end of verse 2, signals a smoother transition between sections (shots 5, 9, 12, 14, and 26).

I was forced backward.
I was forced forward.
I was passed hand to hand
like a bowl of fruit.

Instrumental 1 One hand passes a piece of cloth to another, but the image and music seem disconnected. On the one hand, the visual activity may tempt us to anticipate an approaching event, perhaps a funeral or wedding. On the other hand, the melancholic flute draws our attention to the past. It might remind one of the panpipe solo in Simon and Garfunkel's version of "El Condor Paso," a traditional Peruvian tune, and seems similar in tone to the image of the father pulling the boat in shot 15. (In this instance, material has been carried from image to music.) In addition, the plaintiveness of the Andean flute melody suggests subjectivity and, more strongly, a sense of loss, encouraging us to review what we have seen thus far. Because the image's and music's temporal cues conflict, the viewer's attention is drawn in two directions.[12]

Suddenly
a wave that we go under.
Under. Under. Under.
We are daring the sea.
We have parted it.
We are scissors.
Here in the green room
the dead are very close.
Here in the pitiless green
where there are no keepsakes
or cathedrals

ARRANGEMENT

The image responds to the music in "Mercy St." by reflecting the sense of fullness or emptiness in the musical texture. At the opening of the chorus, the song becomes more densely orchestrated, while the instrumentals are more sparsely textured. This reduction in sound does not work as it might in disco, in which the listener can find pleasure in the thin textures of the "breaks" by inhabiting the song's underlying groove. Rather, in "Mercy St.," the more thinly orchestrated sections constitute moments of abandonment. The bottom drops out, perhaps because one of the most stabilizing musical elements, the synthesizer pad, is removed. Additionally, the voice cracks and almost threatens to break apart, becoming almost inaudible. The video responds to these moments of fullness and emptiness (shots 1, 2, 13, 18, 20, 27, 32, and 37). At the beginnings of the choruses, the image becomes fuller (the shots of water), and in more thinly textured sections, it seems to wane (a searching hand or a murky cross). Another way that the image plays with the music's threat of absence is by itself threatening to blink out. The edits shift from patches of slow dissolves, to quick fades to black, to firm cuts to black. The most frightening moment in the video may be when an image of the father and the boat dissolves into a long stretch of pure black (fig. 13.7).

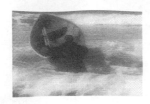

FIGURE 13.7

The content of the image responds to the simplification of the melodic lines and to the harmony. As the video unfolds, the images lose their specific characters, becoming simply undefined shapes. First we see a house, then the shadow of a house, next a rounded head, and finally a hand and a head. This last image, however, is more like two abstract circles of light than a human body. By the time we see the head, it seems like a raised surface with indented areas. Because the video begins with a small cluster of images, the moments when the material flattens out are even more disturbing. First we see two sets of legs, then two kinds of building, then two variations upon a woman's head, each depiction becoming vaguer.

The arrangement is deliberately indistinct at times, despite the clarity of its registral scheme. The arpeggiating synthesizer part blends with the triangle instrumental, and they blend in the song's highest register. Both are faded in and out of the mix instead of having discrete entrances. Gabriel's baritone is often recorded with a lot of reverb, doubled at the octave, and multitracked. In addition, there are three different analog synthesizer patches in the middle register, all of which have long reverberations. A heavily processed sound that seems like backward distorted guitar—but that may in fact be a saxophone—helps to close sections. The conga, surdo, and fretless bass form a murky rhythmic stratum in the lowest register.

The image, too, is indistinct. Though the image relies upon simple forms, photographic techniques render them as vague contours and fields. It can be hard, at first, to make out the figures, both those that are high key against a black background and those shot in very low light and a middle gray. Would the video still work if one or both media were rendered more sharply? Perhaps their indistinct qualities encourage the viewer to do imaginative work.

For months my hand had been sealed off
in a tin box. Nothing was there but subway railings.
Perhaps it is bruised, I thought,
and that is why they have locked it up.
But when I looked in it lay there quietly.

Verse 2 This verse is immediately preceded by an image of textured black that accompanies the "backward guitar" sound. The beginning of verse 2 pulls the viewer over a threshold. This verse contains more reverb, additional vocal samples, and an extra synthesizer pad. The hollow space of the drawer and the blurry images of the hand and paper complement two features of reverb—its distorting effect as well as its sense of space. Not only the music (the isolated words, like "nowhere," overdubbed on separate tracks), and the lyrics ("word upon word"), but also the images point to distant memories (fig. 13.8).

FIGURE 13.8

Both the music and image in verse 2 may evoke moments when dream images seem to take control of the body. The open drawer suggests an abyss. The hand loses control and drops the drawer and the knees give way to soft grass. The flickering light on the sheet of paper resembles water, and the creeping shadow dimly recalls the shadow of the foot in the opening shot. It is important, too, that the paper's text cannot be made out. One becomes a voyeur, hungry for more information. Like verse 1, verse 2's lyrics "like stone," "handle the shocks," and "father" seem to pierce through the texture. The image of feet, wrapped in cloth and stretched out on the linoleum floor, as well as the fragmentation of the text, suggests a woman who is institutionalized and attempting to escape her past, as well as the anointing of feet as part of a funeral rite.

The section closes with three staggered entrances across media: image, lyrics, music. A woman prays, the text "Mary's lips" comes to the fore, and the synthesizer's arpeggiated figure returns, matching the repetitive motion of the lips (fig. 13.9).

FIGURE 13.9

I feel the earth like a nurse,
curing me of winter.
I feel the earth,
its worms oiling upward,
the ants ticking,
the oak leaf rotting like feces
and the oats rising like angels.

LOCAL TRANSFORMATION OF MATERIAL

Gabriel is an avowed tinkerer. He sifts through hours of recorded improvisations, listening for "magical" gestures and then piecing them together against a back-drop provided by prerecorded rhythm tracks.[13] "Mercy St." contains many idiosyncratic details and a mix that changes frequently: notice the raspy sound that appears briefly at the ends of instrumentals and in the chorus; the shifts in the timbres of the synthesizer in each verse; the sudden entrances and exits of the high-pitched synthesizer and the triangle; the changing amounts of reverberation on the vocal tracks; the moments when the conga and surdo are brought up and down in the mix. Like the song, the image seems the result of a careful sifting through much material, and it, too, draws upon a limited set of themes. The shadow of the cloak in the first shot anticipates the cloth imagery. Dark pits in the sand suggest the hollow sockets of the woman's eyes. Certain elements of the song become associated with related visual features: the arpeggiated figure in the synthesizer matches the images of transient phenomena, like rippling water, dappled light, the twirling rosary, the motion of lace and cloth. The long decay of the synthesizer pad reflects slower processes, like the sun setting on still water in the closing shot.[14]

In a video that leaves the motivations of its characters—and even the nature of their actions—vague, the relations between the song and the image help to reveal, at least obliquely, what the figures are doing and thinking. As we see shots of a foot striking sand and an oar pulling through the water, the bass slides up from the seventh scale degree to the tonic. The finality of the tonic lends authority to a gesture that would otherwise seem more perfunctory. In verse 2, the guitar suggests the rough surface of the wooden drawer, and the upper partials of the synthesizer, the softness of the grass. When verse 2 presents images of isolated body parts, the exaggerated, shifting postproduction effects on the voice remind us that these images depict the trials of a complex subject.

Sometimes the video grants agency to objects and to body parts that seem almost autonomous.[15] Because body parts are often depicted separately—hands reaching for unseen objects, feet suspended motionless with soles up, heads drooping toward the bottom of the frame—each, eerily, possesses its own thematic function: the hands function as a vulnerable first line of defense; the feet are cleansed through a series of trials; heads seem to become inert matter.[16]

The video links these images, which are not contiguous, by responding closely to shifts in the musical arrangement. Gabriel's strongest suit as a musician may lie in the realm of timbral nuance. At the level of the small sound or gesture, Mahurin matches the image to the sound. For example, when the production of the voice is more or less flat, we see images of houses. When the multitracked voices overlap, figures meet each other. When the voice sounds tinny and distant, the father is far away, out on the water.

There are brains that rot here
like black bananas.
Hearts have grown as flat as dinner plates.
Anne, Anne,
flee on your donkey,
flee this sad hotel

Chorus 2 The girl of chorus 2 confronts several male figures. Perhaps this is the only moment that functions in the mode of classic Hollywood narrative. The exchange of sightlines between father and daughter grants the viewer's position a momentary stability. For once, the figures' relationship becomes clear. This moment is fleeting, however. Because the image looks like it is projected onto a screen, viewers are reminded of its unreality, and may even become conscious of its proximity to Hollywood film.

Though music and image seem closely related at this point in the video, they are actually far removed from one another in terms of affect. The second chorus becomes warmer and fuller than the first through a vocal arrangement that incorporates countermelodies and heterophony. The image, by contrast, is cold and a bit frightening. Music and image are linked, however, through an association with water. The synthesizer parts, particularly, serve to connote the sea in which the figures float.[17]

On subsequent viewings, we may want to assign characters to the figures. The figures who look at one another are similar to those who appear in Freud's "A child is being beaten." Freud noticed that many of his adolescent patients were haunted by a fantasy in which they would look onto a tableau where their father beat a sibling. The child pleasurably imagines himself as the parent, and then, out of guilt, imagines himself as the beaten child—such an experience produces intense ambivalence. In "Mercy St.," a priest/father may leave a girl to drown, while a sibling or the child's other self watches on. The latter case would be the most disturbing, as it would mean the obliteration of one part of Sexton's self (fig. 13.10).[18]

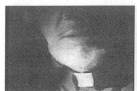 

FIGURE 13.10 (A–B)

This section begins and ends with an image of the boat, but it is dominated by shots of heads against dark or watery backgrounds. Toward the end of the section, most of these images are situated high in the frame. Because it occurs gradually and without apparent design, this process achieves a feeling of suspension. There are parallels in the music: the chorus introduces an additional vocal line in the upper register and contains a prominent upward leap in the main melody.

> but my father
> drunkenly bent over my bed,
> circling the abyss like a shark,
> my father thick upon me
> like some sleeping jellyfish.
>
> Those times I smelled the Vitalis on his pajamas.
> Those times I mussed his curly black hair
> and touched his ten tar-fingers
> and swallowed down his whiskey breath.
> Red. Red. Father, you are blood red.
> Father,
> we are two birds on fire.
>
> In the mind there is a thin alley called death
> and I move through it as
> through water.
> My body is useless.

HARMONY

With its constant Latin percussion tracks and tonic-heavy fretless bass part, "Mercy St." would seem to emphasize unity of affect over internal differentiation. The song's harmony, however, tells a different story. The verse can be described in terms of functional harmony, but it clearly sounds more modal than tonal. Thus, it follows the "exotic" tendencies of the song's texture. The chorus, however, presents a chord progression that recalls Protestant hymnody. This section contains a full, multitracked vocal arrangement that works according to eighteenth- and nineteenth-century rules for voice leading and chord spacing. The word "mercy" falls on the first convincing major tonic as well. It therefore works against the Asian and Latin American elements of the song. This may be why the imagery gradually becomes more Christian toward the middle of the song, with its shots of a confessional and a priest: the chorus is able to assert its harmonic weight, particularly as the verse progressively diminishes in length. By contrast, imagery that might seem to support the song's exotic elements comes at the beginning and the very end of the song. It is at these moments that we see shots of swaddled feet and boats that might look Arabic or Indian. By positing England as the delicate interior of the song and by reflecting the music's ethnic elements in only the vaguest ways, the video raises questions about the song's use of its musical materials.[19]

Perhaps the earth is floating,
I do not know.
Perhaps the stars are little paper cutups
made by some giant scissors,
I do not know.
perhaps the moon is a frozen tear,
I do not know.
Perhaps God is only a deep voice
heard by the deaf,
I do not know.

Bridge 2—Shots 33–37 A shot from the window of a sanatorium, and subsequent shots, might suggest a cleansing—a taking leave of the world—and the field of muddled gray might point to cremation, where the spirit leaves the body, rises above and surveys the world, and then disperses among the elements. Some of the video's power stems from the numerous ways that it depicts a death, or a type of quiescence or blanking out, followed by a sense of rejuvenation or rebirth. Here are four examples:

1. The video seems to wind down and exhaust its small set of materials. Instrumental 2 is approached by means of a shot that is uncharacteristic of the video. The frame fills with a blur of gray and white, and the soundtrack turns into a buzz of white noise. As the boat drifts out of our view, the video seems to come to an end. This is true for the soundtrack as well, for the buzzy white noise functions like a fade at the end of an outchorus. The fact that the video draws upon the resources of previous images and music is surprising.

2. A person's death is depicted four times—in shots 1 and 2, the feet tethered to the end of the boat suggest a drowning; in shot 25, the feet, palms blackened and face up on the floor suggest an electrocution; in shot 37, the turning to dust suggests a cremation; and in shots 39–46, the multiple shots of figures above and below the water suggest a more elaborately staged drowning near the video's end. Like a cat with nine lives, the character lives on.

3. The reconfiguration of past and future also suggests some freedom from time's arrow. The shot of a hand brushing sand off feet carries great thematic weight and deserves special notice.[20] We might read this gesture as the true beginning of the video. Here the character readies herself to begin the journey out to sea. She brushes sand from her feet and then steps into the first shot of "Mercy St." where, swaddled in cloth and veiled in half light, she leans forward and pushes the boat out onto the water. The video's first image functions as a flash forward (a device rarely used in Hollywood cinema); the feet on the floor in the second verse suggest the recovered drowned body in the morgue.

4. The fragmentation and autonomy of individual body parts suggests a preternatural animation that extends beyond death. Let us consider again the shot of the hand brushing sand from the feet. Thus far, the physical contact

between figures or parts of the body has been minimal: one hand lightly taps another, or is moved before a face. The video's closing shots contain a woman's hand moving back and forth before her face; this last image, along with the hand brushing off sand, suggests a sort of character development. The fact that the hand that passes in front of the woman's face may not belong to her also suggests a Catholic ritual associated with death (fig. 13.11; appendixes A and B).

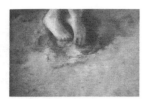

FIGURE 13.11

RHYTHM AND ARTICULATION

In music, the downbeat possesses the authority of the measure. The images in the first half of the video emphasize the downbeat through either editing or movement within the frame. In the second verse, the video's themes—the power of religion to control as well as comfort, death, the family romance—are brought into relation. After this section, the video avoids drawing attention to the downbeat, shifting to an emphasis on beats two and four. This shift gives the image a more relaxed feel and, more importantly, helps to explain why the first half of the video is hard to bear in mind while one views the second.

The arrangement exhibits a considerable amount of rhythmic variety. The triangle and conga articulate the offbeats. Images of dappled light on water and patterned stucco seem to reflect these rhythmic features, but since these images are merely textural, they push the percussion's offbeats into the background. The rhythmic vitality of the song is thereby muted in the video. The image focuses instead upon the trajectory of the voice. This careful tracing of the voice provides continuity across the video.

Although this close tracking of the voice might threaten to become monotonous, the video establishes variety through staggered phrasing among the voice, the synthesizer, and the image. The synthesizer pad tends to move in similar motion with the voice, but it lags a bit behind. The figure in the frame is often revealed through flooding light, and this light appears after the pad enters, creating even greater rhythmic play. Conversely, the revelation of a figure sometimes presages moments of greater activity in the music, as at the end of verse 1, when light fills a face just before the chorus begins.

The surdo was most likely recorded first, along with the other percussion instruments, *while the other parts, including the voice, were added later. Although this sequence conforms to conventional recording practice, it takes on a special role in the context of the song's division between white male subjectivity and "ethnic" percussion. As a result of this division, the percussion seems to inhabit its own conceptual realm, outside of the subject matter of the song. It sounds almost like the percussionist does not know that the song is an elegy for a female European American poet who committed suicide.*[21]

The rhythm of exertion and relaxation governs the phrase structure of the image as well as that of the song. The image follows this rhythm: a person stepping forward, then legs floating passively; the boat going out and then a motionless head. This visual rhythm responds to the mostly symmetrical phrase structure of the vocal line. Finally, the images of figures murmuring out of sync with the music provides an extra rhythmic layer, perhaps outside of the music's grasp.

> Let's face it, I have been momentary,
> A luxury. A bright red loop in the harbor.
> My hair rising like smoke from the car window.
> Littleneck clams out of season.

Chorus 3—Shots 39–46 At the beginning of the third chorus, the electric guitar plays an ascending phrase that reaches past the tonic, while the surdo and bass get louder, the triangle playing becomes more deliberate, and the voice breaks into plaintive moans. The accumulated momentum of the percussion now begins to determine the course of the video. Without representing the will of a particular character or suggesting a specific course of events, the percussion becomes, for a moment, the video's principal voice. As in the previous choruses, we follow the boat's course. At first, since the image is in long shot, the viewer possesses little information about unfolding events. A fragile connection between music and image remains, however: the guitar ascends as a bird flies along the top of the frame.[22] Perhaps because the video has worked so hard to keep viewers adrift, the next series of shots is strangely affective. Not only are the images of hands in these shots evocative in themselves, but the music also carefully tracks their course—hands reach forward in the water, and the boat oars row forward and pull back. A descending vocal line accompanies these shots: the music seems to follow the contours of the figures' arms as the father strokes the oars and the other figure swims. For the first time, the video depicts ongoing, directed activity. (The surdo's increase in volume may also suggest forward motion.) Even though the video may be allowing a woman to drown in the water, it is refreshing finally to be moving somewhere, to be leaving behind the disturbing, static images. We can sense that something lies ahead of us, and the losses for the woman and the benefits for us produce a guilty pleasure.

The use of montage culminates in the juxtaposition of two shots: one of the father in the boat and another of a long hallway with a lighted window at the end. The shadow of the window's crossbars forms a cross on the floor. The path down the hallway, with the "light at the end of the tunnel," suggests that the father is on a quest. The prominent cross, in the context of the video's Christian imagery, lends a religious overtone to his journey. These shots are more balanced than most in the video, and thereby provide a ground: unlike the earlier, spinning cross on a rosary, the cross on the floor gives momentary stability, turning the hallway into an altar. The fact that this is cliché imagery—rowing toward God and finding the light at the end of the tunnel—only adds to its stabilizing effect (fig. 13.12).

FIGURE 13.12

For a moment, when the image of a wave appears, the singer's call of "mercy" is buried in the musical arrangement. It is as if the call concerns not only the woman but also the father or even the singer himself. At this moment, the emphatic articulations of the triangle, the synthesizer's crescendo, and the steady bass and surdo energize the image of a wave, and our contact breaks with whomever we assume is assigned to the surdo, lost in the rush of the oncoming wave. The woman passes her hand before her face as the surdo and triangle drop out: the end of the self. The video concludes with a shot of the father in the boat as the song articulates the tonic.[23]

"Mercy St." focuses our attention on a woman and her travails. Suddenly, in the video's last shot, we are confronted with a man who seems alone, and who may have assisted in the drowning of his daughter. What role did he play in this drama, and what were his experiences? Is he grieving? Although we may wish to understand his predicament, when we watch the video again, the woman's story takes over. Music videos frequently end in a way that tells us we have missed crucial details and need to watch once more (fig. 13.13).

FIGURE 13.13

LYRICS

In "Mercy St.," as with most music videos, the musical and visual flow fractures the continuity of the lyrics, fragmenting text into chunks ranging from two to six words each. Even adjacent words drift away from one another, while other more distant words, linked by some tangential feature in the image or the music—a repeat of a hand tapping another, or the return of a riff—are eerily bound together. Although the lyric's sense fades, moment by moment, the words change into sensual objects, the harsh word "stone" and the softly labial "Mercy Street," wrapped in sound and linked to individual images, become talismanic. While the text's meanings refuse to anchor—is the father a patriarch, a priest, or Dante's Virgil?—the lyrics quickly narrow interpretive possibilities, just as the music assists in coloring the disposition of the depicted forms. The hook line "looking for Mercy St." exhorts us to remain patient while the murky image and music unfold, because we are seeking something, possibly a street, possibly redemption.

> I come like the blind feeling for shelves,
> feeling for wood as hard as an apple,
> fingering the pen lightly, my blade.
> With this pen I take in hand my selves
> and with these dead disciples I will grapple.
> Though rain curses the window
> let the poem be made.

> The woods are underwater, their weeds are shaking
> in the tide; birches like zebra fish
> flash by in a pack.
> Child, I cannot promise that you will get your wish.

Thus far, I have made a point to call the people who appear in "Mercy St." figures rather than characters. What is gained and what lost by describing them as characters? Because the video refers to an actual person, the viewer may be tempted to construct a story, and if she does, the video may gain in sentimentality and lose in shimmer—occasionally, if a viewer stays with a video for a long time, both long enough to attend to music, lyrics, and image and to make good hunches about temporal, spatial, and narrative gaps, the ambiguity abates. However, in "Mercy St.," when the viewer makes up a story about the life of a young Sexton, the video loses its radical edge—in this instance, the video's interest in blanking out, absence and negation. "Mercy St." invites the viewer to read characters, but strongly asks that he not do so. (More than in most videos, its progress is fragmentary, and events are revealed incompletely.) To do so is an act of trespass. However, while constructing scenarios may be an invasion of the director's and possibly Anne Sexton's privacy, to do nothing but simply watch the video is also transgressive. Already implicated for seeing something that should not be shown, the viewer is kept witness to a number of primal scenes, yet neither can she interfere with the unfolding events nor piece out who the victims are in relation to the perpetrators.

THE STRUCTURE OF "MERCY ST."

> looking down on empty streets, all she can see
> are the dreams all made solid
> are the dreams made real

This section explores large-scale form. Without a background into Sexton's life or work, "Mercy St." is dazzling oblique—without the video in hand, it is daunting to reconstruct the order of the images against the music. How and what holds this video together will be discussed in this section. Fragments from Gabriel's "Mercy St." lyrics will be interwoven in the text.

> all of the buildings, all of those cars
> were once just a dream
> in somebody's head

Whereas many videos derive their strength from a tension between musician and videomaker, "Mercy St." benefits from the affinities between Mahurin's and Gabriel's work. Mahurin's dark imagery complements Gabriel's sometimes hermetic style, and, as previously mentioned, this basic similarity allows for divergences at other levels.[24] We can gain insight into the imagery for "Mercy St." by looking at one of Mahurin's drawings.[25] His drawings often contain a rounded representation of a solitary figure standing stiff-limbed against a richly textured background (an overcast, sooty sky). Dim light breaks through the background. There is usually another object in the picture—a cliff, a box, a globe, and so on—frequently drawn with sharper edges.

It cannot be said that Gabriel's music typically works in such dark terms, but "Mercy St." does seem at home in the world of Mahurin's drawings. The song is brooding and grim, constructed without clear outlines. Unlike most of the songs on *So*, the album from which it is drawn, "Mercy St." does not make use of a conventional rhythm section. Instead, its reduced instrumentation consists only of a sparse percussion part (triangle, congas, and surdo, rather than the usual drum set), a fretless bass, and a keyboard pad, along with a few incidental parts that come in and out of the mix. The fretless bass has relatively indistinct attacks and can inflect its pitches. The surdo and bass blend in the mix and appear in so low a register that their precise pitches can be hard to determine. The bass often functions as a pedal or drone, which contributes to the song's dark sense of constancy. These dronelike effects sometimes obscure rather than articulate the chord changes. The synthesizer pad, with its soft attacks, washes over the rest of the musical texture and helps to blur orchestrational distinctions.

Mahurin's lone figure against a darkening sky relates to Gabriel's style of singing and his writing for the voice in "Mercy St." The singing at time is only murmured; the melodic line falls or wanders. The vocal line in the chorus is distinctly hymnlike, composed of several simple lines, with clear voice-leading and without ornamentation. The voice moves impassively and unresponsively through the musical texture toward its own destination: it reminds one of Lutheran hymnody in its steadfastness and purity of style.

Around this unornamented and very "European" vocal line are many instrumental allusions to "non-European" music.[26] The simple fact that the steadfast vocal line does not respond to these exoticized elements creates a sense of isolation. Like the figures in Mahurin's drawings, the voice remains distinct against a shadowy background. One might wonder at this sense of isolation in the music, particularly to the extent that it is created through the opposition of "first world" and "third world" musical elements. Taken with the lyrics and the imagery of the video, however, the hymnlike character of the vocal writing and performance can be heard as suggesting the possibility of redemption, just as Mahurin's luminous backgrounds might be understood to hint at such a possibility.

> she pictures the broken glass,
> she pictures the steam
> she pictures a soul
> with no leak at the seam
> let's take the boat out
> wait until darkness
> let's take the boat out
> wait until darkness comes

NARRATIVE STRANDS

The song is dedicated to American poet Anne Sexton, and named for *45 Mercy St.*, one of her later volumes of poems. The lyrics allude to the poet's characteristic preoccupations and eventual suicide, and echo certain lines from her poems (many of which are autobiographical in nature).[27] Even without knowledge of Sexton's poems or Gabriel's lyrics, however, the video's themes are clear: the family romance; loss of childhood; religion as consolation and as constriction; death and redemption.

The video does not tell a complete story, however. It presents fragments, many of which seem narratively charged, without providing connections among them or showing beginnings and ends of the stories of which they are a part.

Even more than the lyrics, the video evokes things, hints at them, shows them only in part. The camera often seems to be engaged in a kind of witnessing rather than in exposition, and the editing and mise-en-scène emphasize light and shade over sharp contrast, transition over stability, and parts over wholes.

Because the video's themes are of the most serious sort and the visual style is strongly evocative, one might well be tempted to construct a narrative for the video, knowing at the same time that the images will not yield a complete story. "Mercy St." suggests at least three narratives, none of which, I believe, can be given priority. Whereas one interpretation has the largest number of images devoted to it, another receives greater support from the song. And at the same time, the theme that is the most musically integrated is also the most obscure. These three narratives run as follows:

1. Anne Sexton commits suicide with her father's assistance. The story begins when a corpse appears in the second shot. Tantalizing clues about Sexton's suicide come at the end of the tape, encouraging the viewer to reevaluate what has come before in terms of the poet's death.

2. No suicide actually occurs and the drowning is only symbolic, perhaps of spiritual rebirth. Evidence for this interpretation is embedded in the first shot of the corpse. When the feet become still, a "heartbeat"—a musical evocation of movement—kicks in. This reading is grounded in the vitality of the final chorus, and in the gradual diminution of the verse, which contains both somber music and frightening imagery. Many images toward the end of the tape might be considered affirmative of life.

3. The video allows for an identification with the father, an identification partly supported by the lyrics and Gabriel's performance. The father's story might be reconstructed as follows: his role in Sexton's suicide—both as facilitator and as ultimate cause—draws him into her emotional world and sends him into a deep depression. Through a collection of fleeting images, the video shows the father's breakdown, presenting his body as a collection of fragments and his life as the senseless repetition of empty forms. The father's story, though it does not seem the most compelling of the three, nevertheless acquires a kind of prominence in the video. Its importance derives in large measure from the subjectivity of the lyrics and music. The lyrics alternate between addressing the listener and addressing Sexton.[28] The fact of a male singer encourages us to hear the song as from a male perspective. More specifically, the vocal line expresses a kind of vulnerability through its narrow ambitus, falling motives and feminine endings, and the performance brings out this quality through voice-breaks and the almost whispered quality of certain moments.[29]

The conventions of music video create a space for the narrator's story, since a viewer will expect a male figure, if not Gabriel himself, to represent the singer. Almost any male figure in the video will therefore become a candidate. The frequent appearances of the father, along with the possibility of his being the lyric "I" for at least part of the song, give his perspective a particular weight. As I will show, the image seems to embody the narrator's emotional changes by tracking carefully the gradual break-up of the voice. Regardless of the extent to which this subject position can be identified with the father, it becomes the principal subject by the end of the video.

nowhere in the corridors of pale green and gray
nowhere in the suburbs
in the cold light of day

there in the midst of it so alive and alone
words support like bone

dreaming of mercy st.
wear your inside out
dreaming of mercy
in your daddy's arms again
dreaming of mercy st.
'swear they moved that sign
dreaming of mercy
in your daddy's arms

PRIMARY THEMES

The video deals with difficult subjects: incest and suicide. It derives a certain beauty, however, from its capacity to manage two disparate modes—the music is a melancholy lullaby, and the image, a frightening nightmare, replete with flashbacks. Lullaby and nightmare, memory of incest and suicide are suspended within a complex structure where each layer of the form possesses a different mode of organization—background, middle ground, and foreground are organized within a labyrinthine, episodic, and prismatic structure, respectively.[30] The first shot of the video is emblematic of the whole. We see a foot step onto sand in twilight, but the mark of where we are—the circle in the sand that surrounds the foot—will quickly disappear into the sand's surface, while the shadow passing over the foot will render everything obscure. A viewer may have the sense of being led without being given a way back.

pulling out the papers from drawers that slide smooth
tugging at the darkness, word upon word

confessing all the secret things in the warm velvet box
to the priest—he's the doctor
he can handle the shocks

dreaming of the tenderness—the tremble in the hips
of kissing Mary's lips

FORMAL UNITY

It is not unusual for a music video to suggest multiple points of view and
several outcomes. The greatest difficulty, however, lies in grasping the formal
unity of the piece. The difficulty lies in three principal areas: (1) the length and
function of sections and the clarity of sectional divisions, (2) the relations
among shots, both contiguous and noncontiguous, and (3) the role of visual
details.

1. Many visual features of "Mercy St." tend to blur the song's sectional
divisions. The seemingly neutral shots found in each section—water, sky, trees,
and grass—might be expected to perform as establishing shots, or to provide
a relief from those shots that contain a stronger narrative charge, but they are
always photographed with a particularity that renders them unfit to serve such
functions. They are viewed from an extreme high or low angle, or from too
close or too far, which implies a specific point of view. These shots appear
without regard for the song's sectional divisions. Not only does the placement
of these images work against the creation of a unified tone within each section,
it also prevents these images themselves from being seen as related. It is only
later in the tape, in fact, that a viewer can group these images together as a
meaningful collection (shots 3, 13, 17, 23, 27, 32, 34, 35, 36, 37, 39, 48, and 50).

2. The relations between adjacent shots are difficult to ascertain. Many images are brought together through montage, in Russian film director Sergei
Eisenstein's strict sense of the term: when two images come together in montage, a new concept arises which was not contained in either of the original
images. In "Mercy St.," a shot of dogs circling on cement, followed by a shot
of hands brushing off sand, might signify an acceptance of the mundane (shots
34 and 35). The shot of a drawer holding an illegible sheet of paper, followed
by a shot of knees dropping toward the bottom of the frame suggests the
imprisonment of a woman by the church (shots 21 and 22). These shots are
further complicated by the images that precede them. The light that slinks along
the unreadable sheet of paper will connect with earlier images of water and
hunched bodies to suggest a sense of shame.[31] Eisenstein argues that montage
creates a collision that requires the viewer to make an intellectual leap. Because
"Mercy St." provides so few clues to characters and their motivations, such
leaps demand a tremendous cognitive effort. They divert a viewer's attention
from previous images and from the flow of the music, making it difficult to
map the video's progress.

3. The image, like the song, exhibits a high degree of detail. One cannot
determine when a detail serves a structural function, when it works more dec-

oratively, and when it is accidental. Although the video contains no overarching narrative or linear thematic development, it creates continuity through a myriad of local music/image connections. Some of the visual details are easy to see: the image of the dogs turning resembles closely the earlier image of hands passing cloth against a black background, for example. Both figures trace circles, make a quick gestural exchange, accompany the Andean flute melody, and exist in relative isolation from the rest of the piece (shots 18 and 34).

The video also contains a stratum of detail that can be difficult to recognize. The many images of crosses can provide access to this level. At first, the imagery is so submerged in the tape that these crosses seem purely coincidental—an antenna on a falling house, a pattern on the lace that covers a woman's head, a design on a kitchen floor, a misshapen cross, the lines in cement under two circling dogs, the sidewalk from a birds'-eye view, the crossbars in a lit window at the end of a hallway, and a shot of the father in the boat that resembles the top part of a cross. Later, however, it becomes clear that Christian imagery is central to the video (shots 3, 5, 6, 20, 25, 33, 34, 45, and 49).

Some of the song's unusual features help to provide a context for the video's visual techniques. The section lengths of the song vary: each time the verse appears, it is shorter. The chorus is ten measures long, instead of the expected eight, creating a subtle hesitation and keeping the song slightly off-balance. The strong emphasis on the tonic, along with dronelike effects in the bass, creates the ground for a flexible orchestrational approach in which sounds can be brought in and out rather freely. The sparseness of the percussion setup, too, allows for a high level of timbral detail in the studio production of the voice.

With so many incomplete and independent visual processes, one might wonder whether there are strong unifying features in the piece. As I will show, there are indeed features that work toward unity, but their effects remain partial and provisional. Much of the piece is built up through moment-to-moment connections—local music/image relations of different kinds. Mahurin's emphasis on local connections makes the relations between music and image mercurial and transitory. In fact, it is the large-scale narrative and formal concerns that tend to occupy one's attention while the more local issues of continuity move to the background of one's consciousness.

TRANSITION AND TRANSFORMATION

In a video without clear plot points, the very evasiveness of the narrative style requires investigation. If events are not shown with clear beginnings, if effects are not connected with causes, if characters are never shown entirely, what, then, is the video attempting to do? By focusing upon the video's style of depiction, with its emphasis upon continuous transition and transformation, we can begin to answer this question.

dreaming of mercy st.
wear your inside out
dreaming of mercy
in your daddy's arms again
dreaming of mercy st.
'swear they moved that sign
looking for mercy
in your daddy's arms

Figures always appear in the middle of some activity: swimming, rowing, pushing, pulling, waving, falling, stepping, pacing, reaching, dropping, murmuring, carrying, towing, passing, kneeling, tapping, circling, gliding. The video also emphasizes materials that are associated with physical processes: light, water, dust. The dappled patterns in some of the backgrounds and the shift from day to twilight also create a sense of process.[32] Working with the many images of the boat, the camera's continuous movement gives the viewer a sense of motion through the video. If the viewer seems to move, then objects and figures will seem to hover. This effect is caused in part by the placement of objects in the frame—they seem to loom above us, moving slowly, separate from the background.

The meditative character of the video belies its readiness to confront the viewer with disturbing imagery. Some figures move so surely and smoothly that they seem mechanical rather than human. Often, they fall through the frame before they can be identified. The video's indistinct background can make it difficult to determine what moves, the camera or the figure, rendering the figure strange, even threatening. Many images depict the frightening effects of unknown causes—a corpse floats on the water, a severed head lies in a boat, an emaciated arm pulls a drawer all the way out and drops it.

The figures are usually presented only in part, as just a face, a hand, knees, or feet. These images appear noncontiguously, leaving the viewer to determine to whom the body parts belong. Moreover, they never appear the same way twice; instead, they vary in shade, movement, and position in the frame. The viewer may infer that the figures develop between appearances, but the precise nature of their development—and whether some key to it might be found in the lyrics, the music or elsewhere in the image—remains unclear.

A STRUCTURAL OVERVIEW

The video presents a number of visual strands rather than a single, overarching line. It moves unpredictably among four sites: the shore; houses and a hospital; intimate interiors; and above and below the surface of the water. Perhaps the most prominent thread in "Mercy St." is constituted by a boat's going out onto the water. This path represents the video's only consistent, directed motion. The video withholds formal landmarks, instead lightly sketching a number of possible outlines which, when considered together, suggest a structure. I will trace these formal and narrative outlines (appendixes D and E).

mercy, mercy, looking for mercy
mercy, mercy, looking for mercy

At the beginning of the song, the relative speed of the various musical parts is determined by register.[33] The highest register (triangle, arpeggiating synthesizer) moves the most quickly, the mid range (voice, synthesizer pad) moves moderately, and the lowest register (bass) moves at the slowest rate. The image, too, moves at different rates based on the weight and momentum of each object: as the boat goes out onto the water, it gradually increases in speed; unidentified arms move at a moderate pace; the image of a falling head seems to slow down as the light darkens around it.

The video encourages one to hear the song as gradually shifting registral emphasis from low to high. The opening is low, grounded in the bass and surdo. Two-thirds of the way into the song, the congas become thinner, the bass disappears, and the high-pitched synthesizer sequence becomes more insistent. Similarly, the image shifts from an emphasis on the lower part of the frame to and emphasis on the higher part: the hand reaching upward and the boat's setting out from the bottom of the frame in verse 1 gives way to the dogs circling on cement high in the frame in the second instrumental. Because "Mercy St." is dominated by round shapes and soft edges, three rectangular forms stand out: the windows of the building at the beginning of the piece; the drawer in the middle; and the windows and hallway at the end (shots 3, 4, 20, 43, and 45).

"Mercy St." breaks into two parts. Two signposts gird the center—the hand opening the drawer and the feet swaddled in white cloth—yet the precise breaking point is hard to ascertain.[34] The first half of the video expands upon the opening shots, and deals with loss, grief, and death, while the second half drives forth imagery of acceptance and redemption. At any moment, the temporal status of any medium—lyrics, image, or music—remains uncertain.

The video also partitions into sections according to the delineations of chorus, verse, and instrumental. The individual musical sections have unequal lengths (and, as mentioned, the verse gets shorter each time it appears). Each section begins with a suggestion of threshold, and closes with a sense of quiescence. The verses begin with images of falling or reaching—a hand comes forward or pulls down a drawer—lyrics that begin an activity ("looking back on everything"), and an identifiable musical motif. They end with deathly images of women's heads, lyrics that suggest resolution ("words like stone"), and a melody that closes in on itself. Choruses follow the same pattern, moving from a noticeable head motive and oceanic imagery to imagery of closure, like the father rowing away.

The video concerns itself with graphic shapes as a way of transcending the entanglements of people and things to find a purity in forms. This happens not only within the frame but also across frames, through editing. The first third of the video contains images emphasizing circular motion, like the shot of hands. Expanding circular and zigzag shapes begin to form across edited images, blocking the boat's course out to sea. In the second chorus, these images form a circle across several edits (the sightlines among the priest, the child in the water, and the little girl who watches). The overall effect is of time impeded by the bonds among the figures (shots 15, 18, and 27–32). The final third of the video features a horizontal trajectory from screen left to right, followed by one along the z-axis from the center of the frame to the back.

On the one hand, "Mercy St." seems teleologically driven. The video is structured as the search for an altar. It opens with a shot of feet stepping in sand and ends with a cross in a window. Along the way, the doubling of particular images—houses plus hospitals; hands passing cloth paired with circling dogs—forms a symmetrical structure. Yet the piece tends not to present structural signposts. As I have remarked, the connections between music and image are momentary and provisional. As we approach the end of the video, we may feel that we have lost track of the beginning.[35]

The image does not require words to show us where we are and where we will go. A shot of feet guiding us toward a boat that is then launched seems clearly introductory. When a drawer is opened, we sense that a secret will be revealed. When figures gaze at one another through sightlines established across shots, we expect a confrontation. The image of a cross slowly moving in circles draws us under the video's spell. When we move down a hallway toward a source of light—the light at the end of the tunnel—we know that the video is drawing toward closure (shots 1, 20, 33, and 43).

It might be helpful at this point to provide a synopsis of the video in accordance with the sectional divisions of the song. This synopsis should not be taken to imply that these sectional divisions govern the visual track: the video is respectful of the song's formal parts, but it does not seek to emphasize them. The synopsis can provide a map for a video that does not contain many clear landmarks, and give a sense of the way that materials are introduced and transformed across musical sections. For example, the video amplifies the downward motion in verse one to create a sense of vertigo—a loss of balance and spatial control—in verse two (see appendixes).

Anne, with her father is out in the boat
riding the water
riding the waves on the sea

CHARACTER AND GENDER

This chapter, thus far, has focused on music/image relations that might be called formal. The logic of these relations can establish the ground for an investigation of the figures' thoughts and actions. One must begin by noting that the very identity of the characters is not beyond question. The lyrics adopt the perspective of a woman, understood as Anne Sexton, who wishes ambiguously for a return to childhood. The video shows her as both adult and child, although its depictive mode prevents one from saying that the scenes of childhood are flashbacks—they might well be taken as the dreamlike images of an imagined past. The father, who is referred to in the lyrics, appears only in the earlier of the two periods. There is another male character, a priest, in the video's present, and his characterization seems to shade into the father's, inasmuch as both represent figures of authority.

The video complicates the simple structure of real present versus remembered or imagined past, however. The woman's experiences occupy, not the present, but the recent past. They work as a collection of images from a painful adulthood. Without attempting to maintain a temporal sequence, the video presents the woman's medical treatment, institutionalization, confessions, and obsessive prayer. Because these scenes have an inky or murky look, they seem as much like flashbacks as do the scenes of childhood—perhaps more so, judged in purely cinematic terms. By contrast, the scenes that depict the father's taking the daughter out in the boat are more fleshed out, with clearer backgrounds and a higher level of detail. They seem also to possess a linearity and contiguity that the adult scenes do not. It is important to note as well that the scenes of childhood obtain greater weight through their association with the song's chorus. The immediacy of the childhood scenes reverses the logic of the flashback, making the past more real than the scenes of adulthood. This is so despite a viewer's sense that the video's distant past may constitute an imagined childhood while the events depicted in the adult scenes have actually taken place.[36]

The video's complications of its temporal structure invite the viewer to perform a reconstruction of the narrative. Because the figure of Sexton stands fast in the video's constellation of themes, a viewer will tend to imagine her perspective, even—or particularly—in scenes in which she does not appear. That the female protagonist claims a strong narrative presence should not let us forget that her story is clearly gendered as female. The video would work quite differently if it were not telling a "woman's story." (Imagine this scenario: a man suffering from depression prepares for death with the help of his male friends. He is represented by isolated parts of his body and partial selves. A female priest reads his last rites, and another woman assists in his suicide.)

The gender roles in "Mercy St." carry great weight, not only in relation to the video's themes, but also in terms of its formal structure. Images of men tend to begin musical sections, and men are shot in a clearer light, while women recede into darkness, moving toward the ends of sections. The first images of the woman move too slowly, appear too late, and stand against the flow of the images around them. Shots of strong feet and hands become associated with masculinity. This material appears when the voice is strengthened through the use of chorus, thereby confirming this association.[37] The video constructs an image of Sexton that goes beyond hysteria and passivity, however. To the extent that it represents her thoughts and experiences, the video reflects Sexton's psychological incisiveness.

It is useful to remember that "Mercy St.," like many videos, cannot be read simply as a story. Videos often seem to delay or withhold narrative closure. In "Mercy St.," the ending does not sufficiently gloss the beginning. Nor can the images always be understood according to their position in the temporal flow. One way that music videos distinguish themselves from classic Hollywood films is that videos are not built upon a rising narrative curve. This is partly because pop-song structures tend to be nonteleological. Images can be tied to a single musical feature or a group of features and such music/image connections can remain somewhat independent of others. Music videos can thereby hold a constellation of contradictory positions without one having greater authority than another.

Most often, however, if one stays with a music video long enough, a point of view will come forth. Though the video may shift among a number of perspectives, relations between music and image will bring something to the fore. A strength of "Mercy St." lies in its ability to delay one's arrival at a final position. Though the image deals with serious themes—murder, suicide, incest, and religious faith—figures become increasingly fragmented. People and things become abstract shapes. Sections end with less definition than they begin with, and finally threaten to black out. The increasing fragmentation and abstraction, and the threat of annihilation, seem, finally, to constitute more than the frustration of narrative closure and thematic clarity: annihilation and oblivion themselves become the central themes of the video.[38] To the extent that "Mercy St." is a mood piece, it derives some of its power from the seamlessness of its music/image relations, many of which elude conscious grasp. The precise nature of the video's mood is difficult to define, partly because the video seems to move toward oblivion. Although it may recall the muted depressiveness of a Rothko painting, it maintains the dignity of the figures it depicts.

Perhaps "Mercy St." might equally be understood as the site of a conversation among three very different artistic sensibilities. Men write few songs about women artists,[39] and even fewer in which the male singer adopts the subject position of a woman artist. Anne Sexton herself was haunted by other artists, both contemporary, like Sylvia Plath and Robert Lowell, and earlier, like Yeats. Mahurin's encounter with the song reflects yet another subject position. One might wonder whether the sphinxlike aspects of the piece derive from Mahurin's imagining himself as Gabriel, who imagines himself as Sexton, who has her sights set elsewhere.[40]

APPENDIX A: SECTIONAL DIVISIONS

Introduction The music begins before the image, which constitutes a departure from standard practice in music video. Typically, however, the opening shots possess a liminal quality: specifically, the feet seem to lead the viewer into a new realm.

Verse 1 A female figure is introduced. The falling houses produce a subtle sensation of downward motion. The flat, distanced vocal performance in this section underscores the distance between the figures in the video and the narrative voice.

Chorus 1 The father takes the girl out in the boat. The visual scheme emphasizes lateral motion. By the close of the chorus, the viewer's distance from the action is at its greatest. The move toward greater objectivity in the chorus could be understood as coming out of the distanced style of verse 1.

Instrumental 1 A solo is played on a synthesizer, with a breathy wooden flute patch (the "Andean flute" melody). The instrumental disperses the energy of verse 1 and chorus 2 so that verse 2 can begin.

Verse 2 Some of the woman's secrets are revealed. Verse 2 amplifies the feeling of downward motion established in verse 1.

Chorus 2 The girl of chorus 1 confronts several male figures. Like chorus 1, the movement in chorus 2 is primarily lateral, but with a stronger sense of movement towards the top of the frame. The claustrophobic atmosphere of chorus 2 develops from the intimacy of verse 2.

Instrumental 2 The video's central figures do not appear in this section (with the exception of feet that may belong to the woman). Instead, two dogs fight near the top of the frame, echoing the image of hands passing cloth. Like the first instrumental, instrumental 2 uses up the momentum of the sections preceding it before the next chorus begins.

Chorus 3 This section expands upon the previous choruses through greater timbral richness and heightened expressivity of performance. Crosscutting provides a sense of stability in the image, and close tracking between music and image governs the section as a whole. The father and daughter are placed in opposition.

Verse 3 The final appearance of the verse is reduced to a single statement of the "a" section. The father remains alone in the boat.

APPENDIX B: THE SONG'S FORM

TABLE 13.1

The harmony of the verse, I-IV, I-VI with inversions, does not drive toward the chorus. Rather, a thickening in the orchestration at a′ helps move the song into the chorus. The chorus can be heard as containing the procession VI-♭VII-I in C♯ minor, or IV-V-VI in E major. This gives the song its hymnlike quality.

INTRODUCTION								CADENCE
↓	a a a′	b a′	C:‖ d	a a a′	C:‖ d	"e" a	↓	
↓							↓	
↓								
(drone → groove)	verse	(no stepwise motion)	chorus	instrumental ("Andean flute melody")		outchorus ("a" type material")		

APPENDIX C: "MERCY ST.": GENERAL SCHEME

TABLE 13.2

	"MERCY ST." LYRICS	MUSIC	VIDEO	LYRICS IN GENERAL	MUSIC	VIDEO
Verse	story, but as ongoing, circular (private, particular) (3d person)	private, sparse, but also exotic	images of pain from protagonistic life, but reflects circularity of lyrics; no working toward goal of the narrative (i.e., suicide)	narrative (posticular), private	intimate or sparse	performer, protagonist alone, working through situations
Chorus	summing up, but more empathetic, felt (2d person— direct address?) (to protagonist or listener?)	public, full, more "European"	work to goal of narrative; more figures	maxim (general) public	grand or full	groups in tableaux
Bridge	fragmentary (as cry?) (1st person?) more direct, directly personal	more like a final verse with ad-lib replacing vocal melody—not transitional	more toward transcendence, redemption (alternate possibility)	reflection, retrospective view, alternate possibility	transitional as fragmentary or "temporary"	smaller groups? new or alternative space

APPENDIX D: SHOT DESCRIPTION

VERSE 1

a section	b section	a section	chorus	instrumental
foot—sand	foot—sand	hand—darkness	water	hands
feet—drowned	hands—boat	boat—going out	girl with lace	passing
house—falling	head—half lit	woman's—head	boat with father	lace, eye
head—low				man and boat
woman—balled				crest waves
hands head				black

VERSE 2

	chorus 2	instrumental 2	bridge
drawer hand	boat—low in frame	cross	man in boat
paper	girl—under water	dogs	swimmer
knees	priest	foot with sand	hallway
grass	young girl	pan over trees	woman's head
knees	(medallion)	fade to dust	wave
feet—shocked	girl—underwater		
woman—	boat—high in		
murmuring	frame		

VERSE 3

man in boat

AFTERWORD

THIS BOOK focuses on particular aspects of music video—volatility, fragmentation, playfulness, heterogeneity, and density. The text attempts to lay out the basic materials of music video, much as David Bordwell and his colleagues do for cinema in *The Classical Hollywood Cinema* or *Film Art,* or Jan La Rue for Western art music in *Guidelines to Style Analysis.*[1] The preceding chapters describe the ways that music videos are structured, using forms such as the process, the series, the catalogue, and the tableau, and trace the function of individual parameters in music video rather than in a Hollywood film or musical. The elements of music video differ strikingly from those of other genres. Fracturing into a single basic unit of equivalence, the fragments of parameters resemble *"petit-a's"*—empty, desirable particulars that stay a bit out of reach, possess a sheen and fulfill multiple purposes (some musical, some cultural) and that relate to one another along a continuum of conformance and contrast.[2] I have also discussed the ways viewers identify with the body and the music.

This book does not offer a grand theory; that would be best filled in or countered by other models.[3] Because what is most needed is a thick description of a structure that encompasses the large-scale and the local, I have proposed a way to show that music, image, and lyrics make room for one another and perform different functions at different hierarchical levels. Such a thick description would probably not resemble music theorist Heinrich Schenker's foreground, middleground, and background, but rather would reflect music video's interlace of multimedia. For the scholarship to progress, there must also be further close analysis of individual videos, genres, periods, the medium's changing features from the beginning to today, particular directors as auteurs, the role of technology and institutions, and the relations among director, industry personnel, and viewers, as well as the body, dance, and music.

In our excitement and anxiety about new technologies like the internet and robotics, there may be an impulse to push music video aside as unimportant. Surely its relevance to particular age groups, genders, and ethnicities is uncertain and unstable, as is its availability, given the way satellite providers schedule videos and then substitute game shows, situation comedies, and musicians' biographies in their stead. Nevertheless, I predict that music video will continue to play a significant role for a sizable segment of the population (from preteens to college age) and will increase in relevance and importance as new delivery systems like the satellite and the web proliferate, even as viewing audiences become more and more balkanized.

Although the description that I have provided works well for many genres (including country, which I do not discuss) and for both early and more recent videos, more work is needed on the ways a visual style complements approaches to music and lyrics in the same era. As a rudimentary effort, I would point to the pop music of the early 1980s, when digital samples crept into the mix, and the lovely features of disco—lush orchestration and nuanced touches—were left behind. The enormous amount of registral space needed for the new drum sounds meant, at least in the beginning, unsatisfactory arrangements and simplified melodic writing, as well as a basic confusion about what songs should sound like. How did music videos reflect the musical style of the early 1980s? Their imagery could be characterized as emphasizing soft focus, dull pastel tones, empty space within the frame, schematic sets (featuring elements like isolated staircases or gigantic window frames), robotic physical gestures, thin gazelle-like performers, and clothing that seemed to emphasize disparate interests: constraint (the cinching of the waist and the padding of the shoulders), artifice (shiny fabrics, big hair, and excessive makeup), and height (clothing that leads the eye from the bottom to the top). Some obvious one-to-one correspondences between image and sound include the large, schematic set pieces against the enormous empty drum sounds, and the early use of samples alongside the robotic gestures. But some relations are more at odds—for example, the pastel colors and soft focus tended to blunt the hard-edged qualities of the clothing and the synthesizer sounds—contributing to a complicated whole. The relation between image and song in 1980s pop videos is not purely formal, however, and indeed some of these videos' charm stems from the difficulty of ascertaining intentions and influences. The look and sound of these works are, in all likelihood, functions of their place within the life cycle of the genre, as well as cultural, institutional, and economic pressures.

Perhaps their relative newness best explains why image and music video in the early 1980s seemed so fumbling and raw. These videos share much with the beginnings of cinema. The first film directors were unsure how to frame a figure, how to light it, or how to direct the eye in the frame,[4] and there was confusion concerning where characters should be and how they should move. (Music video characters often look suspiciously as if they had been shot up with elephant tranquilizer. This may be a desired stylistic effect; it is hard to tell.)

Considerable institutional and economic pressure resulted from the fact that MTV's early focus was on bands—like Flock of Seagulls and Duran Duran— who were British and white. These bands were emphasized because the already-made promotional material was free, but the whites-only programming continued, in part because the cable-company executives were convinced that the white male suburban audience did not want to hear black music. This screening choice—program white—may have had more influence on the mainstream of 1980s popular music than has ever been acknowledged. Interestingly, blacks in that era were excluded as much visually as musically. The white cyclorama background, huge vacant sets, artificial big hair, and robotic movements seem tied to race. Perhaps the 1980s British pop invasion resembles that of the 1960s inasmuch as both were backlashes against African American music; they both succeeded through exploiting and stripping bare African American music as well as adopting exclusive visual practices. In the case of the 1960s, African Americans could not wear The Beatles' and The Rolling Stones' straight Dutch cuts.

Early 1980s imagery may have been partly a response to the prevailing winds of conservatism in the culture. In the era of Reaganomics, a time for making a quick buck and dismantling the social infrastructure, disco's musical practices (with lush arrangements, seasoned performers, and excellent songwriting values) and a mixed social context (partly gay, partly African American, partly Latin American) was replaced by a conservative European culture. Music videos may serve as a site for rehearsing modes of behavior appropriate to an era. Actors in music video look like zombies because people are becoming automatons; the music video provides an opportunity to practice the hollowing out of human values.

This line of questioning—why the early 1980s videos look and sound the way that they did—leads us to a number of new questions. What will the life cycle of the music-video genre be, and has it already been played out? How much does a change in one medium shape the trajectory of another? Do visual or musical technologies exert a special influence on the other media? Does music video have any lasting truth content, or is it a fragile object threatening to fly apart at the seams?

In response to the question of music video's life cycle, it is important to note that a genre like film noir lasted only twenty years; however, the western has persisted for the duration of cinema's history. The influence of technology on a genre's rise and fall can be seen in the faster lenses, more sensitive film stock, lower production budgets, and portable lights that made film noir possible. Music video was born through a sudden expansion of new broadcast channels in search of cheap programming as well as a boom in new editing equipment and visual postproduction effects. The new tools allowed videomakers to obtain a certain kind of speed and volubility; the image could approach the pace and nuance of speech, even its stutter and slur.[5] Today it is arguable that what can be done with music video has already been accomplished; with the high-bandwidth Internet soon to transform the genre into something unrecognizable, it is quite possible that music video has passed its prime (the high point being Hype Williams's work with LL Cool J's video "Doin' It").

In general, music video seems to have exerted an enormous influence on popular music. Pop songs of the new century routinely clock in at six minutes as opposed to the three-minute pop songs of the 1960s, partly because longer songs are needed for music video's seminarrative form. (Unfortunately, these songs only repeat musical sections rather than treating the listener to new material.) Another change is that songs have become more open, modifiable, and mobile. The song released on the radio is often quite different from the one on the video soundtrack, suggesting that neither possesses a wholeness or integrity. In the last ten years, the number of bridge sections in pop songs seems to have waned significantly. Has music video played a role here? Moreover, music video seems to have set the stage for the explosion of hip-hop today. Given that hip-hop represents a departure from pop songwriting practices—and more broadly incorporates dance, visual imagery, and fashion—it is safe to say that the audience needed to "see" the song in order to understand the genre's concerns and issues.

Do technological changes in the musical or the visual realm affect one another? And are these effects seamless or disjunctive? Some technical effects influence stylistic trends across media—from music to image to lyrics and back. The most striking example of music-video imagery's effect on recent music may be seen in the videos of crossover hip-hop artists like Missy Elliot. Her stylized, jerky dance steps seem to come from the visual language of music video itself—its editing, rapidly shifting source lights, and nuance within the frame. A musical equivalent of her physical gestures—a short, stuttered kind of melodic hook—also permeates her pop songs. These aural fragments become even more heightened and baroque in contemporary R&B songs like those of girl groups such as Destiny's Child.

Sometimes, however, a postproduction technique seems simply faddish. Included because it is a newly available technique, it comes across as incongruous, unintegrated within the video's texture. The quantel of the early 1980s, which foregrounded frames within the frame, looked like just a technique, and a more recent one—panning around a room with the figure suspended in space (the so-called bullet time effect from *The Matrix*)—may also remain unincorporated by either performers or music (although the big aural and visual spaces of N' Sync and the Back Street Boys seem vaguely related). These ploys look even more gimmicky as time passes.

Are visual and musical connections organic or arbitrary? A closer consideration of the shelf life of directors suggests that visual styles might be linked to musical ones. Like a songwriter with a particular harmonic sensibility, a producer with a special ear for timbres, or a fashion designer who chooses the right colors and skirt lengths, a music-video director may make it only by using materials that mesh with the zeitgeist. It is likely that they turn over frequently not because they become weary of the form, opting out for more lucrative and engaging projects in film, but rather because their vision is particularly appropriate for the musical style of a very short, particular time; thus, they, like rock bands, can become outmoded. The 1990s directors Matt Mahurin and Mark Pellington seem well fit for groups like Nirvana, Metallica, and Pearl Jam—and not for Michael Jackson or Duran Duran. The only music-video director who has had real longevity in the business is Wayne Isham, who seems, at first glance, capable of a neutral style. His quite malleable work incorporates either grand set pieces or intimate performance footage—both of which have gone in and out of favor.

As time goes on, what were once organic connections turn out to be purely cultural artifice and begin to fly apart. Two elements that now merge poorly into the texture of a music video are props and costumes. What is the meaning of a horse running through the set, a latrine, or a singer sitting on a throne? Viewers might have understood these motifs as connecting music, image, and lyrics at one time because they were part of a fine skein that ran through the culture, visible as well in fashion photography, compact disc covers, attitudes taken up on the street, and so on. But so many cultural phenomena have evaporated that what once seemed natural no longer makes sense. This loss of meaning is clearly visible when we consider the recurring local audio/visual relations in a video in support of musical structure, like the sudden freeze frames at the ends of song's phrases, that became common in the early 1980s. Did these devices ever hold a specific cultural meaning, or were they more purely musical? What do they mean today? Perhaps image, music, and lyrics have their own half-lives, so their meanings fade at different rates. Is it not true that the big empty sets of the 1980s resonate differently against today's music-video sets than against the music itself? In twenty years, will we not find that the distances among media have become greater?

One recent study stresses that no artistic medium—not a music video, a pop song, or a symphonic work—possesses autonomy.[6] Each medium has ellipses that cannot be filled in. It remains for the viewer to make the piece whole. The questions about music video's permeability to multiple influences in the arrow of time, seems true for individual videos as well.

This book comes out of a fascination with the relations among music, lyrics, and image, and from an acknowledgment of a fundamental contradiction embodied in music video. Although music video is one of the most lowbrow of commercial forms, it is also the most extraordinary by virtue of its use of visual means to reveal musical structure. As I mentioned in the introduction, I would stay up late to watch *Don Kirshner's Rock Concert* as a young girl, and would try to figure out what was going on. (I, and I know many others, chart the passing into adulthood through not only songs but also music videos.) In college, when I saw Steve Winwood's and Chaka Khan's "Higher Love" on cable at a friend's house, I thought America must be wonderful to produce something so lush, ornate, and superfluous. Some of the fascination with synchronism has since worn off for me, and I wish for works that might be more independent of commercialism—video-art pieces in which music, image, and lyrics share a common space and yet where change, experimentation, and difference are manifest. Among the few works in the moving-image genres that are surprisingly effective in the way they integrate music, image, and lyrics are narrative films such as P. T. Anderson's *Magnolia,* Andrei Tarkovsky's *Sacrifice,* Lars Von Trier's *Dancer in the Dark,* and Orson Welles's *Citizen Kane;* outstanding examples of musical film work include Busby Berkeley's sequences in *Footlight Parade,* Maya Deren's *Meshes of the Afternoon,* and Harry Smith's *Heaven and Earth Magic.* (It is my hope that some of this book's techniques might be used to illuminate these works.) The images and sounds that we hear today are clearly a function of consumerist culture, where there is not much support for work outside the mainstream. Perhaps I betray disillusionment with language when I suggest that somehow music, text, and image could express some part of ourselves as yet unrevealed; I still have hope that it will break through.

NOTES

NOTES TO INTRODUCTION

1. Many scholars, including Andrew Goodwin, Ann Kaplan, and Susan McClary, have emphasized the need for a theoretical account of music video. See Goodwin, *Dancing in the Distraction Factory: Music, Television and Popular Culture* (Minneapolis: University of Minnesota Press, 1992); Kaplan, *Rocking Around the Clock: MTV Postmodernism and Consumer Culture* (New York: Methuen, 1987); and McClary, *Feminine Endings: Music, Gender, and Sexuality* (Minneapolis: University of Minnesota Press, 1991). As Goodwin observes, no one has attempted an analysis that takes musical codes, processes, and techniques as providing the means by which video image can be structured. Goodwin, *Dancing in the Distraction Factory,* 2.

2. In the years following 1992, music-video scholarship remained relatively quiescent. See Goodwin, *Dancing in the Distraction Factory,* and Carol Vernallis, "The Aesthetics of Music Video: The Relation of Music and Image" (Ph.D. diss., University of California, San Diego, 1994).

3. Most attentive to visual detail and to the flow of music are Nicholas Cook's chapter on Madonna's "Material Girl," and my analysis of Madonna's "Cherish." Cook, *Analyzing Musical Multimedia* (New York: Oxford University Press, 1998), 147–173; Vernallis, "The Aesthetics of Music Video: An Analysis of Madonna's "Cherish," *Popular Music* 17.2 (1998): 153–185. Cook's *Analyzing Musical Multimedia* also provides a theory of the ways media combine to create new meanings. Other attempts to incorporate music include Tricia Rose's analysis of Public Enemy's "Baseheads," Goodwin's shot-by-shot discussion of George Michael's "Father Figure," and Melanie Morton's analysis of Madonna's "Express Yourself." None of these analyses, however, sufficiently considers the song in relation to the image. Goodwin, *Dancing in the Distraction Factory,* 120–130; Tricia Rose, *Black Noise: Rap Music and Black Culture in Contemporary America* (Hanover, NH: University Press of New England, 1994), 115–118; Melanie Morton, "Don't Go for Second Sex, Baby!" in Cathy Schwichtenberg, ed., *The Madonna Connection: Representational Politics, Subcultural Identities, and Cultural Theory* (Boulder: Westview, 1993), 213–234.

4. John Fiske, "British Cultural Studies and Television," in Robert C. Allen, ed., *Channels of Discourse, Reassembled: Television and Contemporary Criticism,* 2d ed. (Chapel Hill: University of North Carolina Press, 1992), 284–326.

5. Antoine Hennion, "The Production of Success: An Anti-Musicology of the Pop Song," *Popular Music* 3 (1983): 159–193.

6. It would have been cost-prohibitive to produce a tape that contained the clips described here. Nevertheless, many of the videos under discussion can be purchased as part of VHS and DVD compilations and are available on the Internet. Readers who cannot recall a video may have to substitute one that they know in its stead. The Nickelodeon satellite service talks of preserving "our television heritage"—what about our music video heritage?

I chart my music-video viewing history, in part, by the satellite station's programming decisions. When MTV started rolling TRL, which has teens talking over the tapes, I almost threw the remote through the set. My favorite institution, The Box, has vanished. BET succumbed to Viacom, which imposed its MTV format. With a satellite dish that offers five stations devoted to music video programming (BET, MTV, MTV2, Much Music, and VH1), there are so many commercials that I videotape and cue. My students simply download and burn.

Experience Music Project, the popular music museum in Seattle, has considered building a collection, and the Radio, Television and Film Museum in New York City has some videos and interviews with music video directors. When I need a particular video, I find it best to bypass the satellite services and solicit the video production house where the tape was originally made. To locate the production company, I find the song's label, contact the record company, and request the number of the production house. If the production house agrees to send the tape, I offer to pay for stock and postage.

NOTES TO CHAPTER 1: TELLING AND NOT TELLING

1. John Fiske interprets music videos as stories; Marsha Kinder does not. See John Fiske, *Reading the Popular* (Cambridge: Cambridge University Press, 1989); Marsha Kinder, "Music Video and the Spectator: Television, Ideology and Dream," *Film Quarterly* 38.1 (1984): 2–15.
2. An Aristotelian definition is narrower than many. Some people shear off an Aristotelian definition, requiring only some elements, such as a cause-and-effect relation or a number of events in an ordered sequence such as a setting of the scene, introduction, character, rising action, crisis, intensifying action, major crisis, and denouement. Narrative can also be defined etymologically as anything that is recounted or told.
3. David Bordwell and Kristin Thompson, *Film Art: An Introduction* (New York: McGraw-Hill, 1997), 482.
4. "Viewer" is a poor term. People who watch the visuals in music video also listen to the soundtrack. Yet no other term serves as a good replacement: "perceiver" suggests a passive mode of reception, and "participant" and "experiencer" seem vague or un-idiomatic. I use the term "viewer" throughout with the understanding that it encompasses both viewing and listening.
5. These descriptions of videos capture some of the peculiarities and nuances of the genre; however, readers who do not have much familiarity with the music-video canon may choose to skip to section II.
6. The relaxed, episodic structure of "Crazy"—one in which events are pleasurable but little is at stake—raises challenging questions. Could it be that female rather than male lead characters are cast because women have been represented traditionally as possessing fragmentary, nondevelopmental lives? Are we meant to think that the girls were fine before they left school, and that they can always return?

Hollywood film narrative gains steam from sending the protagonist on a twofold quest—solving a problem and finding a mate. The activities in Aerosmith's "Crazy" are compressed into a single trajectory—the girls act naughtily to have fun and sex.

7. Shared genes play a significant role in "Crazy." In Marty Callner's and Bon Jovi's "Always," two sisters struggle to capture some male attention while the band sings on. Despite having the same director, musical style, and premise as "Crazy," "Always" loses its narrative drive, exhibiting the intermittent plot structure that most other videos possess.

8. "Crazy" is just one in a series of unusual videos that Aerosmith has been able to make because they are an unusually long-lived and beloved group. The band does not have to lay claim to the new or the special, nor need it depart from earlier material. Although Aerosmith songs are well written within the current context, their comfortable, functional nature does not compel repeated, close listening. The song title "Crazy" suggests a desire for an instant classic. (Willie Nelson's more famous "Crazy" was recorded not only by Patsy Cline, but also by a host of other country and pop artists). The Aerosmith version functions more as a subtle echo of this earlier composition than as a song with its own agenda. Lead singer Steven Tyler, who wrote "Crazy," says explicitly that he now composes music with a potential video in mind, which suggests that he has distanced himself from the pressures and constraints of traditional songwriting—particularly recognizability and novelty.

9. TLC's "So Damn Pretty" is another example. It suggests a narrative by stringing together three different storylines: (1) Chili prepares to go under the knife for breast implants; (2) a heavyset adolescent girl breaks down because she is overweight; (3) Left Eye witnesses an interracial altercation. TLC's three singers envision these scenarios as they float upon thrones of giant flowers within a hexagonal room. The video can create a strong sense of narrative by shifting at the right moment to the storyline that best fits the contours of the song.

10. Many devoutly religious people, as well as those concerned with representations of women, minorities, and gays, have reason to be alarmed by music videos. The image can shift focus so rapidly and seamlessly. Would Herb Ritts's imagery work in a classic narrative film or a sitcom comedy? Maybe in the right settings (such as a men's locker room or a period piece) or the right genre, yet with a campy, tongue-in-cheek tone. The music video camera alone can become blatantly rhapsodic; the music with the image creates a chance for spectacle. Music videos have license to take several steps from everyday life, to slip into fantasy and desire. How commonly do we see such joyful imagery of men with no shirts on? Perhaps in print ads, and in television commercials, but not on such a quick turn, and with so much celebration. There is a famous scene in Howard Hawks's film *How to Marry a Millionaire* with Marilyn Monroe and Rosalind Russell, which "Love Will Never Do (Without You)" could be said to draw upon, but the original is very arch. See chapter 3 for more on the body and representation.

11. The video is also unthreatening because women are in control. At the concert, the camera peers over the shoulders of a mostly female audience. A multiracial group of women makes up Gaye's backup singers, and it is a woman who watches the porn flick from the limo's backseat.

12. Annabel J. Cohen, "Film Music: Perspectives from Cognitive Psychology," *Music and Cinema* (Wesleyan University Press, 2000), 360.

13. The viewer's impulse to guess at what will happen becomes strongest when the video closes its borders by establishing a clearly demarcated space, a restricted setting, and a limited assortment of props. In Solo's "Heaven, Right Here on Earth," in which the band performs inside a bus, items such as a swing, a twirling bass, a conch shell, a globe, and a butterfly appear in the aisles and on the seats, some objects toward the front, some toward the back. We feel anticipation about what will appear next, whether it will fit in with the other items, and whether the video can play itself out well until

the end. U2's "Numb" and Madonna's "Human Nature," which place the performer before a stark background and where only a few characters appear, are other examples of this phenomenon.

14. Interviews with music-video directors Nispel, Sigismondi, Lawrence, and Kerslake.

15. Strangely, music videos do a poor job of depicting death—that is, that the character was here and is no longer; that we were friends of the character and are now in mourning. In general, pop songs that chart possess a somewhat unified tone; they tend not to encompass the severe shift of emotions linked to an engagement with life and a consideration of death. Death may require silence, but the song keeps chugging along.

16. According to Barney Childs, there is an introduction (involving some question or tension), a statement, a development (possibly of relationships increasing irregularly in complexity and intensity), a climax, a resolution or relaxation or "falling action," and a concluding gesture (possibly a restatement and the renewal of cosmic order). Childs, "Time and Music: A Composer's View," *Perspectives of New Music* 2:15 (1977): 194.

17. Perhaps songs such as The Beatles' "Day in the Life" and Led Zeppelin's "Stairway to Heaven" might suggest one, but they are epic with dramatic shifts in many musical domains. One might argue that the lyrics assist the music in defining a song's narrative. The chapter on lyrics will show that lyrics frequently point in one direction and the music in another. When images are added to music and lyrics, all three media signify differently, and the viewer may struggle to create a unified whole.

18. Jann Pasler, "Narrative and Narrativity," in J. T. Fraser, ed., *Time and Mind: Interdisciplinary Issues* (Madison, WI: International Universities Press, 1989), 233–257.

19. Philip Tagg, *Kojak—50 Seconds of Television Music: Toward the Analysis of Affect in Popular Music* (Goteborg: Musikvetens-Kapliga Inst., Goteborgs University, 1979), 123–124, 142–143.

20. Jean-Jacques Nattiez, *Music and Discourse: Toward a Semiology of Music,* trans. Stewart Spencer and Carolyn Abbate (Princeton: Princeton University Press, 1990), 51.

21. Nattiez, *Music and Discourse,* 51.

22. Theodor Adorno, *Mahler: A Musical Physiognomy,* trans. Edmund Jephcott (Chicago: University of Chicago Press, 1996), 20.

23. Nattiez, *Music and Discourse,* 51.

24. Suzanne Langer, *Philosophy in a New Key: A Study in the Symbolism of Reason, Rite, and Art* (Cambridge, MA: Harvard University Press, 1942), 241.

25. Jean-Louis Comolli, "Contrariwise," *Cahiers du Cinema in English* 3 (1966): 57.

NOTES TO CHAPTER 2: EDITING

1. Theorists such as Roman Jakobson have noted that in classic Hollywood film, all elements—lighting, editing, music—become subsumed under the narrative, which functions as the dominant throughline. Roman Jakobson, in Lataslav Matjeka Krystyna Pomorska, ed., *Readings in Russian Poetics* (Cambridge, MA: MIT Press, 1971), 82–87. In music video, on the other hand, the narrative is only one element among many: any parameter can come to the fore, grab our attention, and then quickly recede from view. We do notice the editing in Hollywood films, but only rarely, as during a frenetic action sequence or at the heightened moment when the camera peers down a gun barrel.

   I refer to classical Hollywood editing in its most generic sense, akin to how Janet Staiger, Kristin Thompson, and David Bordwell define it in their *Classical Hollywood Cinema* (New York: Columbia University Press, 1985), 284–285. There are, of course, a number of directors who highlight editing as a stylistic feature, such as Sergio Leone and Sam Peckinpah, and those who break the rules, like Carl Theodor Dreyer and Yasujiro Ozu. Music-video editing has influenced contemporary filmmaking such that the border between media has become less distinct. The contemporary directors best known for a style reminiscent of music video—Paul Thomas Anderson, Spike Lee, Quentin Tarantino, and Wong Kar-Wai—make frequent use of popular music, and long stretches of their work can resemble music video. They achieve some of music video's effects—a sense of postmodern play, a type of frisson—but not others, such as the foregrounding of the song's structure.

I do not intend to minimize the ways that editing contributes to a narrative film's organization and its effect on spectators. One very good piece on the subject is by Ayako Saito. He argues that three films Hitchcock made in close proximity to one another, *Vertigo, North by Northwest,* and *Psycho,* each focus on a different theme—melancholia, mania, and schizophrenia. Such states of consciousness are evoked almost purely through editing, camera movement, and framing. What makes music video different from film is that the casual viewer notices the edits. Saito, "Hitchcock's Trilogy: A Logic of Mise en Scène," in Janet Bergstrom, ed., *Endless Night: Cinema and Psychoanalysis—Parallel Histories* (Berkeley: University of California Press, 1999), 200–249.

Editing tends to be an undertheorized area of film studies. The most significant texts on film editing are Karel Reisz, *The Technique of Film Editing* (Boston: Focal Press, 1988), and Ken Dancyger, *The Technique of Film and Video Editing* (Boston: Focal Press, 1996).

2. David Bordwell notes that "graphics, rhythm, space, and time, then are at the service of the filmmaker through the technique of editing. . . . Yet most films we see make use of a very narrow set of editing possibilities—so narrow, indeed, that we can speak of a dominant editing style throughout Western film history. . . . The purpose of the system [continuity editing] was *to tell a story* coherently and clearly, to map out the chain of characters' actions in an undistracting way. Thus editing, supported by specific strategies of cinematography and mise-en-scène, was used to ensure *narrative continuity*. . . . The basic purpose of the continuity system is to create a smooth flow from shot to shot. All of the possibilities of editing we have already examined are bent to this end. First, graphic qualities are usually kept continuous from shot to shot. The figures are balanced and symmetrically employed in the frame; the overall lighting tonality remains constant; the action occupies the central zone of the screen.

Second, the rhythm of the cutting is usually made dependent on the camera distance of the shot. Long shots are left on the screen longer than medium shots, and medium shots are left on longer than close-ups. The assumption is that the spectator needs more time to take in the shots containing more details." David Bordwell and Kristin Thompson, *Film Art* (McGraw-Hill, 1997), 280–281.

3. Music videos seldom present a clear path through their structure. Sustained sequences of pure cross-cutting are rare (The classic example is a shot of a man on a horseback racing to the train, then the speeding train, then back to the man on horseback), as is a figure chasing another in a single shot. More levels of activity may be necessary to underscore the heterogeneous quality of the song. At first glance, The Clash's "Rock the Casbah" seems like a simple chase—Egyptians chase Israelis. A closer examination of the video reveals that the armadillo that runs at the bottom of the frame complicates the relations among the figures and the music.

4. Videos establish a sense of continuity on the surface partly by using dissolves. Smoother than cuts, dissolves provide a fuzzy articulation, rather than a sharp one, against the song. They do not therefore require a strong rhythmic commitment to a single musical feature.

Director David Fincher's background is in graphic art. In an interview, he told me that when he shot music videos, he purposely avoided learning the information commonly taught in film schools. He believed he would make more interesting work by not sharing a common background with other filmmakers. Interview with Fincher, spring 1998.

5. Reisz, *The Technique of Film Editing*, 35.

6. In a music video, a graphic match will produce a momentary sense of surprise, a shock of recognition. This edit may take the viewer outside of the tape, yet, without "skipping a beat," he or she will quickly become immersed again in the video's flow. The effect is similar to the small shocks that are associated with a sudden shift in color or a lyric that creates a punning or disorienting effect. Narrative films use graphic matches much more sparingly, because they aim to enmesh the viewer in the constant unfolding of the narrative. To achieve this effect, editing should be as invisible as possible.

7. "The most elementary requirement of a smooth continuity is that the actions of two consecutive shots of a single scene should match . . . if a scene is shot from more than one angle, the background and positions of the players remain the same in each take. . . . A more difficult aspect of the same problem is to keep the action and movement shown in consecutive shots accurately continuous. If an actor starts a movement—say he is half way through opening a door—in one shot, then that movement must be continued in the next from the precise moment it was left." Reisz, *The Technique of Film Editing*, 216–217.

8. "As filmmaking developed, a universal system for classifying shots evolved. These provide convenient quick reference points for all members of the production team—especially for the director and the camera operator.

   "A series of 'standard' terms have evolved for the most effective shots of a single *person*. . . . If in doubt, remember how these shots are framed; e.g. 'cutting *just below* the waist', '*just below* the knees.' Avoid framing that cuts through the body at natural joints." Gerald Millerson, *Television Production* (Boston: Focal Press, 1999), 99.

9. Interview with Nispel, spring 1997.

10. Scott McCloud, *Understanding Comics* (Northampton, MA: Kitchen Sink Press, 1994), 66–72.

11. Christian Metz has noted that when we see a close-up of a gun on top of a bureau, the image can be read as a sentence: "Look, this is a gun." J-P Gorin, similarly attentive to close-ups, remarks that when the camera focuses on a prop, we expect the film to make further use of it—in the case of the gun, for example, a shooting. Unlike classical Hollywood cinema, music video possesses few ways to make an image stand out from the rest of the visual flow. We may reach a peak in a music video, but feel unsure about what has led us to this moment. As we pass through an assortment of images, it can be hard to tell which serve to foreshadow an event and which perform a more purely decorative function. Consequently, our commitment to thinking about future events becomes attenuated. Christian Metz, *The Imaginary Signifier: Psychoanalysis and the Cinema*, trans. Celia Britton et al. (Bloomington: Indiana University Press, 1982).

12. The image of the worm rhymes visually with a bootlace, as well as with the cables that entwine Marilyn Manson's mike stand. The worm, as it dances at the edge of a precipice, seems highly marked, yet also, through its placement, tangential—a thrown-away object. Only after reflecting upon the tape as a whole, might the viewer notice how key the image is. The squirmy worm stands for the spinal cords that Manson steals from his victims.

13. Often, in music video, each visual strand develops in isolation. It may be difficult to gauge when a particular strand will reappear or the degree to which it has changed

during its absence. Each strand may contain clues that shed light on the performer, the supporting characters, or the general context. By piecing these clues together, the viewer will gradually build a composite, if self-contradictory, image of who the characters are and what they tend to do. Assembling such a picture is difficult because some of the clues may link to moments difficult to trace—ones within different domains, music, lyrics, or image, or at a moment difficult to locate (the third beat of the last measure before the bridge). The contradictory clues may each seem to possess truths about the characters; however, they are separated by musical time and space, and there is no way to give the proper weight to one in relation to another.

   The visual strands in music video can bear some similarity to those in popular music. Popular music contains distinct sections, each of which develops in a manner different from that of classical Hollywood narrative. Toward the end of each song section, the music may thicken, intensify, or simply be used up—one can't really say that a particular song section possesses a teleology. Though a verse, chorus, or bridge can be highly differentiated, it can also share materials, and one might be tempted to say that some cross-fertilization has taken place as the song unfolds. Similarly, each visual strand in a music video remains distinct from another, changes over time (though rarely in a narrative fashion), and becomes affected to some degree by the other strands. It is common in music video for one strand to take on a particular patch of color, prop, or disposition from another. It almost seems as if one element from a visual strand had seeped into another and contaminated it. At some point, both strands may return to their original identity, yet, by this point, the viewer will have the sense that some sort of process has taken place and that the video is ready to draw to a close.

14. Andre Bazin observes that the use of the graphic match atrophied once sound became used in film. He notes that the shots of women talking and then chickens clucking in Fritz Lang's *Fury* are a holdover from silent filmmaking. Andre Bazin, *What Is Cinema?* (Berkeley: University of California Press, 1971), 34.

15. Edward Branigan, "Sound and Epistemology in Film," *Journal of Aesthetics and Art Criticism* 47 (1989): 312–324; Michel Chion, *Audiovision: Sound on Screen*, trans. Claudia Gorbman (New York: Columbia University Press, 1990); Walter Ong, *Orality and Literacy: The Technology of the Word* (London: Methuen, 1985).

16. Rudolph Arnheim, *The Power of the Center* (Berkeley: University of California Press, 1988), 53–55.

17. Earlier, I noted that music can seem to leap across frames and link two shots together, thereby connecting one character to another. In this example, the music seems to pierce the viewing plane and pour forth to envelop the viewer.

18. At certain moments in some music videos, a parameter's first-order function is to highlight musical structure, and second, to represent. If it serves as an articulation, it doesn't matter if we are flashed something sexual (a breast or a crotch), or something that is not sexual (an elbow or an ankle). When elbow, breast, flash of light, hip, edit or buttock accentuate the beat or a timbre in the voice, distinctions start to blur, as well as the boundary between gender and sexuality. Some of music video's intense pleasure may stem from a slide into a pre-oedipal state, one of abundance, repetition, and polymorphous perversity.

19. Music-video directors often covet particular editors. Marcus Nispel admires his editor's special sensitivity to the ways an edit falls on or off the beat, perhaps gained from years as a professional drummer. Music-video editing demands skills not taught in film school.

20. Although some types of shot and edit appear more frequently in some genres than in others—a slo-mo, low-angle, long tracking shot followed by a dissolve appears most

frequently in rap—the language of shots and edits does not differ greatly from one musical style to another. Even in country videos (such as Shania Twain's "Looks like We Made It"), the rhetoric remains within the same language. Neither has editing changed noticeably in music video's short broadcast history. While a number of early 1980s videos, such as INXS's "What You Need," may not be as densely articulated as some videos of today, many of the same editing techniques and strategies are present. A study of editing based on genre, period, or director would be fruitful.

NOTES TO CHAPTER 3: ACTORS

1. It is helpful to consider those videos that come closest to erasing or leaving out the star. George Michael's "Freedom" offers an array of the highest-paid fashion models in the industry, and right from the start, the video makes it clear that we will never see Michael. Eminem's "The Real Slim Shady" shows us twenty Eminems, but we can still pick out the real one.

2. Like music video, *Star Trek* and *The Rocky Horror Picture Show* are watched obsessively and constantly by fans, but anyone who pays attention to the soundtrack knows that these two films are operas of, respectively, space and horror, rich in music and sound effects.

3. The close-up may serve as an entrance into a music video, a way to find a connection with the music.

4. Patches of music video can also take on a fetishistic-type appeal—whether a single shot or several. The viewer can try to possess the beloved section, almost as if he were reaching for the brass ring from a moving circus carousel horse: though the hand always slips, the shiny, bright object never loses its allure. I have a soft spot for the last seven shots or thirty seconds of Madonna's "Don't Tell Me."

5. For me, the recent skirmishes with music-video boundaries feel like an act of desperation, a using-up of the last resources of the genre. Directors may no longer experiment with the form—they cannot leave out the stars, stray far from the music, or significantly distort the narrative—hence, the "one trick pony" tapes that push the video's boundaries, such as those by Blink 182. This band's trademark is a mild form of transgression—in one video the male performers are substituted by dwarfs. In another, the band pretends to be Britney Spears and the Backstreet Boys, and in the last, the musicians streak across the settings. Even if boundaries are threatened, propriety is not. Blurry circles chastely follow the boys in the appropriate places.

6. Edward T. Cone, *The Composer's Voice* (Berkeley: University California Press, 1974), 30.

7. In Madonna's "Music," a supporting character turns the music off, and Madonna requests that it be turned back on. However, the fantasy effect is not *really* broken. If the star were to turn the music both off and on or, even better, did so periodically, that might be another thing.

8. In specialized music-video situations, editing can appear to be the cause of change: for example, when a series of rapid edits falls ahead of the beat and pushes the figure forward, editing can do something. In "If," editing moves to the fore and other music video parameters move to the background.

9. In the music video, Madonna, looking buff, perhaps even a bit brutish after her new weightlifting regime, sings from the shoreline, but the elegant, graceful mercurial mermen simply tune her out, staying enchanted with each other instead. The music helps us to read the mermen as uninterested listeners.

10. I am an ardent fan of Madonna and her music. (I believe that she writes her own songs and is a talented musician.) Nevertheless, her songs have a peculiar quality: they seem to be written only for and about her; the music has no reach. It is surprising

that the songs of a star of her stature have so rarely been covered by other musicians. Sonic Youth has made a cover of "Into the Groove" (1988) and Kelly Osbourne of "Papa Don't Preach" (2002)—Osbourne's cover could be said to lampoon the original.

11. Cone, *The Composer's Voice*, 26, 32.

12. A record executive at Motown I spoke with described his quandary over a video for an African American girl group that lacked enough close-ups of the singers. The director liked his edit and threatened to remove his name if the tape were altered. A well-known director, his name carried some weight. Because the group was popular at the time, the lack of a director credit would look suspicious. Should the executive slap in some more close-ups and remove the credit? Ultimately, he did.

13. The relationship between the rapper and his posse is often less wide than between the performer and complementary roles found in other genres, but rap is closer to speech. Perhaps the gap between speaking and silence is less than that of song and silence.

14. Rudolph Arnheim, *The Power of the Center* (Berkeley: University of California Press 1988), 53–55.

15. Herbert Zettl describes these as vectors. Zettl, *Sight, Sound, Motion: Applied Media Aesthetics* (San Francisco: Wadsworth, 1998), 106.

16. Richard Middleton, *Over and Over: Notes Towards a Politics of Repetition* (http://www2.hu-berlin.de/fpm/texte/middle.htm).

17. Other Janus-faced instances include the moment when the rhythm arrangement drops out and the star covers his crotch. Both the singer and the music have lost the phallus.

18. The Robbie Williams video "Rock DJ" has its progressive moments, but it is not really *that* progressive. Richard Dyer points out that sexism affects men as well as women. Whereas women's bodies are often portrayed as valuable, male sexuality is portrayed as driving, tough, aggressive, hard, importunate, randy, and grotty. Dyer, *The Matter of Images* (New York: Routledge, 1993), 113–117. While women's bodies are often menaced in film, men's bodies are meant for abuse—they are cut up, shot, and blown apart.

19. Although directors tend to restrict highly choreographed dance music to a few planes within the frame, more naturalistic movement can be rendered in four or more viewing planes. Whether of conscious or unconscious design, this separation of visual material helps to draw attention to different strata within the music.

20. Sut Jhally, *Dreamworlds 2* (Northampton, MA: Media Education Foundation, 1991).

21. The depictions of race are very carefully handled in this video. Two women, who may be bodyguards, employees, or friends, flank Madonna at all times. One is perhaps Latina and one is black. The dancer for the girly show is a very light-skinned African American woman with short, straight, chestnut hair. The video then quickly moves to a series of white women and one Asian. The video moves away from black representation and, despite the thrilling moment when women create their own sexual and social world, returns to patriarchy, with the European male taxi driver's license plate having the last word. Real transgressions might include African American women looking at and enjoying other African American or European American women or European American men. Similarly, African American men are rarely allowed to enjoy European American women or men of any ethnicity.

NOTES TO CHAPTER 4: SETTINGS

1. Departures from the norm include idealized, abstracted, and postapocalyptic landscapes.

2. If they did, the sequence would function as part of a humorous pastiche or as a jab directed toward the music industry.

3. Tricia Rose notes that the street signs recall a particular place and time in much the way that a borrowed sample does. Rose, *Black Noise: Rap Music and Black Culture in Contemporary America* (Hanover, NH: University Press of New England, 1994), 9–12, 89.

4. Murray Forman provides a description of hip-hop culture, urban centers, and realistic modes of depiction. Of particular interest is his discussion of East Coast and West Coast iconographies. Forman, *The 'Hood Comes First: Race, Space, and Place in Rap and Hip Hop* (Middletown, CT: Wesleyan University Press, 2002), 243–245.

5. In the videotape *bell hooks: Cultural Criticism and Transformation* (Northampton, MA: Media Education Foundation, 1997), bell hooks speaks about the way young European American males use rap music.

6. When we consider the genre as a whole, the sheer number of these representations leads us to conclude that music-video image limits the meaning of the song. What happens at the level of an individual video, however, is harder to ascertain. In any video, the fit among lyrics, music, and image is never exact. Each can be said to embody similar values or characteristics in different ways, and the slight mismatch can be said to complicate or even confuse the matter, rendering each medium unstable. At first glance, Maxwell's "Fortunate" would seem to reflect R&B's interest in consumption, yet a closer look reveals a more complicated message. The video's setting is a beautiful modernist New York apartment with a view of the skyline and a color scheme of blue with a tinge of red. However, other features complicate this. Some enigmatic props— serenely floating jellyfish in the bathtub and butterflies wafting in the air—as well as layers of multitextured glass placed before the camera lens that render the image a bit more unstable, seem to move us past an image of upward mobility to one of desire for some sort of experience beyond which contemporary culture can give us. Maxwell's music suggests the composer/performer's relationship to craft, musical history, sensuality, pride, and constraint.

7. For example, Marcus Nispel describes his struggle to retain control over the imagery in The Fugees' "Ready or Not," a video modeled on action adventure films such as *The Hunt for Red October.* In "Ready or Not," Wycleff Jean, an imprisoned African American rapper, fights back against a white jailer. Even though the jailer is clearly a figure of oppression, the image had to be cut. Another of Nispel's videos focuses on the benign topic of people falling in love. A cupid draws an arrow upon a crowd, and couples randomly fall into each other's arms. The image of two men embracing had to be cut.

8. Jodi Berland argues that in male videos the camera focuses on the guitar, but in female videos the camera obsessively focuses on the woman's neck. Berland, "Sound, Image and Social Space: Music Video and Media Reconstruction," in Simon Frith, Andrew Goodwin, and Lawrence Grossberg, eds., *Sound and Vision: The Music Video Reader* (New York: Routledge, 1993), 39.

9. John Berger, *Ways of Seeing* (New York: Viking Press, 1995), 42. Such representations continue in the photographs of Eadward Muybridge, which anticipate cinema by using strips of successive shots to depict the continuity of an action. In these photographs, a male figure typically throws a discus or wields an axe, while a woman will pose next to an ornamental urn. Linda Williams, "Film Body: An Implantation of Perversion," in Ron Burnett, ed., *Explorations in Film Theory* (Bloomington: Indiana University Press, 1991), 46–71.

10. Examples include Whitney Houston's "I Will Always Love You" and Toni Braxton's "Unbreak My Heart."

11. Lisa A. Lewis, *Gender Politics and MTV: Voicing the Difference* (Philadelphia: Temple University Press, 1990), 109–110.

12. Much as sound passes through and wraps around physical objects, a song may have the uncanny ability to dissolve boundaries. The rhyming imagery of the hand gestures of the stage performers and of the audience seem more closely related than if the setting were silent.

13. James Naremore, *Acting in the Cinema* (Berkeley: University of California Press, 1990), 68–71.

14. I provide a close description of how a sense of place is created through the images' relation to song structure in chapter 11. I argue that a community of gay men (depicted as mermen) finds a safe, private space in a fragment of the verse that is nestled between two bridges.

15. We should remember that the image of the spacefaring African American prophet constitutes an important topos, familiar from musicians such as Sun Ra and Parliament.

16. Camera movement through a setting can reflect ideology. Many rap videos make use of Hollywood mansions, fancy cars, and swimming pools, but they reveal a kind of prudishness by presenting these settings as tableaux. This reticence becomes clear against the sinuous, exploratory camera work one sees in the typical loft settings of R&B.

17. Changing Faces, "G.H.E.T.T.O.U.T.," dir. Marcus Nispel (conversation with Nispel, spring 1997).

18. The commissioner had been claiming that money was not there to pay directors for their treatments, and that a video could be sent back to postproduction only so many times—the case in point involved a video where the chromo had been stripped, and falling dollar bills were to be colorized green.

19. Interview with Sigismondi, fall 1998; interview with Lawrence, fall 2001.

20. In my interviews with music-video directors, I have been struck by how much meaning a director might invest in the setting, all the while knowing that viewers and the record industry will most likely not be able to piece it out. Music video director Kevin Kerslake has spoken about how his set for Nirvana's "Come as You Are" was rich with meaning for him. He designed it as an abandoned Hollywood mansion with holes in the wall, no ceiling, and water pouring down the staircase. A three-legged dog with a scratch collar delicately made its way down the steps. For Kerslake, the setting and the dog represented Cobain's entrapment by the media industry. The setting functioned as a portrait of Cobain's wounded psyche. Interview with Kerslake, spring 1999.

21. Nicholas Cook, *Analyzing Musical Multimedia* (New York: Oxford University Press, 1998), 122.

22. Constance Penley, *The Future of an Illusion: Film, Feminism, and Psychoanalysis* (Minneapolis: University of Minnesota Press, 1989).

23. Henri Lefebvre, *The Production of Space* (Oxford: Blackwell, 1991), 26, 59.

NOTES TO CHAPTER 5: PROPS AND COSTUMES

1. See chapter 9.

2. A list of videos with odd, isolated details includes Nina Howard's "Freak like Me" (long fingernails); Madonna's "Human Nature" (black hair in corn rows); Ol' Dirty Bastard's "Fantasy" (silver-capped teeth); Queen Latifah's "Just Another Day" (woven Peruvian hat); Method Man's "Bring the Pain" (glass eye); Aaliyah's "One in a Million" (eye patch); Green Day's "Misery" (pierced tongue and extracted tooth); Nirvana's "Heart-Shaped Box" (obese woman with painted body suit and old man on cross with Santa Claus hat); Mötley Crüe's "Primal Scream" (necktie without a shirt); and Bush's "Everything Zen" (pig's head).

3. Off-the-record conversation with a Motown music-video executive.

4. Interview with Sigismondi, fall 1998.

5. The costuming, coupled with an alternating high and low-angle camera, leaves the viewer with the sense that they are hovering over the scene and music.

6. James Naremore, *Acting in the Cinema* (Berkeley: University of California Press, 1990), 84–87.

7. Interview with Nispel, spring 1997.

8. For a very long time, music-video director Floria Sigismondi wanted to work with a sequence from the Pilobilus dance troupe, yet until Marilyn Manson, bands turned her down. Similarly, David Fincher wished to make a video where the musicians were as tall as New York City buildings. Megabands such as Aerosmith refused until Rolling Stones singer Mick Jagger said "Sure." Fincher then made "Love Is Strong." Interview with Sigismondi, fall 1998; interview with Fincher, spring 1998.

9. Nicholas Cook, *Analyzing Musical Multimedia* (New York: Oxford University Press, 1998), 69–70.

10. Roland Barthes describes a third layer of meaning that exploits language's polysemy. This layer exceeds and is even opposed to language. Meanings here roam unfixed as pure signifiers. Barthes locates such moments in the texture and materiality of sounds and images. In a music video, do the "third meanings" in music, image, and lyrics mingle to create a new admixture? Does this help explain some of music video's affective power? Barthes, "The Third Meaning," reprinted in *The Responsibility of Forms: Critical Essays on Music, Art, and Representation* (New York: Hill and Wang, 1986), 41–62.

11. In the Macy Gray video "I Try," which contains a flower presented to the singer by a fruit vendor, the flower seems especially round and pink, and the music seems more upbeat; the flower's influence appears to spread further throughout the frame than if there were no soundtrack.

12. At the shoot for Marcus Nispel's music video for k. d. lang's "Sexuality," rows of props were lined up by item—shoes, nighties, coffee mugs, and the like. The director would try out one prop, and then another. Several suitable matches were found based upon the lighting, camera, setting, star, and music, but the best match was uncovered during the editing process.

NOTES TO CHAPTER 6: INTERLUDE: SPACE, COLOR, TEXTURE, AND TIME

1. Yi-Fu Tuan, *Space and Place: The Perspective of Experience* (Minneapolis: University of Minnesota Press, 1977), 12.

2. In classic Hollywood cinema, the last close-ups often reveal an intimacy or crucial plot point.

3. Tuan, *Space and Place*, 34–37.

4. John Ellis, *Visible Fictions: Cinema, Television, Video* (London: Routledge & Kegan Paul, 1982), 112, 137.

5. Eduard Hanslick, *On the Musically Beautiful*, trans. Geoffrey Payzant (Indianapolis: Hackett, 1986), 29.

6. Suzanne K. Langer, *Mind: An Essay on Human Feeling*, vol. 1 (Baltimore: Johns Hopkins University Press, 1967), 109.

7. Langer, *Mind*, 113.

8. Thomas Clifton, *Music as Heard: A Study in Applied Phenomenology* (New Haven: Yale University Press, 1983), 272.

9. Hans Jonas, *The Phenomenon of Life* (Chicago: University of Chicago Press, 1982), 151.

10. Mark Johnson, *The Body in the Mind: The Bodily Basis of Meaning, Imagination, and Reason* (Chicago: University of Chicago Press, 1987), 30–31. "The experiential basis for *in-out* orientation is that of spatial boundedness, of being limited or held within some three-dimensional enclosure, such as a womb, a crib, or a room. You wake *out* of a deep sleep and peer *out* from beneath the covers, *into* your room. You gradually emerge *out* of your stupor, pull yourself *out* from under the cover, climb *into* your robe, stretch *out* your limbs, and walk in a daze *out* of the bedroom and *into* the bathroom. You look *in* the mirror, and see your face staring *out* at you. . . . Once you are more awake you might even get lost *in* the newspaper, might enter *into* a conversation, which leads to your speaking *out* on some topic."

11. In response to what he perceived as a shift in current filmmaking practice, film music composer Bernard Herrmann complained, "Until recently, it was never considered a virtue for an audience to be aware of the cunning of the camera and the art of making seamless cuts. It was like a wonderful piece of tailoring; you didn't see the stitches. But today all that has changed, and any mechanical or technical failure or ineptitude is considered 'with it.'" Film directors in the era Herrmann describes (the 1960s), and even some of the most showy of contemporary popular American directors today, such as Quentin Tarantino, Oliver Stone, and Paul Thomas Anderson, direct segments that draw attention to style and to the process of filmmaking. These directors, however, must still keep long sections of their films seamless in order to draw the viewer into the narrative. David Bordwell points to a contemporary trend where cinema is sped up and stripped down—directors today deploy rapid editing, choose close-ups over wide shots, and compress what would normally comprise several shots into a single one. Yet these new approaches, while they periodically draw the viewer's attention away from the narrative, do not match the levels to which music video calls attention to its own materials and process of production. Bordwell, "Intensified Continuity: Visual Style in Contemporary American Film," *Film Quarterly* 55 (2002): 16–28. Bernard Herrmann, quoted in Roger Manvell and John Huntley, *Technique of Film Music*, 2d ed. (New York: Focal Press, 1975), 244.

12. Exceptions include electronica videos (rave, techno, drum and bass, and house) like those shown on MTV's *Amp*. These videos explore the z-axis much more than the edges of the frame. The sensation is one of barreling down a tunnel. Interestingly, while electronica features the z-axis, rap features the y, or lateral, axis.

13. This setting, which I have described as the "proscenium arch," disposes figures in space so that the viewer can easily procure them. It is a by-product of Western culture—the vanishing horizon and "God's-eye view" perspective techniques first developed in Renaissance painting. We could imagine a different type of music video, perhaps one possessing a similar depiction of space to that of traditional Chinese landscapes, where mountains overlap one another and the small human figures are dwarfed by the environment. Earlier, I argued that music-video space is treacherous, yet some aspects may be rendered overly accessible.

14. David Bordwell and Kristin Thompson, *Film Art: An Introduction* (Reading, MA: Addison-Wesley, 1997), 280–281.

15. This is a strong claim. Pat Aufderhyde argues that music videos cannot encompass great emotional range—authentic anger, joy, or sadness. Videos like Madonna's "Oh Father" or Peter Gabriel's "Mercy St." can leave me in tears, while some of Francis Lawrence's work can leave me with a sense of great joy. Yet in twenty years of watching music videos, I have not seen a truly transformative one, one that might disinter or undermine my worldview. A film like *Meshes of the Afternoon* or some films by Andrei Tarkovsky seem capable of precipitating such a transformation. Perhaps music video's conservatism stems simply from the fact that it functions within a commercial system.

Yet the problem might also be a formal one. The Kuleshov effect may play a role here, as well as the fact that music videos are short forms with figures that are forced to move to the music, and that are transformed into shape, color, and gesture—to some extent figures become slaves to the music. Luis Buñuel's *Un Chien andalou* is an example of a radical film that, I would argue, is a cousin to music video. *Un Chien andalou* is similar to music video but possesses significant differences. This film, seventeen minutes long, contains no dialogue and uses two or more types of music, title cards, moments of silence, and very loose synchronization. Linda Williams's analysis of *Un Chien andalou* can be helpful for understanding music video's processes. She talks in particular about the film's use of similarity and contiguity, and more broadly metaphor and metonymy, to create a sense of form. Williams, *Figures of Desire: A Theory and Analysis of Surrealist Film,* (Urbana: University of Illinois Press, 1981), 53–73.

16. See chapter 2. William Rothman's analysis of *Nanook of the North* reflects a belief that the themes explored within a scene can carry forth from one shot to another. The Eskimo Nanook holds a puppy, and the subtitles claim that he is proud of his Husky. His wife Nyla holds a baby (and the subtitles argue that she is proud of *her* Husky.) When Nanook bites a record to discover how the white male trader can "can his voice," Nanook is doing what a baby or dog would do; hence he is like a baby or a dog. Rothman, *Documentary Film Classics* (New York: Cambridge University Press, 1997), 10–12.

17. Videos that work similarly include Mike and the Mechanics' "In The Living Years," Gloria Estefan's "Turn the Beat Around," and R. Kelly's "I Believe I Can Fly."

18. Albin J. Zak, *The Poetics of Rock: Cutting Tracks, Making Records* (Berkeley: University of California Press, 2001), 77–78.

19. Videos where space and song structure are closely linked include Janet Jackson's "That's the Way Love Goes"; Madonna's "Express Yourself," "Bedtime Stories" and "Rain"; Lisa Loeb's "Stay"; and Candlebox's "Far Behind."

20. Strangely, because of the way that the eyes' cones-and-rods function, blue becomes brighter than other colors at dusk.

21. Sound, like color, does have some contextual properties. Bob Dylan's voice may seem harsher to listeners in tandem with an acoustic guitar than with an electric, and an oboe can be masked by other instruments.

22. Of course, a different musical parameter might be placed in relation with colors. A changing color scheme might be complimented by a shift in the harmony, arrangement, or rhythm.

23. Linda Holtzschue, *Understanding Color* (New York: Wiley, 2002), 41.

24. Janet Eastman, "Special Issue: Crazy for Color; The Basics," in *The Los Angeles Times,* January 8, 2004, Section Home, Part 6, p. 2, Features Desk.

25. Richard Watson, "Learning with Mozart," in *BBC News* (*BBC Online Network*), July 8, 1999.

26. Richard Dyer, *White* (London: Routledge, 1997), 98. See also Charles Kronengold, "Identity, Value, and the Work of Genre," in Shelton Waldrep, ed., *The Seventies: The Age of Glitter in Popular Culture* (New York: Routledge, 2001), 118–119.

27. Nicholas Cook, *Analyzing Musical Multimedia* (New York: Oxford University Press, 1998), 33. Rather than synesthesia being a function of genetics, Cook argues that synesthetic experiences occur in specific cultural contexts. For example, Scriabin's color system reflected the harmonic system in which he composed, and Rimbaud's color-image relations derived from a spelling book he was acquainted with as a child.

28. Cook, *Analyzing Musical Multimedia,* 26.

29. Currently, except for the pentatonic system, no musical system is widely considered innate.

30. One of Mr. Big's inexcusable crimes is having forsaken the beautiful Lila for this cheap, white woman.

31. Jonathan D. Kramer, *The Time of Music* (New York: Schirmer, 1988), 6. Gerard Grisey, "Tempus ex Machina: A Composer's Reflections on Musical Time," *Contemporary Music Review* 2.1 (1987): 239–275.

32. Victor Zuckerkandl, *Sound and Symbol: Music and the External World,* trans. Willard R. Trask (London: Routledge, 1956), 234–235.

33. A good question is whether a viewer can follow two or more strands of information at once or must oscillate between them.

34. Richard Middleton, *Studying Popular Music* (Philadelphia: Open University Press, 1990), 216–217.

35. See the section on tempo in chapter 8.

36. Stanley Cavell, *The World Viewed* (Cambridge, MA: Harvard University Press, 1979), 18, 101–108. William Rothman and Marian Keane provide an excellent reading of this text in *Reading Cavell's "The World Viewed": A Philosophical Perspective on Film* (Detroit: Wayne State University Press, 2000).

37. All of the following videos work accordingly: Guns N' Roses, "November Rain"; No Doubt, "Don't Speak"; Madonna, "Borderline"; and Smashing Pumpkins, "Disarm." Such examples include Boyz II Men, "On Bended Knee"; Mötley Crüe, "Home Sweet Home"; Madonna, "This Used to Be My Playground."

38. Anahid Kassabian describes a scene from the New Zealand horror spoof *Dead Again* that begins with an inexperienced pianist clumsily practicing her scales. The soundtrack shifts to dramatic scoring when the camera moves upstairs to witness a man abusing a woman and the piano writing suddenly becomes virtuosic. When the camera returns to the pianist, the soundtrack again reflects the performer's poor skills. In classic Hollywood cinema, the camera may jump between an objective point of view and that of a character. This example is related but not exactly analogous. Kassabian, *Hearing Film: Tracking Identifications in Contemporary Hollywood Film Music* (New York: Routledge, 2001), 45.

39. Michel Chion, *Audiovision: Sound on Screen,* trans. Claudia Gorbman (New York: Columbia University Press, 1990), 17–19.

40. Henri Bergson, *An Introduction to Metaphysics,* trans. T. E. Hulme (1903; rpt. New York: Library of Liberal Arts, 1955), 23–26.

NOTES TO CHAPTER 7: LYRICS

1. Let me qualify the claim that lyrics play an "essential" role. American audiences may find the lyrics for American music videos to be central. But MTV broadcasts globally, and many countries receive a mix of local and American videos. Perhaps the largest share of the music video viewing audience cannot follow the lyrics. Many satellite viewers also watch Worldlink (among other satellite services) which present videos from around the world, without being able to make out the text.

2. Claudia Gorbman, *Unheard Melodies: Narrative Film Music* (Bloomington: Indiana University Press, 1987), 77.

3. *The Daily Mail* (London), 21 June 1913, cited in Charles Hamm's *Irving Berlin* (New York: Oxford University Press, 1997), 9.

4. Andrew Goodwin, *Dancing in the Distraction Factory: Music, Television and Popular Culture* (Minneapolis: University of Minnesota Press, 1992), 65.

5. Simon Frith, *Music for Pleasure: Essays in the Sociology of Pop* (New York: Routledge, 1988), 119–120, cited in Richard Middleton's *Reading Pop: Approaches to Textual Analysis in Popular Music* (Oxford: Oxford University Press, 2000), 163.

6. Of the two who emphasize antagonism—Kofi Agawu and Lawrence Kramer—the last makes the case most strongly in his book *Music and Poetry.* Agawu, "Theory and

Practice in the Analysis of the Nineteenth-Century *Lied*," *Music Analysis* 11.1 (1992): 5–8; Kramer, *Music and Poetry* (Berkeley: University of California Press, 1984), 125–135.

7. Kobena Mercer, "Monster Metaphors: Notes on Michael Jackson's Thriller," in Simon Frith, Andrew Goodwin, and Lawrence Grossberg, eds., *Sound and Vision: The Music Video Reader* (New York: Routledge, 1993), 93–108.

8. Eduard Hanslick, *The Beautiful in Music/Vom Musikalisch-Schönen*, trans. Gustav Cohen (New York: Library of Liberal Arts, 1957), 144.

9. Peter Kivy, *The Corded Shell: Reflections on Musical Expression* (Princeton: Princeton University Press, 1980), 91–92.

10. Suzanne K. Langer, *Feeling and Form* (New York: Scribner's, 1953), 68, 439. According to Peter Kivy, the music is not really sad; this shape is only one that we recognize as resembling sadness, similar to the face of a Saint Bernard or a weeping willow. Kivy, *Sound Sentiment: An Essay on the Musical Emotions* (Philadelphia: Temple University Press, 1989), 12.

11. Roland Barthes, *Image—Music—Text* (New York: Hill and Wang, 1977), 25–27.

12. Richard Middleton, *Studying Popular Music* (Philadelphia: Open University Press, 1990), 231.

13. Antoine Hennion, "The Production of Success: An Anti-Musicology of the Pop Song," *Popular Music* 3 (1983): 159–193.

14. The isolation of text is similar to what happens in film music. Composers report that viewers are unable to remember more than thirty seconds of the music they hear in a film. They therefore most often rely on short phrases and memorable timbres rather than on a music built on continuity and a logical internal structure.

15. Because elliptical, impinging elements are so crucial to music video and take on as much importance as lyrics, it is fitting here to recount a few examples. The cover art for Nirvana's album cover *In Utero* appeared in "Heart-Shaped Box." Similarly, the cover of Nine Inch Nails' *Downward Spiral* appeared in "Closer," and Metallica's *Load* is referred to in "Hero of the Day." Video imagery that puns on the band's name includes Crystal Waters' "100% Pure Love," Busta Rhymes's "Woo Hah," and C&C Music Factory's "Everybody Dance Now." The role idle conversation can play in the formation of a video is illustrated through the director Marcus Nispel's collaboration with LL Cool J in "Six Seconds of Pleasure." Nispel put LL in a child's playpen because the rapper spoke of "cribs," and the director, a recent émigré from Germany who spoke poor English, thought a child's play space might be an effective setting for the song, as well as a comment on the rapper's machismo. It was only after the completion of the video that Nispel discovered "crib" to be a grown-up reference—slang for a bachelor's apartment. The theme for Garbage's "Stupid Girl" came about when, in conversation, the performers and the director discovered a mutual admiration for the credits of David Fincher's *Seven*. David Bowie's and Floria Sigismondi's "Dead Man Walking" reflects a shared appreciation for the work of the painter Francis Bacon. Interview with Nispel, spring 1997; interview with Sigismondi, fall 1998.

   Equally arbitrary is the choice of imagery for the way it reflects the star's physiognomy. The director Kevin Kerslake chose to shoot most of Bush's "Glycerine" in extreme close-up, anchoring the camera just above the lead singer's eyebrows because Gavin Rosedale's hawklike, piercing eyes and sharply chiseled brow possess a stern unyielding quality that seemed to work well with material in the song. Likewise, Herb Ritts wanted to exploit a newly emergent sexuality he sensed in Janet Jackson that had not yet been revealed. For the video "Love Will Never Do," he dressed Jackson in ripped jeans and a spaghetti-strap tank top and placed her deep in the desert. After numerous takes, while the sun set and the cameras rolled, she began to exude the warm sexuality that Ritts had banked on.

16. J. L. Austin, *Sense and Sensibilia* (New York: Oxford University Press, 1962), 71.

17. Nicholas Cook, *Analyzing Musical Multimedia* (New York: Oxford University Press, 1998), 43.

18. A computer search will bring up most music-video lyrics. (In a search engine such as Google, type in the band's name, the song title, and the word "lyrics"—for example, "alanis morrissette ironic lyrics.") There are several sites where one can view and download music videos off the web—launch.com, Rollingstone.com, GetMusic.com, MTV.com, and Peeps.com are popular ones. It has also become easier to find obscure videos on the web.

19. Kobena Mercer, "Monster Metaphors: Notes on Michael Jackson's Thriller," in Simon Frith, Andrew Goodwin, and Lawrence Grossberg, eds., *Sound and Vision: The Music Video Reader* (New York: Routledge, 1993), 93–109.

20. In a video like TLC's "Waterfalls," the lyrics and the visual track tell the same story. The sung text sounds close to speech, and the duplication of information is comforting, so we listen closely. In a video like Dave Matthews's "I Did It," the lurid and overexcited imagery seems quite distant from the words, and we may attend only haphazardly.

NOTES TO CHAPTER 8: MUSICAL PARAMETERS

1. Musical materials that function as hooks are often depicted in special ways. Recorded popular music in the video era presents a range of hooks in different domains. Charles Kronengold defines the hook as "that feature of a song which is memorable, which distinguishes it from other songs of its kind. It is frequently repeated, but often not; it is usually thought of as being a phrase, but it can also be a single sound, an entire section, or a technique that runs through a song." Videos develop a variety of means to underscore a song's hook. Kronengold, "Excess and the Contract of Genre: Functions of the Hook in Popular Music," paper presented at the Popular Music of the 1970s Conference, University of California, San Diego, spring 1994.

2. See the section on time in chapter 6.

3. Richard Middleton, "Over and Over: Notes Towards a Politics of Repetition," http://www2.huberlin.de/fpm/middle.htm.

4. See chapters 9, 11, and 13.

5. Another video of this sort is Janet Jackson's "Because Love Is Better."

6. Many smooth R&B ballads of the 1990s make use of slo-mo timing.

7. Christina Amphlett's popping her bubble gum in The Divinyls' "I Touch Myself" and a model dropping a bouquet of flowers in Duran Duran's "Ordinary World" are other examples.

8. This, to me, is not unlike the narrative-film star who suddenly lunges for the gun that is out of reach and grabs hold of it, or who leans forward and draws the sword from the stone.

9. Jane Feuer, *The Hollywood Musical* (Bloomington: Indiana University Press, 1982), 3–5.

10. In "Heart-Shaped Box," when carried out by the bass player at the hospital. In "Blackberry Molasses," by one of the boys riding on the back of the bus.

11. They might exemplify what Richard Dyer attributes to whiteness—order and rigidity. Richard Dyer, *The Matter of Images* (New York: Routledge, 1993), 152.

NOTES TO CHAPTER 9: CONNECTIONS AMONG MUSIC, IMAGE, AND LYRICS

1. Michel Chion, *Audiovision: Sound on Screen,* trans. Claudia Gorbman (New York: Columbia University Press, 1990), 63.

2. I am indebted to Edward Branigan's article "Sound and Epistemology in Film," *The Journal of Aesthetics and Art Criticism* 47 (1989): 312–324.

3. Walter Ong, *Orality and Literacy: The Technology of the Word* (New York: Methuen, 1985), 32.
4. Thomas Clifton, *Music as Heard: A Study in Applied Phenomenology* (New Haven: Yale University Press, 1983), 35.
5. Chion, *Audiovision*, 19.
6. Chion *Audiovision*, 144.
7. Chion, *Audiovision*, 47.
8. J. D. Anderson, "Sound and Image Together—Cross Modal Confirmation (Film)," *Wide Angle* 15.1 (1993): 30–43.
9. Chion, *Audiovision*, 16.
10. Chion, *Audiovision*, 26–27.
11. Chion, *Audiovision*, 61.
12. Richard Middleton, *Studying Popular Music* (Philadelphia: Open University Press, 1990), 177.
13. Nicholas Cook, *Analyzing Musical Multimedia* (New York: Oxford University Press, 1998), 84.
14. Cook, *Analyzing Musical Multimedia*, 70.
15. Cook, *Analyzing Musical Multimedia*, 81–82.
16. Cook, *Analyzing Musical Multimedia*, 83.
17. George Lakoff and Mark Johnson, *Philosophy in the Flesh* (New York: Basic Books, 1999), 45–49.
18. Cook, *Analyzing Musical Multimedia*, 104.
19. Personal experience has corroborated this for me. When I edit images onto the music track, some of the image's affective power dissipates as soon as it is slotted in against the music. Music, too, is tainted—spatialized a bit, changed in its proportions, speed, and mood. The previous chapter on props explores some unusual possibilities of recombinance.
20. Do we link moments that are connected through a symbolic connection separately from those that are iconic? (It seems quite likely that such sync points are processed in different parts of the brain.)
21. Roland Barthes describes the punctum in a photograph as that which functions as a "sting, speck, cut, little hole—and also a cast of the dice. A photograph's punctum is that accident which pricks me (but also bruises me, is poignant to me)." Barthes, *Camera Lucida* (New York: Hill and Wang, 1981), 27.
22. Lacan never directly explores how sounds, music, and rhythm might function as *objets petit a*, objects fetishized for the plenitude they represent for the subject, and for the suggestion they bring of bygone wholeness. Other psychoanalytic critics have, however. Gerard Blanchard, *Images de la musique de cinema* (Paris: Edilig, 1984), 101–102.
23. Gestalt theorists have argued that a viewer is more likely to read a pattern as contained within the whole if objects are placed closer together rather than far apart. Albert S. Bergman, *Auditory Scene Analysis: The Perceptual Organization of Sound* (Cambridge, MA: MIT Press, 1990), 18–20.
24. Madonna's "Open Your Heart" depicts a strip show. The characterization of the voyeurs play off Madonna's depiction: a teenager flashing a camera connects to a shot of Madonna pretending to shoot off a gun; a military man's tassels, and a man's dreadlocks relate to the fringe on Madonna's costume; a fat man's thick glasses resemble Madonna's round face staring through the bent cane of a chair; another man's long nose suggests the tip of Madonna's breast; twins whose pressed together faces suggest a new one, and a woman dressed in drag. All congeal to suggest that the image of the stripper is a cultural projection.

25. Lawrence Kramer, *Music and Poetry: The Nineteenth Century and After* (Berkeley: University of California Press, 1984), 104.

26. Cook, *Analyzing Musical Multimedia,* 104.

27. Stefan Sharff defines slow disclosure as a "shot starting in close-up that does not reveal the location of the subject at first. It then moves back or cuts to a full revelation of the geography, which comes as a surprise. A shot typical of cartoons would show an animal sleeping comfortably and then zoom out to reveal that his enemy is lowering an axe over his head." Sharff, *The Art of Looking* (New York: Proscenium, 1997), 194. Sharff's first description of slow disclosure occurs in his excellent book *The Elements of Cinema: Toward a Theory of Synthetics Impact* (New York: Columbia University Press, 1982).

28. Research in cognitive psychology and film seems to verify this. Both short-term and long-term cognitive processing strips both music and image into basic outlines. What we finally come to experience is not the whole artifact. Annabel J. Cohen, "Film Music: Perspectives from Cognitive Psychology," in James Buhler, Caryl Flinn, and David Neumeyer, eds., *Music and Cinema* (Middletown, CT: Wesleyan University Press, 2000), 360–377.

29. Heinrich Schenker, *Five Graphic Music Analyses* (New York: Dover, 1969).

NOTES TO CHAPTER 10: ANALYTICAL METHODS

1. Kobena Mercer, "Monster Metaphors: Notes on Michael Jackson's Thriller," in Simon Frith, Andrew Goodwin, and Lawrence Grossberg, eds., *Sound and Vision: The Music Video Reader* (New York: Routledge, 1993), 105.

2. Angus Fletcher, *Colors of the Mind: Conjectures on Thinking in Literature* (Cambridge, MA: Harvard University Press, 1991), 11.

3. Michel Chion, *Audiovision: Sound on Screen,* trans. Claudia Gorbman (New York: Columbia University Press, 1990), 135.

4. John O. Thompson, "Screen Acting and the Commutation Test," *Screen* 19.2 (1978): 55–70.

5. Philip Tagg, *Kojak—50 Seconds of Television Music: Toward the Analysis of Affect in Popular Music* (Goteborg: Musikvetens-Kapliga inst., Goteborgs University, 1979), 71–77, 99–154.

6. Leo Spitzer, *Essays on English and American Literature* (Princeton: Princeton University Press, 1962), 114–115.

7. Pop songwriters need catchy hooks to sell their song and/or CD, and they will often write a "pop-oriented" song or song section so that they can explore other types of material elsewhere. Film directors frequently shoot their films with an eye to creating imagery they can use in the trailer. (So claimed M. Night Shyamalan about his film *Signs*; Marshall Sella, "The 150-Second Sell, Take 34," *The New York Times Magazine,* 28 July 2002.) I am not sure a music video image can advertise a song or a performer any better than a narrative film can sell a star's image or a soundtrack (such as *The Big Chill* or *Reservoir Dogs*). The New York film critic Armond White likes to say that films are made to sell popcorn in the theaters. Both Ann Kaplan and Andrew Goodwin provide extensive discussions on the topic of music video and advertising.

8. Rob Walser documents the deliberate attempts to broaden metal's appeal during the 1980s. Visual codes are used to address female fans. One reason that "Nothing Else Matters" looks like an ad is that it is unlike any other video that Metallica has made, or any image that had previously defined them. Walser, "Forging Masculinity: Heavy-Metal Sounds and Images of Gender" in Simon Frith, Andrew Goodwin, and Lawrence

Grossberg, eds., *Sound and Vision: The Music Reader* (New York: Routledge, 1993), 155, 163–177. Will Straw provides a description of how the music industry profits by music television. Straw, "Popular Music and Postmodernism in the 1980s," in Simon Frith, Andrew Goodwin, and Lawrence Grossberg, eds., *Sound and Vision: The Music Video Reader* (New York: Routledge, 1993), 123–143.

9. Cook, *Analyzing Musical Multimedia*, 74.

NOTES TO CHAPTER 11: THE AESTHETICS OF MUSIC VIDEO

1. The attempts that come closest are Nicholas Cook's analysis of Madonna's "Material Girl," Tricia Rose's reading of Public Enemy's "Baseheads," Andrew Goodwin's shot-by-shot discussion of George Michael's "Father Figure," and Melanie Morton's analysis of Madonna's "Express Yourself." Cook, *Analyzing Musical Multimedia* (New York: Oxford University Press, 1998), 147–173; Rose, *Black Noise: Rap Music and Black Culture in Contemporary America* (Hanover, NH: University Press of New England, 1994), 115–118; Goodwin, *Dancing in the Distraction Factory: Music Television and Popular Culture* (Minneapolis: University of Minnesota Press, 1992), 120–130; Melanie Morton, "Don't Go for Second Sex Baby!" in Cathy Swichtenberg, ed., *The Madonna Connection: Representation Politics, Subcultural Identities, and Cultural Theory* (Boulder: Westview, 1993), 213–235. None of these analyses, however, is sufficiently attentive to visual detail and to the flow of the music.

2. Goodwin, *Dancing in the Distraction Factory*, 2.

3. Allen Ellenzweig, *The Homo-erotic Photograph* (New York: Columbia University Press, 1992), 188.

4. Walter Ong, *Orality and Literacy: The Technology of the Word* (New York: Methuen, 1985), 32.

5. David Bordwell, in Janet Staiger, Kristin Thompson, and David Bordwell, *The Classical Hollywood Cinema: Film Style & Mode of Production to 1960* (New York: Columbia University Press, 1985), 54.

6. Staiger, Thompson, and Bordwell, *The Classical Hollywood Cinema*, 55–57.

7. Composer and theorist Robert Erickson states: "Any melody is analogous to a moving line. The line is strictly speaking never continuous; there is always a jump from tone to tone, and the visual analogy of a series of dots producing the effect of a line would be more accurate." Erickson, *The Structure of Music: A Listener's Guide: A Study of Music in Terms of Melody and Counterpoint* (New York: Noonday, 1955), 24.

   Visual images can also be said to have fundamental structural contours. Leonardo da Vinci said something very beautiful about this: "The air is full of an infinite number of radiating straight lines which cross and weave together without ever coinciding; it is these which represent the true form of every object's essence." Leonardo da Vinci, *The Genius of Leonardo da Vinci: Leonardo da Vinci on Art and the Artist*, ed. Andre Chastel (New York: Orion Press, 1961), 146.

8. Leonard Meyer, *Style and Music: Theory, History and Ideology* (Chicago: University of Chicago Press, 1989), 128–129.

9. Georges Seurat thought of the horizontal line as passive, the vertical line as active; lines descending from the horizontal seemed lugubrious; lines ascending from the horizontal tended toward joy. "Letter to Jules Christopher. August 28, 1890," in R. Goldwater and M. Traves, eds., *Artists on Art from the XIV to the XXth Century*, ed. (New York: Pantheon, 1972), 375.

10. The song presents the chorus and the complete verse only twice each. This in itself is unusual for a pop song at this tempo as long as the version of "Cherish" used in the video (about four and a half minutes long).

11. I discuss the role of sectional divisions more fully in the second part of this chapter.

12. Rudolf Reti, *The Thematic Process in Music* (Westport, CT: Greenwood, 1985), 13–14.

13. Though a relation, in music video, can exist through similarity or contrast, confluence may be more easily perceived than disjuncture. Similarly, an arch shape is simple to grasp. The "Cherish" video's accessibility derives in part from the video's clear transformations of its basic shape, as well as from its continuity and flow.

14. Note the firm articulations, in both image and music, at the beginnings of phrases (measures 5, 9, 13, and 17). Note also how, throughout each section, the images gradually diminish in force. In the first chorus, the image punches through the section, from Madonna marching up to the camera to the little boy and the mermen surfacing, the mermen pulling through the water, and Madonna crunching her shoulder up and down. As the music in the chorus gradually winds down, the image too, softens; the residual "pop" in the imagery of the older merman nudging the little boy on the nose and the last image of Madonna's knee propped up reflects music that has lost its drive.

    The image slavishly follows the phrase structure of the music in the first verse and chorus. During these two sections, the image supports the song's regular phrase structure and is edited to emphasize meaningful word groupings and motivic cells. In verse 2, however, the image begins to play with the phrase structure—sometimes coming slightly before, sometimes lagging slightly behind the musical phrase. Because we can recognize both the rule and its variation, we still experience the phrasing of the music and the image in verse 2 as contrapuntally related.

15. Although probably produced by a digital synthesizer, this patch is designed to have the richness and grain associated with earlier analog synthesizers. It resembles a Minimoog "lead guitar" timbre popularized by fusion keyboardists such as Chick Corea, Jeff Lorber, and Jan Hammer. On digital synthesizers, this timbre is sometimes referred to as the "Steve Winwood" patch because of its frequent presence on his albums from the early and mid-1980s.

16. The bass line is a very significant feature of the "Cherish" song. Both it and the vocal line are equally charismatic. The bass line is interesting because it is one of the song's few performerly aspects—there is some flexibility in the rhythmic feel, as well as some improvisatory flair in the choice of notes. The vocal line is, as one would expect, in the foreground. "Cherish" is better thought of as a two-voice structure, and not as melody and accompaniment, because the bass line provides so much melodic interest, and seems to carry the harmony, even when it is contradicted by the keyboard pad (as in the bridge).

17. Synthesizer and drum machine–based dance-pop songs with a human feel became a staple on the R&B charts starting in 1982. Examples from 1982–83 include "Sexual Healing" by Marvin Gaye, "Ain't Nobody" by Rufus and Chaka Khan, "Just Be Good to Me" by The S.O.S. Band, and "Yah Mo B There" by James Ingram with Michael McDonald. Examples can be found on the pop charts soon after: Prince's "When Doves Cry" (1984), which reached number one on both the pop and R&B charts, Madonna's own "Borderline" (1984), and Howard Jones's "Things Can Only Get Better" (1985). Madonna's sometime collaborator, Manhattan DJ and producer "Jellybean" Benitez, was instrumental in popularizing this sound and connecting it with certain strands in the British "New Romantic" style. One might say that this sound achieved hegemonic status on American radio from 1986–88.

18. Many aspects of the song are constructed to emphasize sameness over difference, restraint over assertion. The melodic materials of the chorus and bridge relate closely to those of the verse. The pitches G–F♯–A–B, which form the principle motive of the chorus (for example, m. 21), come out of the synthesizer's cambiata figure in the verse, D–C♯–A–B. These connections help to make the similarities among the sections of the

song as important for the videomaker as are the differences among them. The orchestration remains a continuous wall of sound. The only element that seems really to progress in the song is the synthesizer's countermelodies. For example, the synthesized trumpet is buried very deep in the mix in the first verse. It does not come to the fore until the second bridge. Later, it plays a crucial role in bringing the song to a close.

19. One way that the video draws attention to sectional divisions is through shifts in pacing. The imagery of the verse is slowed down, and the imagery for the chorus moves more quickly. The particular pacing of "Cherish" derives from the fact that the chorus has a faster harmonic rhythm than does the verse.

20. This moment illustrates a crucial point about music video: most often, the image can point to but a few musical parameters. At one moment, the image may comment upon the subtle nuances of the music, and at another, it may suggest the way that the music articulates larger sectional divisions. However, by the close of the video, our attention will have been drawn to almost all of the musical parameters. Music video works by saying, "First listen to this, then this, now this."

    Relations between music and image can exist within all degrees of concordance. Some correspondences may be literal one-to-one mappings, like those seen in cartoons (referred to as "mickey mousing"). An example in "Cherish" would be the moment when Madonna raises her shoulders on beats 1 and 3. Yet the most successful connections may be ones that are obscure and enigmatic. Such connections may ask viewers to tease out the relation between music and image, and contribute to an important aspect of music videos—that they encourage us to watch them repeatedly. Some more enigmatic and subtle connections in "Cherish" might include the relation between the sibilants in the voice and the percussion samples, and how they, in turn, relate to the prismatic light on sand and water; how the bass line seems to carry the figures forward; the echo of the theme song from the television series *Flipper,* and the way that the nostalgic elements in the music are paralleled by imagery drawn from beach films and old home movies, myths, and fairytales.

21. Rudolf R. von Laban, *Principles of Dance and Movement Notation* (Boston: Plays Inc., 1974), 10.

22. This image of Madonna makes a vague joke, which would relate the Mermen's coming onto land (as in Hans Christian Andersen's fairytale) to the first amphibian stalking forward without much grace. This kind of oblique association is common in music video. Much of the imagery in music video operates on jokes and associations that are not quite consciously acknowledged. We can turn, however, to the music and to the whole music video to fill in the context, in order to get the tone or flavor of such an association.

23. The expected form for a song of this genre and period would be (introduction)–verse–chorus–verse–chorus–bridge–verse (instrumental)–outchorus. "Cherish" departs from the letter, if not the spirit, of this form by repeating the bridge and adding a break. The presence of a break is somewhat unexpected, in that the break is a formal conceit associated more with dance music than with middle-of-the-road music. The song's most significant modification of formal conventions, however, lies in the internal construction of the third verse.

24. Another director might have emphasized the suspension, say through imagery of unrequited love. Ritts moves past this suspension and draws attention to the verse fragment, thereby underscoring the mermen's collective identity.

25. The gesture of a broad, sweeping arc that resolves into a balanced image of height and depth occurs frequently in "Cherish." Visual arcs imply phrasing that can be shaped either with or against that of the music. One can see an antecedent to this gesture in Ritts's still photography. The photograph "Male Nude with Bubble" (reproduced in

Ellenzweig, *The Homo-erotic Photograph,* 194) bears interesting similarities to "Cherish": many of the qualities of balance in the photo seem, in the video, to be extended in time and placed in relation to the song.

26. The image highlights two falling gestures in the bass (mm. 1–12, 13–20), and the rising line in the melody (mm. 1–17).

27. The Busby Berkeley sequence is much beloved, particularly in the gay community, for its spectacular opulence and willingness to dispense with narrative.

28. Philip Hayward, "Desire Caught by Its Tail: The Unlikely Return of the Merman in Madonna's 'Cherish,'" *Cultural Studies* 5.1 (1991): 98.

29. It is difficult to determine whether we are seeing feet that belong to a child or to an adult. The ambiguity thus created can be expressed as follows: if the legs are a child's, then the merboy meets Madonna as a child; if they are adult legs, he may meet her as a lover. More time will have elapsed, most likely in the company of the mermen.

30. Michael Jackson's "Thriller" provides a good example of this phenomenon, as shown by Kobena Mercer in "Monster Metaphors: Notes on Michael Jackson's Thriller," in Simon Frith, Andrew Goodwin, and Lawrence Grossberg, eds., *Sound and Vision: The Music Video Reader* (New York: Routledge, 1988), 93–109. Mercer points to the many thematic threads in the image and the song that might bear upon the video's ending.

31. Staiger, Thompson, and Bordwell, *The Classical Hollywood Cinema,* 12–23.

32. The expressions on the mermen's faces in the group close-up in the first bridge could be read as an expression of anger at Madonna's having stolen their child from the ocean. The boy's teeth chatter as Madonna reaches to hold him. Yet the imagery in this section also points to the notion that the boy comes ashore of his own accord—here, we see the fishtail moving by its own power toward the shore: the merboy has beached himself. The imagery of Madonna in the second bridge—her shielded breasts, vulnerable belly, and heavy movements—seems campy. Her movements undercut her attempt to look beautiful. In addition, the relationship between the mermen and the merboy looks warm and unconflicted, but the relationship between Madonna and him seems less so.

33. Another example of correspondence between affect and music can be drawn from Madonna's "Open Your Heart" video. Her stiff movements, heavy mascara, and brooding expression, as well as the dark setting (emerald green, deep blue, black) match the severity of the music. Music-video imagery can ignore, match, or supersede various parameters of the music. In "Cherish," the affective character of the image is more extreme than that of the music. The mood of the image seems like a heightened version of the mood of the song—with images of people crashing and diving through frothy water, Madonna's rocking movements, and expressions of elation. At one level, music videos need to exceed the bounds of the music—it gives their existence a raison d'être. The claim of greater affective range is an easy way for the image to show that it is more authoritative than the music. This is an easy way, but not the only one. In U2's "With or Without You," the image envelope the music by moving at pulses both faster and slower than that of the music. In Peter Gabriel's "Mercy St.," a slow song that evokes a sense of solemnity, the slowest pulse is associated with the image.

34. The vocal line here embodies a nontraditional construction. Much of the song, until the high D4, can be heard as a circling around D3. The octave leap up to D4 is not prepared for, in terms either of linear direction or harmonic flow. Its intrinsic appeal is questionable, but it does support the wide-eyed quality of the singer's subject position in this song.

35. *Flipper* may be the most concrete possibility, because its theme song resembles the opening of "Cherish."

36. Hayward, "Desire Caught by Its Tail," 98.

37. There seems to be a very wide range of competence in the ability to view music video, with teenagers who have watched a great deal of television often displaying the greatest visual and musical acuity. My experiences, from speaking with videomakers and their assistants, and with students who watch music video, suggest that their engagement with the medium is quite intense. The students in my undergraduate course on music video often write sustained and incisive analyses of videos. I discovered, further, that their fluency in the medium meant that music videos could be used as a tool for teaching music fundamentals.

38. Ludwig Wittgenstein, *Philosophical Investigations,* trans. G. E. M. Anscombe (New York: Macmillan, 1968), 19.

NOTES TO CHAPTER 12: DESIRE, OPULENCE, AND MUSICAL AUTHORITY

1. For example, the moments when the voice blurs with instrumental elements, or when its gender becomes ambiguous.

2. In African American popular music, it is not uncommon for the singer to offer a clear contract concerning ways of loving. This can be seen as a positive feature. The lyrics for Barry White's song "Never, Never Gonna Give Ya Up," which contains the lines "Gonna give you all of me that you can stand" and "I'm never, ever gonna quit, 'cause quitting just ain't my stick," are an example. When Love Unlimited, also produced by White, sing "Move me no mountain, turn me no tide; swim me no ocean, long, deep and wide; just say you love me, . . ." the lyrics can be seen as a response to these contracts.

3. It is in articulating a reading like this one that the misogyny of the video comes out most strongly—for some viewers, "Gett Off" may indeed be irredeemably sexist.

4. Donald Bogle speaks about the role of the tragic mulatto in the history of American cinema. Bogle, *Toms, Coons, Mulattos, Mammies, and Bucks: An Interpretive History of Blacks in American Films* (New York: Continuum, 1989), 9, 147–154, 175. It is interesting that the tragic mulatto is almost always a woman—Dorothy Dandridge and Lena Horne are the most famous examples. I am indebted to Professor George E. Lewis for making this point and providing me with this reference. Prince, with his Carmen Miranda hair and high-waist pants, borrows from women's culture, but also from the topos of the Latin gigolo—another instance of cultural promiscuity on the part of the video. In "Gett Off," style of dress serves as a source of power and empowerment, a source of safety and difference. If Prince wore the traditional unbuttoned white shirt of the Latin lover, he might have seemed more dangerous. Note that Diamond wears combat boots and shorts. Diamond's hardened edges make her more invincible than Pearl—a diamond, in nature, is a more permanent substance than a pearl.

5. bell hooks, *Black Looks: Race Representation* (Boston: South End Press, 1992), pp. 179–194.

6. Compare Prince's narrating of a sexual tale in the "Little Red Corvette" video, which contains sparse imagery, to this moment in "Gett Off."

7. Success and failure seem like strong terms, yet the video calls for an evaluation, and asks for a judgment. More than other music videos, "Gett Off" asks the viewer to participate in its work. In the introduction to the video, the bouncer asks Diamond and Pearl, "Are you here for the audition?" It can be said also that the video presents itself as "here for the audition."

8. Readers may wonder whether men alone can engage in the primal scene. However, it is a key fantasy in the gay community. Stevan Key, "The Architecture of Social Transgression: Film, Homosexuality and Music," Ph.D. diss., University of California, San Diego, 1994.

9. Method shape analysis, a framework developed by dance and movement therapists for observing and characterizing the lived body over time, might be useful for unpacking what bodily gesture means in "Gett Off." See Irmgard Bartenieff and Martha Ann Davis, "Effort-Shape Analysis of Movement: The Unity of Expression and Function" (1965), in *Research Approaches to Movement and Towards Understanding the Intrinsic in Body Movement* (New York: Arno Press, 1972), 17–27; Cecily Dell, *A Primer for Movement Description Using Effort-Shape and Supplementary Concepts* (New York: Dance Notation Bureau, 1977).

10. I have often considered what could be done differently in the "Gett Off" video. Perhaps both the figures and the decor could be placed more closely together (Prince could be threaded through a hallway of figures), or the lighting could become darker. Our culture has few models for what to do with dense figuration, so any maker who embarked on this project would have had trouble. As evidence of the difficulty, one only has to think of the other popular, contemporary artist who deals with this amount of figuration within a tableau—Peter Greenaway. In terms of how to deal with the conflict between temporal and spatial organization I think St. Nicholas is clearly more successful than Greenaway. Director St. Nicholas clearly knows how to conceive of a video as a whole: Prince's "Insatiable," Toni Braxton's "Breathe Again," and Baby Face's "Keeping No Secrets" are cases in point. Later in the chapter I will argue that something is gained by the misshapen quality of the piece.

NOTES TO CHAPTER 13: PETER GABRIEL'S ELEGY FOR ANNE SEXTON

1. "Mercy St." contains elements held in common by many music videos: a structure built upon the form of the song, the adoption of several of the song's musical features, and a subject position more fluid than that created by Hollywood film. Like many videos, it raises the question of the genre's narrative means and aims. Though the video compilation, *Peter Gabriel CV,* that contains "Mercy St." is out of print, "Mercy St." may appear on www.petergabriel.com.

2. Analyzing the factors that supported Mahurin in making such a tape may provide clues to the development of a viable video production model. Without being held to an early release date, as he would have been with a hit single, Mahurin was able to take his time. Low production costs—the video was shot on Super-8 film—gave him the freedom to shoot until he obtained the image he envisioned. As director of a "filler" on the *CV* tape, Mahurin could make artistic decisions without interference from the artist or the record company. Another source for production models may be collaborations in the Hollywood film industry, like Orson Welles's and Bernard Herrmann's work on *Citizen Kane.* Perhaps video artists, like some film composers, might be brought in at an early stage of production, while the band is still in the studio, for example. Songs might instead be held for release until the videomakers have been given time for their ideas to come to fruition. Record companies might grant video directors final cut in certain cases. In addition, government or corporate funding might be set aside to support the development of an alternative music video practice, much as funding is presently allocated for documentary and experimental film. Mahurin has made some longer, noncommercial music videos (*Tribes* was funded through the NEA), but sources of support and venues are few.

3. We might justify the incorporation of Sexton's poetry within the analysis on a number of grounds. Gabriel and Mahurin use bits and pieces of Sexton's poetry, and the video sits well with the poetry. Sexton herself might have sanctioned such an approach, being quite loose about borders between life experience and art. She often read her poems

live to musical accompaniment (with the musical ensemble called Her Kind). Perhaps the poetry serves as an encouragement to make it through an opaque form. Music videos seem to aim toward the state of poems, and so, too, often does analysis. The Anne Sexton excerpts are from the following poems: "45 Mercy Street" (p. 253), "Water" (p. 255), "The Double Image" (p. 256), "The Truth the Dead Know" (p. 257), "Briar Rose (Sleeping Beauty)" (p. 258), "The Boat" (p. 259), "The Touch" (p. 260), "Letters to Dr. Y" (p. 261), "Flee on Your Donkey" (p. 263), "Briar Rose (Sleeping Beauty)" (p. 264, first stanza), "The Death of the Fathers 6. Begat" (p. 264, second stanza), "For the Year of the Insane" (p. 264, third stanza), "The Poet of Ignorance" (p. 265), "For My Lover, Returning to His Wife" (p. 267), "Mother and Jack and the Rain" (p. 269, first stanza), "The Fortress" (p. 269, second stanza). Anne Sexton, *The Complete Poems* (Boston: Houghton Mifflin Company, 1981).

4. Our understanding of the cultural, economic, institutional, and technical context of "Mercy St." is crucial to a full reading. However, pertinent facts are unavailable. Cable programming stations, record companies, and individual production houses are surprisingly hostile to academic researchers, though I have had some luck with interviewing individual music-video directors. No comprehensive list of music-video production companies is available even within the industry. Nevertheless, broad outlines of a context can be sketched. In the late 1980s, videomakers might still take risks and explore the potential of the genre. A good companion to the "Mercy St." video, R.E.M.'s "Fall On Me," contains only bolded red lyrics against black-and-white footage of buildings and earth, with the background and/or the text sometimes turned upside down. Many musicians in the late 1980s experimented with world beat (Paul Simon, for example). With long, well-established careers, both Gabriel and Mahurin could be said to have entered a period of introspection. Both were committed to social causes. Gabriel played an active role in Amnesty International and in supporting international musicians. Mahurin lobbied to change the ways the industry compensates music video directors for treatments. (Unlike other fields, such as television commercials, film, or print advertising, music-video directors give their initial proposals for music video away free, "on spec.")

5. Because this sequential description differs from most close analyses of film, it will be worth explaining quickly how it is organized. Close analyses of film usually use the shot or the scene as the fundamental unit of analysis, and close readings of music video have tended to do the same. Here, the method of detailed description is similar, but the fundamental unit is the musical section, rather than the scene or the shot. The use of the musical section as the fundamental unit places an emphasis upon varied repetition of materials over linear development of plot. Treating the form of the song as the analytical ground for the video better reflects its semantic and formal structure.

6. In Greek mythology, Laertes damaged his son Oedipus's feet and left him to die to avoid the fulfillment of the prophecy that the King's son would kill the father and marry the mother. One of the themes of "Mercy St." is incest.

7. In "Mercy St.," shapes such as circles, crosses, and lines continually reappear, change, and then thin out. We can trace the gap of the Band-Aids in shots 3, 4, 16, and 17, and the parallel lines in shots 2, 8, 18, 19, 25, 35, 36, and 40–46.

8. The musical lines in a piece of music—the melody, the bass, the inner voices—have contours; composers often talk about these musical lines as visual shapes. In music video, the shape of the musical line can correlate to the shape of the visual image.

9. In traditional Hollywood narrative, the editing techniques work to suggest the viewer's mastery of the space (through shot/reverse shot, 180-degree rule, eyeline match, and point of view. Janet Staiger, Kristin Thompson, and David Bordwell, *The Classical Hollywood Cinema: Film Style & Mode of Production to 1960* (New York: Columbia University Press, 1985), 55–57. Music videos forgo such mastery in order to create the

sense of a continuous line. The editing usually attempts to keep the eye moving fluently through the space in a way that supports the directionality of the song.

10. One striking (if subtle) kind of continuity comes in the second instrumental: continuity is preserved through shape—here, a circle and a cross (shots 33–37). The priest's cross, with its circular movement, reappears as the cross formed by the lines cut into the cement below the dogs. The dogs are echoed in the following image by a circle of sand with two feet and a hand.

11. The foot stepping into sand and the figure tugging a cloak close to the chest are the only two moments closely linked to the music, matched by the bass sliding up to the tonic.

12. Mahurin's preliminary charcoal sketches most likely bear a strong resemblance to the imagery in "Mercy St." These preproduction decisions may have contributed to the refined sense of continuity in the final video. Note that two vertical slashes of black in this shot match the boat oars in the next.

13. D. Milano, "Peter Gabriel's Identity," *Keyboard Magazine* 15 (1989): 32–38.

14. For more about one-to-one connections among music, image, and lyrics, see Michel Chion's work on synchresis, what he calls "the spontaneous and irresistible weld produced between a particular auditory phenomenon and visual phenomenon when they occur at the same time." Chion, *Audiovision: Sound on Screen,* trans. Claudia Gorbman (New York: Columbia University Press, 1990), 63. For more on how synchresis can be used as a means for interpreting music video, see chapter 9.

15. The sand in the first shot can be understood to brush across the woman's face at the close of the first verse. It dissolves the cloth and hand imagery into nothingness as the final instrumental ends. In the "b" section of verse I, we see an assertive hand; in the subsequent "a" section of that verse, a more tentative hand; in verse 3, an emaciated hand.

16. The video almost suggests that the world is animated, not by people, but by cold, platonic forms—spheres and boxes, circles and lines.

17. In *Analyzing Musical Multimedia,* Nicholas Cook provides a description of relations among music, image, and text based on a scale of conformance, complementation, and contrast. How would this section be interpreted through Cook's model of conformance to contest? Because the warm, soothing elements of the music seem distant from the element of terror embedded in visual track, the relation might be considered one of contest. (Because slumber and nightmare are intimately linked, these relations may seem less adversarial than, say, a couple fighting against romantic music.) Within the large-scale form of the video, we might say that this moment creates a snug fit, a relation we might ultimately want to call complement: "Mercy St." establishes a Freudian game of fort/da in which image, lyrics, and music are repeatedly brought into close relation and then pushed apart (the moments of gap and then sync seem to grow more extreme as the video progresses), while the viewer is, at the same time, brought into confidence and then left outside. (The distance between music and image comes at the right time in the right amount—so this is a relation that we might ultimately want to call a complement.) In addition, a shape shared by music and image—the rising contour in the melodic lines and the gradual progression of the boat on the water from the bottom to the top of the frame—suggests a relation of iconicity. The video contains relations based on contest, complement, and congruence. Cook, *Analyzing Musical Multimedia,* (New York: Oxford University Press, 1998), 98–106.

18. Later work on spectatorship by Laplanche and Constance Penley is helpful here. Laplanche noticed that the subjectivity of the adolescent patient in the Freudian scenario shifts—not tethered to any particular point of view, she imagines herself as parent, beaten child, and onlooker. Drawing upon Laplanche, Constance Penley extends the work of earlier psychoanalytic theorists such as Laura Mulvey, who argued

that female film spectators were locked into a masochistic position as the object of the gaze. Penley argued that the female viewer could imagine herself as a man, the camera, or even the image's landscape or set. The multivalent text of "Mercy St." supports a split subjectivity. The viewer can identify with the anonymous voice of the surdo, the foam of the waves, the trajectory of the boat, the isolated circling hands, or even a sense of falling. Penley, "Feminism, Psychoanalysis, Popular Culture," in Lawrence Grossberg, Cary Nelson, and Paula Treichler, eds., *Cultural Studies* (New York: Routledge, Chapman and Hall, 1992), 493, 495.

Sexton believed that her parents molested her, and she, in turn, molested her daughter. More frightening than the witnessing of a primal scene is the video's suggestion of incest. Anxiety about this scene could be said to be displaced onto adjacent imagery in the video—the isolated hands that seem to guiltily and anxiously flutter throughout the video.

19. The chorus could be heard as Protestant hymnody filtered through folk revivalism. This still places the chorus in common practice harmony. See Philip Bohlman, *The Study of Folk Music in the Modern World* (Bloomington: Indiana University Press, 1988), 39.

Gabriel justifies his musical choices by arguing that musical cultures need new influences to remain vibrant. He speaks about how much the musicians from other cultures that he has met hunger to play rock and roll, and how much value he receives from playing with these musicians. He acknowledges that the system of exchange is not equal, and, as an act of appreciation for the opportunity to work with these artists, he records their music on a special label. To stop here, however, would be to beg the question of how the borrowed elements work within "Mercy St." It may be important to point out that Sexton's imagery of other cultures seems naïve and limited by today's standards.

Gabriel's strategies for supporting the distribution of world music suggest possibilities for music video. The distribution of music videos made by world musicians and video artists, however, is even more difficult than that of world music. Currently, world music is most often recorded in such a fashion that the timbral and performerly nuances of particular musics are erased in favor of a sound that is amenable to Western ears. (A comparison of Ry Cooder's recording of the Buena Vista Social Club with more traditional Cuban recordings is a good case in point.) The distribution of locally made world music videos would be positive, partly because international viewers would need to learn not only musical but visual codes—dress, movement, ways of moving the camera, editing practices, and the like.

20. This kind of movement is repeated so frequently that it takes on an articulative and rhythmic function that complements the style of the editing and the slow movement of the figures.

21. Both Black Uhuru and Herbie Hancock have released versions of "Mercy St." Black Uhuru, *Mystical Truth Dub* (Mesa Records, 1993), and Herbie Hancock, *The New Standard* (Verve Records, 1996). It is unusual for African American musicians from two different genres (reggae and jazz) to cover a British contemporary pop song. The questions surrounding representations and the recording of the surdo—a drum which in the context of the song suggests a mute, wild voice—are not present on these covers.

22. The juxtaposition of a bird and a high note may seem hackneyed. If taken seriously, however, it can serve a structural function: it completes a gradual ascent to the top of the frame that starts at the beginning of the video. After this shot, the video winds down toward closure.

Two other subtle details could be said to bracket the image of the bird. In the previous long shot of the man in the boat on the water (opening of chorus 2), a beacon shines in the left-hand side of the frame. In the video's second-to-last shot, of a woman against a textured background, a metal barrette in the woman's hair glimmers on the right side of the frame. These two details, as well as the bird, could sustain a hopeful tone.

23. One might wonder why the song ends on such a strongly emphasized tonic chord since it is pointedly a modal song. Perhaps Gabriel felt a need to contain the song and prevent it from seeping into other tracks on the album. As it stands, the degree of closure that the final chord provides seems excessive, as the song has been brought to completion by other means.

24. Nicholas Cook provides a description of relations among music, image, and text based on a scale of conformance, complementation, and contrast. At a very basic level, the relation between music and image in "Mercy St." might be considered somewhere between conformance and complement. According to Cook, where "an IMM [an instance of multimedia] is conformant, it should be possible to invert such statements without change of meaning; it makes as much sense . . . to speak of the upper *luce* part in *Prometheus* projecting the music, as of the music projecting the upper *luce* part." At some level, the image and song in "Mercy St." are synonymous. Both project a haunting, ghostly quality. Cook, *Analyzing Musical Multimedia,* 98–106.

25. Mahurin has served as a graphic artist for *Time* and *Newsweek* and is a long-standing staff illustrator for the opinion section of the *Los Angeles Times.*

26. The surdo, congas, and triangles suggest the samba; the bass's slide up to the tonic from the seventh sounds like Indian classical music; a flute sound alludes to Andean music.

27. Neither Sexton's poems nor her life provide great insight into "Mercy St." as song or video. One or two lines from the song "Mercy St." may borrow from Sexton's poem "45 Mercy St.": "searching for a street sign" becomes "swear they moved that sign" and "in order not to see my inside out" becomes "wear your insides out." The more outrageous moments of the poem have been left out, however. Later in the poem, Sexton starts pulling fish out of her pocketbook and chucking them at street signs. Her poems are predicated on showing greater aggression. Because the song functions more as elegy than as biography, this analysis will take the video as its primary text.

28. One section, the chorus, might represent the narrator's own desires ("mercy, mercy, looking for mercy"). While the sections addressed to the listener refer to the father in the third person, those written in the second person ("let's take the boat out, dreaming of mercy / in your daddy's arms again") seem to adopt his perspective.

29. A listener may even be tempted to hear the voice as white male subjectivity trying desperately to hold its own against the unyielding percussion.

30. "Mercy St." features three types of experience. The video's fundament feels labyrinthine: the shifting sectional lengths suggest that we, the viewers, are laboratory rats hitting the dead ends in a maze, and the jumbled, blocklike images, resembling the little plastic letters of a children's slide puzzle, add to the confusion. The middle layer feels comforting, composed of the repeated rising and falling of the voice, the drifting up and down of the image within the frame, the periodic phrase structure of the text. Containing a jittery jouissance, the finest level foregrounds the mercurial, prismatic, shifting relations among music, image, and text. Labyrinthine, periodic, and prismatic, each feels present in "Mercy St." Can we say this about a classic Hollywood narrative film?

A music video analysis that loosely borrows from a Shenkarian approach and that takes into account the medium's radically different material might look quite unusual. For example, a visual background might feature a stripped-down narrative—in "Mercy St.," the head in the boat might fall into the water and sink, to rest finally against the base of a cross planted at the bottom of the ocean. (Does the cross's tip extend past the ocean's surface?) The hook line "looking for Mercy St." would reduce to "mer-street," echoing the Latin root "mar" for ocean, or "ocean street." In order to leave space for image and text, the song's musical urlinie might be patchier than urlinies common to music alone. The opening C♯ and the final root of C♯ four octaves below at the video's close might serve as the two fundamental pitches. (While the video's imagery gradually rises in the frame and the song reaches a higher tessitura, the video's concern is with falling.) Layers within the middle ground might shift emphasis completely. To reflect music video's need for a basic temporal-spatial spine (sort of like the girding within a model airplane), the middle ground might contain rising and falling shapes that possess similarity regardless of whether they appear in music, image, or lyrics. The foreground might contain very fine instantiations in timbre, texture, and shade.

31. The correlation between the shapes of the spot and prongs underneath the image of a circling cross and the anuses, penises, and tails of the dogs will make the religious elements seem profane.

32. In a general way, music-video image can adopt the experiential qualities of sound—the objects depicted can become more processual than concrete: they can have soft rather than firm boundaries and can be seen to ebb and flow. "Mercy St." provides good examples of this phenomenon.

33. This is colotomy, a principle that structures musical practices like the Balinese gamelan.

34. When the hand opens the drawer and hangs in the middle of the frame, the image achieves a momentary sense of balance. It presents the only balanced image until the video's final sequence. Another image that helps to create a midpoint is the shot of swaddled white legs on the floor ("he can handle the shocks"). It is the only all-white shot in the video, and the only shot that places a person in a homelike interior (shots 20, 25).

35. If we consider the video played backward, it might suggest a birth. The figure in the boat might suggest an ovum; the woman, the mother; the hall, the birth canal; and the figure in the water, a newborn child. The opening shot of "Mercy St." with the foot stepping into the sand would therefore suggest a desire to return to one's origins.

36. Is it possible to suggest that the video has granted the woman's wish for a second childhood? Such a childhood would thereby occupy the video's present, just as the final stanza of the lyrics ("Anne, with her father is out in the boat") might be understood as recording this transformation from the perspective of the song's present.

37. In my conversation with Mahurin, he noted that the lead characters, most often men, in all of his music videos fade out.

38. One might wonder whether a medium like music video can truly embody the passage to oblivion: the form is short and the music continues without interruption. The constraints upon commercial music video are sufficient to explain the absence of videos that focus upon death and decay. It is easy to think of songs that might support such a focus and to imagine approaches that videomakers might take. We would need a number of these videos to develop a grammar of death in music video—a "slow decay" subgenre?

39. Elton John's "Candle in the Wind" is one such example, but it is a rather one-dimensional homage to Marilyn Monroe (and as a cultural icon, not as an artist).

40. To judge from a recent book on Sylvia Plath's biographers, this line of enquiry might be interesting in itself, especially inasmuch as "Mercy St." involves tracking another poet who left complex traces.

The "Mercy St." video can be used in the classroom as an example of the relations among music, image, and lyrics in music video, perhaps most successfully in courses on media literacy, popular culture, and popular music. (Instructors may wish to refer to my article "Teaching Music Video: Aesthetics, Politics and Pedagogy," *Journal of Popular Music Studies* [2000]: 93–101, 293–295.) In part because the present analysis is so lengthy and detailed, I find it helpful to engage students with the video before assigning the reading. I begin by rolling the video two or three times, each time asking the students to watch in a specific way. First, I ask students to write about what they perceive is the video's story. (These responses as well as later ones are gathered and distributed.) Next, I ask students to report on how the video's structure relates to sectional divisions: verses, choruses, and bridges, as well as which sections reflect the past and which the present. I lecture on a few relations between song and image, such as melodic and visual contour or the song's arrangement and how it relates to what appears within the frame, and ask students to report on how the video draws our attention to particular sounds. Finally, I ask them to write on the board what they would focus on if they were to do an analysis of the video—they might pick themes such as clothing, shadow and light, texture, or gender. The students then break into small groups, the tape rolls, and afterward they share their findings with the rest of the class. When the paper is assigned, the videotape is placed on reserve, and students submit a short write-up and take a quiz. Some students' comments are quite lovely. For instance, one student felt that "the black in the video stretched to infinity"; another that "the images were ghostly and so was the song," and another that "the waves crashing at the end might have been the waking from a dream, hence none of the depicted imagery is real."

NOTES TO AFTERWORD

1. Jan La Rue, *Guidelines for Style Analysis* (New York: Norton, 1971); Janet Staiger, Kristin Thompson, and David Bordwell, *The Classical Hollywood Cinema: Film Style and Mode of Production to 1960* (New York: Columbia University Press, 1985); David Bordwell and Kristin Thompson, *Film Art: An Introduction* (Reading, MA: Addison-Wesley, 1997).
2. I am drawing upon Nicholas Cook's model of how media within a musical multimedia work may enter into relation. Please refer to chapter 9.
3. Such as the debate between the film theorists Sergei Eisenstein and Andre Bazin and the music theorists Rudolph Reti and Heinrich Schenker.
4. Staiger, Thompson, and Bordwell, *The Classical Hollywood Cinema.*
5. Michel Chion, *Audiovision: Sound on Screen,* trans. Claudia Gorbman (New York: Columbia University Press, 1990), 163.
6. Nicholas Cook, *Analyzing Musical Multimedia* (New York: Oxford University Press, 1998), 268–270.

BIBLIOGRAPHY

Adorno, Theodor. *Mahler: A Musical Physiognomy*. Trans. Edmund Jephcott. Chicago: University of Chicago Press, 1996.

Agawu, V. Kofi. "Theory and Practice in the Analysis of the Nineteenth-Century *Lied*." *Music Analysis* 11.1 (1992): 5–8.

Anderson, J. D. "Sound and Image Together—Cross Modal Confirmation (Film)." *Wide Angle* 15.1 (1993): 30–43.

Arnheim, Rudolph. *The Power of the Center*. Berkeley: University of California Press, 1988.

Austin, J. L. *Sense and Sensibilia*. New York: Oxford University Press, 1962.

Bartenieff, Irmgard, and Martha Ann Davis. "Effort-Shape Analysis of Movement: The Unity of Expression and Function." In Martha Ann Davis, ed., *Research Approaches to Movement and Towards Understanding the Intrinsic in Body Movement*, 17–27. New York: Arno Press, 1972.

Barthes, Roland. *Camera Lucida*. Trans. Richard Howard. New York: Hill and Wang, 1981.

——. *Image—Music—Text*. Trans. Richard Howard. New York: Hill and Wang, 1977.

——. *The Responsibility of Forms: Critical Essays on Music, Art, and Representation*. Trans. Richard Howard. New York: Hill and Wang, 1986.

Bazin, Andre. *What Is Cinema?* Berkeley: University of California Press, 1971.

Berger, John. *Ways of Seeing*. New York: Viking Press, 1995.

Bergman, Albert S. *Auditory Scene Analysis: The Perceptual Organization of Sound*. Cambridge, MA: MIT Press, 1990.

Bergson, Henri. *An Introduction to Metaphysics*. Trans. T. E. Hulme. 1903. New York: Library of Liberal Arts, 1955.

Bergstrom, Janet, ed. *Endless Night: Cinema and Psychoanalysis—Parallel Histories*. Berkeley: University of California Press, 1999.

Berland, Jody. "Sound, Image, and Social Space: Music Video and Media Reconstruction." In Simon Frith, Andrew Goodwin, and Lawrence Grossberg, eds., *Sound and Vision: The Music Video Reader*, 25–43. New York: Routledge, 1993.

Blanchard, Gerard. *Images de la musique de cinema*. Paris: Edilig, 1984.

Bogle, Donald. *Toms, Coons, Mulattos, Mammies, and Bucks: An Interpretive History of Blacks in American Films*. New York: Continuum, 1989.

Bohlman, Philip. *The Study of Folk Music in the Modern World*. Bloomington: Indiana University Press, 1988.

Bordwell, David. "Intensified Continuity: Visual Style in Contemporary American Film." *Film Quarterly* 55 (2002): 16–28.

——, and Kristin Thompson. *Film Art: An Introduction*. Reading, MA: Addison-Wesley, 1997.

Branigan, Edward. *Point of View in the Cinema*. New York: Mouton, 1984.

——. "Sound and Epistemology in Film." *Journal of Aesthetics and Art Criticism* 47 (1989): 312–324.

Cavell, Stanley. *The World Viewed.* Cambridge, MA: Harvard University Press, 1979.

Childs, Barney. "Time and Music: A Composer's View." *Perspectives of New Music* 2.15 (1977): 194.

Chion, Michel. *Audiovision: Sound on Screen.* Trans. Claudia Gorbman. New York: Columbia University Press, 1990.

Clifton, Thomas. *Music as Heard: A Study in Applied Phenomenology.* New Haven: Yale University Press, 1993.

Cohen, Annabel J. "Film Music: Perspectives from Cognitive Psychology." In James Buhler, Caryl Flinn, and David Neumeyer, eds., *Music and Cinema,* 360–377. Middletown, CT: Wesleyan University Press, 2000.

Comolli, Jean-Louis. "Contrariwise." *Cahiers du Cinema in English* 3 (1966): 57.

Cone, Edward T. *The Composer's Voice.* Berkeley: University of California Press, 1974.

Cook, Nicholas. *Analyzing Musical Multimedia.* New York: Oxford University Press, 1998.

Dancyger, Ken. *The Technique of Film and Video Editing.* Boston: Focal Press, 1996.

Dell, Cecily. *A Primer for Movement Description Using Effort-Shape and Supplementary Concepts.* New York: Dance Notation Bureau, 1977.

Dyer, Richard. *The Matter of Images.* New York: Routledge, 1993.

——. *White.* London: Routledge, 1997.

Ellenzweig, Allen. *The Homo-erotic Photograph.* New York: Columbia University Press, 1992.

Ellis, John. *Visible Fictions: Cinema, Television, Video.* London: Routledge & Kegan Paul, 1982.

Erickson, Robert. *The Structure of Music: A Listener's Guide: A Study of Music in Terms of Melody and Counterpoint.* New York: Noonday, 1955.

Feuer, Jane. *The Hollywood Musical.* Bloomington: Indiana University Press, 1982.

Fiske, John. "British Cultural Studies and Television." In Robert C. Allen, ed., *Channels of Discourse, Reassembled: Television and Contemporary Criticism,* 2d ed., 284–326. Chapel Hill: University of North Carolina Press, 1992.

——. *Reading the Popular.* Cambridge: Cambridge University Press, 1989.

Fletcher, Angus. *Colors of the Mind: Conjectures on Thinking in Literature.* Cambridge, MA: Harvard University Press, 1991.

Forman, Murray. *The 'Hood Comes First: Race, Space, and Place in Rap and Hip Hop.* Middletown, CT: Wesleyan University Press, 2002.

Frith, Simon. *Music for Pleasure: Essays in the Sociology of Pop.* New York: Routledge, 1988.

——. *Performing Rites: On the Value of Popular Music.* Cambridge, MA: Harvard University Press, 1996.

——, Andrew Goodwin, and Lawrence Grossberg, eds. *Sound and Vision: The Music Video Reader.* New York: Routledge, 1993.

Goodwin, Andrew. *Dancing in the Distraction Factory: Music Television and Popular Culture.* Minneapolis: University of Minnesota Press, 1992.

Gorbman, Claudia. *Unheard Melodies: Narrative Film Music.* Bloomington: Indiana University Press, 1987.

Grisey, Gerard. "Tempus ex Machina: A Composer's Reflections on Musical Time." *Contemporary Music Review* 2.1 (1987): 239–275.

Hamm, Charles. *Irving Berlin.* New York: Oxford University Press, 1997.

Hanslick, Eduard. *The Beautiful in Music/Vom Musikalisch-Schönen.* Trans. Gustav Cohen. New York: Library of Liberal Arts, 1957.

——. *On the Musically Beautiful.* Trans. Geoffrey Payzant. Indianapolis: Hackett, 1986.

Hayward, Philip. "Desire Caught by Its Tail: The Unlikely Return of the Merman in Madonna's 'Cherish.'" *Cultural Studies* 5.1 (1991): 98.

Hennion, Antoine. "The Production of Success: An Anti-Musicology of the Pop Song." *Popular Music* 3 (1983): 159–193.

Holtzshue, Linda. *Understanding Color.* New York: Wiley, 2002.

hooks, bell. *Black Looks: Race and Representation.* Boston: South End Press, 1992.

——. *Cultural Criticism and Transformation.* Videotape. Northampton, MA: Media Education Foundation, 1997.

Jakobson, Roman. "On Realism in Art." In Lataslav Matjeka Krystyna Pomorska, ed., *Readings in Russian Poetics,* 82–87. Cambridge, MA: MIT Press, 1971.

Jhally, Sut. *Dreamworlds 2.* Videotape. Northampton, MA: Media Education Foundation, 1991.

Johnson, Mark. *The Body in the Mind: The Bodily Basis of Meaning, Imagination, and Reason.* Chicago: University of Chicago Press, 1987.

Jonas, Hans. *The Phenomenon of Life.* Chicago: University of Chicago Press, 1982.

Kant, Immanuel. *The Critique of Pure Reason.* Trans. Norman Kemp Smith. New York: St. Martin's, 1965.

Kaplan, E. Ann. *Rocking Around the Clock: MTV Postmodernism and Consumer Culture.* New York: Methuen, 1987.

Kassabian, Anahid. *Hearing Film: Tracking Identifications in Contemporary Hollywood Film Music.* New York: Routledge, 2001.

Key, Stevan. The Architecture of Social Transgression: Film, Homosexuality and Music. Ph.D. diss., University of California, San Diego, 1994.

Kinder, Marsha. "Music Video and the Spectator: Television, Ideology and Dream." *Film Quarterly* 38.1 (1984): 2–15.

Kivy, Peter. *The Corded Shell: Reflections on Musical Expression.* Princeton: Princeton University Press, 1980.

——. *Sound Sentiment: An Essay on the Musical Emotions.* Philadelphia: Temple University Press, 1989.

Kramer, Jonathan D. *The Time of Music.* New York: Schirmer, 1988.

Kramer, Lawrence. *Music and Poetry: The Nineteenth Century and After.* Berkeley: University of California Press, 1984.

Kronengold, Charles. "Identity, Value, and the Work of Genre: Black Action Films." In Shelton Waldrep, ed., *The Seventies: The Age of Glitter in Popular Culture,* 79–123. New York: Routledge, 2000.

Laban, Rudolf von. *Principles of Dance and Movement Notation.* 2d ed. Boston: Plays Inc., 1974.

Lacan, Jacques. *Écrits: A Selection.* Trans. Alan Sheridan. New York: Norton, 1977.

Lakoff, George, and Mark Johnson. *Philosophy in the Flesh.* New York: Basic Books, 1999.

Langer, Suzanne K. *Feeling and Form.* New York: Scribner's, 1953.

——. *Mind: An Essay on Human Feeling.* Baltimore: Johns Hopkins University Press, 1967.

——. *Philosophy in a New Key: A Study in the Symbolism of Reason, Rite, and Art.* Cambridge, MA: Harvard University Press, 1942.

La Rue, Jan. *Guidelines for Style Analysis.* New York: Norton, 1971.

Lefebvre, Henri. *The Production of Space.* Trans. Donald Nicholson-Smith. Oxford: Blackwell, 1991.

Leonardo da Vinci. *The Genius of Leonardo da Vinci: Leonardo da Vinci on Art and the Artist.* Ed. Andre Chastel. New York: Orion Press, 1961.

Lewis, Lisa A. *Gender Politics and MTV: Voicing the Difference.* Philadelphia: Temple University Press, 1990.

Manvell, Roger, and John Huntley. *The Technique of Film Music.* 2d ed. New York: Focal Press, 1975.

McClary, Susan. *Feminine Endings: Music, Gender, and Sexuality.* Minnesota: University of Minnesota Press, 1991.

McCloud, Scott. *Understanding Comics.* Northampton, MA: Kitchen Sink Press, 1994.

McRobbie, A. "Settling Accounts with Subcultures: A Feminist Critique." *Screen Education* 34 (1980): 37–49.

Mercer, Kobena. "Monster Metaphors: Notes on Michael Jackson's Thriller." In Simon Frith, Andrew Goodwin, and Lawrence Grossberg, eds., *Sound and Vision: The Music Video Reader,* 93–108. New York: Routledge, 1993.

Metz, Christian. *The Imaginary Signifier: Psychoanalysis and the Cinema.* Trans. Celia Britton et al. Bloomington: Indiana University Press, 1982.

——. *Language and Cinema.* Trans. Michael Taylor. New York: Oxford University Press, 1974.

Meyer, Leonard. *Style and Music: Theory, History and Ideology.* Chicago: University of Chicago Press, 1989.

Middleton, Richard. "Over and Over: Notes Towards a Politics of Repetition." http://www2 .huberlin.de/fpm/middle.htm.

——. *Reading Pop: Approaches to Textual Analysis in Popular Music.* Oxford: Oxford University Press, 2000.

——. *Studying Popular Music.* Philadelphia: Open University Press, 1990.

Milano, D. "Peter Gabriel's Identity." *Keyboard Magazine* 15 (1989): 32–38.

Millerson, Gerald. *Television Production.* Boston: Focal Press, 1999.

Morton, Melanie. "Don't Go for Second Sex, Baby!" In Cathy Schwichtenberg, ed., *The Madonna Connection: Representation Politics, Subcultural Identities, and Cultural Theory,* 213–235. Boulder: Westview, 1993.

Naremore, James. *Acting in the Cinema.* Berkeley: University of California Press, 1990.

Nattiez, Jean-Jacques. *Music and Discourse: Toward a Semiology of Music.* Trans. Stewart Spencer and Carolyn Abbate. Princeton: Princeton University Press, 1990.

Ong, Walter. *Orality and Literacy: The Technology of the Word.* New York: Methuen, 1985.

Pasler, Jann. "Narrative and Narrativity." In J. T. Fraser, ed., *Time and Mind: Interdisciplinary Issues,* 233–257. Madison, WI: International Universities Press, 1989.

Penley, Constance. "Feminism, Psychoanalysis, Popular Culture." In Lawrence Grossberg, Cary Nelson, and Paula Treichler, eds., *Cultural Studies,* 479–500. New York: Routledge, Chapman and Hall, 1992.

——. *The Future of an Illusion: Film, Feminism, and Psychoanalysis.* Minneapolis: University of Minnesota Press, 1989.

Reisz, Karel. *The Technique of Film Editing.* Boston: Focal Press, 1988.

Reti, Rudolf. *The Thematic Process in Music.* Westport, CT: Greenwood Press, 1978.

Rose, Tricia. *Black Noise: Rap Music and Black Culture in Contemporary America.* Hanover, NH: University Press of New England, 1994.

Rothman, William. *Documentary Film Classics.* New York: Cambridge University Press, 1997.

——, and Marian Keane. *Reading Cavell's "The World Viewed": A Philosophical Perspective on Film.* Detroit: Wayne State University Press, 2000.

Saito, Ayako. "Hitchcock's Trilogy: A Logic of Mise en Scène." In Janet Bergstrom, ed., *Endless Night: Cinema and Psychoanalysis—Parallel Histories,* 200–248. Berkeley: University of California Press, 1990.

Schenker, Heinrich. *Five Graphic Music Analyses.* New York: Dover, 1969.

Sella, Marshall. "The 150-Second Sell, Take 34." *The New York Times Magazine,* 28 July 2002.

Seurat, Georges. "Letter to Jules Christophe. August 28, 1890." In R. Goldwater and M. Traves, *Artists on Art from the XIV to the XXth Century,* 375. New York: Pantheon, 1972.

Sexton, Anne. *The Complete Poems.* Boston: Houghton Mifflin Company, 1981.

Sharff, Stefan. *The Art of Looking.* New York: Proscenium, 1997.

——. *The Elements of Cinema: Toward a Theory of Synthetics Impact.* New York: Columbia University Press, 1982.

Spitzer, Leo. *Essays on English and American Literature.* Princeton: Princeton University Press, 1962.

Staiger, Janet, Kristin Thompson, and David Bordwell. *The Classical Hollywood Cinema: Film Style & Mode of Production to 1960.* New York: Columbia University Press, 1985.

Straw, Will. "Popular Music and Postmodernism in the 1980s." In Simon Frith, Andrew Goodwin, and Lawrence Grossberg, eds., *Sound and Vision: The Music Video Reader,* 3–21. New York: Routledge, 1993.

Tagg, Philip. *Kojak—50 Seconds of Television Music: Toward the Analysis of Affect in Popular Music.* Goteborg: Musikvetens-Kapliga Inst., Goteborgs University, 1979.

Tetzlaff, David. "MTV and the Politics of Postmodern Pop." *Journal of Communication Inquiry* 10.1 (1986): 80.

Thompson, John O. "Screen Acting and the Commutation Test." *Screen* 19.2 (1978): 55–70.

Tuan, Yi-Fu. *Space and Place: The Perspective of Experience*. Minneapolis: University of Minnesota Press, 1977.

Vernallis, Carol. "The Aesthetics of Music Video: An Analysis of Madonna's 'Cherish'." *Popular Music* 17.2 (1998): 153–185.

——. The Aesthetics of Music Video: The Relation of Music and Image. Ph.D. diss., University of California, San Diego, 1994.

——. "The Functions of Lyrics in Music Video." *Journal of Popular Music Studies* 14:1 (Spring 2002): 11–31.

——. "The Kindest Cut: Functions and Meanings of Music Video Editing." *Screen* 42:1 (Spring 2001): 21–47.

——. "Teaching Music Video: Aesthetics, Politics and Pedagogy." *Journal of Popular Music Studies* 9/10 (2000): 93–99.

Walser, Robert. "Forging Masculinity: Heavy-Metal Sounds and Images of Gender." In Simon Frith, Andrew Goodwin, and Lawrence Grossberg, eds., *Sound and Vision: The Music Video Reader*, 153–181. New York: Routledge, 1993.

Williams, Linda. *Figures of Desire: A Theory and Analysis of Surrealist Film*. Urbana: University of Illinois Press, 1981.

——. "Film Body: An Implantation of Perversion." In Ron Burnett, ed., *Explorations in Film Theory*, 46–71. Bloomington: Indiana University Press, 1991.

Wittgenstein, Ludwig. *Philosophical Investigations*. Trans. G. E. M. Anscombe. New York: Macmillan, 1968.

Zak, Albin J. *The Poetics of Rock: Cutting Tracks, Making Records*. Berkeley: University of California Press, 2001.

Zettl, Herbert. *Sight, Sound, Motion: Applied Media Aesthetics*. San Francisco: Wadsworth, 1998.

Zuckerkandl, Victor. *Sound and Symbol: Music and the External World*. Trans. Willard R. Trask. London: Routledge, 1956.

INDEX